# Committee Decisions on Monetary Policy

# Committee Decisions on Monetary Policy

Evidence from Historical Records of the Federal Open Market Committee

Henry W. Chappell Jr.,
Rob Roy McGregor, and
Todd Vermilyea

The MIT Press
Cambridge, Massachusetts
London, England

MIT Press books may be purchased at special quantity discounts for business or sales promotional use. For information, please e-mail special_sales@mitpress.mit.edu or write to Special Sales Department, The MIT Press, 5 Cambridge Center, Cambridge, MA 02142.

This book was set in Palatino on 3B2 by Asco Typesetters, Hong Kong.
Printed and bound in the United States of America.

Library of Congress Cataloging-in-Publication Data

Chappell, Henry W.
Committee decisions on monetary policy : evidence from historical records of the
Federal Open Market Committee / Henry W. Chappell, Jr., Rob Roy McGregor, Todd
Vermilyea.
    p.   cm.
Includes bibliographical references and index.
ISBN 0-262-03330-5 (alk. paper)
1. United States. Federal Open Market Committee. 2. Monetary policy—United States.
3. Federal Reserve banks. I. McGregor, Rob Roy, 1961–. II. Vermilyea, Todd. III. Title.
HG2565.C356   2005
339.5'3'0973—dc22                                                    2004055942

10 9 8 7 6 5 4 3 2 1

To our parents, who inspired us, and our spouses and children, who supported our efforts throughout this project

# Contents

# Tables and Figure

# Preface

In the United States and many other countries, monetary policy decisions are made by committees. Committees' policy choices reflect the preferences of their members as well as the institutional arrangements that govern the aggregation of individual preferences into collective choices. In this book, we examine the monetary policy preferences of members of the Federal Reserve's Federal Open Market Committee (FOMC) and the process by which its members' preferences are translated into policy decisions. In the context of an academic literature that often presupposes the existence of a single policymaker who maximizes a well-defined objective function, our focus on individual preferences and group decisions is unusual and, in some respects, unique. We believe that this perspective is important for understanding the evolution of monetary policy choices.

The book is primarily intended for professional economists and political scientists. Much of our attention is devoted to methodology, both in the collection of data and in its analysis. Nevertheless, the book is broadly readable; anyone interested in the topics we address will find that large portions of the book are accessible. This is particularly true of chapters 9 and 10, which present material that is primarily anecdotal. Although the book is not intended as a text, it could be used as a supplement for courses in monetary theory and policy or political economics.

Our work on topics covered in this book dates back to 1988, when Henry Chappell spent a sabbatical as a visiting scholar at the University of North Carolina at Chapel Hill. Thomas Havrilesky of Duke University presented a seminar there on FOMC voting patterns that eventually led to a collaborative project; Chappell and Havrilesky were joined by Rob Roy McGregor, then a PhD student at the University of South Carolina. Our early work used FOMC voting data to estimate monetary policy reaction functions (empirical relations linking desired policy settings to prevailing economic conditions) that differed across individual members of the FOMC. We also used those reaction functions to investigate the importance of political pressures on the committee. Chapter 4 of this book updates and extends research that uses dissent voting data in this way.

Because dissenting votes occur infrequently, formal voting records provide limited information about the preferences of FOMC members. In the early 1990s, we began to investigate more detailed information about members' preferences derived from the *Memoranda of Discussion* (detailed summaries of deliberations for meetings held up to March 1976) and the *FOMC Transcripts* (edited transcripts available for meetings held after March 1976). Havrilesky's untimely death in 1995 came as we were completing our first paper making use of the *Memoranda*. This book greatly benefits from his contributions to that research.

As we collected data to describe the policy preferences of FOMC members, we became more optimistic about how those data might be used. We became convinced that it would be possible to assemble data sets describing desired interest rate settings for each member of the FOMC in each of a sequence of meetings. With such a data set, it would then be possible to investigate how individual preferences were mapped into committee choices. Todd Vermilyea, then a PhD student at the University of South Carolina, joined us in the mid-1990s as we began the effort to assemble the data for this purpose. Chapters 5 through 8 of this book are a direct result of that data collection effort and the econometric analysis that followed.

As we read documents describing FOMC deliberations, we also became aware of the richness of their anecdotal content. Many professional economists, students of economics, and others concerned with monetary policy are interested in how the FOMC makes its decisions, but most will never read the *Memoranda* or the *Transcripts*. Our book provides some flavor of the anecdotal content of these sources in adopting "narrative" approaches to investigate political influences on the FOMC (chapter 9) and the relevance of the time inconsistency problem for explaining the "Great Inflation" (chapter 10).

Many people have assisted us during our work on this book, but we are particularly indebted to the late Thomas M. Havrilesky. In addition, we would like to acknowledge helpful comments from individuals who have read portions of the book or our published articles from which the book is derived. In particular, we wish to thank William

Dougan, John Gildea, David Gordon, Kevin Grier, William Keech, Roger Waud, Kenneth West, and colleagues at the Federal Reserve Bank of Philadelphia, the University of North Carolina at Charlotte, and the University of South Carolina. Research assistance was provided by Minesh Amin, Matthew Birmingham, Ronald Gill, Susan Harden, Yoko Kawakami, Steven Nape, Matthew Neidell, Michael Nelson, Jane Norton, Ann Poovey, David Ramsey, Paul Prochaska, and Souren Soumbatiants.

We received a number of documents from the Federal Reserve Board, including Green Books, Blue Books, and transcripts associated with meetings of the FOMC. We particularly wish to thank Normand Bernard and Shirley Tabb for their assistance with these documents. We received transcripts of FOMC meetings for portions of the 1976–1978 period from the collection of Arthur Burns's papers housed in the Gerald R. Ford Library; microfilmed copies of the *Memoranda* were obtained from the National Archives. We thank Jeffrey Bucher for information provided via e-mail correspondence and telephone regarding his experiences as a member of the Board of Governors of the Federal Reserve System. Research support was provided by the National Science Foundation (grant numbers SES–9122322, SES–9121941, SBR–9423095, and SBR–9422850), the University of North Carolina at Charlotte, and the University of South Carolina. We are also grateful to The MIT Press, and particularly to Elizabeth Murry and Sandra Minkkinen, who assisted us throughout the publication process.

Several chapters of this book are derived from previously published articles and include material excerpted from those articles. Portions of chapter 4 are drawn from Chappell and McGregor (2000); chapter 7 is based on Chappell, McGregor, and Vermilyea (2004); and chapter 10 is based on Chappell and McGregor (2004). Permission to reprint excerpts from these articles was granted by the *Southern Economic Journal* (Allen Press), *Economics and Politics* (Blackwell Publishers), and the *Journal of Money, Credit, and Banking* (Ohio State University Press).

The views expressed in this book are those of the authors and do not necessarily represent the views of the Federal Reserve Bank of Philadelphia or the Federal Reserve System.

# Committee Decisions on Monetary Policy

# 1    Introduction

*My experience as a member of the FOMC left me with a strong feeling that the theoretical fiction that monetary policy is made by a single individual maximizing a well-defined preference function misses something important. In my view, monetary theorists should start paying attention to the nature of decisionmaking by committee, which is rarely mentioned in the academic literature.*

—Alan Blinder, *Central Banking in Theory and Practice*

In the United States, monetary policy decisions are made by the Federal Reserve's Federal Open Market Committee (FOMC), which consists of the seven members of the Board of Governors and the presidents of the twelve district Federal Reserve Banks. Since any decision made by the FOMC must reflect some aggregation of the preferences of these committee members, the actions and interactions of individuals on the committee could have important consequences for monetary policy. In this book, we investigate the policy preferences of individual FOMC members and describe the manner in which those preferences are aggregated to produce policy outcomes. Thus, a focus on individuals is the distinguishing feature of our work.

## 1.1   Evidence from Historical Records: Individual-Level Data and Analysis

FOMC decisions are formally made by majority vote, and voting records provide an important part of the information available on individuals' monetary policy preferences. Voting records are limited in significant ways, however. Votes reflect only a qualitative preference relative to the adopted policy; recorded votes do not allow us to observe individuals' desired policy settings. Perhaps more important, FOMC members rarely dissent in formal votes on policy directives. Thus, even when there are disagreements within the committee, evidence of these disagreements may not show up in voting records.

Alternative data sources are available that provide a far richer description of FOMC members' policy preferences. From 1936 to March 1976, the FOMC's deliberations at each of its meetings were described in documents called the *Memoranda of Discussion*. The *Memoranda* provide edited summaries of statements made by each committee member in the "policy go-around" preceding the adoption of a formal directive to guide the conduct of policy. Although preparation of the *Memoranda* ceased in 1976, the FOMC continued to tape-record and transcribe its deliberations. Using the *Memoranda* and *Transcripts*, we have been able to code information about committee members' policy preferences that is more detailed than the information contained in formal voting records. Specifically, these documents often reveal individuals' desired policies in the form of quantitative targets for a policy instrument. On those occasions when members are not so precise, qualitative indications of policy preferences can be observed. We have developed procedures for coding these qualitative descriptions of preferences as well as the more numerous quantitative preference statements. The description and presentation of the resulting data sets represent a major contribution of this book.

Econometric techniques that we develop and apply are also distinctive. Empirical descriptions of monetary policy behavior have often been presented in the form of reaction functions—regression equations that explain the setting of a policy instrument with variables that describe prevailing economic and political conditions. In our approach, we retain the reaction function as a tool, but our econometric procedures are especially designed for estimating individual FOMC members' reaction functions based on the descriptions of their preferences—both quantitative and qualitative—that they offer during committee meetings.

Our unique data sets and estimation methods enable us to pursue issues that have not previously been explored in the literature. In particular, we are able to examine hypotheses about monetary policy decisions that involve differences *across* members of the FOMC, and we can study the mechanisms by which individual policy preferences are aggregated into a committee decision. For example, it is generally recognized that the chairman of the Board of Governors is more powerful than other committee members, but we are able to provide a quantitative assessment of the chairman's power.

Finally, we are able to buttress and supplement our econometric investigation with anecdotal evidence from the original textual records. Our primary purpose in reading the *Memoranda* and the *Transcripts* was to produce data for use in analytical work, but we have also found that a narrative approach to interpreting those documents can be revealing. Anecdotal material is often used to supplement analytical evidence and serves as the primary source of evidence in discussions of how political pressures figure into FOMC deliberations and the relevance of the time inconsistency problem as an explanation for the rise of inflation in the 1970s.

## 1.2  Organization of the Book

In chapter 2, we provide background information on the structure and functions of the Federal Reserve, and in chapter 3, we review the academic literature dealing with monetary policy and Federal Reserve decision making. These discussions cover institutional detail and offer theoretical and empirical contexts that are useful for understanding our analyses.

In chapter 4, we explore data on FOMC voting that has often been used in past studies of internal Fed decision making. We begin by describing a method for using voting data to estimate reaction function parameters for individual FOMC members; we then provide two applications of this method to data from the 1966–1996 period. First, we produce a ranking of eighty-three members from that era on a dimension ranging from "easiest" to "tightest." Our rankings are based on an analysis of individuals' behavior in a framework that controls for the state of the economy and the stance of monetary policy over time. Second, we investigate how models of political influence on the Federal Reserve can be extended to incorporate information on the policy preferences of individual FOMC members. We investigate whether governors appointed by Republican and Democratic presidents systematically differ in their monetary policy preferences and assess the relative importance of the power of appointment and direct pressure as channels of influence for U.S. presidents who want to sway the FOMC. We also investigate whether tendencies to favor preelection ease differ by partisan heritage: are Republican-appointed governors, for example, more likely to favor preelection stimulus when the incumbent president is a Republican? Voting data are useful for investigating issues like these, which require long sample periods in order to observe multiple election cycles and instances of partisan change.

In chapter 5, we describe two original data sets we have constructed using the *Memoranda* and the *Transcripts*: one for the 1970–1978 period when Arthur Burns served as Fed chairman and another for the 1987–1996 portion of Alan Greenspan's tenure as chairman. We discuss the important attributes of the source data and the coding schemes we developed for translating verbal descriptions into quantitative and qualitative measures of policy preferences for individual FOMC members. We also highlight differences in operating procedures and committee decision-making practices between the Burns and Greenspan years.

In chapter 6, we explain how the data sets described in chapter 5 can be used to estimate monetary policy reaction functions for individual FOMC members who served under Burns or Greenspan. We then investigate differences in policy perspectives across members. To do so, we estimate reaction functions for the FOMC as a whole and its individual members; we also test whether each individual is statistically different from the committee on which that member served. We use the estimates to characterize the theoretical perspectives that might underlie individuals' policy preferences. For the Burns era, we focus particular attention on the monetarist perspective advocated by representatives from the Federal Reserve Bank of St. Louis. For the Greenspan era, we emphasize the distinctive views of those who were staunch advocates of gearing policy to achieving and maintaining price stability.

In chapter 7, we use the Burns era data set (described in chapter 5) to investigate decision making by the FOMC in the 1970s, focusing on the competing pressures of majority rule, consensus building, and the power of the chairman. We initially describe how the data we have collected can be used to construct complete "preference profiles" for each FOMC meeting held during the Burns years (a preference profile consists of a listing of desired settings for the federal funds rate for all members of the committee). Using this set of preference profiles, we then empirically link individuals' policy preferences to adopted policies, employing generalized versions of the median voter model and alternative specifications. Our analysis characterizes the aggregation of preferences within the committee and quantitatively assesses the weight of the chairman in this process.

In chapter 8, we use the Greenspan era data set (described in chapter 5) to construct complete preference profiles for each FOMC meeting held between August 1987 and December 1996. We then examine committee decision making during this period. Because Greenspan's proposed policy was almost always adopted, and because the median committee member preference and Greenspan's preference almost always coincided, econometric procedures cannot be used to directly estimate the relative power shares of the chairman and the committee. Nevertheless, we are able to investigate the influence of the chairman's proposals on the stated preferences of individual committee members within a given meeting, and we consider how differences of opinion between Greenspan and other members within one meeting might influence the chairman's policy proposal at the next meeting.

Most of the work in this book is econometric and analytical. In reading the *Memoranda* and the *Transcripts*, however, we have gained an appreciation for their content that goes beyond formal data coding. In chapters 9 and 10, we offer a noneconometric description of the content of these records as it relates to the academic literature on monetary policymaking. In chapter 9, we rely on anecdotal evidence to document political pressures exerted on the Fed and recognized by FOMC members in their deliberations during the Burns and Greenspan eras. In chapter 10, we again use anecdotal evidence to buttress an argument in favor of time inconsistency theory as an explanation for the "Great Inflation" of the 1970s. We also contend that time inconsistency analysis can account for the subsequent decline in inflation that occurred in the 1980s and 1990s.

Finally, in chapter 11, we summarize the key contributions and results presented in this book. We also describe important questions that remain for future research and discuss some of the implications of our work for central banking institutions.

# 2

This chapter briefly describes the structure and functions of the Federal Reserve System, focusing attention on institutional arrangements that affect the environment for monetary policymaking. Our discussion will cover the organization of the system, with particular emphasis on the responsibilities of the Board of Governors, the district Federal Reserve Banks, and the Federal Open Market Committee (FOMC), as well as the procedures by which members of the board and presidents of the district Reserve Banks are chosen for their positions. We also look at the process, both formal and informal, used by the FOMC for arriving at monetary policy decisions. Finally, we discuss the operating procedures used for implementing the committee's decisions.

## 2.1 Organization of the Federal Reserve System

The Federal Reserve System was established by the Federal Reserve Act of 1913, and its current structure has been in place since major changes were introduced by the Banking Act of 1935.[1] For carrying out the daily operations of the system, the country is divided into twelve Federal Reserve districts, with banks in Boston, New York, Philadelphia, Cleveland, Richmond, Atlanta, Chicago, St. Louis, Minneapolis, Kansas City, Dallas, and San Francisco. The Federal Reserve System is supervised by the seven-member Board of Governors, which also has the authority to set reserve requirements and approve the discount rates proposed by the district Reserve Banks.

The Banking Act of 1935 also established the FOMC, the Federal Reserve's principal monetary policymaking body. The FOMC is composed of the Board of Governors and the presidents of the district

---

1. For more detailed discussions of the organizational structure of the Federal Reserve System, see Board of Governors (1994) and Mishkin (2003).

Reserve Banks. At its regular meetings, the FOMC adopts monetary policy directives to guide the conduct of open market operations, the primary tool of monetary policy.[2]

The members of the Board of Governors and the presidents of the district Federal Reserve Banks are chosen by different means. Board members are appointed by the president of the United States and confirmed by the U.S. Senate to serve fourteen-year terms. Terms on the board are staggered, with one term expiring on January 31 of each even-numbered year. A member may serve only one full term of office; however, an individual originally appointed to fill an unexpired term may be reappointed to serve a full term. The president also designates one member of the Board of Governors to be the chairman and another member to be the vice chairman, each for a four-year term and subject to Senate confirmation.

The presidents of the district Reserve Banks, on the other hand, are chosen to serve five-year renewable terms by the boards of directors of these banks, subject to approval by the Board of Governors. The board of directors of each district bank has nine members: three class A directors representing banking interests; three class B directors representing industry, agriculture, and commerce; and three class C directors representing the general public interest. Class A and class B directors are elected by the member banks within the Federal Reserve district. Class C directors are appointed by the Board of Governors. Given that governors and bank presidents serving on the FOMC have different appointment mechanisms, statutory powers, organizational bases, and interests to represent, these groups may also differ in terms of their behavior and influence in the policymaking process.

In addition to its role in setting monetary policy, the Board of Governors has regulatory and supervisory responsibilities that cover the domestic operations of U.S. banks and bank holding companies, the U.S. operations of foreign banking organizations, and the foreign activities of U.S. banking organizations. The board also has the authority to set margin requirements that limit the use of credit for purchasing or carrying securities, and it is responsible for the development and administration of banking regulations.

The district Reserve Banks, as the operating arms of the Federal Reserve System, hold reserves for depository institutions in their district

---

2. The FOMC is also responsible for directing Federal Reserve operations in foreign currencies, but our analysis will not focus on this responsibility.

and make discount loans to such institutions. They are responsible for the distribution of currency and coin in their districts as well as check processing, wire transfers, and automated clearinghouse services. The district Reserve Banks provide checking accounts for the U.S. Treasury and issue and redeem government securities. The board has delegated to the district banks the responsibility for supervising and examining bank holding companies and state-chartered member banks located in their districts to ensure their safety and soundness and compliance with banking regulations.[3] In addition, each district bank maintains an independent research staff that monitors and analyzes national and regional economic conditions.

In setting policy, the Federal Reserve System is guided by the objectives set forth in the Employment Act of 1946. This act calls for the achievement of high employment, sustainable economic growth, and stable prices. Monetary policy—the management of interest rates and monetary aggregates—is the Fed's primary tool for achieving these statutory objectives. As noted, the FOMC is the Fed's principal monetary policy decision-making body. In the following section, we look at this important committee in greater detail.

## 2.2 Decision-Making Processes within the FOMC

The FOMC periodically meets to adopt monetary policy directives—formal statements that describe the committee's instructions for conducting monetary policy. Although the FOMC is comprised of all the governors and the district Reserve Bank presidents, the committee's decisions are formally made by majority rule among voting members. Voting members include all seven members of the Board of Governors, the president of the Federal Reserve Bank of New York, and four of the presidents of the remaining eleven district banks. Voting privileges rotate in a prescribed manner among the district banks.[4] Currently,

---

3. The Federal Reserve shares bank supervisory responsibilities with the Office of the Comptroller of the Currency (national banks), the Federal Deposit Insurance Corporation (state-chartered banks that are not members of the Federal Reserve System), and various state regulatory agencies (state-chartered banks).

4. The district banks, other than New York, are divided into four rotation groups: (1) Boston, Philadelphia, and Richmond; (2) Cleveland and Chicago; (3) Atlanta, St. Louis, and Dallas; and (4) Minneapolis, Kansas City, and San Francisco. Within each group, voting privileges rotate annually among the banks. Thus, in the three-member groups, one bank votes for one year and is off for two years while each of the others takes a turn; in the two-member group, the banks vote in alternate years.

meetings occur at intervals of about six weeks; at times in the past, meetings were somewhat more frequent, occurring at roughly monthly intervals. In addition, the committee occasionally has meetings via telephone conference calls, and policy changes can be adopted in this setting as well.

Meetings of the FOMC have usually followed a standard protocol. Prior to the meeting, Federal Reserve staff members prepare several documents for distribution to committee members. These include the Beige Book, the Green Book, and the Blue Book. The Beige Book summarizes prevailing regional economic conditions organized by Federal Reserve district. The Green Book presents national economic data, including current and historical data, as well as staff forecasts for several quarters into the future. The Blue Book presents alternative policy scenarios for the upcoming intermeeting period and sometimes for longer horizons.

The Blue Book scenarios provide options for discussion as the committee proceeds to the selection of a policy directive. These scenarios describe alternative settings for policy instruments, usually with predictions for associated variables. For example, in the 1970s, policy scenarios described target ranges for the federal funds rate and the money growth rates thought to be compatible with them. Frequently, the Blue Book presents three policy scenarios, which can be ordered on an "ease-to-tightness" dimension. Table 2.1 provides an example taken from the Blue Book for the FOMC meeting held on January 16, 1973, in which the committee was presented with three funds rate target ranges and the associated forecasts for money growth. In this case, alternative A has the easiest specifications (with the lowest funds rate target range and the highest money growth targets), alternative C has the tightest specifications, and alternative B is an intermediate option. Although Blue Book alternatives can be thought of as a menu of choices, the committee is not bound to select one of these options per se. It has not

**Table 2.1**
Blue Book policy scenarios for the FOMC meeting on January 16, 1973

| Scenario | Target funds rate range (%) | Target money supply (M1) growth range (%) |
|---|---|---|
| A | 5.375–5.875 | 6.0–7.0 |
| B | 5.625–6.250 | 5.0–6.0 |
| C | 5.750–6.500 | 4.0–5.0 |

been unusual for an adopted directive to include funds rate targets from one alternative and money growth forecasts from another. On still other occasions, the FOMC has adopted options intermediate to those specifically listed.[5]

At the meeting itself, the discussion of monetary policy is preceded by a staff presentation on the state of the economy. After the staff presentation, members discuss their own impressions of economic conditions, with bank presidents normally emphasizing conditions in their regions. The general discussion of economic conditions is then followed by the policy go-around, in which members describe their preferred policy prescriptions, often framing recommendations with references to Blue Book scenarios. Additional discussion may follow, as the committee seeks to arrive at an acceptable directive. Ultimately, a directive is crafted and brought to a formal vote by majority rule. In the formal voting, members can either "assent" or "dissent." When dissenting votes are cast, explanations are recorded in the "Minutes of the Federal Open Market Committee," a brief summary of proceedings published after a one-meeting lag.[6] These explanations almost always characterize dissents as favoring either additional ease or additional tightness in policy.[7] Dissenting votes are rather infrequent, occurring in just 7.8 percent of all votes over the 1966–1996 period.

The role of the chairman in this process has varied. Sometimes chairmen choose to speak first in the policy go-around, offering a clear policy proposal to the committee. Greenspan, for example, generally offers his preferences before other members speak. In contrast, Burns occasionally spoke first but frequently did not. In arriving at a policy directive, it is usually the chairman who crafts the specification of an alternative that will be accepted. The chairman's role in deliberations is

---

5. Karamouzis and Lombra (1989) note that over the 1971–1979 period, the FOMC made adjustments to the Blue Book alternatives in 59 out of 108 meetings (that is, 55 percent of the time).

6. This is the current title of the meeting summary, and it has been in effect since the FOMC meeting of February 2–3, 1993. Prior to that, it was called the "Record of Policy Actions of the Federal Open Market Committee." Meeting summaries were published only in the Board of Governors' annual report until 1967; beginning in July 1967, they were also published in the monthly *Federal Reserve Bulletin*. The practice of publishing the summaries in the *Bulletin* was discontinued after December 2001; they are now available from the Board of Governors' Web site or through links from any of the district Reserve Bank Web sites.

7. On several occasions, members have dissented on the basis of an objection to operating procedures instead of a disagreement about the degree of ease or tightness implicit in the policy stance.

clearly distinct from those of other members, even though it is difficult to point to statutory provisions that endow the chairman with special influence.

Also notable is the lack of a formal mechanism permitting political principals to directly influence FOMC meeting outcomes. The FOMC (as well as the entire Federal Reserve System) was created by the U.S. Congress and could be abolished or restructured if Congress chose to do so. In the absence of legislative change, however, Congress does not have the ability to manipulate the stance of monetary policy on a day-to-day basis. The U.S. president also has limited powers. As mentioned earlier, the president appoints board members (subject to confirmation by the Senate), but once appointments are made, long term lengths would appear to minimize the leverage a president has over the appointees. The terms for chairmen are shorter and reappointment is possible, suggesting more opportunity for political leverage, but overall the Fed enjoys considerable formal independence.

## 2.3   Monetary Policy Operating Procedures

Once a monetary policy directive is adopted by the FOMC, it must be implemented. Although directives may appear to outsiders to be rather vaguely worded, they do reflect an understanding between the FOMC and the open market account manager at the New York Federal Reserve Bank, who implements monetary policy via open market operations (that is, buying and selling government bonds). In carrying out open market operations, the Fed has at times followed different operating procedures—it has chosen to target different instruments under its influence. The following sections briefly describe alternative operating procedures.[8]

### 2.3.1   Targeting Reserves
In conducting open market operations, the Fed buys and sells government bonds. When the Fed buys bonds, the purchase increases reserves in the banking system (banks' holdings of cash or their deposits with the Federal Reserve). Initially, this leaves banks with excess reserves (reserves in excess of regulatory requirements), but because reserves do not yield interest, banks will begin to loan out excess reserves. This

---

8. Our discussion of Federal Reserve operating procedures draws from Board of Governors (1994); Gilbert (1985); and Mishkin (2003).

process creates demand deposits, increasing the supply of money. If the Fed instead sells bonds, the money supply will contract. By targeting reserves, the Fed influences the supply of money and, less directly, other macroeconomic variables. Under a reserve targeting regime, interest rates adjust to equate the quantity of money demanded with the quantity supplied. As a result, interest rates will fluctuate in response to money demand shifts as well as Fed-induced changes in the money supply.

### 2.3.2 Direct Targeting of Interest Rates
When the Fed has targeted interest rates, the specific target has been the federal funds rate, which is the interest rate that banks charge each other for overnight loans. Under this procedure, the Fed selects a target level (or range) for the funds rate that is to apply in the period between FOMC meetings. As conditions vary in this period, the demand for money (and hence reserves) will also fluctuate. In order to maintain the targeted value for the funds rate, the Fed must inject or drain reserves as necessary to meet fluctuations in demand. By targeting the funds rate, the Fed must tolerate fluctuations in reserves and, ultimately, the monetary aggregates.

### 2.3.3 Indirect Targeting of Interest Rates
The Fed has at times followed procedures that can be characterized as indirect interest rate targeting. One of these procedures involves the targeting of borrowed reserves—that is, discount borrowing from the Fed. Behaviorally, borrowed reserves are responsive to the spread between the discount rate and the funds rate. The discount rate is an administratively controlled interest rate at which the Fed lends reserves to banks, while the funds rate is a market rate at which banks lend to each other. Prior to January 2003, the funds rate typically exceeded the discount rate, so when the difference between the two rates was larger, banks wanted to borrow more from the Fed (borrowing remained limited because of administrative disincentives, however).[9] For a given discount rate, it followed that the funds rate and

---

9. Prior to January 2003, discount window regulations required that banks first exhaust other available sources of funds and justify their need for borrowed reserves. This required the Fed to review borrowers' funding situations, and the below-market rate on discount loans necessitated close monitoring of how borrowed reserves were used. Also, banks borrowing repeatedly at the discount window could be viewed as financially weak (hence the existence of an antiborrowing tradition in the banking system). The chief

discount borrowing varied directly, so borrowed reserve targeting was an indirect method of targeting interest rates.

To see this point more clearly, suppose that the discount rate has been set, and that economic fluctuations cause an upward shift in money demand and the demand for reserves. In the absence of an injection of reserves, interest rates would rise, increasing the spread between the funds rate and the discount rate. This would increase discount borrowing, which is not permitted under the borrowed reserve targeting procedure. To hit its borrowing target, the Fed would have to supply additional reserves, keeping the funds rate and the spread essentially unchanged, as it does under a direct funds rate targeting scheme.

Interest rates can also be indirectly targeted when free reserves provide the proximate target. Free reserves are excess reserves in the banking system minus the volume of discount loans. By holding higher levels of free reserves, banks forgo the opportunity to earn interest. This implies that interest rates and free reserves are inversely related, and targeting free reserves results in indirect control of interest rates. Once again, suppose that there is an upward shift in money demand. In the absence of a change in the money supply, this would cause an increase in interest rates, which would in turn cause banks to reduce holdings of free reserves. To maintain the targeted level of free reserves, the Fed would again have to supply additional reserves, keeping the funds rate essentially unchanged.

### 2.3.4 Operating Procedures since 1951

From the establishment of the FOMC by the Banking Act of 1935 until the early 1950s, interest rates were either at Depression era lows or being pegged at low levels to keep down the Treasury's borrowing costs. The interest rate peg began during World War II but continued into the postwar period. By the early 1950s, the Fed's growing dissatisfaction with this arrangement led to the Treasury–Federal Reserve Accord of

---

consequence of these practices was that banks were reluctant to borrow at the discount window even when tight money market conditions made such borrowing appropriate. Under the discount window regulations now in effect, the Fed's lending rate is set as a premium above the target federal funds rate, and discount lending is restricted to generally sound institutions as determined by their examination ratings and capital. Moreover, eligible institutions are no longer required to exhaust other sources of funds before coming to the discount window. These new procedures are expected to reduce the Fed's administrative costs and make the discount window a more attractive source of liquidity when money market conditions become tighter.

1951, which freed the Fed to conduct monetary policy independently of the Treasury's financing needs. The remainder of this section offers a brief description of the operating procedures followed by the Fed during the post-Accord period.

During the 1950s and 1960s, the Fed loosely targeted "money market conditions," either focusing on interest rates directly or indirectly via free reserves.[10] In the 1970s, the Fed moved toward direct interest rate targeting, although it often permitted the federal funds rate to fluctuate within specified bands. When money growth rates were higher (lower) than projected, the funds rate would normally move to the upper (lower) end of its target range.

From October 1979 until October 1982, the Fed appeared to make a radical change, abandoning interest rates as a target in favor of nonborrowed reserves in an effort to gain greater control over money growth and inflation. Nonborrowed reserves is the largest component of total reserves, and this operating procedure approximates that characterized as reserve targeting in section 2.3.1. Despite the apparent change, some (for instance, Greider 1987) have argued that this was primarily a politically motivated choice permitting the Fed to achieve much higher levels for the funds rate, while deflecting responsibility for excessively high interest rates. Fair (1984) makes the case that an interest rate reaction function can accurately describe policy during the period of nonborrowed reserve targeting, as long as one properly accounts for an increased concern with lagged money growth.

In October 1982, the Fed abandoned the targeting of nonborrowed reserves and instead began to target borrowed reserves. As we have noted, this can be characterized as an indirect method of targeting interest rates. Through the 1980s, the Fed gradually moved from indirect to direct targeting of the federal funds rate. This shift was largely completed by 1990, although the Fed did not formally acknowledge that this was the case until 1997.

In sum, the Fed has directly or indirectly targeted the federal funds rate almost continuously since the 1950s, as Goodfriend (1991) and Bernanke and Blinder (1992) have previously argued. The 1979–1982 interval of nonborrowed reserve targeting provides an apparent brief exception, but one that can be interpreted as interest rate targeting if added concern with lagged money growth is recognized and taken into account.

---

10. Romer and Romer (2002) document the importance of interest rates for the implementation of monetary policy during the 1950s.

## 2.4   Conclusions

In this chapter, we have described the institutional arrangements that shape the environment for monetary policymaking in the United States. We have considered the structure and functions of the Federal Reserve System as well as the operating procedures that have been used for implementing the FOMC's monetary policy decisions. With this institutional background, we are now in a position to review the academic literature on monetary policymaking.

# 3                    Analytical Background

We begin this chapter by describing three broad areas of research that are related to the work in this book. The first of these involves the behavior of politicians and their influence on monetary policymaking; specifically, we look at political business cycle models of opportunistic and partisan varieties. The second strand of research views the Federal Reserve as a bureaucracy and focuses on its internal motivations and decision making. Finally, we discuss the theory of the time inconsistency problem, which offers an explanation for the existence of an inflationary bias in monetary policy and has spawned a substantial body of work on the role of central bank independence. These issues are reviewed more comprehensively by Drazen (2000), Keech (1995), and Persson and Tabellini (2000).

We then focus more narrowly on previous studies of monetary policymaking that most closely relate to the inquiry undertaken in this book. We review the literature on monetary policy reaction functions, which empirically describe the Fed's behavior in making monetary policy. We also discuss work that has employed FOMC voting records to analyze preferences and choices made by individual members of the committee.

## 3.1 Political Business Cycles

In this section, we describe theories linking election cycles with cyclical movements in macroeconomic policies and outcomes. We first discuss opportunistic political business cycles and then consider partisan political business cycles.

### 3.1.1 Opportunistic Political Business Cycles
The "opportunistic" political business cycle model predicts that incumbent governments interested in their own electoral advantage may try

to generate favorable economic conditions (that is, high output and employment along with low inflation) as elections approach. This idea was given formal expression by Nordhaus (1975) as the theory of the political business cycle, which says that "within an incumbent's term in office there is a predictable pattern of policy, starting with relative austerity in early years and ending with the potlatch right before elections" (1975, 187). Nordhaus's original model has been criticized for its reliance on an assumption of adaptive expectations that permits voters to be systematically victimized by manipulative politicians in each election. The model was reformulated, however, by Rogoff and Sibert (1988) as a game of imperfect information with an assumption of rational expectations, and it has continued to attract attention in empirical analyses.

Empirically applying the political business cycle model to monetary policy, Grier (1987) provided econometric support for the existence of an electoral cycle in money growth. To do so, he estimated a reaction function explaining money growth with variables describing the current state of the economy and dummy variables to account for electoral timing. Beck (1987) confirmed the presence of a cycle in monetary policy, but argued that the electoral pattern primarily reflected accommodation of fiscal policy pressures. Using more flexible functional forms, Haynes and Stone (1989) and Grier (1989) countered with stronger support for the presence of a cycle; in Grier's later study, evidence for the cycle persisted even when controls for the stance of fiscal policy were introduced into the model. At the very least, this work clearly demonstrates that the hypothesis of a monetary political business cycle cannot be dismissed.

### 3.1.2 Partisan Political Business Cycles

Hibbs (1977) popularized a second genre of political business cycle models based on partisan differences. He argued that left-of-center and right-of-center parties respond to distinct clienteles with different interests and objectives and that macroeconomic policy should shift in predictable ways in response to partisan change brought about by elections. He also offered empirical support for his hypothesis; in a cross-country analysis, he found that unemployment rates were lower under left-leaning political regimes.

Although Hibbs studied unemployment outcomes directly, subsequent research has investigated the existence of partisan patterns in the conduct of monetary policy. For the United States, there is support for the proposition that Republican presidential administrations, on average, have been characterized by more restrictive monetary policies than Democratic administrations (Alesina and Sachs 1988; Beck 1984; Chappell and Keech 1986, 1988; Grier and Neiman 1987; Havrilesky 1987; Hibbs 1986, 1987). Grier (1991, 1996) finds that the partisan composition of congressional oversight committees also affects the stance of monetary policy.[1]

Alesina (1987), Alesina and Sachs (1988), and Chappell and Keech (1986, 1988) developed partisan models with rational expectations (now commonly referred to as "rational partisan" models). In these models, partisan differences and electoral uncertainty combine to create election-related policy surprises with resulting fluctuations in real economic outcomes. Chappell and Keech (1988) specifically estimated the impact of election-related partisan surprises in monetary policy on the path of the unemployment rate for the United States.

## 3.2 The Federal Reserve as a Bureaucracy

Partisan and opportunistic models are driven by the motives of politicians who must influence the Fed via external pressure. Another strand of research examines the Fed as a bureaucracy, emphasizing the objectives of the Fed itself rather than those of its political principals. It is often presumed that bureaucracies maximize their power or budgets, and the Fed is unique among agencies in both its budgeting and policymaking independence.

The Fed's expenses are funded from earnings on its portfolio of government bonds. These earnings are substantial, and the Fed regularly turns over a residual profit to the Treasury after paying its expenses.[2] While this arrangement might appear to have little relevance for monetary policy choices, there is a possible link. Toma (1982) notes that when the Fed exchanges money for bonds (in an open market purchase), it trades an asset that bears no interest for one that does, producing an incentive for monetary expansion. Shughart and Tollison (1983) have provided supporting evidence, observing that increases in Federal Reserve employment (presumably an "expense preference" valued by the Fed) are correlated with expansion of the monetary base.

---

1. This conclusion is not without its critics, however. Beck (1990) and Chopin, Cole, and Ellis (1996a, 1996b), for example, have argued that Congress has relatively little influence on the Fed's monetary policy decisions.
2. In 2002, the Fed turned over in excess of $24 billion to the Treasury (Board of Governors 2002).

For the Fed, power and prestige may be more important bureaucratic concerns than the budget. In the conduct of monetary policy, the Fed's prestige and power stem largely from its independence, which under current arrangements is considerable. Despite its independence, the Fed is aware that its actions are monitored by Congress, which could limit that independence through legislative action. Bills that would alter the Fed's powers are introduced in Congress with some regularity, but legislative threats are most numerous and credible when economic conditions are poor and the Fed's policy actions are scrutinized (Havrilesky 1995).

Woolley's study of Fed policymaking (1984) suggests that bureaucratic motivations might have been responsible for the easy monetary policy stance that enhanced the reelection prospects of Richard Nixon in 1972. Nixon had imposed price controls in 1971, and the FOMC feared that in an era of price controls, increases in interest rates would not be politically tolerable. By avoiding rate increases, the committee hoped to avoid mandatory controls that would have represented a more substantial threat to its independence. Havrilesky (1995) further argues that the president's influence over the Fed may stem from an implicit alliance with the Fed—the president is a valued ally because of the power to veto threatening legislation emanating from Congress.

The Fed's bureaucratic motives can affect its monetary policy strategy in several other ways. Presumably, the Fed's power and prestige are derived from the importance of its monetary policymaking functions. Fed officials frequently cultivate the view that because current economic conditions are uniquely complex, monetary policy decisions should be left to professionals, like themselves, who have the necessary expertise.[3] To further this view, the Fed has historically been secretive, providing little information about its policy decisions or the reasoning behind those decisions (Goodfriend 1986). The Fed has become more open in recent years—by announcing the FOMC's monetary policy decision immediately after each committee meeting, by reporting the specific target adopted for the federal funds rate, and by releasing the voting record immediately after each committee meeting. Neverthe-

---

3. This was true even in the early days of the Federal Reserve System. In 1926, board member Adolph Miller testified that the administration of credit policy had to be based on policymakers' judgment and discretion: "Yes.... I think it is important to realize that no two situations are identical. They do not repeat themselves with such accuracy that the method by which you successfully deal with one situation will insure an equally satisfactory result in another situation" (House Committee on Banking and Currency, 1926, quoted in Meltzer 2003, 186).

less, Greenspan's public statements would never be cited as examples of transparency; indeed, during testimony before the Senate Banking Committee he once famously (and self-deprecatingly) remarked, "If I say something which you understand fully in this regard, I probably made a mistake" (June 20, 1995, quoted in Kahaner 2000, 126).

Mystery and complexity can also be used to justify the use of discretion instead of rules in monetary policymaking. Some economists (for example, Friedman 1960) have argued that the results of monetary policy would be improved if the Fed were to announce and follow simple rules for the setting of a policy instrument. The Fed, however, has rejected mechanical rules, instead taking the view that flexibility is needed to deal with unusual contingencies. This choice may also reflect bureaucratic motives. If the Fed were merely in charge of administering a preformulated rule, its bureaucratic importance would be greatly diminished.

The Fed's bureaucratic goals are further served by its effort to make decisions in a consensual fashion (Krause 1996). Disagreements over policy occasionally surface during FOMC deliberations, but those private disagreements generally do not become public. Efforts are made to craft policy directives that not only gain majority support but, if possible, unanimous support. By making decisions in a consensual manner and keeping disagreements internal, the Fed may reduce the likelihood of external meddling and criticism (Greider 1987; Havrilesky and Schweitzer 1990; Krause 1994, 1996; Knott 1986; Woolley 1984).

### 3.3 The Theory of the Time Inconsistency Problem

The time inconsistency problem provides a third strand of literature that has become important in the study of the politics of monetary policy. In most economies, the price level rises over time. In the absence of a strong case for the desirability of inflation, one is led to suspect a political bias toward inflationary policies. The time inconsistency problem, described by Kydland and Prescott (1977) and applied to monetary policy by Barro and Gordon (1983), offers a possible explanation for such a bias.

According to this theory, policymakers value both low inflation and reductions in unemployment below its natural rate. If the public expects zero inflation, policymakers have an incentive to lower unemployment with a positive money supply surprise. But if the public has rational expectations, this incentive will be anticipated, rendering both the desired unemployment reduction and zero-inflation equilibrium untenable. Rather, inflation will be positive in equilibrium and will persist at a level where the policymaker balances the perceived marginal costs of inflation and marginal (short-run) gains from lower unemployment. Although it is not widely appreciated, a similar result was described by Nordhaus (1975) in a setting where expectations were adaptive rather than rational.

To avoid a suboptimal inflationary equilibrium, some have proposed that politicians should appoint "conservative" central bankers (that is, those who are less concerned with output gains than their political principals) and grant them independence in day-to-day policymaking (Rogoff 1985; Waller 1992b). Subsequently, a substantial empirical literature has developed on the relationship between central bank independence and inflation across countries (Alesina and Summers 1993; Cukierman 1992; Cukierman, Webb, and Neyapti 1992; Havrilesky and Granato 1993). Cukierman (1992) concluded that the preponderance of the evidence supports the view that independence and low inflation are connected, but that evidence is not overwhelming.

## 3.4 Committee Reaction Function Studies

We will next describe two strands of the empirical literature on monetary policy that are closely related to the work undertaken in this book. In this section, we discuss reaction function studies; in the following section, we consider studies that have used dissent voting data to investigate internal decision making by the FOMC.

Reaction functions are empirically estimated equations that describe the behavior of monetary policymakers by linking the setting of a policy instrument to prevailing levels or forecast values of macroeconomic variables that the policymakers ultimately want to influence. Early applications of the reaction function technique include studies by Dewald and Johnson (1963) of the objectives of U.S. monetary policy over the 1952–1961 period and by Reuber (1964) of the objectives of Canadian monetary policy over the 1949–1961 period. Khoury (1990) has surveyed the results of a number of reaction function studies of monetary policy.

Our discussion of operating procedures in chapter 2 made the case that over most of the post-Accord period, it is reasonable to regard the

federal funds rate as the Fed's operating instrument, making it a leading candidate as the dependent variable in a reaction function (Havrilesky, Sapp, and Schweitzer 1975; Abrams, Froyen, and Waud 1980;
Beck 1982). However, previous reaction function studies have also
used the M1 money supply (Dewald and Johnson 1963; Christian
1968), the monetary base (Barth, Sickles, and Wiest 1982), total reserves
(Beck 1984; Havrilesky 1967), free reserves (Dewald and Johnson 1963;
Christian 1968; Friedlaender 1973), or the Treasury bill rate (Dewald
and Johnson 1963; Christian 1968; Fair 1984) as the dependent variable. The Employment Act of 1946 made the federal government responsible for maintaining high employment consistent with stable
prices, suggesting that (un)employment and inflation should be included as independent variables in estimated reaction functions. In
some cases, variables indicating exchange rates or the balance of pay-
ments have also been included.

Although findings differ somewhat depending on the period covered and the precise empirical specification, in general the reaction
function literature supports the proposition that the Fed "leans against
the wind" in conducting monetary policy—that is, the adopted policy
stance is "easier" during recessions and "tighter" when the economy is
at full capacity or inflation is high (Dewald and Johnson 1963; Christian 1968; Havrilesky, Sapp, and Schweitzer 1975; Abrams, Froyen,
and Waud 1980; Barth, Sickles, and Wiest 1982; Beck 1982, 1984; Havrilesky 1967). The empirical evidence is also consistent with the idea
that the Federal Reserve seeks interest rate stability, but it generally
does not support the notion that international factors weigh significantly in the Federal Reserve's decision process.[4]

Important methodological issues in the estimation of reaction functions were identified by Abrams, Froyen, and Waud (1980). They
noted that most previous reaction function studies had used past or
current values of targets as independent variables in empirical specifications, even though the FOMC formulates policy on the basis of *forecasts* of these variables. The failure to use the appropriate forecast
variables implies that the explanatory variables are subject to measurement error, which in turn implies that reaction function estimates will

---

4. Exceptions are Havrilesky, Sapp, and Schweitzer (1975), who found that international
factors were occasionally significant during the 1964–1974 period; and Abrams, Froyen,
and Waud (1980), who found that during the 1970s, international considerations were
significant, but only after the United States moved to floating exchange rates in March
1973.

be biased. In addition, the use of current values in place of forecasts of the target variables produces a simultaneity bias if policy choices affect the target variables within the current period. As a remedy, Abrams, Froyen, and Waud (1980) proposed an instrumental variables technique for constructing *consistent forecasts* to be used as explanatory variables in place of current or lagged values of target variables. In the work that follows in this book, forecast variables included in reaction functions are the "real-time" Green Book forecasts that were available to FOMC members at the time of the meeting. These forecasts were based on information available prior to the meeting, thereby avoiding the simultaneity problem. Also, because they are the exact forecasts that were available to the committee, measurement error should be minimal.

In recent years, it has become fashionable to estimate reaction functions that take the form of a "Taylor rule." On a normative basis, Taylor (1993) argued that a simple, specific interest rate targeting rule would provide desirable macroeconomic outcomes. His rule links the federal funds rate to the deviation of inflation from a target value and to the gap between actual and potential output. Other analysts have estimated reaction functions that adopt this specification, usually finding that they provide reasonably accurate descriptions of the historical behavior of the Federal Reserve (for instance, Judd and Rudebusch 1998). Orphanides (2001), however, has shown that while estimated Taylor rules employing ex post revised data seem to capture historical behavior well, those employing real-time data are less satisfactory.

The empirical specifications we employ in this book generally do not adopt the Taylor rule specification, although they can approximate it closely. The primary differences are that our reaction functions use the unemployment rate as an indicator of capacity utilization instead of the output gap and that we also include output growth as an explanatory variable. Given that unemployment forecasts have been more readily available and more frequently discussed in FOMC meetings than the output gap, this is a reasonable choice.

Alt and Woolley (1982) noted an important caveat that should be remembered when interpreting reaction functions. Reaction function parameters reflect not only preferences over outcomes but also perceptions of relevant macroeconomic constraints (that is, the correct macroeconomic model). For example, if the monetary authority's reaction function were to indicate greater sensitivity to inflation in recent than in past years, that might indicate that the authority has become more inflation averse, or it might mean that it has come to believe that inflation is controllable but other variables are not.

## 3.5   Analysis of FOMC Voting Records

As we have noted, at each of its regular meetings, the FOMC adopts a monetary policy directive by majority vote. Any member who objects to the adopted policy may cast a dissenting vote, and dissenting members typically provide a written explanation of their dissent. With only a few exceptions, the written explanations that members provide when they dissent permit their votes to be further classified as "dissents favoring additional tightness" or "dissents favoring additional ease" relative to the adopted directive. A number of studies have investigated the internal dynamics of decision making at the Fed by analyzing dissent voting patterns. Most of these studies investigate differences in the voting behavior of various groups of committee members, offering evidence of behavioral differences across FOMC members that are related to status as a governor or a Reserve Bank president, partisan heritage, and educational and career background characteristics.

The pioneering work of Canterbery (1967) and Yohe (1966) first noted differences in the voting behavior of governors and Reserve Bank presidents. Subsequent work examining this distinction has revealed that governors have tended to prefer more expansionary monetary policy than the Reserve Bank presidents (Belden 1989; Gildea 1990; Havrilesky and Gildea 1991a; Havrilesky and Schweitzer 1990; Puckett 1984; Woolley 1984). Other analyses have indicated that governors appointed by Democratic presidents have tended to be more ease-oriented in their monetary policy preferences than governors appointed by Republican presidents (Havrilesky and Gildea 1991b, 1992; Puckett 1984; Woolley 1984).

Canterbery (1967) also analyzed the effects of backgrounds in law, banking, and economics on FOMC voting behavior. Analyses by Gildea (1990) and Havrilesky and Gildea (1991b) have suggested that career backgrounds in central government are associated with preferences for easier monetary policies. In addition, Havrilesky and Gildea (1992) have found that governors who are professional economists have tended to be especially "reliably partisan" in their monetary policy voting behavior (that is, their voting records are predictable based on partisan affiliations).

In a series of articles, Tootell (1991a, 1991b, 1996, 1999) has used dissent voting data in the estimation of monetary policy reaction functions in order to assess differences in individuals' policy preferences. He begins by classifying the adopted monetary policy directive for each FOMC meeting according to its proposed movement relative to the status quo: easier, tighter, or unchanged. He then classifies the policy positions of each individual member of the FOMC in a similar fashion. If a voter assents, that member is attributed the same preference as that adopted in the directive. If a voter dissents, that member's explanation is used to categorize policy preferences as favoring an easier, tighter, or unchanged policy. Tootell then estimates a reaction function that explains the categorical policy preference variable using a set of standard indicators of macroeconomic conditions. An important limitation of Tootell's data coding scheme is that it fails to recognize the distinctiveness of dissent votes. A dissent favoring a move to tighten is behaviorally different from an assent that *concurs* with a committee move to tighten—dissents indicate greater strength of preference. Following an approach similar to that of Tootell, Chang (2003) has also used the dissent voting record and a reaction function framework to describe individuals' policy preferences. Her coding of the data, like Tootell's, does not fully account for the unique behavior that produces dissents.

Regardless of the scheme employed to categorize choices, voting data have crucial limitations. First and most important, dissent votes are unusual—in most cases, individuals assent in the formal vote even when they have expressed reservations about the proposed policies. As we noted in chapter 2, dissents represent only 7.8 percent of the voting observations over the 1966–1996 period. Second, dissenting votes are expressions of preference relative to the adopted policy of the committee as a whole, but the adopted policy is itself a function of the preferences of the individual FOMC members. The failure to recognize and account for the endogeneity of the adopted directive when modeling individual choices could potentially produce misleading inferences. Third, dissent voting records provide no information about the preferences of nonvoting members, even though these members attend meetings, discuss policy issues, and might influence the committee's decisions.

Moreover, most studies of the FOMC voting record have suffered from a failure to control for the state of the economy and the prevailing policy stance when comparing committee members. A dissent in favor of ease when the current policy stance is restrictive is different from a dissent for ease when policy is already expansionary. Further, the tendency of a given member to dissent must indirectly depend on the relationship of that individual's preferences to those of other committee members. As the composition of the committee changes, this will affect committee choices as well as individuals' tendencies to dissent. Laney (1990) and Tootell (1991a, 1991b, 1996) examined FOMC voting records to detect differences across members while controlling for prevailing economic conditions, and Havrilesky and Schweitzer (1990) explained dissent voting patterns on the basis of differences between the characteristics of an individual and those of the rest of the committee. These studies, however, have not estimated individual reaction functions of a conventional form in which an individual's desired setting for a policy instrument is specified to be a function of forecast values of macroeconomic target variables.

In sum, the information content of the voting data is limited, and correctly interpreting the information these data do contain is more complex than one might expect. Nevertheless, the dissent voting data are easy to obtain and provide an objective and consistent record of individuals' monetary policy preferences over long periods of time. In chapter 4, we will use dissent voting data to investigate some prominent theories related to political influences over monetary policymaking. To do so, we employ a methodology that permits the estimation of individual reaction function parameters using dissent voting data, while accounting for the endogeneity of the adopted directive and for the state of prevailing economic conditions.

## 3.6   Conclusions

In some fashion, this book is related to all of the major themes and more specialized research genres described above. A distinguishing feature of our work is the effort to provide empirical analysis of the microfoundations that underlie the politics of monetary policymaking. If political influences are important, they must be important for particular individuals who serve on the FOMC, and we examine influence at the level of individuals. In some cases, a focus on individuals may suggest reformulations of existing theories.

For example, consider the opportunistic political business cycle model. If an incumbent president is to contrive a preelection expansion of monetary policy, which members of the FOMC will engineer that expansion? Theory and previous empirical studies have treated the Fed as a monolithic actor, but political loyalties are likely to differ across individual committee members. Similarly, models of partisan change implicitly assume that when presidential administrations change, the FOMC will respond, even if the composition of the committee has not changed. Our analysis in chapter 4 investigates political models of monetary policymaking while distinguishing the incentives of different individuals.

Voting theory implies that the median voter's preference should prevail when decisions made by a committee follow a majority voting rule. On the other hand, bureaucratic theories suggest that the Fed will value consensus, and institutional practices provide a distinctive role for the FOMC's chairman. Given these alternative perspectives on decision making, we seek to describe how the preferences of individual committee members are linked to the decisions taken by the committee, recognizing separate pressures for majoritarian, consensual, or chairman-dictated outcomes.

Although the time inconsistency problem and central bank independence are less central to the pursuits of this book, we also address these topics. As we have noted, the theory of the time inconsistency problem offers a potential explanation for the existence of an inflationary bias to monetary policy. In chapter 10, we evaluate this explanation by examining the textual records of FOMC deliberations during the years when Arthur Burns chaired the committee. The Burns years were characterized by high and volatile inflation, so an examination of the reasoning of policymakers, as revealed in recorded deliberations, may provide insights about the relevance of the time inconsistency problem as an explanation for the rise of inflation.

Our methods and data also place the analysis in this book in the literatures on monetary policy reaction functions and dissent voting patterns. One significant contribution of the book is the development of methods that permit econometric estimation of monetary policy reaction functions for individual members of the FOMC. A second important contribution involves the development of original data characterizing the policy preferences of FOMC members. These data supplement and enrich the dissent voting data that have been used in previous studies that have described the preferences of individual monetary policymakers.

# 4    A Long History of FOMC Voting Behavior: Individual Reaction Functions and Political Influence on the Monetary Policy Decision Process

In this chapter, we use dissent voting data to investigate the monetary policy preferences of individual FOMC members over the 1966–1996 period.[1] We begin the chapter by describing a methodology for using dissent voting data to estimate monetary policy reaction function parameters for individuals. We then employ that method in two applications. The first application produces an ease-to-tightness ranking of eighty-three members who served on the FOMC during our sample period. In the second application, we investigate extensions of the opportunistic and partisan political business models that permit political pressures to vary for different individuals. Testing these model extensions requires the use of data that describe individual policy preferences.

In the preceding chapter, our literature review listed key limitations and problems associated with the use of dissent voting data. Most important, members of the FOMC rarely cast dissenting votes even when they have reservations about adopted directives—in our complete sample of 3,339 voting observations drawn from the 1966–1996 period, dissents were observed in only 262 cases (7.8 percent). Because of the limitations of the voting data, most of the analysis in this book makes use of the richer data sets we have constructed using the *Memoranda* and *Transcripts*.

There are nevertheless good reasons for using voting data for some purposes. First, almost all of the previous literature that has examined the behavior of individual FOMC members has relied on voting records as a primary data source. To facilitate comparisons, it is helpful to use data that have commonly been employed by previous researchers.

---

1. The material in this chapter draws heavily from Chappell and McGregor (2000). It also extends our earlier work in Chappell, Havrilesky, and McGregor (1993) and McGregor (1996).

Second, voting records provide a description of preferences in a form that can be interpreted in a consistent fashion over time. In the formal vote at each meeting, members either concur with the adopted directive or they dissent, with dissents normally expressing a preference for either additional ease or additional tightness. Even if operating targets change over time, this characterization of voting outcomes remains appropriate. Finally, voting data are available promptly after meetings, while transcripts are available only after a five-year holding period. If one wishes to analyze the choices of individual FOMC members for recent periods, voting data provide the only option.

In this chapter, the availability of a long sample is an especially important issue. We will investigate partisan and electoral pressures on members' voting decisions, focusing attention on how these political pressures differ for members with different political loyalties. The use of voting data is attractive in this context because the available sample includes multiple elections and multiple instances of partisan turnover. Specifically, between 1966 and 1996, the White House was occupied by three Democrats (Lyndon Johnson, Jimmy Carter, and Bill Clinton) and four Republicans (Richard Nixon, Gerald Ford, Ronald Reagan, and George H. W. Bush), and there were eight presidential elections.

Our analysis uses dissent voting data to estimate individual reaction function parameters. Analyzing voting behavior in a reaction function context offers three fundamental advantages over descriptive analyses of the dissent voting record. First, our empirical model links policy outcomes to the reaction functions of FOMC members, providing microfoundations for aggregate reaction functions. Second, specifying differences across members as differences in reaction function parameters implicitly controls for prevailing policy and the state of the economy when evaluating members' voting records. Third, differences across FOMC members can be interpreted as differences in desired settings of a policy instrument, which are more meaningful indicators of policy preferences than dissent voting frequencies. The development of an econometric method for estimating individual reaction function parameters using dissent voting data therefore represents a key contribution of this chapter.[2]

We begin by explaining our econometric methodology for estimating individual reaction functions in the first section of this chapter. The

---

2. The method presented here was previously employed in Chappell and McGregor (2000). Similar, but not identical, procedures were used by McGregor (1996) and Chappell, Havrilesky, and McGregor (1993, 1995, 1997).

second section further describes the data employed and the empirical specifications for reaction functions. In the third section, we estimate reaction functions that permit intercepts to differ across FOMC members; the results are used to produce our ranking of members according to preference for monetary ease. The fourth section builds on the work of Chappell, Havrilesky, and McGregor (1993) and McGregor (1996) and uses the individual reaction function methodology to investigate partisan and opportunistic political pressures that affect different committee members in different ways.

## 4.1   A Model of FOMC Decision Making

This section describes an econometric model of FOMC decision making. In the model, each FOMC member's policy preferences are represented by a monetary policy reaction function in which parameters are permitted to vary across individuals. The dependent variable of each individual's reaction function is an unobserved "desired" federal funds rate. Dissent voting decisions are assumed to depend on the distance between an individual's unobserved desired rate and the rate that is actually adopted, enabling us to model voting decisions with an ordered probit model. By further specifying a process by which individual preferences are aggregated to produce a collective choice, we introduce model restrictions that are sufficient to determine the scale of the probit model's underlying "latent propensity," permitting identification of the individual reaction function parameters.

### 4.1.1   Individuals' Reaction Functions

Although operating procedures employed by the FOMC have varied over the 1966–1996 period, we follow the literature in describing policymaking in this period primarily as an interest rate targeting regime (see chapter 2). Consequently, each of the $N$ members of the committee is assumed to have a desired interest rate reaction function of the following form:[3]

---

3. A notational convention should be emphasized here. The variable $N$ (indexed by $i = 1, \ldots, N$) refers to the number of committee member positions excluding the chairman. If there are no absences or vacancies, $N = 11$. Because there are occasional absences and vacancies, $N$ varies over time. For expository purposes, we ignore this complication and drop the time subscript on $N$. In contrast, the variable $K$ (indexed by $k = 1, \ldots, K$) indicates specific individuals (for example, Wayne Angell, Henry Wallich, Nancy Teeters, and so on) who served on the committee. Over an extended period of time, many specific individuals occupy the $N$ positions on the committee, so $K$ is larger than $N$.

$$R_{it}^* = \alpha_0 + \sum_{k=1}^{K} \alpha_k D_{kit} + \sum_{j=1}^{J} \beta_j X_{jt} + e_{it}, \ i = 1, \ldots, N, \ t = 1, \ldots, T. \qquad (4.1)$$

The dependent variable, $R_{it}^*$, is member $i$'s desired federal funds rate for the period between meeting $t$ and meeting $t+1$ (referred to hereafter as the intermeeting period). This variable is unobserved. The independent variables $X_{jt}$, $j = 1, \ldots, J$, vary over time but not across members. The variables $X_{jt}$ include forecast values of macroeconomic variables of concern to the Fed (for example, inflation, unemployment, and economic growth). The remaining independent variables, $D_{kit}$, $k = 1, \ldots, K$, vary across both members and time. In section 4.3 below, the $D_{kit}$ will consist of dummy variables indicating specific individuals who served on the committee. Their inclusion permits individual-specific reaction function intercept shifts. In section 4.4, these individual-specific intercepts will be replaced with dummy variables designed to capture the influence of political considerations on individuals' FOMC voting behavior. The coefficients of the macroeconomic indicators, the $\beta_j$s, are assumed to be identical across committee members. This assumption is not required by our estimation technique but has been imposed as a reasonable restriction given the limited information content of the voting data.

Our model also includes a reaction function for the chairman (who is indicated by the position index 0):

$$R_{0t}^* = \delta_0 + \sum_{m=1}^{M} \delta_m C_{mt} + \sum_{j=1}^{J} \beta_j X_{jt} + e_{0t}, \ t = 1, \ldots, T. \qquad (4.2)$$

Equation (4.2) contains a series of dummy variables, $C_{mt}$, $m = 1, \ldots, M$, indicating specific chairmen (for instance, Burns, G. William Miller, Paul Volcker, and Greenspan). We assume that coefficients of the $X_{jt}$ are identical for chairmen and other members.

Error terms for the reaction functions (4.1) and (4.2) are assumed to be identically distributed normal random variables that are uncorrelated over time but correlated across individuals at a given meeting:

$$E(e_{it}) = 0, \ E(e_{it}^2) = \sigma^2, \text{ for } i = 0, \ldots, N, \ t = 1, \ldots, T,$$

$$E(e_{it}e_{js}) = 0 \text{ for } t \neq s, \ E(e_{it}e_{jt}) = \rho\sigma^2 \text{ for } i \neq j.$$

### 4.1.2  Monetary Policy Choices and FOMC Voting

Monetary policy directives are adopted by a majority vote at regularly scheduled FOMC meetings. Although the chairman has just one vote, it is generally recognized that he exerts additional influence, perhaps via control of the agenda or direction of staff activities.[4] To allow for this enhanced power, we specify that the proposed funds rate, $R_t$, is a weighted average of the chairman's own desired rate and the mean desired rate of all other members:

$$R_t = \gamma R_{0t}^* + (1 - \gamma)\left(\frac{1}{N}\right) \sum_{i=1}^{N} R_{it}^*, \ 1/12 \leq \gamma \leq 1.0, \tag{4.3}$$

where $\gamma$ is the weight attached to the chairman's desired interest rate. In practice, the proposed rate is put to a formal vote only when its adoption is assured, so the proposed interest rate is also the adopted target rate. Further, we assume that $R_t$ is observed as the average funds rate prevailing in the subsequent intermeeting period.

Once the chairman has proposed a federal funds rate target to the committee, a formal vote follows. The summary records for FOMC meetings provide brief descriptions of members' reasons for dissenting votes, permitting us to classify votes as dissents favoring ease, dissents favoring tightness, or assents. The discrete variable $V_{it}$, referring to the vote by member $i$ in meeting $t$, is defined to equal $-1$, 1, or 0 in these three cases.

Because dissents apparently occur only when disagreements are acute, we assume that a member dissents when the difference between the proposed federal funds rate and that individual's desired federal funds rate exceeds a threshold level $\lambda > 0$:[5]

If $R_t - R_{it}^* > \lambda$, then $V_{it} = -1$ (dissent favoring ease), $\qquad$ (4.4.a)

If $R_t - R_{it}^* < -\lambda$, then $V_{it} = 1$ (dissent favoring tightness), $\qquad$ (4.4.b)

If $-\lambda \leq R_t - R_{it}^* \leq \lambda$, then $V_{it} = 0$ (assent). $\qquad$ (4.4.c)

---

4. For a more detailed discussion of the role and influence of the chairman in the monetary policy decision process, see chapters 7 and 8.

5. Anecdotal evidence concerning motives for dissent and pressures for consensus are presented in Havrilesky and Schweitzer (1990); Chappell, Havrilesky, and McGregor (1993); and Krause (1994). Havrilesky and Schweitzer (1990) also develop a net utility maximizing model of FOMC dissent voting.

Condition (4.4.a) says that if the proposed rate exceeds the desired rate by more than $\lambda$ units, then member $i$ will dissent favoring ease. Similarly, (4.4.b) says that if the proposed rate is less than the desired rate by more than $\lambda$ units, then member $i$ will dissent favoring tightness. Finally, (4.4.c) says that if the difference between the desired and proposed rates is less than or equal to $\lambda$ in absolute value, then member $i$ will assent.

### 4.1.3 Estimation of the Model

Substituting (4.1) and (4.2) into (4.3) yields a reduced form equation for the postmeeting federal funds rate:

$$R_t = \gamma \delta_0 + (1 - \gamma)\alpha_0 + \gamma \sum_{m=1}^{M} \delta_m C_{mt} + \sum_{j=1}^{J} \beta_j X_{jt} + (1 - \gamma) \sum_{k=1}^{K} \alpha_k \bar{D}_{kt} + u_t,$$

(4.5)

where

$$\bar{D}_{kt} = \left(\frac{1}{N}\right) \sum_{i=1}^{N} D_{kit}, \quad u_t = \gamma e_{0t} + (1 - \gamma)\bar{e}_t,$$

and

$$\bar{e}_t = \left(\frac{1}{N}\right) \sum_{i=1}^{N} e_{it}.$$

This equation explains the postmeeting interest rate as a function of exogenous economic variables and variables describing the composition of the committee. Its reduced form coefficients can be estimated by ordinary least squares (OLS). Note that estimates of the structural coefficients of the economic variables in the reaction function (that is, the $\beta_j$s) are obtained directly from this regression.

Once again considering voting behavior, we substitute (4.1) and (4.5) into conditions (4.4) to obtain the following conditions:

$$\text{If } \gamma(\delta_0 - \alpha_0) + \gamma \sum_{m=1}^{M} \delta_m C_{mt} + (1 - \gamma) \sum_{k=1}^{K} \alpha_k \bar{D}_{kt} - \sum_{k=1}^{K} \alpha_k D_{kit} + v_{it} > \lambda,$$

then $V_{it} = -1$,

(4.6.a)

If $\gamma(\delta_0 - \alpha_0) + \gamma \sum_{m=1}^{M} \delta_m C_{mt} + (1 - \gamma) \sum_{k=1}^{K} \alpha_k \bar{D}_{kt} - \sum_{k=1}^{K} \alpha_k D_{kit} + v_{it} < -\lambda,$

then $V_{it} = 1,$                                          (4.6.b)

If $-\lambda \le \gamma(\delta_0 - \alpha_0) + \gamma \sum_{m=1}^{M} \delta_m C_{mt} + (1 - \gamma) \sum_{k=1}^{K} \alpha_k \bar{D}_{kt} - \sum_{k=1}^{K} \alpha_k D_{kit} + v_{it} \le \lambda,$

then $V_{it} = 0,$                                          (4.6.c)

where $v_{it} = \gamma e_{0t} + (1 - \gamma)\bar{e}_t - e_{it}$. Conditions (4.6) characterize a reduced-form ordered probit model, which can be estimated using voting data pooled over members and time.[6] The model explains members' voting decisions as a function of variables indicating the identity or characteristics of a particular voting member (the $D_{kit}$) as well as variables describing the composition of the full committee (the $\bar{D}_{kt}$).

To gain some intuition for the effect of committee composition variables on individual voting decisions, consider a simple example. Suppose that individual $i$ is a Democrat-appointed governor. Further, suppose that Democratic appointees tend to favor monetary ease, while Republican appointees tend to favor monetary tightness. If Democrats currently dominate the FOMC, policy should be easy, and the individual should not need to dissent frequently for ease. In contrast, if Republicans dominate the committee, policy should be tighter, and a single Democratic appointee would more frequently dissent for ease.

Probit models generally require a normalization in order to identify the scale of a latent propensity that determines values of an observable discrete variable. In our model, the latent propensity is measured in interest rate units, and its scale can be identified via cross-equation restrictions implied by the model. Appendix 2 provides additional details on this issue and others associated with the estimation of the model.

## 4.2   Data Considerations

We adopt a conventional empirical specification for members' reaction functions. The dependent variable is the postmeeting federal funds

---

6. McKelvey and Zavoina (1975) describe the ordered probit model and provide an application to roll-call voting in the U.S. Congress.

rate, denoted $R_t$, and measured as the average rate between meetings $t$ and $t + 1$. Among the independent variables included in the $X_{jt}$ variables in equation (4.5) is the lagged federal funds rate, $R_{t-1}$. This variable captures inertial dynamics in the movement of interest rates. Also included is recent money growth, $\dot{M}_t$, defined as the average growth rate of M1 over the three months prior to the month of the meeting. Money growth is included because of its presumed link to future inflation; at times, it was also an explicit intermediate target. The remaining elements of $X_{jt}$ are two-quarter-ahead forecasts of macroeconomic goal variables thought to influence monetary policy: $\hat{P}_t$, the annualized percentage inflation rate calculated from the implicit price deflator for real gross national product (GNP); $\hat{U}_t$, the civilian unemployment rate; and $\hat{Y}_t$, the annualized percentage growth rate of real GNP.[7] These forecasts are taken from the projections presented to the FOMC in the Green Book prepared for each committee meeting by the Federal Reserve Board staff.

It is likely that the desired policies of different individuals respond to economic conditions in different ways; it is also likely that individuals' policy preferences change over time. Unfortunately, limitations of the voting data prohibit us from being very general in permitting coefficients to vary over time and members. We do, however, investigate a possible structural break of some importance.

Following the FOMC meeting of October 6, 1979, the Federal Reserve announced a change in operating procedures that was intended to give the committee better control of money growth in its efforts to slow the rate of inflation. We attempt to capture this shift in focus by creating a dummy variable for the period following October 1979 (POST79) and augmenting the reaction function with interactions of this dummy variable with each of the economic variables in the specification. In addition, because the Federal Reserve placed particular emphasis on its money growth targets during the period from October 1979 through September 1982, we define a dummy variable for this specific period (D7982) and include in the reaction function an interaction of this dummy variable with money growth. The latter modification follows the example suggested by Fair (1984). Our later empirical results support both of these modifications to account for regime changes.

---

7. Our forecasts are generally calculated as an average of forecasts for the current quarter and the upcoming quarter. For several meetings where only the current quarter forecast is available, that measure is employed.

The data set used in the empirical analysis includes the previously described variables and individual voting records linked to 319 regular FOMC meetings over the 1966–1996 period.[8] The votes of the chairman (who always assented) are excluded, as are observations associated with vacancies, absences, and uncodable dissents. The final sample contains 3,339 voting observations; among these, there are 85 dissents for ease (2.5 percent), 177 dissents for tightness (5.3 percent), and 3,077 assents (92.2 percent). In appendix 1, we provide a list of all individuals who served on the FOMC during the 1966–1996 period along with their voting records on the monetary policy directive.

## 4.3  Empirical Results: Individual FOMC Members

We first specify the $D_{kit}$ in the ordered probit model (4.6) as dummy variables for the eighty-three individual FOMC members who voted five or more times on the monetary policy directive during the 1966–1996 period. The remaining members are represented in the intercept, $\alpha_0$. The variables $C_{mt}$ indicate the identity of the current chairman; dummies for Burns, Miller, Volcker, and Greenspan are included, with William McChesney Martin captured by the intercept, $\delta_0$.

Table 4.1 provides estimates of the empirical model, including OLS estimates of (4.5) and ordered probit estimates of (4.6). The reported estimation imposes values for $\rho$ (the correlation between different individuals' contemporaneous reaction function error terms) and $\gamma$ (the chairman's voting weight), with the selected values ($\rho = 0.70$ and $\gamma = 0.50$) based on estimates and data discussed in chapters 5 and 6. Appendix 2 provides additional details on this issue, but substantive conclusions of the analysis are not sensitive to these parameter choices.

The results for the economic variables offer support for the view that the Fed leans against the wind. The coefficient on the growth rate of real GNP is positively signed and statistically significant, suggesting that the Fed tightened when output growth accelerated and eased when it slowed. The results for the *POST79* interaction terms support the hypothesis of a regime change, with significantly stronger responses to inflation and output growth following the October 1979 change in operating procedures. The inflation result, especially, is

---

8. Although more recent voting data are available, Green Book forecasts are subject to a five-year lag. At the time of this writing, 1996 is the latest year for which these forecasts are available. Also, our sample does not include telephone meetings that have been held between regularly scheduled FOMC meetings.

**Table 4.1**
Monetary policy reaction functions with individual-specific effects[a]

| Variable | Coefficient | $p$-value |
| --- | :---: | :---: |
| *OLS estimates* | | |
| $R_{t-1}$ | 1.0148** | 0.000 |
| $\dot{M}$ | 0.0352** | 0.013 |
| $\hat{\dot{P}}$ | 0.0352 | 0.537 |
| $\hat{\dot{Y}}$ | 0.0620** | 0.004 |
| $\hat{U}$ | −0.0785 | 0.208 |
| $R_{t-1} \cdot POST79$ | −0.1784** | 0.000 |
| $\dot{M} \cdot POST79$ | −0.0411* | 0.022 |
| $\hat{\dot{P}} \cdot POST79$ | 0.3134** | 0.000 |
| $\hat{\dot{Y}} \cdot POST79$ | 0.2136** | 0.000 |
| $\hat{U} \cdot POST79$ | −0.0810 | 0.248 |
| $\dot{M} \cdot D7982$ | 0.0940** | 0.000 |
| $\sum_{k=1}^{K} \alpha_k \overline{D}_{kt}$ | 0.1154 | 0.715 |
| *Ordered probit estimates of individual intercepts* | | |
| INTERCEPT $[\gamma(\delta_0 - \alpha_0)]$ | −0.1192 | 0.459 |
| Burns | 0.1669 | 0.402 |
| Miller | −0.9356* | 0.012 |
| Volcker | −0.8038** | 0.004 |
| Greenspan | −0.7485* | 0.015 |
| Angell | 0.0176 | 0.967 |
| Balles | −0.2916 | 0.548 |
| Baughman | 0.2728 | 0.515 |
| Black | 0.6093 | 0.067 |
| Blinder | −0.7002 | 0.059 |
| Boehne | −1.1692** | 0.004 |
| Bopp | 0.1485 | 0.634 |
| Boykin | 0.2579 | 0.522 |
| Brimmer | 0.1800 | 0.586 |
| Broaddus | 1.0095 | 0.070 |
| Bucher | −0.8121* | 0.047 |
| Clay | 0.4377 | 0.247 |
| Coldwell | 0.2960 | 0.460 |
| Corrigan | −0.7836* | 0.016 |
| Daane | 0.1888 | 0.582 |
| Debs | 0.2258 | 0.556 |
| Eastburn | −0.8741* | 0.038 |
| Ellis | −0.0018 | 0.995 |
| Ford | 1.4416** | 0.007 |

**Table 4.1**
(continued)

| Variable | Coefficient | $p$-value |
| --- | --- | --- |
| Forrestal | −0.7612* | 0.023 |
| Francis | 1.4160** | 0.001 |
| Galusha | −0.2083 | 0.505 |
| Gardner | −0.1342 | 0.635 |
| Gramley | −0.1792 | 0.663 |
| Guffey | −0.2461 | 0.592 |
| Hayes | 1.0828** | 0.001 |
| Heflin | −0.1557 | 0.641 |
| Heller | −0.6157 | 0.057 |
| Hickman | 0.5986 | 0.146 |
| Hoenig | −0.1075 | 0.841 |
| Holland | −0.2130 | 0.638 |
| Horn | −1.6135** | 0.001 |
| Hoskins | 1.2344** | 0.006 |
| Irons | 0.9902* | 0.050 |
| Jackson | 0.1636 | 0.686 |
| Johnson | −1.0504* | 0.018 |
| Jordan | −1.2303 | 0.093 |
| Keehn | −0.7263* | 0.026 |
| Kelley | −0.7412 | 0.100 |
| Kimbrel | 0.2408 | 0.523 |
| Laware | 0.1643 | 0.674 |
| Lilly | −0.6349 | 0.191 |
| Lindsey | −0.8497 | 0.143 |
| Maclaury | 0.4928 | 0.265 |
| Maisel | −0.7108* | 0.042 |
| Martin, P. | −2.0172** | 0.000 |
| Mayo | −0.1706 | 0.572 |
| McDonough | −0.8650* | 0.014 |
| McTeer | −1.0518** | 0.005 |
| Melzer | 0.4451 | 0.343 |
| Meyer | −1.2107** | 0.003 |
| Minehan | −0.6169 | 0.102 |
| Mitchell | −0.3904 | 0.248 |
| Morris | −0.3358 | 0.477 |
| Moskow | −0.6169 | 0.102 |
| Mullins | −0.8162* | 0.020 |
| Parry | 0.1130 | 0.802 |
| Partee | −1.1399** | 0.001 |
| Phillips | −0.8770* | 0.013 |

**Table 4.1**
(continued)

| Variable | Coefficient | $p$-value |
|----------|-------------|-----------|
| Rice | −1.5010** | 0.000 |
| Rivlin | −1.2107** | 0.003 |
| Roberts | −0.4291 | 0.270 |
| Robertson | 0.0435 | 0.894 |
| Roos | 0.3860 | 0.539 |
| Scanlon | 0.6467 | 0.111 |
| Schultz | −0.8350* | 0.014 |
| Seger | −2.3382** | 0.000 |
| Sheehan | −0.5212 | 0.232 |
| Shepardson | 0.8980 | 0.057 |
| Sherrill | −0.0864 | 0.776 |
| Solomon | −0.8777 | 0.103 |
| Stern | −0.0631 | 0.884 |
| Swan | −0.0778 | 0.800 |
| Syron | −0.7273 | 0.061 |
| Teeters | −1.9843** | 0.000 |
| Timlen | −0.7779* | 0.026 |
| Treiber | 0.4995 | 0.311 |
| Volcker | 0.3564 | 0.345 |
| Wallich | 0.5588 | 0.095 |
| Wayne | −0.2437 | 0.447 |
| Willes | 1.6086** | 0.001 |
| Winn | 0.3994 | 0.261 |
| Yellen | −0.8297* | 0.022 |
| $\lambda$ | 2.0417** | 0.000 |

[a] Estimates for $\rho = 0.70$ and $\gamma = 0.50$
*Significant at the 0.05 level, two-tailed test
**Significant at the 0.01 level, two-tailed test

consistent with our expectations. The lagged federal funds rate is also highly significant, reflecting substantial inertia in the path of the funds rate; however, the significant negative coefficient on the interaction term involving the funds rate suggests that the Fed has placed less emphasis on interest rate stability since October 1979. The money growth coefficient is positive and significant; however, the combination of dummy variable interactions indicates especially large responses to money growth during the October 1979–September 1982 period and essentially no response to money after 1982.

The constant term reported in table 4.1 is the composite intercept, $\gamma(\delta_0 - \alpha_0)$, that appears in conditions (4.6), but the remaining parameter estimates are those for the model's structural parameters, $\lambda$ (the dissent threshold parameter) and the $\alpha_k s$ (the individual-specific intercepts).[9] The point estimate of $\lambda$, 2.04, appears to be large, but this is not surprising given the paucity of dissenting votes in the sample. If dissents are infrequent, this must be explained in the model by a strong aversion to dissent. Estimates of the individual-specific intercepts reveal considerable variation in preferences across committee members.

To facilitate comparisons across individuals, we use the estimates in table 4.1 and mean values of the economic variables to compute average desired interest rates for each individual who voted five or more times during the 1966–1996 period. Based on these average desired interest rates, table 4.2 ranks committee members from "easiest" to "tightest." For comparison, each member's net ease dissent frequency and rank by this measure are also provided (where the net ease dissent voting frequency is defined as dissents for ease minus dissents for tightness, divided by total votes). A positive value for the net ease dissent frequency indicates that the member dissented for ease more often than for tightness, while a negative value means that the member dissented for tightness more often than for ease.

In table 4.2, the ease tendencies of most governors are apparent, as are the tightness tendencies of most Reserve Bank presidents. These findings confirm results that have been noted in previous studies of dissent voting patterns and that are readily verified in our sample: governors account for 79 percent of the ease dissents, while Reserve Bank presidents account for 68 percent of the tightness dissents.[10] Rankings by average desired interest rates are similar to rankings by net ease dissent frequencies; the correlation coefficient between members' average desired interest rates and net ease dissent frequencies is −0.81 (the negative correlation reflecting the fact that low values of

9. The intraequation restrictions relating coefficients of the $\bar{D}_{kt}$ and the $D_{kit}$ variables in (4.6) are imposed in the estimation.

10. Previous studies have noted that Reserve Bank presidents, on average, appear to favor a more anti-inflationary policy stance than governors. See Puckett (1984); Woolley (1984); Belden (1989); Laney (1990); Havrilesky and Schweitzer (1990); Havrilesky and Gildea (1991a); Chappell, Havrilesky, and McGregor (1993); and McGregor (1996). Tootell (1991a, 1991b) fails to find significant differences between governors and Reserve Bank presidents; however, he employs a coding procedure that fails to account for the added intensity of preference revealed by dissents. More detailed descriptive statistics on our voting sample are provided in appendix 1.

**Table 4.2**
Federal Reserve governors and bank presidents ranked by average desired interest rates
and dissent voting frequencies, 1966–1996

| Member | Type | Average desired interest rate | Rank by average desired interest rate | Rank by net ease dissent frequency | Net ease dissent frequency (%) |
|---|---|---|---|---|---|
| Seger | Governor | 4.74 | 1 | 1 | 29.63 |
| Martin, P. | Governor | 5.06 | 2 | 3 | 16.13 |
| Teeters | Governor | 5.10 | 3 | 2 | 18.00 |
| Horn | Bank president | 5.52 | 4 | 8 | 5.26 |
| Rice | Governor | 5.58 | 5 | 7 | 6.35 |
| Jordan | Bank president | 5.85 | 6 | 12 | 4.35 |
| Rivlin | Governor | 5.87 | 7 | 17 | 0.00 |
| Meyer | Governor | 5.87 | 7 | 17 | 0.00 |
| Boehne | Bank president | 5.91 | 9 | 16 | 2.13 |
| Partee | Governor | 5.94 | 10 | 8 | 5.26 |
| McTeer | Bank president | 6.03 | 11 | 17 | 0.00 |
| Johnson | Governor | 6.03 | 12 | 15 | 2.86 |
| Solomon | Bank president | 6.20 | 13 | 17 | 0.00 |
| Phillips | Governor | 6.20 | 14 | 17 | 0.00 |
| Eastburn | Bank president | 6.21 | 15 | 5 | 8.57 |
| McDonough | Bank president | 6.22 | 16 | 17 | 0.00 |
| Lindsey | Governor | 6.23 | 17 | 17 | 0.00 |
| Schultz | Governor | 6.25 | 18 | 17 | 0.00 |
| Yellen | Governor | 6.25 | 19 | 17 | 0.00 |
| Mullins | Governor | 6.26 | 20 | 17 | 0.00 |
| Bucher | Governor | 6.27 | 21 | 4 | 10.00 |
| Corrigan | Bank president | 6.30 | 22 | 17 | 0.00 |
| Timlen | Bank vice president | 6.30 | 23 | 17 | 0.00 |
| Forrestal | Bank president | 6.32 | 24 | 17 | 0.00 |
| Kelley | Governor | 6.34 | 25 | 17 | 0.00 |
| Syron | Bank president | 6.35 | 26 | 17 | 0.00 |
| Keehn | Bank president | 6.35 | 27 | 17 | 0.00 |
| Maisel | Governor | 6.37 | 28 | 6 | 6.74 |
| Blinder | Governor | 6.40 | 29 | 17 | 0.00 |
| Lilly | Governor | 6.45 | 30 | 11 | 5.00 |
| Minehan | Bank president | 6.46 | 31 | 17 | 0.00 |
| Moskow | Bank president | 6.46 | 31 | 17 | 0.00 |
| Heller | Governor | 6.46 | 33 | 17 | 0.00 |
| Sheehan | Bank president | 6.56 | 34 | 8 | 5.26 |

**Table 4.2**
(continued)

| Member | Type | Average desired interest rate | Rank by average desired interest rate | Rank by net ease dissent frequency | Net ease dissent frequency (%) |
|--------|------|------|------|------|------|
| Roberts | Bank president | 6.65 | 35 | 17 | 0.00 |
| Mitchell | Governor | 6.69 | 36 | 13 | 3.20 |
| Morris | Bank president | 6.74 | 37 | 17 | 0.00 |
| Balles | Bank president | 6.79 | 38 | 52 | −2.08 |
| Guffey | Bank president | 6.83 | 39 | 57 | −4.35 |
| Wayne | Bank president | 6.84 | 40 | 17 | 0.00 |
| Holland | Governor | 6.87 | 41 | 14 | 2.94 |
| Galusha | Bank president | 6.87 | 42 | 17 | 0.00 |
| Gramley | Governor | 6.90 | 43 | 65 | −7.69 |
| Mayo | Bank president | 6.91 | 44 | 17 | 0.00 |
| Heflin | Bank president | 6.92 | 45 | 17 | 0.00 |
| Gardner | Governor | 6.95 | 46 | 17 | 0.00 |
| Hoenig | Bank president | 6.97 | 47 | 61 | −6.25 |
| Sherrill | Governor | 6.99 | 48 | 17 | 0.00 |
| Swan | Bank president | 7.00 | 49 | 17 | 0.00 |
| Stern | Bank president | 7.02 | 50 | 68 | −9.38 |
| Ellis | Bank president | 7.08 | 51 | 17 | 0.00 |
| Angell | Governor | 7.10 | 52 | 68 | −9.38 |
| Robertson | Governor | 7.12 | 53 | 49 | −1.02 |
| Parry | Bank president | 7.19 | 54 | 66 | −8.00 |
| Bopp | Bank president | 7.23 | 55 | 17 | 0.00 |
| Jackson | Governor | 7.24 | 56 | 53 | −2.56 |
| LaWare | Governor | 7.25 | 57 | 71 | −11.32 |
| Brimmer | Governor | 7.26 | 58 | 50 | −1.79 |
| Daane | Governor | 7.27 | 59 | 51 | −2.00 |
| Debs | Bank vice president | 7.31 | 60 | 17 | 0.00 |
| Kimbrel | Bank president | 7.32 | 61 | 58 | −4.69 |
| Boykin | Bank president | 7.34 | 62 | 75 | −15.63 |
| Baughman | Bank president | 7.35 | 63 | 55 | −4.17 |
| Coldwell | Bank president and governor | 7.38 | 64 | 60 | −5.68 |
| Volcker | Bank president | 7.44 | 65 | 63 | −6.67 |
| Roos | Bank president | 7.47 | 66 | 73 | −13.64 |
| Winn | Bank president | 7.48 | 67 | 67 | −8.47 |
| Clay | Bank president | 7.52 | 68 | 54 | −3.64 |

**Table 4.2**
(continued)

| Member | Type | Average desired interest rate | Rank by average desired interest rate | Rank by net ease dissent frequency | Net ease dissent frequency (%) |
|--------|------|------------------------------|----------------------------------------|-------------------------------------|-------------------------------|
| Melzer | Bank president | 7.53 | 69 | 78 | −22.58 |
| Maclaury | Bank president | 7.57 | 70 | 55 | −4.17 |
| Treiber | Bank vice president | 7.58 | 71 | 59 | −5.00 |
| Wallich | Governor | 7.64 | 72 | 77 | −18.03 |
| Hickman | Bank president | 7.68 | 73 | 64 | −7.32 |
| Black | Bank president | 7.69 | 74 | 76 | −17.91 |
| Scanlon | Bank vice president | 7.73 | 75 | 61 | −6.25 |
| Shepardson | Governor | 7.98 | 76 | 70 | −11.11 |
| Irons | Bank president | 8.07 | 77 | 72 | −13.33 |
| Broaddus | Bank president | 8.09 | 78 | 80 | −37.50 |
| Hayes | Bank president | 8.16 | 79 | 74 | −15.53 |
| Hoskins | Bank president | 8.32 | 80 | 81 | −43.75 |
| Francis | Bank president | 8.50 | 81 | 79 | −28.57 |
| Ford | Bank president | 8.52 | 82 | 83 | −62.50 |
| Willes | Bank president | 8.69 | 83 | 82 | −54.55 |

the individual average desired interest rates are associated with high net ease dissent frequencies). By either measure, governors Martha Seger, Preston Martin, and Nancy Teeters are the most ease-oriented FOMC members, while Reserve Bank presidents Mark Willes, William Ford, Darryl Francis, Lee Hoskins, Alfred Hayes, and Alfred Broaddus are among the most tightness-oriented members. There are, however, other comparisons that illustrate advantages of our ranking method over rankings based on dissent voting frequencies.

Consider Reserve Bank presidents David Eastburn of Philadelphia and Karen Horn of Cleveland. Eastburn dissented for ease more often than Horn, but our method ranks Horn as the easier of the two. The logic of the model implies that Horn's ease dissents came at a time when the committee had already adopted a more expansionary policy stance. More strikingly, neither William Sherrill nor Alice Rivlin ever dissented during the 1966–1996 period, and they tie for seventeenth in the ranking by net ease dissent frequency. Nevertheless, Rivlin ranks seventh easiest according to our estimates, while Sherrill is forty-eighth; again, this reflects the differences in prevailing policy stances across their tenures.

Our method also permits statistical tests of reaction function differences between pairs of individual FOMC members. With eighty-three individual intercepts, there are 3,403 possible pairwise comparisons. We do not report all of these test results here. There are, however, a number of significant differences. For example, Seger prefers significantly lower interest rates than thirty other governors (at the 0.10 level), while Henry Wallich prefers significantly higher interest rates than twenty-eight others.

Finally, we note one particularly interesting feature of our results. During the 1966–1996 period, seven women—governors Seger, Teeters, Rivlin, Susan Phillips, and Janet Yellen along with Reserve Bank presidents Horn and Cathy Minehan—have served on the FOMC. Our method ranks six of these women among the eighteen most ease-oriented members. In the past, concerns have been raised about the underrepresentation of women on the Board of Governors and as presidents of district Federal Reserve Banks. Given the small number of women in the sample, any conclusions would be speculative, but we cannot dismiss the possibility that greater representation of women in the Fed's monetary policy decision process would have an important effect on policy outcomes.

The results reported in this section lend support to the idea that an accurate characterization of differences in policy preferences across individual FOMC members is a necessary first step in the process of carefully describing the forces underlying the policy choices made by the committee. In the next section, we continue our analysis of dissent voting patterns, focusing on systematic political influences on monetary policy choices.

## 4.4    Political Influences on the Monetary Policy Decision Process

We turn now to an examination of how partisan and opportunistic political pressures might affect the FOMC's monetary policy decisions. While political business cycles have been widely studied, the models we develop are distinctive in recognizing that political pressures do not affect all FOMC members in the same way. We first investigate the relative importance of two possible channels through which partisan pressures might be exerted. Partisan influence could be a result of either direct presidential pressure exerted on all members of the FOMC or partisan considerations in presidential appointments to the Board of Governors. We then investigate how the timing of elections plays a role in the monetary policy decision process. We begin that analysis with a straightforward application of the opportunistic political business cycle model, which suggests that policy should move toward ease in preelection periods. That model is then reformulated in order to permit the political incentives of FOMC members to differ according to their partisan heritage. Essentially, we investigate partisan-opportunistic business cycle interactions in which the tendency to favor the incumbent president with expansionary policies before elections is tempered (or amplified) by considerations of partisan loyalty. An investigation of these extensions to the original partisan and opportunistic models *requires* an analysis of individual FOMC members' decisions—differences across individuals are fundamental to our hypotheses.

### 4.4.1   Political Influences on Monetary Policy: Analytical Background

The partisan business cycle model suggests that incumbent presidents will influence monetary policy in an ideological fashion, with Democratic administrations tending to support easier policies than Republican ones. This follows from Hibbs's (1977, 1987) argument that the distributional effects of easier monetary policy favor the working-class clienteles of Left parties relative to the higher-income clienteles of Right parties. If presidents directly influence monetary policy, then partisan turnover in the presidency should be accompanied by changes in monetary policy.[11]

The president can also exert partisan influence over the Fed indirectly via the appointments process. In our voting sample, evidence of partisan differences is readily apparent. About 74 percent of dissents by Democratic appointees favored ease compared to only 48 percent for Republican appointees. Opportunities to appoint governors occur infrequently, however, and gaining control of the FOMC by packing the board with reliable ideologues takes considerable time (Keech and

---

11. Despite the Fed's formal independence, there is a strong presumption that presidents do influence monetary policy. For example, Woolley (1984, 109) reports that "there is substantial consensus that presidents generally get the monetary policy they want from the Federal Reserve." Beck (1982), Havrilesky (1988), Kane (1980), and Weintraub (1978) have also argued that presidents have substantial influence over the Fed.

Morris 1997; Waller 1989). Further, the role of the Senate in confirming appointments can moderate partisan influence from the president (Chang 2003; Morris 2000; Waller 1992a). If appointments provide a means of partisan control, one would not expect to see immediate policy responses following turnover in the presidency. Rather, one would expect a delayed policy response following a series of appointments. Extending our earlier work (Chappell, Havrilesky, and McGregor 1993), we will explore channels of partisan influence, distinguishing direct influence from the president from influence exerted through the power of appointment.

The opportunistic political business cycle model focuses on electoral timing rather than partisan ideology. In this model, incumbent governments interested in their own electoral advantage try to generate favorable economic conditions (that is, high output and employment along with low inflation) as elections approach. Once again, application of this model to monetary policymaking requires an implicit assumption that presidents control the Fed. When elections approach, monetary policy responds in a way that favors the incumbent president.

This argument ignores the possibility that FOMC members may have distinct interests and loyalties. Because governors have long terms, it is not unusual for some of them to be appointees of presidents who preceded the incumbent. These governors' partisan loyalties may lie with the out-party rather than the incumbent, complicating the successful pursuit of an opportunistic political business cycle. The importance of partisan loyalties on the FOMC was explicitly noted in the *Wall Street Journal* of April 5, 1991, when Alan Murray reported a split between Reserve Bank presidents and Republican-appointed governors during election year 1988:

It was a presidential election year. And while few would acknowledge it, politics exacerbated the split between the Fed's governors and district-bank presidents. Led by the presidents, the policy committee pushed the fed funds rate up steadily through the year to combat potential inflation. But the governors in Washington by and large remained reluctant participants. They refused to raise the discount rate. The presidents were worried. Although they never said so in meetings, some wondered privately whether the governors—all of them Republican appointees—were holding down the discount rate to help George Bush win the coming presidential election.

In this case, nearing the end of eight years of a Republican presidency, the board was dominated by Republican appointees. But partisan dominance is the exception rather than the rule, and manipulating policy for the benefit of an incumbent might frequently meet with resistance from governors appointed by the opposition party. Extending McGregor's analysis (1996), we investigate interactions between pressures for preelection stimulus and partisan loyalties of governors.

### 4.4.2  Empirical Evidence: Direct Partisan Influence and Partisanship in Appointments

To investigate the impact of partisan political pressures, we again use the method developed in section 4.1 for estimating parameters of individual reaction functions. Now, however, we specify differences across individuals to reflect their political affiliations. Specifically, we replace the individual-specific dummy variables used in the previous section with group-specific dummy variables indicating governors appointed by Democratic and Republican presidents (bank presidents are represented in the intercept, $\alpha_0$).[12] These variables are intended to capture the influence that results from partisan patterns in the appointment of governors. We also now include among the $X_{jt}$ the dummy variable *DEMOPRES* to indicate that a Democrat currently holds the presidency. The latter variable should capture direct partisan influence from the executive branch.

The results obtained from estimating this model are presented in the model (1) column of table 4.3.[13] The results provide evidence of presidential influence over monetary policy in a systematically partisan fashion, with suggestions that both direct influence and the power of appointment are important channels. The coefficient of *DEMOPRES* indicates that an FOMC member's desired funds rate is about seventeen basis points lower when the current president is a Democrat; the coefficient falls just short of significance at the 0.10 level. There is

---

12. Havrilesky and Gildea (1991b, 1992) found that the "supply-side" appointees of Ronald Reagan differed notably from the appointees of other Republican presidents in their predilection for monetary ease. In our earlier work (Chappell, Havrilesky, and McGregor 1993; McGregor 1996), we distinguished Reagan's appointees from other Republican appointees and found the difference to be significant; indeed, the Reagan appointees were even more ease-oriented than Democratic appointees over the 1960–1987 period. In the late 1980s and early 1990s, several of Reagan's appointees became staunch advocates of *tighter* monetary policy; thus, the importance of the supply-sider distinction appears to have been a sample-specific phenomenon. As a consequence, we have not adopted it for our work here.

13. We proceed by estimating the reduced-form interest rate equation (equation 4.5) by OLS and the ordered probit model (conditions 4.6) by maximum likelihood, again using the values $\gamma = 0.50$ and $\rho = 0.70$.

slightly stronger evidence that desired funds rates differ according to the partisan affiliation of appointees. The results imply that a typical Democrat-appointed governor prefers a funds rate that is about twenty-two basis points lower than a typical Republican colleague, and this difference is significant at the 0.05 level.

The results also confirm that governors and Reserve Bank presidents behave differently. The negative coefficients on the dummy variables for Democratic and Republican appointees indicate that governors of each party prefer a lower federal funds rate than Reserve Bank presidents. These differences are significant at better than the 0.01 level.

### 4.4.3 Empirical Evidence: Electoral Influences on Monetary Policy

We next consider the role of elections in monetary policy decisions. We first modify the model to permit a conventional opportunistic cycle in which all members' policy preferences shift as an election approaches. Then we investigate whether specific individuals on the FOMC may be more inclined than others to vote the cause of the incumbent president.

The model (2) column of table 4.3 alters the model of the previous section by adding a variable to the $X_{jt}$ to capture the effects of electoral timing. We create a dummy variable ELCYCLE, which equals one for the two years preceding a presidential election and is otherwise equal to zero.[14] The results show that the coefficient of this variable is significantly negative (at the 0.05 level), supporting the hypothesis that members generally favor an easier policy stance prior to an election. When ELCYCLE is included in the model, the effect of DEMOPRES also becomes significant at the 0.05 level, strengthening support for conventional partisan differences.

To permit incentives for preelection ease to differ according to partisan loyalties, in the specification reported in the model (3) column, two additional variables are included among the $D_{kit}$. Democratic governors voting under Democratic presidents and Republican governors voting under Republican presidents are designated as INPARTY governors. Democratic governors voting under Republican presidents and Republican governors voting under Democratic presidents are designated as OUTPARTY governors. Each of these variables is interacted with the ELCYCLE dummy variable. These interactions permit differences in the voting behavior of in-party and out-party governors in the last two years of an administration.

---

14. We obtain similar results when the preelection period is limited to the year before the election rather than the two years before the election.

**Table 4.3**
Monetary policy reaction functions with partisan and electoral influences, 1966–1996[a]

| Variable | Model (1) | | Model (2) | | Model (3) | |
|---|---|---|---|---|---|---|
| | Coefficient | p-value | Coefficient | p-value | Coefficient | p-value |
| *OLS estimates* | | | | | | |
| INTERCEPT | 0.0155 | 0.982 | 0.2234 | 0.740 | 0.3049 | 0.733 |
| $R_{t-1}$ | 1.0022** | 0.000 | 0.9679** | 0.000 | 0.9683** | 0.000 |
| $\dot{M}$ | 0.0364* | 0.012 | 0.0375** | 0.009 | 0.0376** | 0.010 |
| $\hat{P}$ | 0.0458 | 0.489 | 0.0678 | 0.306 | 0.0681 | 0.306 |
| $\hat{Y}$ | 0.0659** | 0.003 | 0.0671** | 0.002 | 0.0668** | 0.003 |
| $\hat{U}$ | −0.0871 | 0.184 | −0.0501 | 0.452 | −0.0513 | 0.445 |
| $R_{t-1} \cdot POST79$ | −0.1969** | 0.000 | −0.1865** | 0.000 | −0.1867** | 0.000 |
| $\dot{M} \cdot POST79$ | −0.0477* | 0.013 | −0.0516** | 0.007 | −0.0515** | 0.008 |
| $\hat{P} \cdot POST79$ | 0.3439** | 0.000 | 0.3593** | 0.000 | 0.3593** | 0.000 |
| $\hat{Y} \cdot POST79$ | 0.2100** | 0.000 | 0.2260** | 0.000 | 0.2256** | 0.000 |
| $\hat{U} \cdot POST79$ | −0.0823 | 0.242 | −0.1256 | 0.081 | −0.1236 | 0.090 |
| $\dot{M} \cdot D7982$ | 0.0995** | 0.000 | 0.1058** | 0.000 | 0.1056** | 0.000 |
| DEMOPRES | −0.1712 | 0.123 | −0.2220* | 0.047 | −0.2241* | 0.049 |
| ELCYCLE | | | −0.2140* | 0.013 | −0.3369 | 0.752 |
| *Ordered probit estimates of individual intercepts* | | | | | | |
| INTERCEPT $[\gamma(\delta_0 - \alpha_0)]$ | −0.2959** | 0.000 | −0.2933** | 0.000 | −0.3191** | 0.000 |
| Burns | 0.2431 | 0.072 | 0.2410 | 0.072 | 0.2979* | 0.029 |
| Miller | −0.6618* | 0.037 | −0.6561* | 0.037 | −0.5746 | 0.067 |
| Volcker | −0.0552 | 0.747 | −0.0547 | 0.747 | 0.0067 | 0.968 |
| Greenspan | 0.0493 | 0.757 | 0.0489 | 0.757 | 0.0806 | 0.611 |

| | | | | | | |
|---|---|---|---|---|---|---|
| DEMOCRATIC GOVERNOR | -0.5555** | 0.000 | -0.5507** | 0.000 | -0.6468** | 0.000 |
| REPUBLICAN GOVERNOR | -0.3364** | 0.000 | -0.3335** | 0.000 | -0.3886** | 0.000 |
| INPARTY · ELCYCLE | | | | | -0.0369 | 0.729 |
| OUTPARTY · ELCYCLE | | | | | 0.4576** | 0.001 |
| $\lambda$ | 1.7263** | 0.000 | 1.7713** | 0.000 | 1.7295** | 0.000 |
| *Additional tests of hypotheses* | | | | | | |
| $\alpha_{Democratic\ governor} - \alpha_{Republican\ governor} = 0$ | -0.2191* | 0.016 | -0.2172* | 0.016 | -0.2582** | 0.004 |
| $\alpha_{Out\text{-}party\ cycle} - \alpha_{In\text{-}party\ cycle} = 0$ | | | | | 0.4945** | 0.000 |

[a] Estimates for $\rho = 0.70$ and $\gamma = 0.50$
* Significant at the 0.05 level, two-tailed test
** Significant at the 0.01 level, two-tailed test

The coefficient on the interaction of *OUTPARTY* with the cycle variable is positive and significant, while the coefficient on the interaction of *INPARTY* with the cycle variable is negative but insignificant. More important, the former coefficient is significantly greater than the latter coefficient at better than the 0.01 level. Therefore, in-party and out-party governors do behave differently prior to elections in a fashion consistent with expectations—out-party governors are less likely to support easy policies that might benefit the incumbent. Further, in this estimation, the original *ELCYCLE* variable is no longer significant, suggesting that the political monetary cycle is driven primarily by the behavior of in-party appointees. These results confirm similar patterns in the dissent voting record. Both ease and tightness dissents are roughly evenly divided between in-party and out-party governors in the first half of presidential election cycles. In the second half of these cycles, however, in-party governors cast about 79 percent of the ease dissents, while out-party governors cast 61 percent of the tightness dissents.[15]

### 4.4.4   Monetary Policy Signaling: An Alternative Measure of Direct Presidential Influence

As Havrilesky (1995) has argued, it is also possible that presidential pressures are effective *without* being systematically partisan. To permit this possibility, we have replicated the results of the preceding two sections while adding Havrilesky's *SAFER* (Signaling from the Administration to the Federal Reserve) index to the variables in $X_{jt}$. The *SAFER* index measures presidential preferences by coding statements made by administration officials and reported in the financial press. It is calculated as the sum of *Wall Street Journal* articles reporting statements advocating easier monetary policy (coded +1.0) or tighter monetary policy (coded −1.0) over the intermeeting period prior to each FOMC meeting. A complete list of the signal events that comprise the index is provided in Havrilesky (1995). The statements coded by *SAFER* need not follow consistent partisan patterns, and, in fact, frequencies of ease and tightness signals are similar across administrations. Because the *SAFER* index is available only through May 1994,

---

15. While political timing seems to matter for governors, the behavior of Reserve Bank presidents, who are not presidential appointees, has differed little over the election cycle. During the 1966–1996 period, the bank presidents' ease and tightness dissents were about evenly divided between the first and second halves of presidential terms. See appendix 1 for details.

we employ a truncated sample in estimations in which it is included. Results of the model with *SAFER* included are provided in table 4.4.

When *SAFER* is added to our model, we find that its coefficient is negative and significantly different from zero at the 0.01 level. This finding is in accord with the view that monetary policy accommodates the desires expressed by presidential signaling (recall that positive values for *SAFER* imply a desire for a lower funds rate) and confirms results reported by Havrilesky (1988, 1995). More important, introducing *SAFER* into the model has little effect on our conclusions about the partisan and electoral patterns present in monetary policymaking. Coefficients and significance levels for the variables indicating the party of the president, preelection periods, partisan appointment status, and cycle-related in-party and out-party effects are similar to those reported in table 4.3. This further suggests that *SAFER* primarily captures idiosyncratic policy preferences rather than those that are systematically related to elections or partisanship.[16]

As we conclude our discussion of political pressures, we should note that the results reported here differ in one way from those reported in Chappell, Havrilesky, and McGregor (1993). There, results indicated that the primary channel of partisan influence was the power of appointment. While the work in this chapter continues to find important partisan patterns in appointments, it also reveals strong evidence of conventional partisan shifts associated with influence from the incumbent president. This difference could be attributable to any of several changes we have made in our modeling methods, all adopted with the aim of improving the specification for individual reaction functions.[17]

---

16. This finding might be a result of an endogenous process generating signals. When presidents' preferences are in accord with usual political patterns, there may be little need for signaling. Hence, signals are observed only when they are idiosyncratic. A similar logic suggests that signaling might be most frequent when presidents are unhappy with the current state of policy; indeed, Havrilesky (1995) found some evidence that the misery index (the sum of the inflation and unemployment rates) does affect the amount of administration signaling. If presidents agree with the current policy stance, there should be little need to signal. This would suggest that the estimated *SAFER* coefficient is likely to be biased toward zero.

17. Five innovations in the current chapter are noteworthy: (1) we use an extended sample period, updating the data set on FOMC voting through 1996; (2) our analysis simultaneously accounts for opportunistic and partisan pressures rather than partisan pressures only; (3) the classification of partisanship no longer maintains a distinction between "ordinary" and "supply-side" Republicans; (4) the basic reaction function specification now permits a structural shift, recognizing the greater importance attached to price stability after 1979; and (5) forecast values of economic variables in the reaction functions are now "real-time" forecasts obtained from the Green Books available at FOMC meetings.

**Table 4.4**
Monetary policy reaction functions with partisan and electoral influences, 1966–1994[a,b]

| Variable | Model (1) | | Model (2) | | Model (3) | |
|---|---|---|---|---|---|---|
| | Coefficient | p-value | Coefficient | p-value | Coefficient | p-value |
| *OLS estimates* | | | | | | |
| INTERCEPT | 0.0172 | 0.980 | 0.2410 | 0.728 | 0.5770 | 0.522 |
| $R_{t-1}$ | 0.9848** | 0.000 | 0.9413** | 0.000 | 0.9415** | 0.000 |
| $\hat{M}$ | 0.0425** | 0.004 | 0.0449** | 0.002 | 0.0438** | 0.003 |
| $\hat{P}$ | 0.0311 | 0.639 | 0.0577 | 0.382 | 0.0580 | 0.381 |
| $\hat{Y}$ | 0.0616** | 0.006 | 0.0637** | 0.004 | 0.0637** | 0.004 |
| $\hat{U}$ | −0.0920 | 0.162 | −0.0438 | 0.511 | −0.0428 | 0.525 |
| $R_{t-1} \cdot POST79$ | −0.1941** | 0.000 | −0.1836** | 0.000 | −0.1819** | 0.000 |
| $\hat{M} \cdot POST79$ | −0.0505* | 0.013 | −0.0532* | 0.008 | −0.0518** | 0.010 |
| $\hat{P} \cdot POST79$ | 0.3871** | 0.000 | 0.4203** | 0.000 | 0.4174** | 0.000 |
| $\hat{Y} \cdot POST79$ | 0.2132** | 0.000 | 0.2358** | 0.000 | 0.2344** | 0.000 |
| $\hat{U} \cdot POST79$ | −0.1010 | 0.157 | −0.1618* | 0.027 | −0.1624* | 0.029 |
| $\hat{M} \cdot D7982$ | 0.0956** | 0.000 | 0.1007** | 0.000 | 0.1004** | 0.000 |
| DEMOPRES | −0.2776* | 0.026 | −0.3642** | 0.004 | −0.3617** | 0.004 |
| SAFER | −0.1087** | 0.000 | −0.1137** | 0.000 | −0.1154** | 0.000 |
| ELCYCLE | | | −0.2737** | 0.002 | −0.9456 | 0.391 |
| *Ordered probit estimates of individual intercepts* | | | | | | |
| INTERCEPT $[\gamma(\delta_0 - \alpha_0)]$ | −0.2902** | 0.000 | −0.2859** | 0.000 | −0.3209** | 0.000 |
| Burns | 0.2398 | 0.068 | 0.2363 | 0.068 | 0.3186* | 0.017 |
| Miller | −0.6439* | 0.039 | −0.6343* | 0.039 | −0.5146 | 0.093 |

| | | | | | |
|---|---|---|---|---|---|
| Volcker | −0.0502 | 0.763 | −0.0495 | 0.763 | 0.0408 | 0.803 |
| Greenspan | 0.0621 | 0.732 | 0.0612 | 0.732 | 0.0882 | 0.623 |
| *DEMOCRATIC GOVERNOR* | −0.5512** | 0.000 | −0.5430** | 0.000 | −0.6774** | 0.000 |
| *REPUBLICAN GOVERNOR* | −0.3226** | 0.000 | −0.3179** | 0.000 | −0.3596** | 0.000 |
| *INPARTY · ELCYCLE* | | | | | −0.0475 | 0.658 |
| *OUTPARTY · ELCYCLE* | | | | | 0.5873** | 0.000 |
| $\lambda$ | 1.7074** | 0.000 | 1.6820** | 0.000 | 1.7042** | 0.000 |
| *Additional tests of hypotheses* | | | | | | |
| $\alpha_{Democratic\ governor} - \alpha_{Republican\ governor} = 0$ | −0.2285* | 0.017 | −0.2251* | 0.017 | −0.3178** | 0.001 |
| $\alpha_{Out\text{-}party\ cycle} - \alpha_{In\text{-}party\ cycle} = 0$ | | | | | 0.6348** | 0.000 |

[a] Estimates for $\rho = 0.70$ and $\gamma = 0.50$

[b] The sample period is from January 1966 through May 1994, the interval for which the *SAFER* index is available

*Significant at the 0.05 level, two-tailed test

**Significant at the 0.01 level, two-tailed test

## 4.5   Conclusions

In this chapter, we have used dissent voting data to estimate monetary policy reaction functions that permitted parameters to differ across FOMC members. Our analysis covered the complete record of voting on monetary policy directives in the 1966–1996 period and consisted of two distinct applications of our method. In our first application, we estimated individual-specific intercepts for eighty-three FOMC members who served in our sample period. The results of this exercise documented considerable diversity in policy preferences across members. As in other studies, our evidence suggested that as a group, members of the Board of Governors systematically differ from Reserve Bank presidents, with bank presidents usually preferring a tighter policy stance. However, there were individual exceptions within each of these groups.

Our second application investigated two prominent hypotheses suggested by the literature on political economics. The first was the hypothesis that macroeconomic policy stances reflect systematically partisan preferences of politicians; the second was that opportunistic motives produce policy stances that fluctuate in association with the electoral calendar. Unlike most previous work investigating these hypotheses, our analysis has employed FOMC voting data to assess the effect of political pressures on the policy choices of individual policymakers.

We have found support for the conventional hypotheses that FOMC members' reaction functions shift toward ease when the Democrats assume the presidency and when elections are approaching. By focusing on the policy decisions of individuals, however, we have been able to provide a richer description of these political forces. First, we have shown that partisan pressures work both through direct influence from the president and indirectly through the power of appointment—governors appointed by Democratic presidents tend to favor easier policies than those appointed by Republicans. Second, opportunistic motives are tempered by partisan loyalty. In presidential election years, preelection stimulus is largely a result of pressure from in-party appointees; out-party appointees are more likely to favor a tight preelection policy stance that would undermine the incumbent. Each of these results reflects the presence of political pressures that vary across individuals in ways that generalize the conventional partisan and political business cycle models. Empirical tests of these model generalizations require data and methods like those that we have developed to detect differing policy preferences across individuals.

# 5  Data from the *Memoranda of Discussion* and *FOMC Transcripts*

*People think reading the raw transcripts is a way of learning things; I would suggest that if they spend six or eight months reading through some of this stuff, they won't like it.*

—Alan Greenspan, quoted in the *Transcripts*, October 22, 1993

Like most previous work describing the preferences of individual FOMC members, chapter 4 of this book used dissent voting data as the primary source of information. While voting data are revealing and useful, they are nevertheless limited—members dissent infrequently even when they hold differences of opinion. Records of FOMC deliberations contained in the *Memoranda of Discussion* and *FOMC Transcripts* provide more detailed descriptions of individual member preferences, albeit in a less easily quantified form. Interestingly, one of the earliest studies of FOMC decision making, Canterbery (1967), used the *Memoranda* to code "informal dissents" to supplement the record of formal dissents contained in the voting record.

In this chapter, we extend Canterbery's effort by systematically coding information from the textual records of FOMC deliberations in meetings held when Arthur Burns and Alan Greenspan served as chairmen. We describe our data sources and the procedures we followed for extracting information from these sources. The data sets that we compile are used later in the book to produce complete preference profiles for Burns and Greenspan era FOMC meetings, respectively. Those profiles and the original codings described here are available in appendixes 4 and 5. In chapters 6, 7, and 8, we employ these data to more carefully investigate individual policy preferences and FOMC decisions.

## 5.1 Data from the Textual Records of FOMC Meetings

The *Memoranda* and the *Transcripts* provide detailed records of FOMC deliberations on monetary policy. Beginning in 1936 and continuing until March 1976, the FOMC published (after a five-year lag) records of each of its meetings in the *Memoranda*. In 1976, the Fed announced that it would discontinue publication of the *Memoranda*, apparently in response to threats from pending legislation and a lawsuit that would have required a more timely release. The FOMC, however, secretly continued its practice of recording meetings on audiotape and later producing transcripts from these recordings for internal use in preparing the "Record of Policy Actions." In 1993, Greenspan publicly acknowledged the existence of these transcripts, and soon after the Fed agreed to publish edited versions of them. The Fed has not released these records quickly, though. As this is written, official transcripts for 1976 through 1980 remain unpublished, and transcripts covering the period since 1996 are still subject to the five-year holding period. We have filled part of the gap in the data with transcripts for April 1976 through February 1978 that were obtained from Burns's personal papers, archived in the Gerald R. Ford Library in Ann Arbor, Michigan.[1]

Although detailed records exist for most of the 1936–1996 period, in this book we will examine data only for the Burns era (February 1970 through February 1978) and a portion of the Greenspan era (August 1987 through December 1996). For the Burns years, we combine the 1970–1976 *Memoranda* with the 1976–1978 *Transcripts* to obtain detailed records of all ninety-nine FOMC meetings held during that period. The *Transcripts* provide all of the data for the Greenspan years.

These two periods were selected for several reasons. The operating procedures adopted by the Fed and the decision-making procedures followed by the committee facilitated accurate coding of member preferences. During both periods, the FOMC primarily targeted the federal funds rate, and members frequently spoke in terms of quantitative

---

1. The Burns era transcripts are derived from audiotapes just as those available for the Greenspan era. The Ford Library edited the Burns era transcripts to remove references to specific individuals, governments, and businesses; otherwise, these records appear to be copies of the raw internal documents. The Greenspan era transcripts were officially released by the Fed after some additional editing. That additional editing improves the presentation by correcting errors in spelling, punctuation, and form in the original internal documents, but presumably does not alter the text of members' remarks.

funds rate targets. This makes coding members' funds rate preferences relatively straightforward. Furthermore, the resulting data are generally comparable across the two periods.

In contrast, prior to 1970, the committee loosely targeted money market conditions, but often did so in a fashion that did not always provide readily quantifiable funds rate targets. In the interval between Burns and Greenspan, two chairmen served, G. William Miller and Paul Volcker. No transcripts are available for the brief period in which Miller served. Transcripts are also missing for the historically important early Volcker years (years featuring high inflation, reserve aggregate targeting, historically high nominal interest rates, and the beginning of a severe recession). For the later Volcker years, transcripts exist, but the FOMC targeted borrowed reserves rather than the funds rate. That scheme eventually evolved back into interest rate targeting, but coding preferences in a consistent fashion in the early and mid-1980s would be difficult.

The Burns and Greenspan eras are also of interest because of the diversity of macroeconomic conditions that prevailed. The Burns era was characterized by a severe recession and subsequent recovery, a period of accelerating inflation, and unusual political pressures. The Greenspan years were marked by declining inflation, improving productivity growth, sustained growth of real output, and a crash in the stock market that was followed by an extraordinary bull market. These events presented a variety of challenges for the FOMC policymakers who were attempting to respond with appropriate monetary policy actions.

## 5.2 Coding FOMC Members' Monetary Policy Preferences: The Burns Years

Our purpose in coding data from the *Memoranda* and the *Transcripts* is to provide a detailed and accurate representation of the policy preferences of individual FOMC members over the periods we study. Since the Fed targeted the federal funds rate during these periods, ideally we would like to produce a data set that provides a desired target for the funds rate for each member in each meeting. The records that supply our raw data often report individuals' desired funds rates directly; in other cases, we are able to extract qualitative information that we later use to make inferences about individuals' preferred rates.

Although monetary policy operations and committee decision-making procedures were in many respects similar under Burns and Greenspan, there were also some differences. Because of this, the procedures we have employed to code individuals' policy preferences also differ slightly, as do some features of the subsequent empirical analyses. In this section, we describe data coding procedures for the Burns era; in the following section, we look at how coding procedures differed for the Greenspan years.

During the 1970s, the FOMC met at approximately monthly intervals. At each meeting, the Federal Reserve staff presented the committee with alternative policy options and associated forecasts. These alternative policy options usually became a focus of subsequent discussion. After the presentation of the staff report, the chairman called for the policy go-around, in which members of the committee, including both voting and nonvoting district Reserve Bank presidents, presented views on appropriate policy choices. Sometimes Burns spoke first and offered a policy prescription, but on other occasions, especially early in his tenure, he encouraged other committee members to speak first. When called on by the chairman, members usually identified themselves with one of the staff proposals or offered an alternative position. Frequently, members were explicit about their desired ranges for the federal funds rate. Based on the textual record, we have attributed desired federal funds rate targets to individuals when any of the following circumstances prevailed:

1. The individual explicitly stated a desired range for the federal funds rate.

2. The individual stated a preference for a staff policy scenario that had an explicit target range for the federal funds rate.

3. The individual stated that his preference coincided with that of another committee member whose desired funds rate could be inferred by way of either of the two circumstances above.

We then calculated each individual's desired funds rate as the midpoint of the reported range.

Our ninety-nine-meeting sample generated a total of 1,782 observations of voting and nonvoting members. We were able to code a desired federal funds rate directly from information provided in the meeting records 1,427 times (80.1 percent of all observations). During the Burns years, adopted directives were also associated with funds rate target ranges, so we were able to code adopted funds rates for the entire committee in a manner that mirrors the procedure used to code individuals' preferences.

For the 355 (19.9 percent) member observations for which rates were not directly observed, we have recorded qualitative information regarding member preferences. To do so, we first established a benchmark policy with which members' preferences could be compared for each meeting. We used a board staff proposal for this purpose. Although the board staff usually presented several policy scenarios ranging from easier to tighter, we defined a composite proposal as our benchmark. In quantitative terms, the interest rate associated with our benchmark proposal was measured as the midpoint of the funds rate target range in the staff's median proposal. When the staff presented an odd number of scenarios, our benchmark was the midpoint of the range prescribed by the median proposal. When the staff presented an even number of proposals, our benchmark was the midpoint of the range defined by the union of the ranges in the two median proposals.

We then used the textual record of committee deliberations to code member policy positions into three categories. In the policy go-around following the staff presentation, members' comments were coded to indicate one of the following positions:

1. Lean for ease: a preference for a policy that is easier than the staff proposal.

2. Lean for tightness: a preference for a policy that is tighter than the staff proposal.

3. Assent: no clear direction of preference relative to the staff proposal.

In practice, members' statements were frequently framed in comparison to staff proposals, and, with few exceptions, classifying positions was straightforward. One can think of the staff proposals as points on an interest rate number line. Members' comments typically placed them in particular intervals along that line. For example, the staff may have offered scenarios A, B, and C, ranging from easiest to tightest. Without stating a specific target, a member may have indicated a preference "close to A, but shaded in the direction of B." We took this verbal statement to indicate a desire for ease relative to the benchmark staff proposal, which in this case was B. Of the 355 member observations (again including voting and nonvoting members) where desired funds rates were not directly inferred, leans for ease were coded in 88

**Table 5.1**
Burns and Greenspan era data

|                                              | Burns era       | Greenspan era  |
| -------------------------------------------- | --------------- | -------------- |
| Sample start date                            | February 1970   | August 1987    |
| Sample end date                              | February 1978   | December 1996  |
| Number of meetings                           | 99              | 75             |
| Number of voting observations                | 1153            | 771            |
| Observed desired interest rates              | 910             | 719            |
| Qualitative interest rate preferences        | 243             | 52             |
| Leans toward ease                            | 61              | 21             |
| Assents                                      | 141             | 6              |
| Leans toward tightness                       | 41              | 25             |
| Number of nonvoting observations             | 629             | 521            |
| Observed desired interest rates              | 517             | 475            |
| Qualitative interest rate preferences        | 112             | 46             |
| Leans toward ease                            | 27              | 12             |
| Assents                                      | 45              | 7              |
| Leans toward tightness                       | 40              | 27             |
| Total number of observations                 | 1782            | 1292           |
| Total observed desired interest rates        | 1427            | 1194           |
| Total qualitative interest rate preferences  | 355             | 98             |
| Total leans toward ease                      | 88              | 33             |
| Total assents                                | 186             | 13             |
| Total leans toward tightness                 | 81              | 52             |

cases (24.8 percent), leans for tightness were coded in 81 cases (22.8 percent), and assents were coded in the remaining 186 cases (52.4 percent). Table 5.1 provides additional descriptive statistics for the data set, including separate breakdowns for voting and nonvoting Reserve Bank presidents.

While our procedures are meant to assure accuracy and consistency, some subjectivity is inherent when verbal descriptions must be quantified or categorized. One issue that arose in several meetings during the Burns years concerned policy proposals involving "asymmetric midpoints." An asymmetric midpoint represented a primary target value for policymakers that was not strictly the midpoint within the proposed target range. For example, at its meeting on March 9, 1971, the FOMC adopted a monetary policy directive that included a federal funds rate target range of 3.375 to 3.75 percent. Yet instead of viewing this range as having a midpoint of 3.5625 percent (the arithmetic midpoint), the committee explicitly stated that the adopted target range should be seen as having a slightly lower midpoint of 3.50 percent. Whenever asymmetric midpoints were explicitly mentioned, we regarded those as the targets for the given proposals (and for individuals who espoused those proposals). Each Burns era meeting was independently read and coded at least twice following these procedures. Any coding discrepancies that existed between the two independent sets of codings were resolved by the authors after an additional review of the source data.[2]

Given the unique role played by the chairman in committee functions, some special issues arose regarding appropriate coding of his preferences. At many meetings Burns spoke last, proposing language for a directive. Such proposals, coming from Burns, might be construed as an indication of his preferences. On the other hand, if he were simply summarizing the committee view, this interpretation would be misleading. Furthermore, if Burns's policy preferences were inferred on the basis of such statements, his measured preference could be spuriously correlated with the adopted target. In chapter 7, where we attempt to estimate the power of the chairman, this could lead to an overstatement of the chairman's influence over the committee.

To avoid this problem, we reviewed each of Burns's statements to ensure that we did not code a desired funds rate for him when he was actually summarizing the committee view. We had two criteria for distinguishing such cases. First, when Burns spoke early in the meeting (operationally, in the first half of the speaking order), he could not

---

2. The January 11, 1972, meeting required an exception to these coding procedures. At this meeting, there were two target proposals, I and II, and two operating proposals, A and B. Target I was tied to operating procedure A, which was essentially a funds rate targeting procedure. The funds rate range was 3.00 to 3.25 percent, with a midpoint of 3.125 percent, and the accompanying money growth target was 6 percent. Target II was associated with operating procedure B, which called for monetary targeting. This target specified money growth of 8 percent, which would make it appear to be the easier alternative. However, its funds rate range of 2.00 to 5.00 percent had a higher midpoint (3.50 percent), which would make it appear to be the tighter alternative. The committee's discussion revealed that target I was considered the tighter option. For those members who favored target I (which also emphasized the funds rate target), coding was straightforward; they were assigned the midpoint of the associated funds rate range, 3.125 percent. For those who preferred target II, however, there was a problem with applying the usual coding procedure. Those favoring target II clearly wanted greater ease; a strict application of our midpoint rule, though, would have assigned these individuals a midpoint of 3.50 percent, which was higher (that is, tighter) than target I. To resolve this problem, those who favored target II or a nonspecific proposal between targets I and II were coded as "leans for ease" relative to target I, which was employed as the benchmark.

have been summarizing. This was the case in forty-three of the ninety-nine meetings in our sample.

Second, when Burns spoke late, he sometimes explicitly noted that his proposed targets reflected his personal desires. For example, at the November 1972 FOMC meeting, Burns spoke last and proposed the adopted policy calling for a federal funds rate range of 4.75 to 5.50 percent, as associated with alternative B in the staff proposals. The *Memorandum* described Burns's statement as follows: "Chairman Burns then said that in deliberating on the problem *before the meeting* he had found himself inclined toward the directive language, longer-run targets, and federal funds rate constraint of alternative B" (November 20, 1972, 1121, emphasis added). In this case, Burns was clearly indicating that alternative B was his personal preference and not simply the consensus view of the committee. If we include these cases, we can directly infer desired funds rates for Burns in sixty-three of the ninety-nine meetings. In our empirical work, particularly when we estimate Burns's influence over the committee, we use the smaller forty-three- and sixty-three-observation samples in which the Burns preference is more reliably inferred.

## 5.3   Coding FOMC Members' Monetary Policy Preferences: The Greenspan Years

Institutional arrangements governing the conduct of monetary policy were similar in the Greenspan era. The FOMC again met regularly, although less frequently, at six-week intervals. Meetings followed a similar pattern, with staff reports on economic conditions and alternative policy scenarios preceding a policy go-around in which members offered their own policy views in turn. Our coding procedures for the Greenspan era were also similar to those for the Burns years, but some changes were required by differing circumstances. This section describes the collection of data for the Greenspan era, emphasizing the differences in comparison to the Burns era.

Once again, we employed the textual record of deliberations to infer indications of the funds rate preferences of individual FOMC members. The possible codings are like those employed for the Burns years. When a member's statement was clearly aligned with a specific target for the federal funds rate, we directly coded that rate as the member's preferred policy. If no target rate was identified, the preference was

again characterized as "leaning toward ease," "leaning toward tightness," or "assenting."

One change in coding procedures was required by a difference in
the monetary policy operating procedures. When Greenspan assumed
the chairmanship in 1987, the Fed was formally targeting borrowed
reserves, which provided indirect control of the federal funds rate. Policy scenarios presented to the committee by the staff normally described borrowing targets as well as funds rate forecasts associated with
the borrowing levels. As the policy go-around proceeded, some members stated preferences in terms of borrowing targets and some stated
them directly in terms of levels for the funds rate. For consistency, we
coded only interest rate targets, making use of the mapping between
funds rates and borrowing targets provided by the board staff in the
Blue Book prepared for the meeting.[3] As a matter of practice, the committee had completed the shift to direct funds rate targeting by 1990,
and thereafter there was no need for mapping borrowing levels and
funds rates.

A second difference in coding procedures involves the selection of
a benchmark funds rate when coding leaning positions. For the Burns
years, we employed a measure of the board staff's median policy option for this purpose. During the Greenspan years, the scenarios presented by the board staff followed a predictable pattern; in most cases,
the staff offered an alternative corresponding to the "status quo" along
with alternatives involving modest tightening and easing moves. The
federal funds rate alternatives were usually single valued (rather than
ranges) and involved twenty-five- or fifty-basis-point moves relative to
the status quo. An implication was that, in any meeting, there were a
small number of discrete policy options under realistic consideration.
As the policy go-around proceeded, members usually expressed preferences for one of those discrete options or a leaning position relative
to one of them. In coding leaning positions for the Greenspan years, we
employ individual-specific benchmarks, with the chosen benchmarks
depending on how members framed their statements of preference.
Members typically indicated preference for ease or tightness relative to
the prevailing rate, and in these cases, the status quo serves as the

---

3. In a few cases, the Blue Book did not provide a complete mapping. In these instances,
comments by staff representatives or committee members usually revealed the implied
mapping, or we used the committee's usual rule of thumb in constructing the mapping
(normally, a variation of twenty-five basis points in the funds rate was associated with a
variation of $100 million in the borrowing target during the relevant period).

benchmark. On occasion, however, a member might propose "an increase of twenty-five basis points or a bit higher." In such a case, the twenty-five-basis-point increase defines a benchmark rate (distinct from the status quo), and the member would be coded as leaning toward tightness relative to that rate. As a practical matter, this difference in procedures affects few observations. In our sample of 1,292 member-meeting observations, leaning and assenting positions were coded only 98 times, and the benchmark differed from the status quo in only 9 of those 98 observations.

The tendency for policy options to be associated with discrete twenty-five- or fifty-basis-point movements relative to the status quo naturally led members to frame their statements of preference in these terms as well. As options became more discrete, members tended not to state preferences in terms of ranges but to instead choose one of the obvious alternatives. Although we have retained the rule of mapping stated ranges into a single midpoint value when coding preferences, as a practical matter this rule became less important during the Greenspan years.

A third difference involves the speaking order in the policy go-around. Burns sometimes spoke early and sometimes spoke late. When he spoke late, an issue arose regarding whether his stated preference was truly his or whether it was his interpretation of the committee's consensus view. In contrast, Greenspan routinely spoke first (with two meetings early in his tenure providing the only exceptions) and presented a policy proposal. Consequently, for the Greenspan years there is generally no need to divide observations according to the speaking order or the manner in which a proposal was offered (although for some purposes, we do exclude the two meeting observations where Greenspan spoke late).

Finally, a fourth difference involves the adoption of a statement of "bias" to accompany policy directives during the Greenspan era. Beginning in 1983 and continuing until 1999, the FOMC included such statements in each of its adopted policy directives. Consider the following example, taken from the policy directive adopted at the March 28, 1989, meeting of the FOMC: "In the implementation of policy for the immediate future the Committee seeks to maintain the existing degree of pressure on reserve positions. Taking account of indications of inflationary pressures, the strength of the business expansion, the behavior of the monetary aggregates, and developments in foreign exchange markets, somewhat greater reserve restraint would or slightly lesser reserve restraint might be acceptable in the intermeeting period" (*Transcripts*, March 28, 1989, 41). This language indicates a bias toward tightness, with the asymmetry revealed by the words "somewhat greater" versus "slightly lesser" and "would" versus "might." Alternative wording could produce an asymmetry toward ease or a symmetric outlook.

The bias was intended to give an indication of the direction of likely future policy moves; however, its precise interpretation was not always clear. Sometimes it apparently referred to planned intermeeting moves; sometimes it was meant to describe constraints on the chairman's discretionary actions during the intermeeting period; and sometimes it vaguely described anticipated future directions for policy that extended beyond the upcoming intermeeting period (even though the wording suggested the narrower time frame). Members' policy preferences usually included recommendations for both the target funds rate and the bias to be associated with that rate. Although the bias often had implications about expected intermeeting movements in the funds rate, we have treated the coding of desired funds rates and the bias separately. We interpreted the desired funds rate as referring to the rate intended to prevail immediately after the meeting, but prior to any intermeeting moves anticipated in the statement of the bias.[4] This does give a somewhat different interpretation to the adopted funds rate in the Burns and Greenspan eras. Under Burns, the committee adopted ranges in which the funds rate might fluctuate in the upcoming intermeeting period, but under Greenspan the committee adopted a more precise target to prevail immediately after the meeting. That rate might or might not be adjusted by the chairman or by a committee action before the next meeting, but any change would be considered a separate policy action.

Whenever committee members stated preferences on the bias, we have coded that information in our data set. Although most of our attention will be given to the selection of funds rate targets, in chapter 8 we will also investigate whether the adopted bias appears to be a

---

4. We made exceptions to this principle for coding two meetings (October 1990 and December 1991). In these two cases, the discussion in the meeting made it clear that the movement called for in the bias was expected to be quick and nearly automatic, so that it would be best to consider the adopted rate to be that which would prevail after the move. In fact, in one case the expected movement was delayed. Nevertheless, we believe the best representation of the committee's a priori intent was reflected by the rate that embodied a move.

meaningful indicator of future policy shifts and whether individuals'
biases predict future proposals from Greenspan to the committee.

Some of the changes in institutional arrangements and our coding
schemes are reflected in summary statistics describing data for the
Greenspan era. The sample for the Greenspan years includes seventy-
five meetings (although the Greenspan era covers more years, meetings were less frequent, coming at six-week intervals rather than
monthly).[5] For those seventy-five meetings, we coded 1,292 observations of individual preferences regarding policy choices, including voting and nonvoting members. In 1,194 cases (92.4 percent), we observed
individuals' federal funds rate targets directly. In the 98 observations
(7.6 percent) where rates were not observed, we coded 33 leans for ease
(2.6 percent), 52 leans for tightness (4.0 percent), and 13 assents (1.0
percent). Summary statistics for the Greenspan era data are also provided in table 5.1, alongside those for the Burns years.

The most striking difference in comparison to the Burns years is the
greater percentage of directly observed desired funds rates. In those
cases where rates are not observed, the fraction of assenting positions
is also much lower. There are several reasons why desired interest
rates might have been stated more frequently during the Greenspan
years. First, the fact that Greenspan led the go-around with an initial
proposal made it clear that members should indicate either agreement
or disagreement, which required clarity. The availability of obvious
discrete options also facilitated making a clear choice; members knew
that they should select from among the available options, and they
usually did so.

Not only did members state positions more clearly during the
Greenspan years but they also tended to agree with Greenspan frequently (see the discussion in chapter 8 and the data in appendixes 4
and 5). The fact that policy options were more discrete may have made
any disagreements more visible, and the desire to avoid disagreement
may have encouraged members to coalesce around a focal point, specifically the chairman's proposal.

One final issue also deserves comment. Because we use members'
statements to infer their desired policy preferences, the question of
whether members might misstate their true preferences naturally
arises. If choices are made by majority voting and preferences are sin-

---

5. The March 1988 meeting is missing from our sample because the committee's tape re-
corder malfunctioned and no transcript of the policy go-around is available.

gle peaked (as they are likely to be in a one-dimensional "interest rate" issue space), members should have no incentive to misrepresent their preferences. Still, the operative collective choice rule for the FOMC may be more involved than simple majority rule, so truthful revelation need not be an equilibrium strategy. Although we recognize that strategic misrepresentation is a theoretical possibility, we suspect that it was not a pervasive phenomenon. Further, it is not an issue that is central to our purposes. Members' stated preferences, truthful or not, represent their choice of an action in the committee setting. The statements we read in the *Memoranda* and *Transcripts* contain the same expressions of preferences that members revealed to their colleagues when collective decisions were made. In examining the mapping from individual preferences to collective choices, these stated preferences are the actions that are relevant.

## 5.4   Conclusions

Previous studies of the monetary policy preferences of individual FOMC members have almost exclusively relied on dissent voting patterns. Because dissenting votes are rare, voting records provide a limited source of information. Available textual records of committee deliberations offer more detailed descriptions of individual preferences. This chapter has described the methodology we have used to code textual records into rich quantitative data sets that we use in the remainder of this book to test hypotheses about decision making within the FOMC.

Ideally, we would like to identify the desired policy settings of each FOMC member in each committee meeting. In subsequent chapters, we use the data we have collected to move toward that goal. In chapter 7, we describe methods that permit us to impute individuals' desired funds rate targets for the cases where they are not directly observed. When we combine all observed and imputed funds rates, we are able to produce complete preference profiles for the meetings in our samples. Appendixes 4 and 5 present those preference profiles for the Burns and Greenspan meeting samples as well as the original codings used to produce them. These data are the direct product of the work reported in this chapter and, by themselves, represent an important contribution of this book.

# 6

## Estimating Reaction Functions for Individual FOMC Members

In chapter 4, we employed dissent voting data to estimate individual reaction function intercepts for FOMC members who served during the 1966–1996 period. Yet the empirical specification used in that chapter permitted limited characterizations of differences across members because of the infrequency of dissent votes. In chapter 5, we described the construction of rich data sets distinguishing the policy preferences of FOMC members who served during the 1970–1978 and 1987–1996 periods in which Burns and Greenspan chaired the FOMC. These data sets were derived from textual records of FOMC deliberations contained in the *Memoranda* and the *Transcripts*. In this chapter, we use those data to characterize differences in individuals' policy preferences in a more comprehensive fashion than was permitted by our earlier investigation.

Specifically, we again estimate reaction functions for members of the FOMC, but now we permit all coefficients to vary across individuals, and we test for statistical differences between individual members and the committee as a whole. We then examine how estimated reaction functions compare with anecdotal descriptions of individuals' preferences contained in the records of meeting deliberations and other sources. For the Burns years, reaction function estimates can be used to distinguish members with "monetarist" and "Keynesian" views. For the Greenspan era, the reaction functions reveal distinctions between members who advocated an elevated status for price stability and others who promoted broader objectives.

The first section of this chapter discusses issues associated with modeling and estimating individual reaction functions. Empirical results for Burns era FOMC members are presented in the second section. In the third section, we explore the Burns era reaction function estimates in light of information about individual policy preferences provided by other sources, focusing attention on the monetarist-Keynesian debate. In the fourth section, we briefly compare data and specification differences for the Burns and Greenspan eras, and then present individual reaction function estimates for the Greenspan years. A discussion of those results in relation to other sources describing member policy preferences follows in the fifth section, and conclusions are offered in the final section.

## 6.1   Individual Reaction Functions

This section explains the econometric methods we employ to estimate reaction functions for individual FOMC members using the data sets described in chapter 5. The original source data consisted of transcripts or summaries of statements made by FOMC members during committee deliberations. From the statements, we recorded either a continuous desired funds rate or a categorical indicator to describe a member's policy preference. In the latter case, preferences were coded into three categories: leans toward tightness, leans toward ease, or assents, each defined in relation to a benchmark funds rate proposal.

Our econometric model specifies that an individual's reaction function is given by

$$R_{it}^* = \mathbf{X}_t \boldsymbol{\beta}_i + e_{it}, \ e_{it} \sim N(0, \sigma_i), \tag{6.1}$$

where $R_{it}^*$ is member $i$'s desired federal funds rate target for the policy directive to be chosen in meeting $t$, and the vector $\mathbf{X}_t$ includes indicators of macroeconomic conditions that are thought to influence policy decisions. If $R_{it}^*$ were always observed, then equation (6.1) could be estimated by OLS. FOMC members, however, do not always clearly state preferred funds rate targets, so $R_{it}^*$ is not always directly observed.

The observability of $R_{it}^*$ depends on the nature of member $i$'s statement in the policy go-around. When members fail to state explicit target rates, they almost always provide meaningful qualitative information about their views, suggesting that the failure to reveal explicit numerical targets is more a matter of their manner of expression than one of manipulative secrecy. We therefore assume that individual choices to state (or not state) explicit target rates are nonstrategic and that the observability of desired funds rates is econometrically exogenous.

When $R_{it}^*$ is not observed, we instead observe leaning or assenting positions defined in relation to a benchmark rate, denoted $\tilde{R}_{it}$.[1] We assume that leaning positions are generated when an individual's preference deviates sufficiently from the benchmark in accordance with the following conditions:

if $R_{it}^* - \tilde{R}_{it} > \lambda_i$, then $V_{it} = 1$ (member $i$ leans for tightness); $\qquad$ (6.2.a)

if $R_{it}^* - \tilde{R}_{it} < -\lambda_i$, then $V_{it} = -1$ (member $i$ leans for ease); $\qquad$ (6.2.b)

if $-\lambda_i \leq R_{it}^* - \tilde{R}_{it} \leq \lambda_i$, then $V_{it} = 0$ (member $i$ assents). $\qquad$ (6.2.c)

Substituting (6.1) into conditions (6.2) yields:

if $e_{it} > a_{it}$, then $V_{it} = 1$ (member $i$ leans for tightness); $\qquad$ (6.3.a)

if $e_{it} < b_{it}$, then $V_{it} = -1$ (member $i$ leans for ease); $\qquad$ (6.3.b)

if $b_{it} \leq e_{it} \leq a_{it}$, then $V_{it} = 0$ (member $i$ assents); $\qquad$ (6.3.c)

where $a_{it} = \lambda_i + \tilde{R}_{it} - \mathbf{X}_t \boldsymbol{\beta}_i$ and $b_{it} = -\lambda_i + \tilde{R}_{it} - \mathbf{X}_t \boldsymbol{\beta}_i$.

Given the normality of $e_{it}$, conditions (6.3) describe an ordered probit model. If our data set contained only categorical preference indicators, ordered probit would be a suitable estimator. Yet because our data set includes a mixture of continuous and categorical preference indicators, we will employ a hybrid OLS-ordered probit model to estimate reaction functions.

In addition to estimating reaction functions for individuals, we wish to test whether particular individuals are different from their colleagues. To do so, suppose that the behavior of the FOMC as a whole can be described by a conventional "aggregate" reaction function in which the committee's target, $\bar{R}_t$, is also specified to be a function of macroeconomic indicators:[2]

$$\bar{R}_t = \mathbf{X}_t \boldsymbol{\beta} + u_t. \qquad (6.4)$$

---

1. Details on the coding of benchmark rates were provided in chapter 5. The benchmark rate differs across individuals in a meeting for some Greenspan era observations, so the benchmark rate is subscripted with both $i$ and $t$.
2. In contrast to the analysis in chapter 4, we make a distinction between the adopted target rate and the observed postmeeting interest rate. $\bar{R}_t$ refers to the target funds rate associated with the adopted monetary policy directive; in chapter 4, $R_t$ referred to the average value of the funds rate in the postmeeting period. For the sample employed in chapter 4, postmeeting funds rates could always be measured, but clear target rates were not always associated with directives.

The committee reaction function mirrors those for individuals, except that the dependent variable is the committee's target rather than the rate preferred by an individual, and the parameters, $\beta$, are the reaction function coefficients for the committee rather than those for a single individual. By testing whether elements of $\beta_i$ are identical to the corresponding elements of $\beta$, we can test for differences between member $i$ and the committee on which that member served.

Appendix 3 provides additional discussion of issues related to the estimation of the model. It first describes a single-equation method for the estimation of individual reaction functions, then a two-equation method for the joint estimation of individual and committee reaction functions. The latter method facilitates testing for individual-committee differences, as described above, and is used for the empirical analysis presented in this chapter.

## 6.2   Individual Reaction Function Estimates: The Burns Era

Because of differences in committee operations and related differences in our data collection procedures for the Burns and Greenspan eras, we have chosen to separate our analyses of individual reaction functions for these two sample periods. This section and the next examine individual reaction functions for the Burns years; these are followed by two sections examining the Greenspan years.

Our empirical specification for Burns era individual reaction functions is similar to that employed in chapter 4. Explanatory variables include a premeeting funds rate, now measured as the average rate prevailing during the week before the meeting $(R_t^p)$, the average growth rate of M1 over the three months prior to the month of the meeting $(M_t)$, and two-quarter-ahead forecast values for the rate of inflation $(\hat{P}_t)$, the rate of growth of real GNP $(\hat{Y}_t)$, and the civilian unemployment rate $(\hat{U}_t)$, all measured as percentages. Data for all forecast variables were obtained from the original Green Books available to FOMC members at the time of the meeting.

Table 6.1 presents estimates of individual reaction functions for thirty-four FOMC members who served between February 1970 and February 1978. The list includes all members for whom at least ten observations were available.[3] Each member's reaction function was

---

3. The estimation method described in section 6.1 requires observations in at least two of the three qualitative measurement categories characterizing preferences. For three individuals, this condition was not met. For these individuals, we instead employed a

estimated jointly with an equation for the committee as a whole, and tests of differences in coefficients were undertaken. To facilitate comparisons, we have ordered members in the table from low to high according to the average difference between the member's desired interest rate and the committee's target rate, $R_{it}^* - \overline{R}_t$ (with the averaging performed over each member's sample of observations). Thus, the ordering roughly arranges members from easy to tight in relation to their colleagues.

Because members joined and departed the committee at different dates and because of occasional absences, samples differ across individuals.[4] For the purpose of testing differences between a member and the committee, we chose to always estimate the committee reaction function with the sample of observations available for the member. A consequence is that committee reaction function estimates are different for each member. This choice assures that we are conservative in concluding that a member's preference differed from that of the committee on which that member served (we avoid confounding shifts in committee parameters over time with differences between an individual and the committee).

Table 6.1 does not report the committee estimates associated with each individual; however, the first line of the table reports OLS estimates of a committee equation obtained using the complete sample of ninety-nine meeting observations. That estimation shows that the premeeting interest rate and money growth coefficients differ significantly from zero. Coefficients of the forecasts for unemployment, inflation, and output growth have signs consistent with the hypothesis that the Fed leans against the wind, but none of them is significantly different from zero. The coefficient of the premeeting funds rate, $R_t^p$, is significantly less than one (at the 0.01 level), and there was no indication of serial correlation.

Each individual reaction function coefficient in table 6.1 is associated with three tests. In conventional fashion, we first test the null hypothesis that each coefficient is equal to zero. We then test whether each individual coefficient is equal to the corresponding coefficient in the

conventional seemingly unrelated regressions (SUR) estimation, using only the observations where an interest rate was explicitly stated.

4. Although bank presidents rotate in and out of voting positions on the committee, they attend and participate even when they are not voting. Policy preferences are coded in the same way for voting and nonvoting committee members, and all observations are employed in estimation. Pooled estimations did not show evidence of statistical differences in the behavior of members serving in voting and nonvoting capacities.

**Table 6.1**
Estimates of individual FOMC member reaction functions: The Burns era

| Member | Rank | $R^*_{it} - \bar{R}_t$ | Constant | $R^p_t$ | $\dot{M}1_t$ | $\hat{U}_t$ | $\hat{P}_t$ | $\hat{Y}_t$ | $\lambda$ | $\rho$ | $\sigma_e$ | $\sigma_u$ | $\chi^2(6)$ | N |
|---|---|---|---|---|---|---|---|---|---|---|---|---|---|---|
| Committee (OLS) | | | 0.521 | 0.929** | 0.030** | -0.067 | 0.029 | 0.011 | | | | | | 99 |
| Bucher | 1 | -0.286 | 1.994**## | 0.711***†† | 0.022 | -0.286**†† | 0.232**## | 0.050**# | 0.358** | 0.709 | 0.298 | 0.243 | 104.494** | 41 |
| Maisel | 2 | -0.233 | 3.164 | 0.787** | 0.033 | -0.591** | 0.243# | -0.013 | 0.109 | 0.843 | 0.298 | 0.276 | 58.843** | 29 |
| Galusha | 3 | -0.227 | -3.236† | 1.150**## | -0.034 | 0.112 | 0.315 | 0.124 | 0.108 | 0.929 | 0.358 | 0.345 | 51.490** | 12 |
| Sheehan | 4 | -0.226 | 3.055 | 0.755**† | 0.058* | -0.470* | 0.164### | -0.047 | 0.166* | 0.773 | 0.399 | 0.270 | 33.874** | 38 |
| Morris | 5 | -0.140 | -0.018†† | 0.957** | 0.048**# | -0.027 | -0.025† | 0.055**## | 0.099 | 0.799 | 0.332 | 0.263 | 133.980** | 93 |
| Mayo | 6 | -0.056 | 0.299 | 0.894** | 0.037** | -0.066 | 0.065 | 0.033**# | 0.183** | 0.716 | 0.265 | 0.221 | 29.962** | 89 |
| Holland | 7 | -0.036 | 2.534** | 0.777** | 0.031**† | -0.225** | 0.071* | -0.001 | 0.094 | 0.847 | 0.207 | 0.238 | 19.164** | 34 |
| Mitchell | 8 | -0.035 | 1.120* | 0.898** | 0.013 | -0.127* | 0.043 | 0.011 | 0.205** | 0.809 | 0.370 | 0.309 | 2.523 | 66 |
| Balles | 9 | -0.034 | 2.076** | 0.808** | 0.068**# | -0.270**† | 0.100 | 0.003 | 0.121* | 0.383 | 0.358 | 0.222 | 15.976** | 56 |
| MacLaury | 10 | -0.030 | 0.253 | 0.901** | 0.050** | -0.075 | 0.074 | 0.042**# | 0.132* | 0.749 | 0.282 | 0.217 | 37.476** | 63 |
| Lilly | 11 | -0.024 | -2.001 | 1.124** | 0.019 | 0.132 | -0.088 | 0.149** | NA | 0.505 | 0.073 | 0.072 | 3.120 | 15 |
| Daane | 12 | -0.020 | 0.815† | 0.916** | 0.020 | -0.243 | 0.181* | 0.046# | 0.197** | 0.874 | 0.310 | 0.310 | 17.494** | 48 |
| Heflin | 13 | -0.012 | 5.130** | 0.722** | 0.041**† | -0.614** | 0.008 | -0.097* | 0.082 | 0.818 | 0.197 | 0.199 | 6.148 | 32 |
| Partee | 14 | -0.007 | -0.825 | 1.054** | 0.025** | 0.014 | -0.055 | 0.114** | 0.049 | 0.705 | 0.087 | 0.076 | 6.784 | 25 |
| Black | 15 | 0.002 | 0.926* | 0.898** | 0.006†† | -0.083* | 0.037 | 0.011# | 0.144* | 0.889 | 0.241 | 0.250 | 17.905** | 63 |
| Burns | 16 | 0.003 | 0.008†† | 0.936** | 0.035** | 0.015## | 0.011 | -0.007 | 0.194** | 0.685 | 0.237 | 0.194 | 19.276** | 77 |
| Baughman | 17 | 0.004 | 0.437†† | 1.061**# | 0.054**# | -0.003 | -0.042# | 0.029**## | 0.339** | 0.941 | 0.231 | 0.188 | 58.261** | 44 |
| Jackson | 18 | 0.013 | -0.543 | 1.035** | 0.024** | 0.003 | -0.051 | 0.097** | 0.303** | 0.703 | 0.107 | 0.089 | 4.521 | 31 |
| Gardner | 19 | 0.014 | 0.071 | 1.021** | 0.003 | -0.040 | -0.040 | 0.068 | 0.132 | 0.792 | 0.084 | 0.082 | 4.059 | 23 |
| Volcker | 20 | 0.031 | -0.264 | 1.016** | 0.013* | 0.024 | -0.054 | 0.054** | NA | 0.581 | 0.070 | 0.085 | 19.850** | 30 |
| Coldwell | 21 | 0.032 | 1.309** | 0.898** | 0.041** | -0.172**† | 0.038 | 0.010 | 0.203** | 0.873 | 0.281 | 0.270 | 26.205** | 96 |
| Eastburn | 22 | 0.037 | 2.067***## | 0.818***† | 0.063**# | -0.258**†† | 0.081 | -0.002 | 0.188** | 0.462 | 0.354 | 0.251 | 31.501** | 86 |

| | | | | | | | | | | | | | |
|---|---|---|---|---|---|---|---|---|---|---|---|---|---|
| Winn | 23 | 0.043 | 2.015**# | 0.843** | 0.058** | −0.237**† | 0.064 | −0.025 | 0.457** | 0.808 | 0.306 | 0.218 | 15.693* | 70 |
| Guffey | 24 | 0.052 | 2.743**# | 1.003** | 0.019* | −0.187 | −0.263**†† | 0.021 | NA | 0.676 | 0.072 | 0.074 | 28.537** | 22 |
| Swan | 25 | 0.056 | −0.371 | 0.986** | 0.031 | −0.177 | 0.271* | 0.048# | 0.353* | 0.753 | 0.258 | 0.281 | 6.348 | 29 |
| Robertson | 26 | 0.074 | 5.911** | 0.693** | 0.064** | −0.886** | 0.152 | −0.031 | 0.235** | 0.720 | 0.306 | 0.271 | 4.626 | 40 |
| Wallich | 27 | 0.078 | 0.208 | 0.924** | 0.059**# | 0.019 | −0.012 | −0.020 | 0.156 | 0.846 | 0.341 | 0.196 | 17.239** | 48 |
| Brimmer | 28 | 0.082 | 4.039** | 0.776** | 0.027* | −0.597** | 0.163* | −0.022 | 0.157** | 0.826 | 0.298 | 0.288 | 11.053 | 54 |
| Roos | 29 | 0.155 | −1.090 | 0.950** | 0.053**## | −0.041 | 0.158 | 0.090 | 0.067 | 0.644 | 0.113 | 0.080 | 78.769** | 18 |
| Willes | 30 | 0.160 | −2.159# | 1.010**†† | 0.050*# | −0.101†† | 0.311**## | 0.113 | 0.079 | 0.053 | 0.110 | 0.057 | 56.255** | 11 |
| Kimbrel | 31 | 0.179 | 1.515** | 0.866** | 0.033** | −0.156** | 0.064 | −0.003 | 0.300** | 0.775 | 0.319 | 0.272 | 45.950** | 91 |
| Hayes | 32 | 0.183 | 1.497** | 0.881** | 0.007 | −0.194** | 0.111** | −0.001 | 0.142* | 0.777 | 0.290 | 0.310 | 42.684** | 56 |
| Clay | 33 | 0.207 | 1.072* | 0.877** | 0.045* | −0.140* | 0.096 | 0.006 | 0.095 | 0.518 | 0.368 | 0.274 | 25.842** | 65 |
| Francis | 34 | 0.432 | 0.986 | 0.791**†† | 0.086**# | −0.048 | 0.118* | −0.009 | 0.287** | 0.653 | 0.426 | 0.310 | 67.556** | 59 |

*Coefficient is significantly different from zero, 0.05 level, two-tailed test

**Coefficient is significantly different from zero, 0.01 level, two-tailed test (one-tailed for $\chi^2$)

#(†)Member coefficient is higher (lower) than the committee coefficient, 0.05 level, two-tailed test

##(††)Member coefficient is higher (lower) than the committee coefficient, 0.01 level, two-tailed test

NA: Ordinary seemingly unrelated regressions (SUR) estimates; $\lambda$ not estimated

accompanying committee reaction function. Finally, for each individual, we test the joint hypothesis that all individual coefficients are equal to the corresponding committee coefficients. Not surprisingly, the table indicates substantial variety in the policy preferences of FOMC members. Almost all members' reaction functions indicate significant nonzero responses to one or more macroeconomic indicators, but there is variety in terms of which indicators are important. Of 204 individual coefficient estimates, we reject (at the 0.05 significance level, two-tailed test) equality of the member and committee coefficients fifty times. The joint hypothesis tests, reported in the column labeled $\chi^2(6)$ in the table, show stronger evidence of differences between members. We reject (at the 0.05 significance level) the hypotheses that all coefficients for an individual are equal to those of the committee in twenty-five of thirty-four cases. Note that most members for whom we reject the joint hypothesis of identical reaction functions tend to be clustered at the top and the bottom of the table. This suggests that some differences can easily be described in terms of an ease-versus-tightness dimension. Nevertheless, other members (for example, Ernest Baughman and Robert Black) who differ significantly from the committee are located near the middle of the table. On average, these individuals have preferred targets close to those of the committee, but they respond in different ways to the macroeconomic indicators in the reaction function.

Several other features of the estimation are of interest. First, $\lambda$ is the interest rate threshold parameter in the model. It indicates what difference in desired funds rates is necessary to induce an individual to lean toward ease or tightness. Its average value across members is 0.185, indicating that if an individual's desired funds rate differs from the benchmark level by 18.5 basis points, this is sufficient to induce a leaning statement (when an explicit rate is not given). Our estimation also produces an estimate of the correlation between the error term for an individual's reaction function and that for the committee as a whole. On average, that correlation is 0.719, indicating that random events not captured by the model's explanatory variables usually affect members similarly. For several individuals, the estimated coefficient of the pre-meeting interest rate exceeds one (suggesting the potential for instability); however, none of these estimates ever significantly differed from one. Given the increases in inflation and interest rates that occurred in some subperiods of the Burns era, some indications of instability are not surprising.[5] Finally, we note that the estimates reported in table 6.1 are similar to those we obtain using OLS over samples that drop observations where explicit funds rate targets are missing (the OLS results are not reported here).

## 6.3 Burns Era Econometric Results in Historical Perspective

In this section, we place some of the results of the Burns era econometric analysis in historical perspective. In the 1970s, the monetarist-Keynesian debate provided an important theme for macroeconomic discourse. Chicago school monetarists argued that managing monetary aggregates was crucial, and that money growth should be steady and predictable. Keynesians attached less significance to the monetary aggregates and favored greater policy activism. Reflecting the balance within the economics profession, the Federal Reserve was predominantly Keynesian and nonmonetarist, perhaps even antimonetarist. A monetarist enclave flourished at the Federal Reserve Bank of St. Louis, however, and, consequently, the monetarist-Keynesian debate surfaced within the FOMC. St. Louis Fed presidents Darryl Francis and Lawrence Roos persistently pressed the monetarist view as money growth and inflation rose and the FOMC primarily targeted the funds rate. According to monetarists, by targeting a short-term interest rate and failing to adjust the target promptly in the face of money growth overshoots, the FOMC lost control of the monetary aggregates and produced inflation.

The following excerpt from the *Memorandum* summarizes the monetarist perspective advocated by Francis, speaking in 1970, in advance of the Great Inflation.

Mr. Francis remarked that the rapid growth in money had resulted from both a desire for quick economic expansion and the emphasis since last fall on money market conditions. A quick economic response from monetary actions had seldom occurred; yet, to his knowledge, every experience of prolonged rapid monetary injection had been followed by an intensification of inflation.

In recent months, Mr. Francis continued, concern had been expressed by members of the Committee that monetary expansion might have been too rapid, despite intentions to the contrary. That had led some to conclude that the Committee was not able to control money growth adequately. He attributed

5. Judd and Rudebusch (1998) report similar results for empirically estimated Taylor rules for the Burns era.

the apparent lack of success in controlling money to the method used. Emphasis had been on influencing money market conditions as a means of achieving a desired rate of monetary expansion. Those market conditions had been permitted to tighten somewhat in recent months; at each occasion, however, there had been a fear that a rise in interest rates might choke off the fragile recovery, and the step had been taken very cautiously. It was his belief that interest rates had continued to be held below equilibrium levels by the Committee's massive injection of Federal Reserve credit since January. The growth of those funds had also encouraged inflationary expectations which, in turn, pushed equilibrium interest rates even higher. With current underlying economic conditions and rising inflationary expectations, the result had been higher rates of money growth than the Committee had specified.

Mr. Francis said he would suggest that the Committee stop the course toward greater inflation and higher interest rates now by directly placing stress on achieving moderate growth in the monetary aggregates rather than by making adjustments in money market conditions. (July 27, 1970, 782–784)

Francis's perspective is also highlighted by the manner in which he revealed his preferences in the committee. Because he favored targeting monetary aggregates rather than the funds rate, he did not speak in terms of funds rate ranges as often as other members. We were able to code explicit funds rate targets for Francis in only thirty-five (59.3 percent) of his fifty-nine meeting observations.[6]

Later in the decade, Roos continued the monetarist crusade of the St. Louis bank. For several meetings in 1977, he pushed the committee to control the growth of the money stock rather than keep interest rates low. For example, at the September meeting, he asked, "Can [we] have it both ways? In other words, can we have low interest rates and low rates of aggregate growth or are these things not inconsistent? and doesn't one have to make a choice sometimes of not having, trying to have the best of both worlds?" (*Transcripts*, September 20, 1977, tape 6, 12).

Despite the advocacy of the St. Louis bank presidents, monetarist thinking usually met with skepticism in most other corners of the Federal Reserve System. Consider the views of New York Fed president Alfred Hayes: "As [Fed] governor [Dewey] Daane has suggested several times, the System runs the risk of falling into the trap of overemphasizing small variations in the aggregates. I would hope we could find a way to downgrade them somewhat in the public mind. I am by no means convinced that there is as close a relationship between money supply growth and subsequent economic conditions as

---

6. Jordan (2001) describes Francis's views and a history of his experiences on the FOMC.

the Monetarists would have us believe" (*Memorandum*, December 15, 1970, 1119). A month later, Fed governor George Mitchell offered similar thoughts, agreeing "that there was a problem of too much emphasis on the performance of M1 as an indicator of monetary policy. The problem was compounded by the fact that some of Professor Friedman's disciples had given the Monetarists' position an aura of religious dogma" (*Memorandum*, January 12, 1971, 55–56). Burns often led the opposition to monetarist thinking. In 1975, he admonished the committee that "members had to remind themselves continually that they should not become prisoners of particular projections [for monetary aggregates] that the Committee had adopted. Those projections merely indicated the members' best thinking at the time they were made, and the Committee should feel free to change them as conditions changed" (*Memorandum*, November 18, 1975, 1244). In other words, Burns took the Keynesian position favoring "discretion" rather than the simple monetary growth rules favored by monetarists.[7]

Even in the late 1970s, after leading the FOMC through a period of dubious success in macroeconomic management, Burns could not resist an opportunity to deride his monetarist critics. Following a comment from Roos to the effect that his personal forecast differed a bit from that of the staff, Burns responded, "I think that's entirely valid but I would have liked your comments better if you had not based it on the model. The St. Louis model does not get high marks for its predictive power. In fact, it gets very low marks in the economics profession. Am I right on that?" (*Transcripts*, January 17, 1977, tape 6, 20). Federal Reserve Board staff member Lyle Gramley then confirmed the chairman's suspicion of monetarist analysis.

It is natural to ask if the econometric estimates of reaction functions presented in this chapter are consistent with anecdotal descriptions of differences in theoretical perspectives. The results in table 6.1 suggest that this is the case. First, we are able to reject the hypothesis that all coefficients for the St. Louis bank presidents, Francis and Roos, were identical to those of the committee (at the 0.01 significance level for each). More important, individual coefficient estimates for the St. Louis presidents are consistent with the distinctions noted above. Both Francis and Roos have significantly larger (0.05 significance level or higher) coefficients on money growth than the committee as a whole. When money growth was high, the committee responded with higher

---

7. Hetzel (1998) documents Burns's antimonetarist views on inflation.

interest rates, but both the Francis and Roos reaction functions indicate a desire for a more aggressive response. In addition, Francis has a significantly smaller coefficient attached to the premeeting funds rate. A key feature of the monetarist critique was that there was excessive inertia in the adjustment of the target funds rate; a smaller coefficient on the premeeting funds rate corresponds to a desire for less inertial policymaking. Although Roos's reaction function does not differ significantly on this coefficient (perhaps in part because there are few observations in the Roos sample), the sign on the difference was again consistent with the monetarist prescription.

Estimates for Burns, Mitchell, Daane, and Hayes, mentioned above as monetarist critics, are consistent with more conventional perspectives.[8] None of these four has a money growth coefficient or a premeeting funds rate coefficient that is different from that for the committee as a whole.

Results for several other individuals are also of interest. Mark Willes served as president of the Minneapolis Federal Reserve Bank from 1977 to 1980 and had previously been a vice president of the Philadelphia Federal Reserve Bank. During our sample period, he was never a voting member of the committee and attended just eleven meetings.[9] After Burns's departure, though, he did vote at eleven meetings and cast dissenting votes six times. As we have noted, a dissent frequency of this magnitude is unusual. The reaction function estimates presented here are based only on statements made in a nonvoting capacity, but they give ample warning of Willes's future contrarian attitude: five of his six coefficient estimates differ significantly from those of the committee.[10] Of particular interest, he had a significantly higher intercept, a significantly lower coefficient on the premeeting interest rate,

8. As we noted in chapter 5, Burns presents a special problem in coding. When he spoke late in the order, he sometimes offered a consensus view, so it was difficult to distinguish the true Burns preference from the committee selection. To avoid a spurious correlation, we use a sample of observations where Burns spoke early in the meeting (and could not have been summarizing) or where he specifically stated that the position proposed was his own preference. These conditions were met in seventy-seven of the ninety-nine meetings. This includes sixty-three observations where Burns directly stated a target rate and fourteen additional observations where he was coded with a leaning position or an assent.

9. Recall that we code preferences for all members who speak within a meeting, including voting and nonvoting members.

10. All of our reported significance levels are based on asymptotic standard errors obtained via maximum-likelihood estimation. Given the lack of observations for the Willes estimation, these should be interpreted with particular caution.

and significantly higher coefficients for money growth and expected inflation. Such estimates suggest monetarist leanings and a concern with inflation.[11] Furthermore, the correlation between the Willes error term and the committee error term is 0.053 (the lowest value in the table), suggesting that Willes responded differently to shocks than the committee did.

External sources confirm Willes's anti-inflationary bent and monetarist tendencies. In contrast to Francis and Roos, however, his theoretical perspective tended toward new classical views spawned by the rational expectations hypothesis. Writing in the 1978 annual report of the Federal Reserve Bank of Minneapolis, Willes (1978) provided a rationale for his decisions over the preceding year:[12]

During the last year, while serving as a voting member of the Federal Open Market Committee, I have tried to apply the theory of rational expectations to policy-making ... if in fact decision makers are rational then restrictive policy actions when implemented properly can lower inflation without severely disrupting the economy. The efficiency with which decision makers process information ultimately determines the costs of fighting inflation with tighter macroeconomic policies.

What policymakers must do to fight inflation effectively, in other words, is to eliminate, whenever possible, surprises in monetary and fiscal policies.... In short, policy must be credible. And the only way to make policy credible is to announce it, implement it faithfully, and avoid shifting it abruptly. (Willes 1978)

Some years later, reflecting on his differences with his colleagues, Willes had this to add:

That was, of course, a time when there were some fairly sharply divergent views about how to manage things domestically. Even though I was president a relatively short period of time, I tended to get more than my share of attention, because I disagreed often with what the System was doing and how it was dealing with what I thought was a policy that was not going to deal with inflation as effectively as we ought to. I believed that if we dealt with it more effectively at that point, we could deal with it at lower cost than if we waited and tried to deal with it when the problem was bigger. (Federal Reserve Bank of Minneapolis 1992)

---

11. One odd result involved the unemployment forecast. For this short sample period, the committee coefficient for the unemployment forecast was perversely positive. Willes had a coefficient near zero, which turned out to be significantly different from that of the committee.

12. Our sample ends with the February 1978 meeting, when Burns left the committee. Willes rotated into a voting position later in 1978.

Our estimates suggest that at least one other committee member, Jeffrey Bucher, was strikingly different from most of his colleagues. His position in table 6.1 indicates that on average, he preferred an easier policy stance. Coefficient estimates would characterize him as a Keynesian activist whose preferred funds rate responded in strong countercyclical fashion to unemployment, inflation, and output growth. Coefficients on each of these variables are significantly larger (in absolute value) than those for the committee. In contrast to the monetarists, Bucher has a significantly smaller coefficient on money growth than his colleagues.

Prior to his appointment to the board, Bucher was a lawyer by training and a banker by profession. Following his term, he returned to the practice of law. In these capacities, he did not leave a paper trail with which we can easily verify his theoretical perspectives on monetary policy. Yet comments recorded in the *Memoranda* confirm his generally Keynesian outlook. The following remarks are attributed to Bucher at the March 1973 FOMC meeting:

Mr. Bucher observed that he had been struck by certain views of Professors Eckstein and Samuelson cited in the current red book. Professor Eckstein was quoted as expressing confidence that "we have learned how to apply the monetary brakes gently." He (Mr. Bucher) shared that hopeful view. The statement by Professor Samuelson which had particularly impressed him was that "cost-push inflation is not something that the monetary authorities can or ought to do a lot about." Both of those statements lent support to the suggestion that the Committee should exercise caution. (*Memorandum*, March 20, 1973, 334)

In January 1974, Bucher expressed similar views about the intractability of the inflation problem and his concern with the level of real activity in the short run:

Mr. Bucher remarked that he was extremely concerned about inflation. In his view, however, it was a long-term problem and one that had resulted in part from some unusual factors; it could not be solved in a relatively short period of time. On the other hand, a problem of fairly immediate concern was the heavy calendar of prospective new issues in the corporate bond market. Expansion in business expenditures for plant and equipment—one of the few expansive areas—was being counted on to temper recessionary developments.... Therefore Mr. Bucher concluded, the Committee should make another move in the direction of ease. (*Memorandum*, January 22, 1974, 98)

Bucher also explicitly advised against monetarist prescriptions that focused undue attention on money growth: "He agreed that the war against inflation should be the number one priority. However, the

Committee might very well lose that war by focusing too intently in the short run on the battle of the monetary aggregates" (*Memorandum*, July 16, 1974, 76–77). Further, "he disagreed with the position that monetary policy had been a major cause of the inflation" (*Memorandum*, September 10, 1974, 75).

In a telephone interview (February 21, 2002), Mr. Bucher noted that before FOMC meetings, he usually consulted both Jerry Jordan, a monetarist associated with the St. Louis Federal Reserve Bank, and Lyle Gramley, a Fed staff member with more Keynesian leanings. He confirmed that in most cases, his recommendations coincided with those of Gramley.

## 6.4   Individual Reaction Function Estimates: The Greenspan Era

This section presents reaction function estimates for individuals who served during the Greenspan era. As chapter 5 has described, there were differences in the way the FOMC operated under Burns and Greenspan, with resulting differences in the character of the data collected for the two regimes. Greenspan routinely spoke first and advocated a position, while Burns only occasionally did so. Policy options were more discrete under Greenspan, focusing on particular target values for the funds rate rather than ranges. The status quo and well-defined twenty-five- or fifty-basis-point moves from it were generally recognized as the obvious options from which members should choose. The clarity of options, as well as the tendency to voice support for the chairman's stated position, meant that it was usually easy to associate target funds rates with individuals; as a result, the fraction of cases in which individuals' preferred targets were observed was higher.

We have made two small changes in our empirical specification for Greenspan era reaction functions. First, we include the Blue Book's status quo funds rate as our measure of the premeeting funds rate rather than the average funds rate prevailing during the week before the meeting. As a practical matter, the status quo rate was almost identical to the week-before average. The second change is that we base our measure of money growth on M2 instead of M1. This reflects the increasing attention given to M2 in staff documents and discussion during this period. Neither M1 nor M2 was accorded much attention over the Greenspan years, so the change in specification is of little consequence.

The nature of the data also requires a minor change to the estimation procedure that was employed for the Burns years, at least for most individuals. During the Greenspan years, members were likely to state a position that could be directly coded as a desired funds rate target. This in turn implies that there are few observations where we see leaning positions or assents; most individuals had no assenting positions coded. Still, to estimate all model parameters for an individual (in particular, the threshold parameter, $\lambda_i$), it is necessary to have at least one observation in a leaning category and at least one observation that is an assent. For individuals where this requirement was not met, we imposed a parameter value for $\lambda_i$ obtained from a sample pooled over all individuals. Remaining parameters were estimated in the manner described in appendix 3.[13]

Table 6.2 presents estimates of individual reaction functions for thirty FOMC members who served during the Greenspan era between August 1987 and December 1996 and for whom at least ten observations were available. The organization of table 6.2 is identical to that of table 6.1, which provided the Burns era results. In many respects, the results in table 6.2 are similar to the Burns era estimates. Although members frequently aligned themselves with Greenspan's recommendations, evidence of policy differences remains abundant. Of the thirty members whose reaction functions are reported in the table, in sixteen cases we can reject the hypothesis that all of the member's reaction function coefficients were identical to those of the committee over the same sample of meetings. Of 180 individual coefficient estimates, we reject (at the 0.05 significance level, two-tailed test) the equality of member and committee coefficients thirty times. Detectable differences were a bit more frequent in the Burns era sample, but that may in part have been a consequence of the larger samples available for most members.

In the Burns years, only two explanatory variables were significantly different from zero in the committee reaction function for the complete period. These variables, the premeeting funds rate and the rate of growth of the money supply, were also usually significant in individ-

---

13. The estimate for $\lambda$ obtained from the pooled regression was 0.037, which is smaller than corresponding estimates from the Burns era. Given the infrequency of assenting positions, this is a sensible result. A low value of $\lambda$ implies that it is easy to cross the threshold for generating leans, so we should not observe many assents. Estimates of other coefficients are not sensitive to the value imposed for $\lambda$, and in all cases, estimates are close to OLS results obtained when we use only the sample of observed target funds rates.

ual reaction functions. While the status quo interest rate remains a significant variable in the Greenspan committee reaction function, money growth does not (this result also holds when M1 growth is used in place of M2 growth). This reflects the fact that the FOMC attached less importance to the monetary aggregates as guides for policymaking during the Greenspan years. Nevertheless, the Greenspan FOMC was more responsive to business cycle conditions—coefficients for unemployment and output growth differed significantly from zero and were signed in a manner consistent with efforts to lean against the wind (the unemployment coefficient was negative and the output growth coefficient was positive).[14]

As with the Burns era estimations, some differences across individuals can be characterized in a simple ease-to-tightness dimension. The members who differ significantly from their committee (based on a rejection of the test of equality of all coefficients) tend to be located at either the top or the bottom of table 6.2, with members at the top tending to favor easier policies and those at the bottom tighter policies. A few members in the middle of the table, however, also differed significantly from their colleagues. The average error correlation reported in table 6.2 is 0.67, compared to 0.72 for the Burns era.

### 6.5  Greenspan Era Econometric Results in Historical Perspective

During the Burns era, it was possible to distinguish members by monetarist and Keynesian perspectives, both in terms of reaction function estimates and verbal descriptions of policy preferences. This is more difficult for the Greenspan years. The monetarism of the Burns years was characterized by a desire to guide monetary policy via simple rules for growth of the monetary aggregates. By the end of the Greenspan years, though, there was near unanimity that the monetary aggregates were not useful guides to short-run policymaking and were of only limited value for longer-term policymaking. Alan Blinder (1998, 27), a Fed governor during the Greenspan era, noted that "ferocious instabilities in estimated LM curves in the United States, United Kingdom, and many other countries, beginning in the 1970s and continuing to the present day, led economists and policymakers alike to conclude that money-supply targeting is simply not a viable option."

---

14. In the committee reaction function for the Greenspan sample, the Durbin-Watson statistic was in the inconclusive range for testing for serial correlation. Corrected estimates, however, were almost identical to the OLS results presented here.

**Table 6.2**

Estimates of individual FOMC member reaction functions: The Greenspan era

| Member | Rank | $R^*_{it}-\bar{R}_t$ | Constant | $R^p_t$ | $\dot{M2}_t$ | $\hat{U}_t$ | $\hat{P}_t$ | $\hat{Y}_t$ | $\lambda$ | $\rho$ | $\sigma_e$ | $\sigma_u$ | $\chi^2(6)$ | N |
|---|---|---|---|---|---|---|---|---|---|---|---|---|---|---|
| Committee (OLS) | | | 0.582 | 0.954** | −0.011 | −0.091* | 0.052 | 0.058** | NA | 0.004 | 0.126 | 0.096 | 43.204** | 75 |
| Seger | 1 | −0.175 | 1.568 | 0.835** | −0.023 | −0.214 | 0.165*# | 0.112** | NA | 0.685 | 0.161 | 0.146 | 13.756** | 28 |
| Blinder | 2 | −0.083 | 5.236 | 0.496** | 0.007 | −0.500 | 0.204 | −0.057 | NA | 0.795 | 0.095 | 0.105 | 17.688** | 13 |
| Heller | 3 | −0.058 | 4.165* | 0.914** | −0.012 | −0.541* | −0.115 | 0.006 | NA | 0.740 | 0.138 | 0.174 | 9.721 | 14 |
| Yellen | 4 | −0.056 | 2.221* | 0.707** | −0.019 | −0.094 | −0.050 | 0.032 | NA | 0.852 | 0.199 | 0.169 | 12.358* | 20 |
| McTeer | 5 | −0.022 | 1.419** | 0.874**† | −0.015 | −0.199**† | 0.118 | 0.068* | NA | 0.889 | 0.196 | 0.174 | 36.921** | 47 |
| Phillips | 6 | −0.021 | 1.321** | 0.878**† | −0.073 | −0.244**†† | 0.183## | 0.131## | NA | 0.563 | 0.140 | 0.110 | 15.137* | 41 |
| Keehn | 7 | −0.019 | 1.414* | 0.935** | 0.005 | −0.212** | 0.037 | 0.058** | NA | 0.588 | 0.091 | 0.076 | 12.003 | 55 |
| Syron | 8 | −0.019 | 0.152 | 0.971** | −0.001 | −0.061 | 0.068 | 0.070**# | 0.031 | 0.975 | 0.093 | 0.099 | 0.013 | 41 |
| Johnson | 9 | −0.011 | 4.263* | 0.886** | −0.010 | −0.521** | −0.150* | 0.071* | NA | 0.862 | 0.169 | 0.144 | 16.719* | 22 |
| Forrestal | 10 | −0.009 | 1.348** | 0.919** | −0.013 | −0.208** | 0.096# | 0.072**## | NA | | | | | 65 |
| McDonough | 11 | 0.000 | 0.686 | 0.932** | −0.031 | −0.091 | 0.035 | 0.099 | NA | NA | 0.221 | NA | NA | 27 |
| Greenspan | 12 | 0.000 | 0.548 | 0.957** | −0.012 | −0.087 | 0.050 | 0.059** | NA | 0.979 | 0.150 | 0.148 | 2.781 | 75 |
| Kelly | 13 | 0.004 | 0.506 | 0.961** | −0.013 | −0.076 | 0.041 | 0.049**† | NA | 0.960 | 0.149 | 0.149 | 8.248 | 74 |
| Boehne | 14 | 0.006 | 0.437 | 0.965** | −0.010 | −0.097* | 0.066 | 0.094**# | NA | 0.789 | 0.152 | 0.147 | 11.862 | 73 |
| Lindsey | 15 | 0.007 | 0.898 | 0.908** | −0.014 | −0.157† | 0.134## | 0.097*## | 0.030 | 0.949 | 0.182 | 0.174 | 23.724** | 41 |
| Jordan | 16 | 0.010 | 1.915* | 0.860** | −0.006 | −0.174* | −0.177 | 0.140* | 0.065 | 0.956 | 0.207 | 0.191 | 5.811 | 38 |
| Corrigan | 17 | 0.012 | 0.915 | 0.951** | −0.001 | −0.133 | 0.031 | 0.062** | NA | 0.160 | 0.107 | 0.093 | 2.311 | 46 |
| Guffey | 18 | 0.020 | 0.944 | 0.935** | 0.007# | −0.130 | 0.051 | 0.040** | NA | 0.465 | 0.085 | 0.097 | 8.715 | 32 |
| Hoenig | 19 | 0.022 | 1.511* | 0.912** | −0.008 | −0.220** | 0.088 | 0.060 | NA | 0.797 | 0.184 | 0.173 | 11.502 | 43 |
| Boykin | 20 | 0.023 | 1.368 | 0.920** | 0.004 | −0.180 | 0.047 | 0.053* | NA | 0.795 | 0.111 | 0.099 | 9.372 | 27 |
| LaWare | 21 | 0.024 | 2.497**† | 0.917** | −0.003 | −0.291** | −0.053 | 0.249 | NA | 0.846 | 0.150 | 0.148 | 10.837 | 53 |
| Moskow | 22 | 0.026 | 0.548 | 0.805** | −0.024 | −0.096 | 0.380* | 0.099 | NA | 0.907 | 0.150 | 0.165 | 6.970 | 19 |

| | | | | | | | | | | | | | | |
|---|---|---|---|---|---|---|---|---|---|---|---|---|---|---|
| Stern | 23 | 0.033 | 0.854* | 0.956** | −0.012 | −0.116* | 0.024 | 0.055** | NA | 0.810 | 0.157 | 0.148 | 13.729* | 75 |
| Black | 24 | 0.033 | 1.226 | 0.910** | 0.006 | −0.185 | −0.185 | 0.103 | NA | 0.468 | 0.109 | 0.096 | 13.616* | 39 |
| Angell | 25 | 0.046 | 2.272**## | 0.908**†† | −0.013* | −0.258**†† | −0.017 | 0.022 | NA | 0.405 | 0.115 | 0.091 | 27.322** | 51 |
| Parry | 26 | 0.066 | 1.183** | 0.930** | −0.017 | −0.222**† | 0.157**# | 0.113**# | 0.030 | 0.612 | 0.201 | 0.150 | 31.983** | 75 |
| Melzer | 27 | 0.075 | 1.801**†† | 0.916** | −0.007 | −0.215**†† | 0.017 | 0.029 | NA | 0.517 | 0.169 | 0.148 | 31.364** | 75 |
| Minehan | 28 | 0.101 | 1.276 | 0.903** | −0.024 | −0.207 | 0.060 | 0.209** | NA | 0.730 | 0.158 | 0.184 | 21.591** | 23 |
| Broaddus | 29 | 0.148 | 3.986**## | 0.825** | −0.031** | −0.392**† | −0.294**† | 0.085 | NA | 0.644 | 0.158 | 0.185 | 52.714** | 33 |
| Hoskins | 30 | 0.203 | 1.476 | 0.903** | 0.027*# | −0.300 | 0.244**# | 0.058* | 0.272 | 0.142 | 0.160 | 0.100 | 53.344** | 30 |

*Coefficient is significantly different from zero, 0.05 level, two-tailed test

**Coefficient is significantly different from zero, 0.01 level, two-tailed test (one-tailed for $\chi^2$)

#(†) Member coefficient is higher (lower) than the committee coefficient, 0.05 level, two-tailed test

##(††) Member coefficient is higher (lower) than the committee coefficient, 0.01 level, two-tailed test

NA: $\lambda$ not estimated; a value for $\lambda$ was obtained from an estimation pooling over individuals

Our results seem to confirm this shift in thinking: money growth is a significant positive regressor in only one individual reaction function reported in table 6.2 (that for Cleveland Fed president Lee Hoskins). By contrast, money growth was significant in the majority of individual reaction functions for members who served during the Burns era.

The early monetarist focus on monetary aggregates was derived from a belief that the Fed had limited ability to stabilize business cycles and should instead concentrate on long-run price stability. Targeting the monetary aggregates was thought to be an effective strategy for achieving that result. During the Greenspan years, the aggregates were considered to be less reliable as policy guides, but a distinct bloc of FOMC members continued to focus on long-run price stability as a primary objective for monetary policy.

Some of these individuals had links to the monetarist tradition—for example, Cleveland Fed president Jerry Jordan had been a director of research at the St. Louis Fed and was well-known for his work developing the monetarist-oriented "St. Louis" econometric model (Andersen and Jordan 1968). St. Louis Fed president Thomas Melzer inherited the monetarist legacy there and continued to occasionally draw attention to the behavior of the money supply in his remarks to the committee. Yet both Jordan and Melzer acknowledged that price stability was the key objective. In 1994, Jordan lamented the loss of money as a nominal anchor and anticipated a possible inflation targeting regime:

I think the main part of our problem right now is inflation psychology. It certainly reflects the lack of a nominal anchor. . . . If somehow we could achieve the conditions of a true gold standard—without gold but the steady purchasing power of money in the minds of people—over time it would make some of these short-term things that we go through a lot easier to deal with. . . . I still feel that the numbers we put together for the Humphrey-Hawkins process *should not be people's predictions* of what is going to happen with regard to inflation, but rather a reflection of *what we intend to try and achieve* by our monetary policy actions. (*Transcripts*, December 20, 1994, 36, emphasis added)

Some months later, Melzer reinforced this position while adding a conventional monetarist jibe at "fine-tuning": "I think our focus in this Committee ought to be on long-term price stability, not short-run fine-tuning of the real economy. That is really what we ought to be thinking about—whether we are on a course that is really going to achieve price stability" (*Transcripts*, March 28, 1995, 45).

Jordan and Melzer were often joined by other Reserve Bank presidents in promoting the goal of price stability. Alfred Broaddus of the

Richmond district noted that "it would be very nice if we could find some longer-term nominal anchor for monetary policy" (*Transcripts*, May 23, 1995, 34). Lee Hoskins, Cleveland Fed president and another inflation hawk, indicated frustration with the committee's unwillingness to tackle price stability more forcefully: "There are some who want zero inflation and there are others who want one or two percent inflation. And I don't see us moving in that direction with the current recommendation on the table" (*Transcripts*, December 18–19, 1989, 97).

In May 1994, Jordan observed that this split in perspective tended to pit governors against Reserve Bank presidents: "It struck me in the go-around earlier that at least some of you looking at the world *from inside the beltway*—Governors Kelley, LaWare, and Phillips—have a different feel of the economy than what I sense from the other twelve of us" (*Transcripts*, May 17, 1994, 37, emphasis added). The propensity of bank presidents to support tighter policies is also evident in the results provided in table 6.2. The four members at the top of the table (that is, those typically advocating lower rates) are all governors, while the five members at the bottom (advocating higher rates) are all bank presidents.

While no central banker would renounce price stability as an objective, some Greenspan era FOMC members were more willing than others to acknowledge the dual objectives of price stability and full employment. Janet Yellen, a Clinton appointee who served on the board from 1994 to 1997, was known for her "new Keynesian" perspective. In 1995, she described her monetary policy views as follows:

Like most mainstream economists these days, I think the "natural rate theory" fits the data for the United States reasonably well, suggesting that there is, to a first approximation, no long-run tradeoff between inflation and employment.... I would agree that the Fed probably cannot achieve permanent gains in the level of employment by living with higher inflation. But the Federal Reserve can, I think, make a contribution on the employment side by mitigating economic fluctuations—by stabilizing real activity. I thus translate the "maximum employment" proviso of the Federal Reserve Act as a mandate for the Fed to lean against the wind, stimulating the economy when the economy is in recession or unemployment is clearly in excess of the NAIRU (the non-accelerating inflation rate of unemployment—the minimum rate of unemployment consistent with stable inflation), and restraining the economy through tighter policy when economic activity is pushing against the limits of capacity with inflationary implications. This is what the Federal Reserve has traditionally done and it is what I think the Fed should continue to do. There is no tradeoff in my view between this stabilization objective and the objective of price stability. We can achieve whatever inflation rate we desire, on average, while acting to stabilize the economy. (Federal Reserve Bank of Minneapolis 1995)

Yellen distinctly maintained that her position need not involve any compromise on price stability and, as she claims, her views were decidedly mainstream in the economics profession. Nevertheless, similar remarks by Alan Blinder, a Fed governor and frequent Yellen ally, had once created controversy. Shortly after assuming his position at the Fed, Blinder delivered a speech in which he acknowledged the existence of a short-run Phillips curve trade-off and asserted that the Fed should take seriously its legal mandate to promote full employment. The press had already adopted the notion that Blinder was a dove on inflation, and the speech was taken as confirmation of the view that he rejected the primacy of price stability as an objective.[15] Although Yellen and Blinder had conventional rather than radical views, both pushed in the direction of ease more often than most of their colleagues.

The reaction functions presented in table 6.2 provide at least mild support for the differences in policy perspectives that we have noted. A group of Reserve Bank presidents—including Gary Stern, Robert Black, Robert Parry, Melzer, Cathy Minehan, Broaddus, and Hoskins—are located at the bottom of the table, indicating a preference for tighter policies. They are joined by Governor Wayne Angell, another champion of the price stability objective. In contrast, governors Yellen and Blinder appear near the top of the list, along with their board colleagues Susan Phillips and Martha Seger. With the exception of Yellen, who served for only fourteen meetings, we reject the hypothesis of equal member and committee reaction function coefficients for each of these individuals.

While the overall ranking in table 6.2 supports a division between those who gave priority to price stability and those who voiced broader concerns, specific coefficient estimates are less revealing. Yellen and Blinder served for short periods, and none of their individual coefficient estimates differed significantly from those of the committee. Judging from her reaction function estimates, Phillips fits the Keynesian stereotype; she responded more actively to unemployment, output growth, and inflation than her colleagues. Although Jordan (see above) had distinguished Phillips's view from that of his cadre of bank

---

15. Blinder's encounter with the press is described in greater detail in Woodward (2000, 131–133).

presidents, meeting transcripts do not give a clear indication of her theoretical perspective. Similarly, Seger routinely proposed easier policy stances than her colleagues, but neither her statements nor her reaction function coefficient estimates reveal much about her theoretical orientation.[16]

Among those who championed price stability, patterns displayed by the individual coefficients are at least mildly puzzling. Hoskins and Parry are more responsive to the inflation forecast than the committee as a whole, and Hoskins also reacts to rapid M2 growth, as one might expect if price stability were a primary objective. Angell and Broaddus have higher intercepts than the committee; other things being equal, this also implies a desire for tighter policy. Yet Angell, Parry, and Broaddus all have unemployment coefficients that are significantly larger (in absolute value) than the corresponding committee coefficients. Minehan, Hoskins, and Melzer also have unemployment coefficient estimates that are larger (in absolute value) than those for the committee, but the differences are not statistically significant.

Although one would not normally expect a commitment to price stability to be reflected in responsiveness to unemployment, there is an interpretation of events under which that might be reasonable. As unemployment trended downward in 1995 and 1996, Greenspan argued that heightened productivity growth was offsetting the potential inflationary effect of tightening labor markets. He also contended that despite low unemployment, workers had been unusually reticent in demanding wage increases because of their concerns about job security. Greenspan used these arguments to defend a delay in any monetary tightening. But the comments of some of the inflation hawks indicate that they were not convinced by Greenspan's reasoning. In the latter half of 1996, Minehan, Broaddus, Melzer, Parry, and Stern frequently advocated higher rates, as Greenspan and the committee held steady. Consider the comments of Broaddus in July 1996:

I am reluctant at this point to deemphasize what you refer to as the "old model." It seems to me that the information we heard yesterday suggests that the economy is currently robust, with the risks dominating on the up side rather than the down side. Moreover, in the Bluebook discussion of short-run alternatives, the point is made that if we want to tilt inflation down, we may have to raise the federal funds rate "considerably." . . .

---

16. Seger was sometimes characterized as a supply-sider, but this label was also occasionally applied to Lawrence Lindsey, Manuel Johnson, and Wayne Angell. Judging from our reaction function estimates, these four individuals shared little beyond the label.

... I personally believe that a solid case can be made for an increase of 50 basis points in the federal funds rate. (*Transcripts*, July 2–3, 1996, 85)

In August, Stern agreed with Broaddus and specifically noted labor market conditions: "There has been a lot of discussion of productivity and, of course, productivity is important.... But the productivity performance notwithstanding, whether we have mismeasured it or not, we do know for sure that output growth so far this year is unsustainable because employment growth thus far this year has been roughly twice the sustainable growth of the labor force" (*Transcripts*, August 20, 1996, 39). It seems clear that during at least one extended episode, declining unemployment was associated with support for higher funds rates among the group characterized as inflation hawks. This behavior could account for the pattern in unemployment coefficients shown in table 6.2.

In addition, it seems likely that in the absence of a clearly accepted nominal anchor, some committee members would have relied on indicators that were not included in our reaction function specification. For example, in committee deliberations Angell often mentioned commodity prices, Broaddus and Melzer commented on spreads between long-term and short-term interest rates, and Melzer discussed growth of the monetary aggregates over longer backward horizons than those employed in our specifications. Future research on individual reaction functions might benefit from the use of a larger set of potential explanatory variables, with variables matched to individuals according to available prior knowledge of their views.

## 6.6   Conclusions

Using detailed records of FOMC deliberations for the Burns and Greenspan eras, we have estimated monetary policy reaction functions for individual committee members. Our results provide information about differences in policy preferences across members as well as evidence confirming the usefulness of our methodology. Where external sources tell us about known policy differences, our estimates usually reveal them as well. The rankings of individuals on an ease-to-tightness scale are generally consistent with those presented in chapter 4 (see table 4.2), which were based on voting data. In this chapter, however, we were able to learn more about the underlying causes of the broad distinctions revealed by voting records.

From an historical perspective, the description of preferences is important in documenting the reasoning that leads to key policy choices. In the 1970s, the monetarist-Keynesian policy split is of interest in the context of both the rise of inflation and a severe contraction. Our estimates confirm the split between the monetarists of the St. Louis Federal Reserve Bank and the rest of the committee; they are also informative about the perspectives of other committee members with distinctive views. During the Greenspan era, traditional monetarism fell into decline as the monetary aggregates came to be viewed as unsatisfactory guides to policy. Nevertheless, both anecdotal evidence and reaction function estimates are consistent with the existence of a division between members who advocated the primacy of price stability as a goal and those who favored a more traditional weighing of the price stability and full employment objectives.

Majority Rule, Consensus
Building, and the Power of
the Chairman: Arthur
Burns and the FOMC

*The reasons are not at all clear for the almost uncanny record of the chairman in never having been on the losing side of a vote on the policy directive. While there is no evidence to support the view that the directive always voted upon and passed on the first ballot merely reflects the chairman's own preference, there is also no evidence to refute the view that the chairman adroitly detects the consensus of the committee, with which he persistently, in the interests of System harmony, aligns himself.*

—William Yohe, "A Study of Federal Open Market Committee Voting"

As the quote above acknowledges, assessing the relative power of the chairman and the committee is a difficult task. In the years since Yohe's (1966) observation, remarkably little has been learned about the pressures that are at play as policy preferences are aggregated to produce a monetary policy decision by the FOMC. In this chapter, we investigate these issues, focusing on the competing pressures of majority rule, consensus building, and the preeminence of the chairman in decision making.[1] In constructing the data sets described in chapter 5, we were able to characterize the policy preferences of each FOMC member in each meeting during the 1970–1978 and 1987–1996 periods. By examining links between individual preferences and committee decisions, it may be possible to learn much more about preference aggregation and FOMC power sharing than Yohe had imagined.

In this chapter, we examine only the 1970–1978 period when Burns served as chairman. Although we have collected data on individual preferences for the Greenspan era as well, the character of the data differs in an important way in the latter period. As mentioned earlier, Greenspan regularly spoke first in the policy go-around, and there was a pronounced tendency for other committee members to align

---

1. This chapter is drawn from Chappell, McGregor, and Vermilyea (2004).

themselves with his preferences. Greenspan's preferred federal funds rate differed from the recorded committee median on only three occasions. Given that the series for the Greenspan and median policy positions are almost identical, it is not possible to carry out a direct econometric assessment of the relative power shares of Greenspan and the committee. In the Burns years, however, the stated preferences of the chairman do not routinely match those of mean or median committee preferences, so a revealing econometric analysis of preference aggregation within the committee is possible. We carry out such an analysis in this chapter.

Burns era records of FOMC deliberations describe policy preferences in a manner that permits us to infer individuals' preferred funds rate targets in about 80 percent of all member-meeting observations. Where preferred funds rates are not directly stated, qualitative indications of preferences are recorded instead. In this chapter, we begin by describing how one can use individual reaction function estimates and qualitative preference indicators to impute individuals' preferred funds rates when they are not directly stated. Combining imputed funds rates with those that are directly stated, we then construct a data set consisting of complete profiles of committee member preferences and use this data to investigate the collective choice process.

Given that the FOMC uses majority voting, the median voter model provides a conceptual starting point for our empirical analysis. We then extend the median voter model to permit an enhanced role for the board chairman and to capture the influence of minority views. Although our focus is on monetary policy, the analysis of committee decision making here should be of independent interest in the field of public choice. The median voter model is the workhorse of empirical public choice, but most empirical applications of that model have been severely constrained by data limitations.[2] Because the FOMC regularly votes on a one-dimensional issue (the degree of ease or tightness of policy) and because we have obtained complete profiles of committee member preferences, the setting is ideal for testing the median voter theorem as well as alternative hypotheses.

---

2. Most empirical applications of the median voter model have analyzed expenditures on public goods across local governmental units. Prominent examples include studies by Borcherding and Deacon (1972) and Bergstrom and Goodman (1973). In such studies, the empirical implementation of the model requires that strong ancillary assumptions be made to identify the preferences of the median voter. For a detailed critique of empirical median voter models, see Romer and Rosenthal (1979).

In the first section of this chapter, we discuss the roles of majority voting, consensus building, and the power of the chairman in FOMC decision making, drawing from both the existing academic literature and anecdotal evidence. The second section briefly reviews the nature of the raw data employed (previously described in chapter 5) and explains how these data can be used to construct complete profiles of FOMC members' policy preferences. The third section introduces empirical models that relate individual preferences to adopted policies, and estimates of those models are presented and discussed in the fourth section. Several model extensions are considered in the fifth section, with conclusions following in the sixth.

## 7.1    The Power of the Chairman and the Allure of Consensus

Journalistic accounts of Federal Reserve decision making often portray the chairman as a monetary policy dictator. For example, the May 10, 1982, issue of *U.S. News and World Report* listed then-chairman Paul Volcker second behind President Reagan in its annual ranking of the most powerful individuals in the United States. The academic literature on monetary policymaking also indicates a prominent role for the chairman. Woolley (1984) has suggested that the chairman's roles as liaison with external clients and resource allocator within the Fed give him leverage over the committee. Other research has documented both the influence of various chairmen on monetary policy decisions and the factors that have shaped their policy positions.[3]

Nevertheless, the need to produce a majority in support of each policy directive suggests that the chairman is unlikely to be a true dictator. On this point, the remarks of Sherman Maisel (1973, 124), a member of the Board of Governors during the Burns era, are instructive:

While the influence of the Chairman is indeed great, he does not make policy alone. At times he may even feel that he is a prisoner of the staff, the other members of the Board, or the Federal Open Market Committee. The limits on his time and energy force him to depend on others for advice and for operations. While any policy he believes in strongly is likely to be adopted in the end, the influence of his colleagues has a great deal to do with its form and timing.

---

3. See, for example, Hakes (1990); Havrilesky (1995); Kettl (1986); Krause (1994); and Peek and Wilcox (1987). The voting weight of the chairman has been econometrically estimated by Chappell, Havrilesky, and McGregor (1993), but that analysis relied on less revealing data than those employed in this chapter.

Maisel (1973, 110) has subjectively estimated that the chairman has about 45 percent of the policymaking power in monetary policy decisions.

Differences in the behavior of Reserve Bank presidents and governors have been noted earlier in this book (chapters 4 and 6) and elsewhere in the literature (see Belden 1989; Chappell, Havrilesky, and McGregor 1993; Krause 1996), and a preponderance of the evidence suggests that bank presidents prefer tighter monetary policy than governors. The reasons for such differences could be grounded in institutional arrangements: bank presidents and governors are chosen by different procedures and have different clienteles and responsibilities. These differences may also be significant for the issues addressed in this chapter, since institutional arrangements may also produce different degrees of policymaking power. Governors may be more powerful because of their proximity to the chairman and because they have the authority to set reserve requirements and approve the discount rates proposed by the district Reserve Banks. Alternatively, because bank presidents do not depend on the chairman for staff support, they may confront the chairman more effectively when disagreements arise.[4]

Bank presidents also differ from governors in another way. Although bank presidents attend all FOMC meetings, they do not always serve as voting members. This invites the question of whether they have any influence on policy choices while serving in a nonvoting capacity. Although Burns specifically referred to the views of nonvoting bank presidents in crafting a directive on at least one occasion (*Memorandum*, January 11, 1972, 95), it seems that in other instances only the views of the voting members were considered.[5]

Despite occasional disagreements, it is apparent that the FOMC values consensus. Internal consensus gives the Fed power and credibility in dealing with external clients, including the president and Congress as well as the public. A transcript of the September 20, 1977, FOMC meeting provides a discussion of the chairman's attempts to orchestrate consensus in a meeting in which views were deeply divided. After a close seven to five vote in favor of the first proposed directive, Burns reacted as follows:

---

4. Maisel (1973, 110) subjectively estimated that, as a group, governors had twice as much influence over monetary policy as the bank presidents.
5. On October 17, 1977, the committee adopted a federal funds rate target range centered on 6.50 percent. Half of the voting members, including Burns, favored this range, while the other half of the voting members and *all* of the nonvoting members preferred higher rates. Clearly, the preferences of the nonvoting members were ignored in this instance.

Well let's stop and deliberate it. I think that would be a very unfortunate vote. To me the Committee is split badly. It would mean that this would excite a great deal of discussion that would not bring honor or credit to the Committee and therefore I think we must seek to accommodate one another. I didn't think our differences were that large. Let's try again. Does anyone have a proposal to make, one of the dissenters? (*Transcripts*, September 20, 1977, tape 8, 16–17)

After several unsuccessful attempts to craft a more universally acceptable alternative, Burns admonished the committee: "Gentlemen, the original vote stands. The first vote. We're divided. I think it is unfortunate, I think it is undesirable and I don't know what has gotten into this group" (*Transcripts*, September 20, 1977, tape 8, 19). Conflicts are usually muted, but this episode reveals that efforts to reach consensus are sometimes abruptly confronted by majoritarian pressures.

The need to gain majority support limits the power of the chairman; however, the presence of an ethic favoring the achievement of consensus might accentuate it. If members are reluctant to challenge proposals offered by an agenda-setting chairman, then he should be able to tilt outcomes toward his favored positions. The following summary of Burns's statement at the FOMC meeting of May 15, 1973, illustrates this phenomenon:

Chairman Burns remarked that a majority of the Committee was clearly in favor of the specifications of alternative B and of some version of the B language for the operational paragraph of the directive. He did not find the majority's position unacceptable, but for reasons which he would not elaborate on at this point, he would prefer a somewhat different course. Perhaps the best procedure would be for him to describe the directive language and specifications he favored and determine whether they would be acceptable to the committee. (*Memorandum*, May 15, 1973, 560)

Burns then proposed specific targets for the federal funds rate, which were later accepted by the committee, despite deviating slightly from the position favored by the majority.

## 7.2   Constructing Preference Profiles for the FOMC

To investigate how individuals' preferred funds rates are aggregated to produce the target rates adopted by the FOMC, it is important that we have complete profiles of individual policy preferences (that is, complete listings of preferred funds rates for all members attending a meeting). For about 20 percent of the observations in the Burns era sample, we do not observe stated rates but instead observe categorical indicators of preferences (leaning and assenting positions). In this section, we describe how we impute individuals' rate preferences for those observations. To do so, we first estimate monetary policy reaction functions for each committee member in a manner similar to that described in chapter 6; we then use the reaction functions to calculate expected values for desired funds rates, conditional on the information provided by leaning positions. This section discusses the calculations involved and the attributes of the data set produced.

### 7.2.1 Individuals' Reaction Functions: Empirical Models

Following the analysis of chapter 6, recall that committee member $i$ has a desired interest rate reaction function of the form

$$R_{it}^* = \mathbf{X}_t \boldsymbol{\beta}_i + e_{it}, \; e_{it} \sim N(0, \sigma_i). \tag{7.1}$$

In this equation, $R_{it}^*$ is member $i$'s desired federal funds rate target for the policy directive to be chosen in meeting $t$, and right-hand side variables include indicators of macroeconomic conditions that are thought to influence policy decisions. $R_{it}^*$ is often observed, but sometimes only qualitative leaning indications of preferences are available.

The empirical specification for the individual reaction functions to be used in making imputations is similar to that employed in chapter 6 for the Burns era. Explanatory variables again include the actual federal funds rate prevailing during the week before the FOMC meeting ($R_t^p$), the average growth of M1 rate during the three months prior to the month of the meeting ($\dot{M}_t$), and two-quarter-ahead forecast values for the rate of inflation ($\hat{P}_t$), the rate of growth of real GNP ($\hat{Y}_t$), and the civilian unemployment rate ($\hat{U}_t$), all measured as percentages. For the analysis in this chapter, however, our reaction function specification includes an additional explanatory variable: the midpoint of the board staff's target range for the funds rate, $\tilde{R}_t$. This variable captures two effects: (1) the influence that the staff exerts on members' subsequently stated preferences and (2) the effect of omitted economic variables that influence the desired funds rates of both the staff and committee members. Although we cannot disentangle these effects empirically, that is not our purpose—for our purposes here, we simply wish to specify a model that has good predictive power.[6] The individual reaction

---

6. It appears that the reaction functions fit the data well. Using only observations where desired interest rates were directly observed, OLS estimates produced $R^2$ values at 0.979 and above for all individuals. For the mixed OLS-probit estimation procedure that used all observations, $R^2$ is not an available statistic.

function estimations undertaken for the analysis in this chapter are not reported here, but they are broadly similar to those reported in chapter 7.[7]

### 7.2.2   A Method for Imputing Desired Interest Rates

When $R_{it}^*$ is not observed, we instead observe leaning or assenting positions defined in relation to the benchmark rate, $\tilde{R}_{it}$. Since the leaning positions contain information about an individual's preferences, we wish to use that information when we calculate imputed desired funds rates for individuals who did not directly state them. Recall from chapter 6 that leaning positions are generated when an individual's preference deviates sufficiently from the benchmark, in accordance with conditions (7.2):

if $R_{it}^* - \tilde{R}_{it} > \lambda_i$, then $V_{it} = 1$ (member $i$ leans for tightness);       (7.2.a)

if $R_{it}^* - \tilde{R}_{it} < -\lambda_i$, then $V_{it} = -1$ (member $i$ leans for ease);       (7.2.b)

if $-\lambda_i \leq R_{it}^* - \tilde{R}_{it} \leq \lambda_i$, then $V_{it} = 0$ (member $i$ assents).       (7.2.c)

Given this model of the data-generating process, our imputations are calculated as expected values of $R_{it}^*$ conditional on exogenous variables, model parameters, and leaning positions. Expressions for the expected values are provided by conditions (7.3):

if $V_{it} = 1$, then $E(R_{it}^*) = \mathbf{X}_t \boldsymbol{\beta}_i + \sigma_i \dfrac{f(\tilde{a}_{it})}{1 - F(\tilde{a}_{it})}$;       (7.3.a)

if $V_{it} = -1$, then $E(R_{it}^*) = \mathbf{X}_t \boldsymbol{\beta}_i - \sigma_i \dfrac{f(\tilde{b}_{it})}{F(\tilde{b}_{it})}$;       (7.3.b)

---

7. The newly included staff midpoint, $\tilde{R}_t$, is now always a significant variable, and some of its explanatory power comes at the expense of the remaining economic variables included in the model. Several additional estimation issues should be noted. First, estimating the combined OLS-probit model requires leans in at least two of the three categories. For a few members, this requirement was not met. For those individuals, we use their OLS results, along with $\lambda$ and/or $\sigma$ values taken from a pooled estimation using data for all members, to impute desired interest rates. Second, some individuals do not have enough observations to allow us to estimate the combined OLS-probit model. Since these individuals were all vice presidents of district Reserve Banks, to impute their desired interest rates, we combined these individuals with the presidents under whom they served. Finally, for the analysis in this chapter, we have used the single-equation estimator described in the first section of appendix 3 rather than the two-equation model used for the results reported in chapter 6.

if $V_{it} = 0$, then $E(R_{it}^*) = \mathbf{X}_t\boldsymbol{\beta}_i + \sigma_i \dfrac{f(\tilde{b}_{it}) - f(\tilde{a}_{it})}{F(\tilde{a}_{it}) - F(\tilde{b}_{it})}.$                     (7.3.c)

In conditions (7.3), $f(\cdot)$ is the standard normal density function, $F(\cdot)$ is the standard normal cumulative distribution function, $\tilde{a}_{it} = (\lambda_i + \tilde{R}_{it} - \mathbf{X}_t\boldsymbol{\beta}_i)/\sigma_i$, and $\tilde{b}_{it} = (-\lambda_i + \tilde{R}_{it} - \mathbf{X}_t\boldsymbol{\beta}_i)/\sigma_i$. These conditions, described at greater length in the third section of appendix 3, can be derived in a manner that follows the example of Tobin (1958). We employ estimated parameters in conditions (7.3) when calculating imputed values of desired funds rates.

The important attribute of the imputation procedure we have developed is that it accounts for the information revealed by leaning statements of preference. If a member leans toward tightness relative to a benchmark rate of 5.0 percent, then that member's imputed desired interest rate will (necessarily) be higher than 5.0 percent.

### 7.2.3   Special Issues Concerning the Chairman

In chapter 5, we noted that because our empirical investigation focuses attention on the influence exerted by Burns in committee deliberations, it is particularly important to measure his preferences accurately. In empirical models used in subsequent sections, we therefore wish to restrict the sample to observations where (1) Burns directly stated a funds rate target and (2) he stated a funds rate target that reflected his own preference rather than the consensus of the committee. To do so, we employ two alternative subsamples of meetings in which Burns stated specific target rates. First, we use a forty-three-observation subsample in which he spoke in the first half of the order and could not have been summarizing the positions of others. Alternatively, we use a sixty-three-observation subsample that adds another twenty observations in which Burns spoke late in the order, but specifically noted that the proposal reflected his own preference.[8]

### 7.2.4   Preference Profiles for Selected Meetings

Using the methods described above, we have imputed desired interest rates as needed and constructed complete preference profiles for all of the FOMC meetings included in our sample. A complete listing of preference profiles for the Burns years is provided in appendix 4. For

---

8. Because the chairman chooses when to speak and what to say, selection into the smaller subsamples is not strictly exogenous. We have estimated models correcting for selection bias and have obtained results that are similar to those reported in this chapter.

**Table 7.1**
Federal funds rate preferences and outcomes: Examples

| May 15, 1973 | | March 18, 1975 | | January 17, 1977 | |
|---|---|---|---|---|---|
| Member | Desired funds rate | Member | Desired funds rate | Member | Desired funds rate |
| Mayo | 7.8750 | Wallich | 5.5000 | Wallich | 4.7500 |
| Hayes | 7.8750 | Hayes | 5.5000 | Volcker | 4.7500 |
| Francis | 7.8750 | Burns | 5.5000 | Partee | 4.7500 |
| Sheehan | 7.6250 | Holland | 5.3750 | Lilly | 4.7500 |
| Morris | 7.6250 | Mitchell | 5.2500 | Gardner | 4.7500 |
| Daane | 7.6250 | Mayo | 5.2500 | Coldwell | 4.7500 |
| Bucher | 7.6250 | MacLaury | 5.2500 | Burns | 4.7500 |
| Brimmer | 7.6250 | Eastburn | 5.0000 | Balles | 4.7500 |
| Balles | 7.6250 | Baughman | 5.0000 | Kimbrel | 4.6560* |
| Burns | 7.5625 | Coldwell | 4.8750 | Winn | 4.6250 |
| | | Sheehan | 4.5000 | Jackson | 4.6250 |
| | | Bucher | 4.5000 | Black | 4.6224* |
| Median | 7.6250 | Median | 5.2500 | Median | 4.7500 |
| Mean | 7.6938 | Mean | 5.1250 | Mean | 4.7107 |
| Adopted target | 7.5625 | Adopted target | 5.2500 | Adopted target | 4.6875 |

*Indicates an imputed desired interest rate

illustrative purposes, in table 7.1 we present preference profiles for three meetings. These examples show that there is considerable variation in members' desired funds rates over time. For instance, in March 1975, all members' desired rates were between 4.50 and 5.50 percent, but in May 1973, desired rates were all between 7.5625 and 7.875 percent. The intertemporal variation in interest rates, along with the tendency for members to state preferences close to prevailing rates, leads to high correlations between the time series for individuals' desired rates. Table 7.1 also shows that there are smaller, but notable, differences across individuals within meetings. For example, at the March 1975 meeting, the range in desired rates was a full percentage point. The existence of preference variation across members within a meeting is necessary if we are to draw inferences about the distribution of influence within the committee.

The patterns of influence suggested by these examples are varied. At the March 1975 meeting, the adopted funds rate was exactly equal to the median of the desired rates of the committee's members; the median was also close to the mean. In May 1973, however, the chosen target of 7.5625 percent was less than both the median and the mean. The target was instead set equal to the rate advocated by Burns, whose preferred rate was lower than that of all other voting members. Yet another scenario is suggested by the January 1977 data. At that meeting, the median desired rate was 4.75 percent, with Burns concurring. However, a sizable minority of four members advocated a lower rate. The chosen target of 4.6875 percent appears to reflect a willingness of the majority to accommodate the views of a strong minority, perhaps in an effort to achieve unanimity in the formal vote. Mirroring the earlier anecdotal discussion, these examples suggest that committee dynamics may be complex and varied, with the views of the chairman as well as the majority and minority factions of the committee all exerting influence.

### 7.3   FOMC Decision Making: Empirical Models

We next investigate econometric models of committee decision making, beginning with the median voter model. This model specifies that the FOMC decision will be equal to the median of the desired policy positions of the voting members, leading to the following regression specification:

$$\bar{R}_t = \phi_0 + \phi_1 MEDIAN_t + u_t. \tag{7.4}$$

In this equation, $MEDIAN_t$ is the median of the desired federal funds rates of members voting in meeting $t$, and $\bar{R}_t$ is the target federal funds rate adopted in the monetary policy directive.[9] The median voter hypothesis requires that $\phi_0$ equal zero and that $\phi_1$ equal one.

If decision making at the FOMC follows a more consensual pattern, one would expect the adopted policy directive to reflect the views of all committee members, not just those of the median voter. To incorporate the Fed's concern for consensus, we propose a model in which the mean of the desired positions of the voting committee members replaces the median:

$$\bar{R}_t = \phi_0 + \phi_1 MEAN_t + u_t. \tag{7.5}$$

The mean voter hypothesis also requires that $\phi_0$ equal zero and that $\phi_1$ equal one.

---

9. When the number of voters is even, $MEDIAN$ is measured as the midpoint of the two median positions.

The simple median and mean voter models can easily be altered to permit augmented power of the chairman, influence of nonvoting members, and differential impacts of governors and bank presidents. A simple way to permit added influence of the chairman is to add his desired funds rate, *BURNS*, to equations (7.4) and (7.5), our base specifications. In similar fashion, by adding an appropriate variable, we can test whether nonvoting members have any influence on policy and whether their influence is as great as members with formal voting rights. Further, by separately including mean desired funds rates for governors and bank presidents, we can test the hypothesis that members of these groups wield equal power within the committee.

## 7.4    FOMC Decision Making: Empirical Results

In this section, we describe empirical results for the models of FOMC decision making we have formulated. For this analysis, we use our sample of ninety-nine observations on FOMC meeting outcomes over the 1970–1978 period as well as selected subsamples where the chairman's preferences are measured more accurately.

### 7.4.1    Mean and Median Voter Models

The first two columns of table 7.2 provide OLS estimates of equations (7.4) and (7.5), the simple median and mean voter models, for the complete sample of ninety-nine meeting observations.[10] The results are consistent with the predictions of both models. In both the median and mean voter specifications, we fail to reject the key model implications: $\phi_0$ is not significantly different from zero, and $\phi_1$ is not significantly different from one.[11] For all specifications, adjusted-$R^2$ values are above 0.990.

---

10. The results in the second column have been corrected for first-order serial correlation, whose presence was indicated by the Durbin-Watson statistic in the original OLS results.
11. We have also corrected for another econometric complication. If the interest rate variables appearing in equations (7.4) and (7.5) are $I(1)$ and cointegrated (as statistical tests suggest), then OLS estimates will be consistent, but standard inference procedures will not always be appropriate. Specifically, standard procedures will not be appropriate for testing the null hypothesis that $\phi_1$ equals one, nor will they be appropriate for testing the null hypothesis that the coefficients sum to one in specifications in which we have two or more $I(1)$ regressors. The Monte Carlo methods that we have used for calculating standard errors for these cases are described in appendixes to Chappell, McGregor, and Vermilyea (2004). When there are two or more $I(1)$ regressors, standard OLS $t$-tests of the significance of individual coefficients are correct, however (see Hamilton 1994; Sims, Stock, and Watson 1990; and West 1988).

**Table 7.2**
Mean and median voter models (dependent variable: target federal funds rate)[a]

| Variable/ equation | Mean $N = 99$ | Median $N = 99$ | Mean with chair $N = 63$ | Median with chair $N = 63$ | Mean with chair $N = 43$ | Median with chair $N = 43$ |
|---|---|---|---|---|---|---|
| Constant | −0.077 (0.310) | −0.016 (0.769) | −0.045 (0.061) | −0.043 (0.085)* | −0.061 (0.029)* | −0.060 (0.055) |
| MEAN | 1.012** (0.000) | | 0.552** (0.000) | | 0.630** (0.000) | |
| MEDIAN | | 0.999** (0.000) | | 0.583** (0.000) | | 0.655** (0.000) |
| BURNS | | | 0.455** (0.000) | 0.422** (0.000) | 0.378** (0.000) | 0.352** (0.001) |
| $\sum_{i=1}^{k} \phi_i$ | 1.012 | 0.999 | 1.006 | 1.006 | 1.008 | 1.007 |
| $\sum_{i=1}^{k} \phi_i = 1$ (Test) | (0.1964) | (0.912) | (0.168) | (0.233) | (0.216) | (0.290) |
| $\rho^b$ | | 0.295 | | | | |
| D.W. | 1.713 | | | | | |
| $\bar{R}^2$ | 0.997 | 0.998 | 0.999 | 0.999 | 0.999 | 0.999 |

[a] $p$-values in parentheses; Monte Carlo methods are used to calculate $p$-values for individual coefficients in the first two columns and for the test that the sum of the coefficients equals one in all columns; variables and parameters are defined in section 7.3
[b] Serial correlation coefficient (when estimates are corrected for serial correlation)
*Significant at 0.05 level, two-tailed test
**Significant at 0.01 level, two-tailed test

### 7.4.2 The Power of the Chairman

In the remainder of the chapter, we investigate specifications that permit an enhanced role for the chairman. To avoid the measurement error problems identified earlier, we employ either the forty-three-observation subsample in which Burns spoke in the first half of the order (and presumably was not summarizing) or the sixty-three-observation subsample, which adds observations in which he spoke late but noted that his proposed range reflected his own preference.[12]

---

12. If we do employ the full sample of ninety-nine observations, including thirty-six observations with imputed values for the chairman's position, then the estimated coefficient of BURNS is smaller. This result is consistent with the existence of a bias toward zero in the presence of measurement error. The BURNS coefficient estimate remains significantly different from zero, however.

The last four columns of table 7.2 report results of regressions that add *BURNS* to the base specifications for the two subsamples.[13] While our estimation does not impose a restriction that coefficients on the chairman and the mean or median sum to one, in practice they come close to doing so; in all cases, we fail to reject the null hypothesis that the relevant coefficients sum to one.[14] Coefficients therefore approximate relative weights in the policy process. In each equation, the *BURNS* coefficient is significantly different from zero at the 0.05 level or better, and the implied voting weight of the chairman (including his contribution to the mean or the median) is approximately 40 to 50 percent.[15] On the basis of these results, we can strongly reject the hypothesis that the impact of the chairman is no different from that of rank-and-file committee members. The evidence also rejects the view that the chairman is dictatorial. The coefficients on committee mean and median positions are significantly different from zero in all equations, and the implied voting weights are usually larger than the chairman's.

### 7.4.3  The Influence of Nonvoting Members

Although Reserve Bank presidents attend all FOMC meetings, they do not always serve as voting members. This invites the question of whether they have any influence on policy choices while serving in a nonvoting capacity. In the first four columns of table 7.3, we provide results for models that permit nonvoting committee members to influence the policy outcome.[16] In the first two columns we add *ALTMEAN*, the mean position of the nonvoting alternates who spoke at a meeting,

---

13. Because of gaps in the data series, the Durbin-Watson statistic is not appropriate for testing for serial correlation in the subsamples. In addition to the reported OLS estimations, we have estimated all equations reported in this chapter under an assumption of first-order serial correlation and adjusting for gaps in the data. In all cases, we find that results are essentially unchanged when serial correlation is assumed.

14. Estimates change very little when the coefficients are constrained to sum to one. Constant terms are often significantly different from zero, but are nevertheless small in magnitude.

15. These results are similar to those of Maisel (1973), who subjectively estimated that the chairman had 45 percent of the voting weight. Maisel's estimates are not strictly comparable to ours, however. Maisel divided power between the chairman, bank presidents, governors, and board staff, while our models do not incorporate an independent role for the staff.

16. At two meetings, no alternates spoke, and *ALTMEAN* and *ALTMED* are therefore missing. This results in different sample sizes in some estimations in table 7.3.

**Table 7.3**
Model extensions (dependent variable: target federal funds rate)[a]

| Variable/equation | Mean N = 62 | Mean N = 42 | Median N = 62 | Median N = 42 | Presidents and governors N = 63 | Presidents and governors N = 43 | Hybrid N = 63 | Hybrid N = 43 |
|---|---|---|---|---|---|---|---|---|
| Constant | −0.045 | −0.053 | −0.043 | −0.062* | −0.045 | −0.069* | −0.048* | −0.063* |
| | (0.079) | (0.078) | (0.091) | (0.045) | (0.086) | (0.029) | (0.042) | (0.025) |
| BURNS | 0.435** | 0.357** | 0.370** | 0.255** | 0.507** | 0.440** | 0.380** | 0.334** |
| | (0.000) | (0.000) | (0.001) | (0.016) | (0.000) | (0.000) | (0.000) | (0.000) |
| MEAN | 0.550** | 0.680** | | | | | 0.347** | 0.492** |
| | (0.000) | (0.000) | | | | | (0.003) | (0.002) |
| MEDIAN | | | 0.538** | 0.546** | | | 0.279* | 0.182 |
| | | | (0.001) | (0.003) | | | (0.027) | (0.274) |
| ALTMEAN | 0.022 | −0.030 | | | | | | |
| | (0.763) | (0.717) | | | | | | |
| ALTMED | | | 0.097 | 0.207 | | | | |
| | | | (0.548) | (0.228) | | | | |
| MEANBP | | | | | 0.254** | 0.226* | | |
| | | | | | (0.003) | (0.028) | | |
| MEANGOV | | | | | 0.245** | 0.343** | | |
| | | | | | (0.009) | (0.002) | | |
| $\sum_{i=1}^{k} \phi_i$ | 1.007 | 1.007 | 1.006 | 1.008 | 1.006 | 1.010 | 1.007 | 1.008 |
| $\sum_{i=1}^{k} \phi_i = 1$ (Test) | (0.162) | (0.253) | (0.220) | (0.229) | (0.201) | (0.152) | (0.172) | (0.219) |
| $\bar{R}^2$ | 0.999 | 0.999 | 0.999 | 0.999 | 0.999 | 0.999 | 0.999 | 0.999 |

[a] $p$-values in parentheses; Monte Carlo methods are used to calculate $p$-values for the test that the sum of the coefficients equals one; variables and parameters are defined in section 7.3; * significant at 0.05 level, two-tailed test; ** significant at 0.01 level, two-tailed test

to a base model that already includes the mean position of voting members. In the next two columns we add *ALTMED*, the median position calculated over all members, to a model that already includes the median calculated over voting members only.

The results indicate that nonvoting alternates have no appreciable influence over policy outcomes. In all cases, measures of mean and median positions including alternates are dominated by those including voting members only; none of the variables measuring alternate preferences has a coefficient significantly different from zero. If policy-making in the FOMC is consensual, that consensus does not appear to encompass the views of nonvoting members.

### 7.4.4   The Relative Power of Governors and Bank Presidents

The fifth and sixth columns of table 7.3 report the results of specifications that generalize the mean voter model to permit differential power for governors and bank presidents. These specifications include *BURNS, MEANGOV* (the mean desired rate for governors, excluding the chairman), and *MEANBP* (the mean desired rate of voting bank presidents) as explanatory variables.[17] In both subsamples, coefficients of the mean positions of governors and bank presidents are significantly different from zero, so both groups have an impact on outcomes. Assessing whether governors and bank presidents have differential power is slightly complicated by the fact that the groups are typically not of the same size. If individual governors and bank presidents are equally powerful, coefficients should be proportional to group size, and the following restriction should hold:

$$\frac{\beta_G}{\beta_{BP}} = \frac{N_G}{N_{BP}}. \tag{7.6}$$

In this condition, $\beta_G$ and $\beta_{BP}$ are coefficients for the two added variables, and $N_G$ and $N_{BP}$ are the average numbers in the governor and bank president groups. Because of vacancies and absences, the number of governors (excluding the chairman) in each meeting varies. In the forty-three-observation sample, the average value for $N_G$ was 5.69; in the sixty-three-observation sample, it was 5.60. The number of voting bank presidents is always five, since absent bank presidents are replaced by substitutes. For the estimations reported in table 7.3, the

---

17. Similar results are obtained when median positions of the bank presidents and the governors are used instead of means.

equal power restrictions cannot be rejected, although the power of the test to discern such differences appears to be low.[18]

### 7.4.5 Tests of Nonnested Hypotheses: Median and Mean Voter Models

In the preceding analysis, we have used both the mean and the median to measure group preferences in our empirical models. Both measures perform well in terms of explaining outcomes, but it may be revealing to formally test median and mean voter models against one another. For this purpose, we compare the generalized mean voter model, which includes BURNS and MEAN, to a generalized median voter model, including BURNS and MEDIAN. The simplest way to do so is with a nonnested F-test. To perform this test, we include BURNS, MEAN, and MEDIAN together in a hybrid "supermodel." Estimates of such a model are provided in the last two columns of table 7.3. In the case at hand, with one regressor unique to each hypothesis, a nonnested F-test is equivalent to a t-test of the significance of the regressor originating with the "alternative" model (each hypothesis is in turn treated as the "null" or "alternative" hypothesis). In the sixty-three-observation sample, both MEAN and MEDIAN are significant, implying that each model is rejected in light of information provided by the alternative hypothesis. In the forty-three-observation sample, only the MEAN coefficient is significantly different from zero, implying that the median voter model is rejected in favor of the mean voter model.[19] While these results give a bit more support to MEAN than MEDIAN, it would be premature to conclude that majoritarian pressures are absent.

### 7.5  FOMC Decision Making: Extensions

In this section, we investigate two extensions of the models developed in the previous section. In the first extension, we examine a hypothesis

---

18. The $t$-statistic for the test of the equal power hypothesis is $-0.418$ for the forty-three-observation sample and $0.232$ for the sixty-three-observation sample. The tests are not extremely discriminating, since we also are unable to reject the hypothesis that governors are twice as powerful as bank presidents.

19. We obtain similar results using a Cox test for nonnested hypotheses. For the forty-three-observation sample, the mean voter hypothesis is not rejected, but the median voter hypothesis is rejected (at the 0.05 significance level). For the sixty-three-observation sample, mean and median voter models are each rejected in light of information provided by the alternative (again at the 0.05 significance level). For further details on these tests, see Davidson and MacKinnon (1981); MacKinnon (1983); and Cox (1961).

suggested by Blinder (1998), who argued that committee decisions are subject to greater "inertia" than those that would be made by a single policymaker. In the second extension, we consider the possibility that the chairman influences the preferences of committee members *before* any aggregation of preferences by collective choice procedures occurs.

### 7.5.1   The Blinder Hypothesis

Alan Blinder served as a member of the Board of Governors in 1994 and 1995. In a subsequent book (Blinder 1998), he maintained that committee decision making, specifically FOMC decision making, tends to be inertial:

> While serving on the FOMC, I was vividly reminded of a few things all of us probably know about committees: that they laboriously aggregate individual preferences; that they need to be led; that they tend to adopt compromise positions on difficult questions; and—perhaps because of all of the above—that they tend to be inertial. Had Newton served on more faculty committees at Cambridge, his first law of motion might have read: A decision-making body at rest or in motion tends to stay at rest or in motion in the same direction unless acted upon by an outside force. (Blinder 1998, 20)

In part, Blinder's argument relies on the observation that the "central tendency" of a committee will tend to be less variable than the position of an individual. At any given meeting, the desires of some to move in one direction are likely to be balanced by the opposing opinions of others, with a resulting tendency for the mean or the median to change less than individual preferences do. As Blinder (1998, 21) says, "monetary policy decisions tend to regress to the mean." If committee inertia is only a result of the inertia embodied in individual preferences or of the "regression to the mean" phenomenon, the models we have estimated already should adequately account for it—our measures of the mean and the median already account for individual preferences and the averaging process that tends to eliminate the impact of extreme individual variations. We interpret Blinder's contention, however, to suggest that inertial forces reflect more than just regression to the mean.

The Blinder hypothesis could be operationalized in a number of ways, but we undertake a simple test. In the previous section of this chapter, our final specification explained the FOMC's target funds rate, $\bar{R}_t$, with measures of the mean and median positions as well as the position of the chairman. We now augment this model with two additional explanatory variables—the previous meeting's target rate, $\bar{R}_{t-1}$,

Table 7.4
The Blinder hypothesis (dependent variable: target federal funds rate)[a]

| Variable | $N = 63$ | $N = 43$ |
|---|---|---|
| Constant | −0.023 | −0.045 |
| | (0.315) | (0.082) |
| $\bar{R}_{t-1}$ | 0.037* | 0.064** |
| | (0.034) | (0.006) |
| $\bar{R}_{t-1} - \bar{R}_{t-2}$ | 0.057** | 0.054** |
| | (0.001) | (0.007) |
| BURNS | 0.353** | 0.273** |
| | (0.000) | (0.001) |
| MEAN | 0.312** | 0.462** |
| | (0.004) | (0.002) |
| MEDIAN | 0.299* | 0.206 |
| | (0.012) | (0.189) |
| $\bar{R}^2$ | 0.999 | 0.999 |

[a] $p$-values in parentheses
*Significant at 0.05 level, two-tailed test
**Significant at 0.01 level, two-tailed test

and the change in the target rate over the two preceding meetings, $\bar{R}_{t-1} - \bar{R}_{t-2}$.[20] These terms should capture inertial tendencies beyond those already captured by the variables summarizing members' preferences. The lagged target rate should capture pressures that favor no change, while the lagged change in the target should capture momentum associated with change in a given direction.

Table 7.4 reports the relevant estimates. In both the forty-three- and sixty-three-observation samples, coefficients of both added variables differ significantly from zero (at the 0.05 significance level for two-tailed tests). The results continue to show that member preferences account for most of the variation in selected targets, but the impact of the inertial variables is clear. Thus, we find favorable evidence for a strong version of the Blinder hypothesis. After accounting for both inertia in individual preferences and the regression to the mean phenomenon, committee choices reflect added inertial forces.

### 7.5.2 The Chairman's Influence on Other Members' Preferences
It is difficult to assess how the chairman might influence members' preferences prior to a meeting. The chairman can informally com-

---

20. The resulting specification is identical to one that simply adds the levels of the lagged targets, $\bar{R}_{t-1}$ and $\bar{R}_{t-2}$, to the original model, but the chosen presentation permits a convenient interpretation of level and change effects.

municate with members between meetings, but the content of these communications is not observable to researchers.[21] In addition, staff recommendations may reflect input from the chairman, and these, in turn, may influence members' positions. Again, the extent to which a chairman has influenced staff recommendations is not observable to researchers.

Meeting records nevertheless offer some opportunity for measuring how Burns affects the preferences reported by other members of the committee. As we have mentioned, Burns sometimes spoke early in the policy go-around. If other members find his comments persuasive, there should be a tendency for those who follow Burns in the speaking order to report preferences closer to his. As noted by Maisel (1973, 127), "A strong statement by the Chairman early in the meeting is influential and transforms the debating atmosphere."

Because textual records provided by the *Memoranda* and the *Transcripts* indicate the order in which members spoke, it is possible to distinguish whether a member's stated preference was revealed before or after Burns offered his own recommendation. By comparing Burns-member policy differences for those who spoke before and after Burns within a meeting, it is possible to gain some insight into the extent of Burns's persuasive powers.

To investigate the "persuasive chairman" hypothesis, we initially estimate the following simple regression:

$$ABSDIFF_{it} = \beta_0 + \beta_1 BURNS1ST_{it} + e_{it}. \tag{7.7}$$

In this equation, $ABSDIFF_{it}$ is the absolute value of the difference between member $i$'s desired interest rate and Burns's desired interest rate in meeting $t$. On the right-hand side, $BURNS1ST_{it}$ is a dummy variable equal to one if Burns speaks before member $i$ in meeting $t$ and otherwise equal to zero. If members are influenced by Burns's within-meeting statements, then $ABSDIFF$ should be smaller when Burns speaks first, so $\beta_1$ should be negative.[22]

---

21. In a telephone interview, Burns era governor Jeffrey Bucher has informed us that Burns respected a "no-lobbying" rule that was effective at the FOMC at that time. Burns did not attempt to influence others' positions or mobilize support for his own position prior to meetings.

22. Of course, if Burns purposely reported preferences different from other committee members when he spoke last, this would produce a similar result. We believe that this is an implausible hypothesis. If Burns instead tended to summarize the positions of others when speaking late, this would produce a bias against finding a Burns influence.

**Table 7.5**
Persuasiveness of the chairman (dependent variable: absolute difference in desired funds rates between Burns and other members)

| Variable | Parameter estimate | $p$-value |
|---|---|---|
| Constant | 0.154** | 0.000 |
| BURNS1ST | −0.042** | 0.001 |
| $R^2$ | 0.0130 | |
| Number of times Burns speaks before a member | 553 | |
| Number of times Burns speaks after a member | 325 | |

**Significant at 0.01 level, two-tailed test

To estimate the equation, we use a sample of 878 pairs of Burns-member observations in which both individuals stated a desired funds rate.[23] The regression results in table 7.5 show that $\beta_1$ is negative and significantly different from zero at the 0.01 level for a two-tailed test. The coefficient estimate implies that the Burns-member differential is lower by about four basis points when Burns states a preference first, consistent with the hypothesis that the chairman can influence the stated preferences of members.[24] The $R^2$ value for the regression is quite low, indicating that the order of speaking explains only a small fraction of the variation in Burns-member differences. The latter result is not surprising, since many other factors might account for these differences.

Interestingly, by estimating equation (7.7) for individuals separately, we found that three members had *larger* differences when following the chairman, suggesting an effort to move away from Burns. These three members were St. Louis Fed president Darryl Francis and governors Jeffrey Bucher and Andrew Brimmer (with each of these differences being statistically significant at the 0.10 level). In an interview, Bucher confirmed his perception that both Francis and Brimmer had contentious personal relationships with Burns. Bucher described his own relationship with Burns as one characterized by occasional differences but not persisting acrimony.

---

23. In 553 cases, Burns was the first speaker in the pair, while in 325 cases he spoke later. Also, recall that we code a desired rate for Burns only when he speaks in the first half of the order or explicitly notes that his proposed target is his own preference.
24. This test is equivalent to a simple *t*-test of a difference in means in samples in which Burns spoke before and after a member.

## 7.6  Conclusions

Employing original data sets and estimation methods, we have measured desired federal funds rate targets for each FOMC member over a sequence of meetings when Burns chaired the committee. We then investigated how collective choices made by the FOMC were related to the stated preferences of its members.

The formal operating procedures of the FOMC require that adopted policy directives be approved by a majority vote of its members, so the median voter model provided a starting point for our analysis. Because observers of monetary policymaking emphasize the importance of the role played by the chairman and the desire for achieving consensus, our analysis also investigated these aspects of the policy process.

Our empirical results substantiate the claim that Burns carried greater policymaking weight than rank-and-file committee members. The estimated voting weight for the chairman (including his contribution to the mean and median positions) is approximately 40 to 50 percent. Additional results show that Burns directly influenced the stated preferences of other committee members. Although we confirm the view that the chairman wields enhanced power, we are also able to refute the view that Burns was dictatorial, since median or mean voter positions are also significant in explaining policy outcomes. Neither the mean nor median voter position is a clearly preferable indicator of committee sentiment, suggesting that both majoritarian and consensual pressures may be important. We also find that nonvoting bank presidents had no influence over outcomes, and detect no significant differences in the power of governors and voting bank presidents. Finally, we find support for the Blinder hypothesis, which we interpret to imply that committee decisions exhibit more inertia than would be expected based on an aggregation of individual preferences alone.

*CHAIRMAN GREENSPAN:* In the immediate period ahead, it strikes me that the general outlook is extraordinarily benevolent and one that I view at the moment as pointing to no change in policy. That is, "B" and symmetrical seems to me the most sensible approach until the next meeting.

*MR. HOENIG:* Mr. Chairman, I support your policy proposal.

*MR. LINDSEY:* I support your policy proposal.

*VICE CHAIRMAN MCDONOUGH:* As do I, Mr. Chairman.

*MR. KELLEY:* As do I, Mr. Chairman.

*MS. MINEHAN:* As do I, Mr. Chairman.

*MR. BOEHNE:* I support your proposal.

*MR. FORRESTAL:* Ditto, Mr. Chairman.

*MR. PARRY:* The same.

*MR. MELZER:* I support it, Alan.

*MR. STERN:* I support it as well.

*MR. BROADDUS:* Me, too.

*MR. JORDAN:* I agree.

*MS. PHILLIPS:* I also.

*MS. YELLEN:* I support your proposal, too.

*MR. MOSKOW:* I support it, Mr. Chairman.

*MR. BLINDER:* So do I.

*CHAIRMAN GREENSPAN:* We'll have lunch earlier than usual!

—*Transcripts*, August 22, 1995, 36–37[1]

In many ways, FOMC operations were similar under Burns and Greenspan. In both eras, the committee primarily targeted the federal funds rate, and policy was carried out in a discretionary fashion with an objective of leaning against the wind. Both chairmen played an important role in achieving consensus and crafting policy decisions in the presence of a diversity of opinion across members. Yet the policy-making environment was not unchanged. There were differences in

---

1. This excerpt omits Greenspan's comments recognizing members in turn.

the economic conditions that prevailed, in the decision-making procedures of the committee, and in the nature of monetary policymaking operations. These differences affect the attributes of the data we have been able to collect for these years as well as the questions we can investigate.

One of the striking characteristics of data describing individual preferences for the Greenspan years is the degree of solidarity expressed in support of the chairman. The excerpt that heads this chapter summarizes an unusually tranquil committee meeting, but it does provide a reminder of the considerable support that Greenspan seemed to be able to count on at each meeting. Greenspan regularly spoke first in the FOMC meeting policy go-around, and at almost every meeting, a majority of voters aligned themselves with the position he advocated. Because of the near uniformity of Greenspan and median voter preferences, an econometric decomposition of power shares like that described in chapter 7 for the Burns era is not possible for the Greenspan years.

This chapter examines committee decision making during the Greenspan era, but adopts an approach that is less direct than the one employed for the Burns years. In the first section, we investigate how individual members of the committee responded to Greenspan's proposals. Although Greenspan almost always had support from a majority, it was not unusual to observe diversity of opinion. This raises the issue of whether Greenspan had a stable coalition of dependable supporters or whether the makeup of supporting coalitions tended to vary from meeting to meeting. In the second section, we evaluate evidence of influence in the reverse direction; specifically, we collect data to summarize the direction and strength of pressure the committee exerted on Greenspan, and we investigate his responses. The third section discusses the roles of the chairman and other members of the committee. Relying on anecdotal evidence from the *Transcripts*, we identify institutional procedures and strategic choices that accentuated or diminished the influence of the chairman, and we describe how members viewed their own roles in the policy process. Concluding comments follow in the fourth section.

## 8.1   Greenspan's Influence on the Committee

In our sample of seventy-five meetings from 1987 to 1996, the position of the median voting member of the committee coincided with the position of the chairman seventy-two times. At his first meeting in August 1987, Greenspan passively listened as others spoke first. He went along with the majority, but late in the meeting he casually mentioned that he would have preferred slightly different specifications. A few months later, in February 1988, Greenspan again spoke late, failed to state a position with clarity, and was coded with an assent. His imputed desired rate at that meeting differed slightly from the median, but there was no direct evidence suggesting that he was unhappy with the outcome. In February 1994, a majority of six committee members indicated a preference for a fifty-basis-point increase in the funds rate. Greenspan was in a minority of four who preferred a tightening of only twenty-five points. In this case, Greenspan appealed for support and his proposal passed without a dissenting vote.[2]

Given the near uniformity of preferences for Greenspan and the median, we cannot use statistical methods to disentangle the relative power of the chairman and the committee. As the results in chapter 6 illustrated, however, support for Greenspan was not always unanimous, and individual reaction functions detected notable differences across members. Of the 1,292 observations of member preferences at meetings, in 984 cases (76.2 percent) members reported a funds rate identical to that of Greenspan, leaving 308 cases (23.8 percent) where members differed with Greenspan (or failed to indicate clear agreement with him). In this section, we analyze patterns of support for Greenspan within the committee, again using the data set derived from the *Transcripts* that we first described in chapter 5.

Greenspan usually spoke first and offered a policy proposal in the policy go-around held at each meeting; other members then either voiced agreement or offered an alternative recommendation. To gauge the impact of Greenspan's proposal on the preferences reported by others, we extend the individual reaction function model employed in chapter 6. For each individual, we now estimate a reaction function that has been augmented with Greenspan's proposed target rate, denoted *GREENSPAN*, as an explanatory variable. The size and significance of the Greenspan coefficient should give some indication of his influence over each member.

As we use this approach to investigate Greenspan's influence, two caveats should be noted. First, Greenspan's proposed funds rate

---

2. Because Cleveland Fed president Lee Hoskins had indicated a willingness to support Greenspan early in the meeting, even though his preference differed, Greenspan's informal count of the committee would probably have shown a tie before he made his appeal.

reflects his reactions to incoming data, and those data also influence other committee members. While some incoming information is captured by the reaction function's explanatory variables, other variables may have been omitted from the model. Because of this, significance of the Greenspan proposal would not unambiguously indicate that Greenspan influences a member. It might instead indicate that Greenspan and a member respond to the same omitted variables. Second, if Greenspan anticipates members' preferences, his proposals might reflect an assessment of what would be acceptable to the committee. High correlations between Greenspan's preferences and those of individuals might, in part, be a consequence of reverse causality. Despite the noted caveats, variations in individuals' *GREENSPAN* coefficients will give some indication of a member's tendency to move in concert with the chairman, whether it derives from deference or likemindedness.

Table 8.1 provides estimates of the *GREENSPAN* policy coefficients in individuals' augmented reaction functions (the remaining reaction function parameter estimates are not reported). The committee members listed in the table are the same as those for whom we reported reaction functions in table 6.2, and the sample for each individual includes all meetings in which the member was present and Greenspan both spoke first and stated a target rate. Members are arrayed from highest to lowest coefficients, so those who appear to be most responsive to Greenspan are listed at the top of the table. A coefficient of 1.0 implies that a member varies point for point with variations in Greenspan's target rate. Two committee members, William McDonough and David Mullins, agreed with Greenspan whenever he stated a rate. Because the Greenspan variable alone explains all of the variation in their desired rates, we cannot estimate regressions for them, but we have recorded the implied Greenspan coefficients of 1.0 in the table.

For purposes of comparison, we also report an alternative measure of agreement. The Greenspan "agreement frequency" reports the ratio of the number of instances in which a member reports a desired target identical to that of Greenspan to the number of meetings that the member attended. In principle, the agreement frequency and the reaction function measure different dimensions of similarity with the chairman. For example, if a member always proposed an interest rate target exactly twenty-five basis points below the rate proposed by Greenspan, that individual should have an agreement frequency of zero, but a reaction function coefficient of 1.0 (the member never

**Table 8.1**
Responsiveness to Greenspan

| Member | Greenspan coefficient | Agreement frequency | N |
|---|---|---|---|
| Forrestal | 1.025** | 0.800 | 63 |
| Corrigan | 1.007** | 0.891 | 44 |
| McDonough | 1.000 NA | 0.964 | 27 |
| Mullins | 1.000 NA | 0.966 | 29 |
| Jordan | 0.997** | 0.632 | 38 |
| McTeer | 0.988** | 0.872 | 47 |
| Kelley | 0.968** | 0.919 | 72 |
| Lindsey | 0.968** | 0.780 | 41 |
| Phillips | 0.957** | 0.805 | 41 |
| Johnson | 0.930** | 0.773 | 20 |
| Moskow | 0.881** | 0.895 | 19 |
| Parry | 0.874** | 0.667 | 73 |
| Boykin | 0.864** | 0.704 | 25 |
| Stern | 0.854** | 0.827 | 73 |
| LaWare | 0.847** | 0.925 | 53 |
| Boehne | 0.813** | 0.849 | 71 |
| Keehn | 0.757** | 0.818 | 53 |
| Hoenig | 0.756** | 0.651 | 43 |
| Syron | 0.689* | 0.805 | 41 |
| Blinder | 0.683 | 0.692 | 13 |
| Heller | 0.665 | 0.429 | 12 |
| Minehan | 0.636* | 0.609 | 23 |
| Yellen | 0.621 | 0.750 | 20 |
| Broaddus | 0.614** | 0.545 | 33 |
| Melzer | 0.580** | 0.640 | 73 |
| Angell | 0.523** | 0.784 | 49 |
| Black | 0.479** | 0.718 | 37 |
| Guffey | 0.407 | 0.719 | 30 |
| Seger | 0.125** | 0.357 | 26 |
| Hoskins | 0.014 | 0.367 | 29 |

*Significant at the 0.05 level, two-tailed test
**Significant at the 0.01 level, two-tailed test
NA: Regression could not be estimated because member and Greenspan targets were identical over the available sample

agrees with Greenspan, but always responds to him with point-for-point changes). Although McDonough and Mullins always agreed with Greenspan when he clearly stated a rate, there was one meeting where Greenspan's position was ambiguous. Because of this, their agreement ratios are less than one.

Despite the conceptual difference, table 8.1 shows that the agreement frequency and the Greenspan regression coefficient are related empirically. Those with large regression coefficients typically have high agreement frequencies.[3] The Greenspan regression coefficients range from near zero to just over 1.0, and agreement frequencies range from 0.35 to 0.97. Among the most dependable supporters of the chairman are the vice chairmen, McDonough and Gerald Corrigan, and members Mullins, Edward Kelley, Michael Moskow, and John LaWare. These individuals have both regression coefficients and agreement frequencies exceeding 0.84. Despite the caveats we noted earlier, agreement of this magnitude almost surely reflects a conscious willingness to follow the chairman. There are no plausible omitted variables that would explain the precise congruence of the Greenspan and McDonough (or Mullins) positions over twenty-seven (or twenty-nine) consecutive meetings. Reverse causality is also implausible, unless one believes that Greenspan was receiving his instructions from McDonough or Mullins (instead of anticipating the consensus of the complete committee).

The table also distinguishes some notable mavericks. Among the more independent members are Reserve Bank presidents Alfred Broaddus, Thomas Melzer, Robert Black, and Lee Hoskins along with governors Martha Seger and Wayne Angell. Seger and Hoskins have agreement frequencies below 0.40 and Greenspan regression coefficients below 0.15. These findings reinforce those presented in chapter 6, which indicated that each of these members had preferences notably different from their colleagues.

Overall, the results suggest that agreement was not so automatic that Greenspan could be assured of majority support whenever he offered a proposal. At times, though, especially when dependable supporters Kelley, LaWare, and Mullins served together (July 1990

---

3. San Francisco Fed president Robert Parry is an exception. His regression coefficient of 0.874 indicates that he responds almost point for point to Greenspan positions; however, he frequently favored a tighter posture and agreed with Greenspan only 66.7 percent of the time.

through December 1993), he would have approached a high level of certainty. With those three members, his own vote, and that of one of his vice chairmen, Corrigan or McDonough, he would need just one more supporter to secure at least a tie.

## 8.2   The Committee's Influence on Greenspan

There is a strong presumption that Greenspan is a powerful leader, but he is not likely to be a dictator. The *Transcripts* sometimes show that members fall in line to support him, but on other occasions diverse views are openly discussed, and the requirement that he get a majority of the votes is a constraint that must be considered. Evidence reported in the preceding section supports the proposition that members follow the lead of the chairman; in this section, we look for evidence of influence in the opposite direction.

Even when Greenspan has a majority supporting his current proposal, the distribution of preferences in the committee can be skewed, and the resulting pressures for future change unbalanced. For example, in December 1993, Greenspan and seven colleagues favored keeping the funds rate target at 3.00 percent. The four other voting members of the committee all favored a move to tightness, but Greenspan and the majority prevailed. At the next meeting, though, in February 1994, Greenspan proposed a tightening. That move might have been made independently, but it could also have been a response by the chairman to committee pressures for tightness.

In an attempt to characterize the direction and strength of committee sentiment that might have guided Greenspan, we have constructed several variables measuring differences between Greenspan and the committee. For each member at each meeting, we first code a variable called *LEAD* (for "leading" Greenspan). We code a member as "leading Greenspan to tightness" (+1) if we can infer that the member prefers, either currently or for the near future, a tighter policy stance than Greenspan. Thus, any member who currently advocates a funds rate higher than the one proposed by Greenspan would be coded as (+1). This coding would apply for directly stated rates as well as leaning positions that indicate greater tightness than Greenspan. In addition, we code members as leading Greenspan to tightness if they agree with Greenspan on the current target but advocate a bias toward tightness when he does not. We would code members as "leading Greenspan to ease" ($-1$) in analogous situations where the direction of preference is reversed. Finally, members who either agree with Greenspan completely or whose differences are unclear receive a *LEAD* coding of zero.

Once we measure *LEAD* for each individual, we can construct a summary measure of the committee's leading tendency. To do so, we first determine who will be voting at the upcoming committee meeting, meeting $t$. For those members who also attended meeting $t - 1$, we calculate their value for *LEAD* based on meeting $t - 1$ preferences, as described above. We then sum *LEAD* values across those members, and express the sum as a ratio of the number of members comprising the sum. This ratio, *LEADR*, provides a measure reflecting the balance of pressure on Greenspan to alter policy. We have also used a variant of this variable that is defined by summing *LEAD* values over the three previous FOMC meetings. The latter variable is denoted *LEADR3*.

Possible influence of committee preferences on Greenspan's proposal is investigated in two ways. We first test whether *LEADR* (or *LEADR3*) has an influence on the rate proposed by Greenspan for the current meeting. We then test whether these variables affect discretionary moves made by Greenspan during the subsequent intermeeting period. For the first test, we specify a reaction function for Greenspan, using the funds rate proposal he advocated at each meeting as the dependent variable and including the same explanatory variables we have used before. We augment that equation with *LEADR* or *LEADR3* to measure the pressure from the committee on Greenspan. The results of the estimation, which are presented in table 8.2, show no evidence that members' differences with Greenspan at previous meetings have any impact on his current proposals. In each estimation, the relevant coefficient is neither correctly signed nor does it differ significantly from zero. Results are unchanged when *LEADR* and *LEADR3* are redefined to include all FOMC members instead of only voting members (results of the latter exercise are not reported).

For the second test, we examine the behavior of the funds rate over the postmeeting period rather than the target adopted at the meeting. Our indicator of the postmeeting interest rate is the recorded status quo funds rate for the subsequent meeting—that is, the rate prevailing after all intermeeting policy shifts. Greenspan often exercised discretion in making intermeeting policy shifts, but these shifts may have been responsive to the tone and content of the remarks made by others. We specify that the postmeeting interest rate is a function of the adopted target rate, a discrete variable indicating the adopted bias ($+1$

**Table 8.2**
Leading Greenspan

| | Greenspan $R$ | Greenspan $R$ | Postmeeting $R$ | Postmeeting $R$ |
|---|---|---|---|---|
| *Constant* | 0.681 | 0.626 | −0.042 | −0.050 |
| | (0.060) | (0.099) | (0.573) | (0.479) |
| $R_{SQ}$ | 0.943** | 0.950** | | |
| | (0.000) | (0.000) | | |
| $\dot{M}2$ | −0.012 | −0.013 | | |
| | (0.113) | (0.109) | | |
| $\hat{U}$ | −0.106* | −0.097 | | |
| | (0.033) | (0.059) | | |
| $\hat{P}$ | 0.074 | 0.060 | | |
| | (0.141) | (0.251) | | |
| $\hat{Y}$ | 0.056** | 0.057** | | |
| | (0.002) | (0.003) | | |
| *Adopted R* | | | 1.003** | 1.005** |
| | | | (0.000) | (0.000) |
| *BIAS* | | | 0.180** | 0.167** |
| | | | (0.000) | (0.000) |
| *LEADR* | −0.110 | | −0.018 | |
| | (0.185) | | (0.857) | |
| *LEADR3* | | −0.015 | | −0.011 |
| | | (0.753) | | (0.822) |
| $\bar{R}^2$ | 0.994 | 0.994 | 0.990 | 0.992 |

*Note:* $p$-values in parentheses
*Significant at the 0.05 level, two-tailed test
**Significant at the 0.01 level, two-tailed test

for asymmetric toward tightness, −1 for asymmetric toward ease, and 0 for symmetric), and the *LEADR* ratio based on the current meeting's preferences. Results in table 8.2 again show no impact of committee preferences on subsequent Greenspan actions; the relevant coefficients fail to differ significantly from zero.

While members' leading preferences have no notable effects on future policies, the results do confirm that the bias associated with the directive is a meaningful predictor. The dummy indicating the state of the bias is significant (at the 0.01 level) in each of the equations explaining intermeeting rate moves. This confirms earlier findings by Lapp and Pearce (2000).

As we have noted, our inability to detect a relationship between the leading preferences of committee members and subsequent Greenspan actions does not imply that members have no influence on Greenspan. If the committee exerts influence, however, it seems likely that the influence comes via premeeting negotiation or through Greenspan's ability to divine committee sentiments in the absence of overt signals.

## 8.3   Sources of Greenspan's Influence

For reasons we have described, we cannot econometrically estimate Greenspan's share of the power in FOMC decision making. Yet circumstantial evidence supports the view that he has considerable influence. At almost every meeting in our sample, Greenspan spoke first, offered a proposal, and defended it. Other committee members followed him and offered support or suggested differences, but Greenspan's original proposal regularly won. In the remainder of this chapter, we investigate anecdotal data from the *Transcripts* to explore the ways in which Greenspan was able to exert influence over the FOMC. We frequently adopt a comparative perspective, focusing attention on differences between the Burns and Greenspan eras in terms of committee decision-making procedures, operational differences in monetary policymaking, the behavior of the chairman, and the committee's external environment.

### 8.3.1   Taking Charge

When Burns chaired the FOMC, he sometimes spoke early in meetings, and he sometimes waited and spoke after everyone else. His behavior on this matter changed as time passed. Early in his tenure, he tended to speak at the conclusion of a meeting and craft a consensus; late in his tenure, he more frequently spoke first and defined the terms of discussion. As chapter 7 showed, when Burns offered a clear indication of his preference, he did have an important weight in the aggregation of preferences, and he also appeared to sway some other members to alter their own recommendations. It should not be surprising that a new chairman would exercise caution early in his term. The formal leadership authority granted the chairman is rather limited and derives more from tradition than statute. A newcomer to the position might gain power in the long term by showing deference to more senior members on arrival.

At his first meeting, in August 1987, Greenspan also deferred to the committee, permitting others to speak before he did. When he did speak, he offered a slightly different preference than that espoused by the majority (a borrowing target of $600 million rather than $525 million), but willingly proposed the majority position for a vote. Prior to

voting, he asked for advice about how to handle preference aggregation, posing this question: "I don't know what the convention is here—
whether you average these things [members' preferred borrowing tar-
gets], which you can, or whether you take the majority. What has been
the convention?" (*Transcripts*, August 18, 1987, 36). Vice Chairman
Corrigan advised the chairman against averaging, implying that the
majority ruled. He then gave Greenspan a brief lesson on the chairman's role:

I think it is hard to average it. One other thing that is done in terms of trying to
sense where the critical mass is, if I could put it that way, or where the Committee might stand, is that the Chairman has been known from time to time to
ask people what their preferences are as opposed to what they could live with.
In this particular case, you may have some shadings of opinion around those
borrowing numbers, for example, based on the question of symmetry or tilt
that would go with them—in other words, the "woulds" and the "mights." I,
myself, certainly would not dissent, at this meeting, over the difference between $600 million and $500 million in the context in which there was some tilt
along the lines that Governor Johnson has suggested. So, you do have some
play; but I don't think that most members of the Committee would be com-
fortable with averaging the borrowings. I think that can get to be quite awkward when there are larger differences, as there may be, than the difference
between $500 million and $600 million. (*Transcripts*, August 18, 1987, 36)

Corrigan's assessment that the median rather than the mean position
was the relevant indicator of committee sentiment appears to have
been an accurate one for the Greenspan years. Greenspan and median
positions were generally congruent and were also identical to the
adopted target. In contrast, the mean position was often different, but
when it was, it never prevailed as the committee choice.

At his second meeting, Greenspan was again cautious, but he did
speak first and offer a proposal, while again showing deference to
the committee. Referring to the discussion of economic conditions that
preceded the policy go-around, he firmly placed himself with the committee: "I find myself probably about in the middle of much of what I
have been listening to" (*Transcripts*, September 22, 1987, 33). He then
diplomatically noted that this left him inclined to make no change in
policy:[4] "Consequently, as far as policy is concerned, where we are at

---

4. Note also that Greenspan now refers to $600 million as the status quo borrowing tar-
get. At the preceding meeting, Greenspan had preferred $600 million, but the committee
choice had been $525 million. How the Greenspan position came to be the status quo by
the second meeting is not addressed in the transcripts, but the result suggests that
Greenspan had quickly learned how to exert influence over committee choices.

the moment strikes me as quite appropriate to the outlook. I don't feel terribly strongly about it, but I would be inclined to start off merely by assuming that we stay at 'B,' and that we stay with the $600 million on the borrowing requirement.... I don't know where that will fit me in the rest of this group, but I'd love to hear" (*Transcripts*, September 22, 1987, 34).

By Greenspan's third meeting, in November 1987, external events had played a role in changing how he managed the committee. Two weeks earlier, the stock market had crashed and the Dow Jones Industrial Average had plunged 508 points (22.6 percent) in a single day. During the intermeeting period, the FOMC had responded by permitting extensive discount window borrowing, de-emphasizing the borrowing target in favor of a funds rate target, and permitting that target rate to fall by about fifty basis points. It seems clear that these events played a role in elevating Greenspan's status in the committee. The Fed was widely praised for its actions in the wake of the crash, and Greenspan received much of the credit for the Fed's success in this incident. At the first regular FOMC meeting after the crash, Greenspan spoke first and at some length, and appeared to be more assertive. With one exception, he always spoke first at subsequent meetings and offered a clear proposal that the committee would ultimately adopt.

### 8.3.2   Intellectual Leadership and the Fruits of Success

Burns was known as an intellectual and an expert on business cycles, and by all accounts he was endowed with a strong personality. Greenspan, however, may have used both his intellectual leadership and management skills to greater advantage than Burns did. Once Greenspan exerted his leadership, he tended to dominate committee discussions in two ways. First, he exhibited an extraordinary knowledge of the details of macroeconomic data; second, he was not inclined to be brief. These remarks from July 1996, discussing the puzzling absence of inflationary pressures in a period of tight labor market conditions, are illustrative:

We obviously are viewing an economy that at the moment does not resemble most of our textbook models. The unemployment rate is low and has remained low for quite a while. Anecdotal evidence continues to indicate tight labor markets, but with little evidence of significant wage acceleration. We also have a strong economic expansion under way, with industrial commodity prices falling even excluding the plunge in copper prices. Broader measures of price inflation are, if anything, still declining. There are, however, two disturbing numbers that suggest the old model may be operative. The first, of course, is the very disturbing ECI wage and salary figure for the first quarter. The second is the recent fairly significant rise in delayed deliveries in the June NAPM report. Most other data, however, are not supportive of a rising inflation trend. To be sure, average hourly earnings have been rising at a fairly pronounced pace in the last two or three years. But as we discussed yesterday, that series shows very little change when we look at the conversion by the BLS to a chain-weighted basis. Indeed, in the 12 months ended in May, it was up 2.9 percent versus 3.4 percent for the published average hourly earnings. The CPI is becoming increasingly obsolete, as I explained yesterday. The more analytically accurate core PCE chain-weighted price index is increasing now at a rate of about 2 percent, as is the core gross domestic purchases chain-weighted price index, with the increase in both measures declining since 1995. The hypothesis that the inflation rate has stabilized is very difficult to sustain with this data system. (*Transcripts*, July 2–3, 1996, 82–83)

The previous excerpt is typical in revealing Greenspan's immersion in the nuances of macroeconomic data sources. The fact that it accounts for less than a fifth of the text of his opening statement gives an indication of his ability to dominate through willpower as well as intellectual ascendancy. In fact, over the 1987–1996 period, Greenspan's remarks came to take up a larger and larger portion of the time spent on the monetary policy go-around. Figure 8.1 illustrates this by plotting the percentage of the text in the policy go-around that was attributed

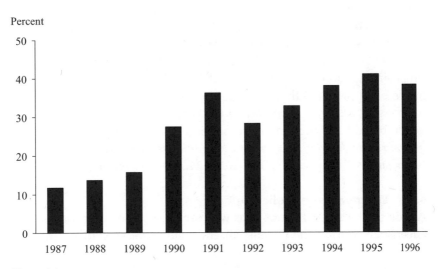

**Figure 8.1**
Average length of Greenspan's opening comments in the policy go-around
Source: *FOMC Transcripts*

to Greenspan's opening statement.[5] In 1987, his opening statement accounted for about 12 percent of the discussion, but from 1990 on, he accounted for at least 25 percent of the total. From 1994 to 1996, Greenspan's opening statement averaged nearly 40 percent of the policy go-around. In addition to his opening statement, Greenspan typically made additional comments during policy deliberations, often responding directly when a committee member stated an opposing view. By doing so, he may have altered the flow of debate in a manner that enhanced his influence over the policy outcome.

Although Greenspan did not have an academic reputation to rival that of Burns or some of his colleagues on the committee, he is frequently credited with having an uncanny ability to interpret economic conditions correctly (see, for example, Woodward 2000). During the 1990s, he staked out controversial positions on several occasions. In 1994, he advocated a "preemptive" tightening of policy to avoid rekindling inflation. In 1995 and 1996, he resisted tightening moves, arguing that the absence of inflationary pressure in a period of tight labor markets reflected an absence of wage pressure due to the insecurity of workers (who had been subjected to downsizing as corporations attempted to slash costs) and a trend toward higher productivity growth driven by gains in information technology. In both of these cases, as well as in the aftermath of the stock market crash, he seems to have made the correct calls. For whatever reason, his policies were successful, and his successes gained him support within the committee, as illustrated by Governor Lawrence Lindsey's comments in September 1996: "Having said that, Mr. Chairman, I believe that what you are proposing is more reflective of what I would call an entrepreneurial, hands-on approach. I think it is built frankly out of self-confidence and nimbleness, and you have earned the capacity to have self-confidence and to be a little more nimble in the conduct of policy. *I will be supporting your recommendation based on what I think is a very well-earned reputation of success*" (*Transcripts*, September 24, 1996, 38, emphasis added).

### 8.3.3 Discreteness of Policy Options

Although the federal funds rate was targeted under both Burns and Greenspan, during the Greenspan era policy choices evolved into in-

---

5. The figures are based on computational word counts for all meetings except those from March 1993 through February 1994. For these latter meetings, the fraction is approximated by page counts, with fractional pages based on visual assessments. Meetings at which Greenspan did not speak first (August 1987 and February 1988) are excluded from these calculations.

creasingly "discrete" options. During the 1970s, policy options were generally framed as ranges, and the funds rate fluctuated within the adopted range over the postmeeting period. As the FOMC moved to more explicit funds rate targeting under Greenspan, the targets themselves were usually single valued. Movements in the target were almost always in twenty-five- or fifty-basis-point increments relative to the status quo. Within meetings, members reported preferences similarly, usually favoring one of these well-defined alternatives. We have already argued that the presence of well-defined discrete alternatives may account for differences in some characteristics of the data sets that we have constructed for the Burns and Greenspan eras. In particular, we observe individuals' directly stated interest rate targets more frequently in the Greenspan years than the Burns years because members found it straightforward to choose from a set of well-defined alternatives. It is also possible that the increasing discreteness of policy options affected the balance of power between the chairman and the committee.

One consequence of having a small set of discrete policy options is that disagreements become more obvious. Once Greenspan stated a preferred rate, each succeeding speaker either agreed with that rate or advocated an alternative. If a member failed to completely agree, then it was clear that the individual had disagreed. In contrast, during the Burns years, if the chairman advocated a range of funds rates, and if another member advocated a range that was identical except that one endpoint of the range was slightly perturbed, there was little sense of disagreement. Burns would have the flexibility to move within ranges that were overlapping anyway, so ranges that were similar could be seen as being supportive of the chairman. Given this perception, Burns era members probably felt less pressure to align themselves precisely with the chairman.

Another consequence of the move toward single-valued targets is that a more prominent distinction arose between policy shifts adopted within a meeting and those adopted at the discretion of the chairman between meetings. During the Burns years, it was normal for rates to fluctuate somewhat within the adopted range as the chairman and the account manager implemented policy between meetings. Intermeeting movements in funds rates were the norm rather than the exception, and the notion that an intermeeting "policy move" was distinct from the policy adopted at the meeting was not always recognized. But as funds rate options became more discrete and more tightly targeted during the Greenspan years, any movement was interpreted as a shift of policy. The discretion delegated to the chairman for making inter-meeting policy moves was a matter of frequent FOMC discussion during the Greenspan years.

It is difficult to determine the overall impact of the increasing discreteness of policy options on the power of the chairman. It probably did increase the tendency of members to align themselves with Greenspan's choice, and this may have added to his influence. The implicit restrictions applied to intermeeting policy moves, however, may have reduced the chairman's power. It was less important for Burns to always "win" on the specification of policy in the directive because that specification would not constrain him as tightly over the upcoming intermeeting period.

### 8.3.4   The Bias and Consensus

From 1983 to 1999, a period that encompasses the Greenspan years included in our sample, the FOMC included a statement of "bias" with each of its adopted policy directives. The bias was intended to give an indication of likely future policy moves, although the precise interpretation was sometimes unclear (see the discussion in chapter 5). Our analysis in section 8.2 showed that the bias had real predictive content for intermeeting shifts in the federal funds rate; that is, it is an important aspect of the decision made at an FOMC meeting. Nevertheless, Thornton and Wheelock (2000) have argued that the bias has also served as a device for orchestrating consensus. By properly framing the bias to associate with a particular funds rate target, the chairman might be able to assemble a more inclusive coalition than would have been possible otherwise. For example, in the last half of 1996, the FOMC held the funds rate steady at 5.25 percent. Several voting members advocated moves toward tightness during this period, and the committee maintained a bias toward tightening. Yet the tightening never occurred—Greenspan was able to maintain a steady funds rate in the presence of at least fringe opposition, with only two dissents recorded in the final five meetings of the year. The setting of the bias to tightness may have discouraged those who would otherwise have dissented.

### 8.3.5   The Committee and the Chairman: Inside Views

Committee discussions sometimes directly address the issue of the roles of the chairman and the committee. In July 1992, Lindsey left little doubt that Greenspan's preferences received added weight simply because he was the chairman: "Mr. Chairman, I very much appreciate your efforts to find a consensus. What has struck me about the challenge to the independence of the Federal Reserve is a need for us to speak with one voice as much as possible. Frankly, I find myself torn between your recommendation, which I will support, and President Jordan's recommendation, which I also could support were he Chairman!" (*Transcripts*, June 30–July 1, 1992, 73–74). Committee members do not simply see the chairman as a dictator and themselves as ineffective bystanders, though, and on occasion the power of the majority was apparent. In November 1992, Governor Wayne Angell questioned Greenspan's informal tally of preferences on the setting of the bias. A lengthy discussion and an additional straw poll were required before the issue was decided by Greenspan's tie-breaking vote (*Transcripts*, November 17, 1992, 46–47):

*CHAIRMAN GREENSPAN:* Listening to the comments on the short term, especially if we [include] the three members of the Committee who are significantly desirous of easing now, it's fairly clear that we have a central tendency toward asymmetry ... as I read it we would be close [to] the average [view] of this Committee if we voted "B" asymmetric toward ease, and I would propose that to the Committee.
*MR. ANGELL:* How do we make it soft asymmetric? I counted six who preferred symmetric and then you said either way.
*CHAIRMAN GREENSPAN:* No, that's not the way I got it.
*MR. ANGELL:* I've got Corrigan—
*CHAIRMAN GREENSPAN:* Corrigan is either way.
*MR. ANGELL:* He said symmetric but he could accept.
*VICE CHAIRMAN CORRIGAN:* I would accept asymmetric because of my concern about the international side.
*MR. ANGELL:* Right, you said symmetric but could accept asymmetric.
*MR. KELLEY:* You might take a poll.
*CHAIRMAN GREENSPAN:* That's the simple way. Why don't we just poll the members?

Further, it seems clear that Greenspan valued consensus enough to avoid heavy-handedness, especially when his preferences were not strongly felt. In July 1992, he clearly indicated that his proposal was intended to reflect his expectation of the consensus view of the committee:

I conclude by saying that, after listening to the general views regarding what this Committee is concerned about and adding up the number of people on the Committee who have taken different views, I am led, as I try to find the central tendency, to [propose] a mildly asymmetric directive toward ease but with the requirement that before any action is taken there be a telephone conference to explain why. I'm not sure that captures everybody; I suspect it probably does not. But having thought about trying to find where the central tendency is—where one captures the largest number of views and concerns of this Committee—that's pretty much where I come out. (*Transcripts*, June 30–July 1, 1992, 67)

On other occasions, Greenspan made efforts to build inclusive coalitions in support of his positions. Woodward (2000), for example, reports that Greenspan successfully lobbied Governor Alan Blinder for support several days before proposing a preemptive fifty-basis-point rate hike in August 1994. Blinder agreed to support Greenspan's proposed tightening, but on the condition that it be accompanied by an announcement that no additional tightening moves were anticipated. Greenspan agreed—the rate was hiked, the announcement was made, and both Blinder and Greenspan had made an impact.

Premeeting negotiations were apparently not always necessary for members to communicate their preferences to Greenspan. Even though he spoke first in the policy go-around, the chairman may have been able to infer members' views in part from statements that they made during earlier stages of the meeting in which economic conditions were discussed. Over time, Greenspan eventually learned enough about individuals' views to confidently predict them without consultation. In May 1993, he remarked: "Well, let me put it this way. I've been around this Committee for a number of years and I think I can say that I pretty much know how every single member of this committee would come out under [any given hypothetical] event. In other words, I could take the vote myself if I had to and I bet I'd get it on the nose three times out of four. The reason for that is that I know where you're all coming from" (*Transcripts*, May 18, 1993, 54).

Greenspan may have been an enthusiastic majoritarian or consensus builder when members agreed with him, but he was willing to push hard to overcome opposition when he had strong preferences. In February 1994, Greenspan was in a minority of four members who favored a twenty-five-basis-point tightening. Six members preferred a larger fifty-basis-point movement. Greenspan made a compelling appeal for support and unity, which was followed by a unanimous vote in his favor:

Let me make the suggestion then that we move 25 basis points with symmetry, that we watch this process very closely, and that if the evidence suggests that this situation is not simmering down, that we have a telephone conference at the appropriate time.... So I would request that. I don't request often that we try to stay together.... I would request that, if we can, we act unanimously. It is a very potent message out in the various communities with which we deal if we stand together. If we are going to get a split in the vote, I think it will create a problem for us, and I don't know how it will play out. I rarely ask this, as you know. This is one of those times when we really are together and I'd hate to have our vote somehow imply something other than the agreement for a tightening move that in fact exists in this Committee. (*Transcripts*, February 3–4, 1994, 57)

## 8.4 Conclusions

During the portion of the Greenspan era that we examine, the position of the chairman and the median voter on the FOMC almost always coincided. Because of this, a statistical decomposition of the power shares of the chairman and the rest of the committee was not feasible. Indirect evidence does support the hypothesis that Greenspan was powerful, however. Econometric estimates show that committee members were responsive to the positions advocated by the chairman, even after controlling for macroeconomic conditions. There was little evidence of influence in the reverse direction; leading measures of committee sentiments did not affect proposals made by Greenspan.

Greenspan initially gained influence by successfully managing policy during a critical period following the 1987 stock market crash. His reputation was further enhanced by a series of good (or fortuitous) decisions that contributed to a prolonged period of growth with declining inflation. His successes earned him respect and support from his colleagues, and as his time on the committee accumulated, he increasingly dominated FOMC deliberations both through intellectual leadership and skillful management of deliberations.

Several changes in committee procedures may also have increased the chairman's power. First, during the Greenspan era, policy options became more discrete, and this, in turn, made disagreements more noticeable. To avoid the appearance of conflict, committee members were led to coalesce on the chairman's position. Second, Greenspan inherited the Volcker regime's practice of including a statement of bias in monetary policy directives. By skillfully crafting the bias associated with a funds rate proposal, Greenspan may have been able to maintain consensus while pursuing his preferred policy options.

# 9      Political Influences on Monetary Policy Decision Making: Evidence from the *Memoranda* and the *Transcripts*

Chapter 5 described the construction of original data sets to character-ize the monetary policy preferences of individual FOMC members during the Burns and Greenspan eras. To produce these data sets, we read the records of committee deliberations contained in the *Memo-randa* and the *Transcripts* for each meeting during the selected periods. Our primary purpose in reading the source documents was to produce data suitable for the analytical work subsequently presented in chap-ters 6–8. As we proceeded, however, we also collected a file of textual excerpts that are related to issues addressed in this book. In many cases, the anecdotal content of these excerpts provides insight into the way individuals and the committee made decisions.

We have used anecdotal excerpts for illustrative purposes through-out the book, but in this chapter and the next, anecdotal material serves as the primary source of evidence. In this chapter, we discuss the political context of FOMC decision making; in the following chap-ter, we evaluate the applicability of time inconsistency theory in explaining the rise of inflation over the Burns years. In both chapters, anecdotal evidence permits us to document the reasoning and motiva-tions of policymakers by reporting the arguments members advanced to support their policy positions.

We begin in the first section of this chapter with a discussion of external political pressures applied to the FOMC by the president, Congress, and the public. In the second section, we consider the im-portance of the electoral calendar and whether FOMC members be-have differently when elections are imminent. Finally, in the third section, we examine the provision of information by the FOMC and document its efforts to limit public knowledge of its motives and actions.

## 9.1 External Political Pressures on the FOMC

It is clear from the textual record of FOMC deliberations that the Federal Reserve takes pride in its independence. In February 1975, for example, Burns argued that the committee should stand firm against political pressures: "It would be a tragic mistake to yield to political pressures [for ease]; the political pressures of today would not necessarily be those of tomorrow. The Congress had established the System as an independent entity, and the Committee ought to live up to the responsibility imposed by that independence" (*Memorandum*, February 19, 1975, 215–216). In our reading of the *Memoranda* and the *Transcripts*, we have not seen comments that suggest that the committee ever felt compelled to follow instructions from any outside authority. Although politically motivated statements were infrequent, the record nevertheless indicates that members were, at times, mindful of the preferences of their external clients (the president, Congress, and the public). In this section, we explore the importance of these influences.

### 9.1.1 Pressure from the President
The 1972 presidential election provided inspiration for models of political business cycles, and the relationship between Nixon and Burns is often cited as an example of presidential influence over the Fed. While administration preferences are not routinely discussed at FOMC meetings, the Nixon-Burns era does provide several examples. In January 1971, Burns reported to the committee that administration "confidence" in the Federal Reserve was diminishing as money growth failed to keep up with announced targets:

As far as society as a whole was concerned, confidence in the Federal Reserve appeared to be strong and growing. However, the Administration's confidence in the System was weakening as a result of the shortfalls that had occurred in the rates of monetary growth. He [Burns] was not concerned so much about the loss of System prestige and credibility as he was about the possible impact on other governmental policies.... The credibility of the Federal Reserve would be greatly strengthened if it became apparent that the Committee was seeking to make up the recent shortfalls. (*Memorandum*, January 12, 1971, 41)

Note that Burns implicitly couched his support for additional ease on the premise that failure to support the administration might result in a more harmful stimulative fiscal policy. Later during the same meeting, however, Chicago Fed president Robert Mayo warned that the committee should also be wary of appearing to cave in to administration pressures: "Adoption of alternative C [the easiest policy option proposed by the staff] might also undermine confidence in the System *by suggesting that it had succumbed to Administration pressure;* and it might damage confidence in the economic outlook by suggesting that the Committee thought conditions had deteriorated to the point where a very large injection of funds was needed" (*Memorandum*, January 12, 1971, 60, emphasis added). At the next month's meeting, Burns again voiced concern with low money growth rates, adding that failure to correct them might lead to undesirable consequences for the Fed:

Personally, the Chairman continued, he believed that monetary policy had been basically sound over the past year, and he had no quarrel with the policy of the last few months. However, the shortfalls from the Committee's targets for the monetary aggregates that had occurred had caused difficulties for the System, and further shortfalls would cause continuing difficulties. He did not agree with those who thought that some particular growth rate in the narrowly defined money supply in 1971 would insure a strong economic expansion this year, and in his judgment the heavy emphasis that many people were placing on the behavior of M1 involved an excessively simplified view of monetary policy. *But however unfortunate such views might be, the fact that they were widely held had consequences for the System.* (*Memorandum*, February 9, 1971, 187, emphasis added)

After the 1972 election, there is little discussion of pressure from the administration regarding monetary policy. Nixon's concerns lay elsewhere once he had been reelected—Watergate events quickly began to occupy his administration.[1] There is also little discussion of executive branch pressures from President Gerald R. Ford during the 1974–1976 period.[2] But after Jimmy Carter took office in 1977, Burns again appeared to be responsive to implicit administration concerns. Carter had campaigned on a promise not to reappoint Burns, but Burns hoped he might yet be retained. Thus, in January 1977, the chairman was ready to extend a signal of goodwill to the incoming president:

1. In 1973, the FOMC acted to slow the rate of money growth in an attempt to prevent further accumulation of inflationary pressures. Wells (1994) reports that the White House supported Burns in this effort, despite even more intense opposition from Capitol Hill to the higher interest rates that it required.
2. Wells (1994, 145) says that after President Nixon's resignation, "Burns lost no time ingratiating himself with Gerald R. Ford's new administration. He would not repeat the mistakes of 1969 and take his relationship with the chief executive for granted." Kettl (1986) and Wells (1994) both note that President Ford and Burns held similar views about the appropriate course for economic policy, and both document the extraordinary degree of cooperation between the administration and the Fed chairman. Kettl (1986, 132) observes that the Ford-Burns period was characterized by "the closest relationship between a president and a Fed Chairman in history."

We have a new administration—the new administration has proposed a fiscal plan for reducing unemployment and any lowering of monetary growth rates at this time would, I'm quite sure, be very widely interpreted, and not only in the political arena, as an attempt on the part of the Federal Reserve to frustrate the efforts of a newly elected President [and a] newly elected Congress, to get our economy, to use a popular phrase, "moving once again." (*Transcripts*, January 17–18, 1977, tape 7, 2)

Indeed, following President Carter's election in 1976, monetary policy shifted toward ease as the Fed cut the discount rate and allowed money growth to accelerate. Greider (1987) confirms that this was calculated to ingratiate Burns with Carter and improve the chairman's chances of reappointment. In the end, Burns was not reappointed, but the excessive monetary stimulus he provided during his campaign for reappointment contributed to the subsequent acceleration of inflation that played a major role in Carter's defeat in the 1980 election.

Administration interest in reaching understandings with the Federal Reserve—and particularly with the chairman—has been an enduring feature of the U.S. political economic landscape. Woodward (2000) reports that during 1991, there was some concern inside the Federal Reserve that Greenspan's aggressive push for lower interest rates was motivated, at least in part, by his desire to be reappointed by President Bush.[3] The Bush administration had relentlessly signaled a desire for easier policy from inauguration day through the reelection campaign.[4] For some FOMC members, the administration "jawboning" appears to have been counterproductive. In the middle of 1992, Boston Fed president Richard Syron suggested that while conditions might warrant an easing move, the visible administration pressure made him hesitant to take that action: "To tell you the truth, in the absence of the jawboning that we've had from the Administration—if we weren't in such an awkward position—I would generally prefer to do something at this meeting.... [U]nder ordinary circumstances I would have preferred [a cut of] 25 basis points at the meeting today. But in the environment we're in, with this amount of jawboning, I'd be cautious about pushing too hard for that" (*Transcripts*, June 30–July 1, 1992, 72). In subsequent months, the committee did lower the target funds rate several times, but it is not clear that the political environment expedited those moves.

3. Woodward (2000) also quotes a *New York Times* editorial from 1991 that expressed doubts about Greenspan's independence from the Bush administration.
4. Havrilesky's (1995) *SAFER* index reports forty-two signals from the administration to the Fed for easier policy over the 1989–1992 period, and no signals for tighter policy.

Given the sluggishness of the recovery at that time, there were good economic reasons to ease monetary policy, as Greenspan noted in October 1992:

I don't think the markets have been viewing anything we have been doing as politically motivated. There are obviously those who make those statements, but I don't think that's a serious issue confronting us.... But if the money supply weakens and the markets behave poorly and we have the evidence that we're getting cumulative deterioration or more exactly that the economy is not picking up, which is I think the main criterion at this particular stage—I do think that we should move toward ease. (*Transcripts*, October 6, 1992, 42–43)

Under the Clinton administration, jawboning for easy policy was much reduced. The administration's "bond market strategy" envisaged that deficit reduction would permit lower long-term rates; overt lobbying for easier monetary policy would undermine that objective by sustaining high inflation expectations. Nevertheless, the Clinton administration felt that it had an understanding with Greenspan and presumably expected cooperation from him. In 1993, it was widely believed that if the administration and Congress produced budgets that incorporated credible deficit reductions, the Fed would provide a reward in the form of interest rate reductions. Under similar circumstances in 1995, Greenspan clearly noted that there was no quid pro quo:

We have argued in the past, and I think quite correctly, that it has never been appropriate for the Federal Reserve to "make a deal" with the Congress or the Administration to take some action if a budget is produced and irrespective of whether it is credible or not credible.... [T]he mere fact of negotiations should not induce us to take action because I think that could turn out to be very unfortunate monetary policy. I think we all have agreed, as best I can judge, that the response that we make is to the markets. If the markets believe that the budget deal is credible, long-term rates will come down and we will get an abnormality in the term structure of rates if short-term rates remain unchanged. So the pressures on us to ease policy would come from the markets and the term structure, not from the budget deal. The market is what would induce us to make a move. (*Transcripts*, November 15, 1995, 46)

While Greenspan advocated no change in monetary policy in November 1995, the committee subsequently adopted two more twenty-five-basis-point reductions in the funds rate—one in December 1995 and the other in January 1996. The additional easing in late 1995 and early 1996 no doubt met with the administration's approval. Indeed, Woodward (2000) reports that by the time President Clinton reappointed Greenspan in 1996 to another term as chairman, the members of the

Clinton economic team had come to view Greenspan almost as one of their own.

### 9.1.2  Pressure from Congress

According to Kettl (1986) and Wells (1994), the Burns years were marked by consistent and intense congressional scrutiny of the Federal Reserve. It is not surprising that FOMC records from that period contain intermittent references to congressional concerns, almost invariably indicating that Congress wanted lower interest rates. In June 1971, Burns commented on the risks of an increase in the discount rate: "For the Federal Reserve to raise the discount rate at a time when unemployment was so high would lead many observers to wonder about the nature and purposes of the System and would produce strongly negative reactions in the Congress and the Administration.... [A]t present he [Burns] would expect to oppose such an action" (*Memorandum*, June 8, 1971, 594–595). In February 1974, Governor Jeffrey Bucher noted that it was important to consider how Congress might respond to the committee's monetary policy decisions: "Committee members needed to be concerned about the effects that System policies might have on Congressional actions to deal with high unemployment and to recognize that, in the long run, the adverse effects of such actions on prices could be much greater than those of any marginal measures the System might take at this point" (*Memorandum*, February 20, 1974, 191).

On occasion, the possible countermoves from Congress included direct legislative remedies aimed at the Fed, not just alternative macroeconomic policies. In April 1973, a measure introduced in the Senate that would have lowered interest rates failed by only four votes (45–41), "a close call that rattled the Fed" (Wells 1994, 113). Four years later, when Richmond Fed president Robert Black commented on the political difficulty faced in lowering target rates of money growth, Burns responded:

As far as our doing something, we do what we think is right. Now there are no political factors that make it hard to reason. To the extent that there are political factors, I think they're of another kind. We have very troublesome legislation in the Congress, and what we do and the way our testimony goes on the 29th when these targets will be announced may have some effect on the course of the legislation in the Congress. I think to the extent that there is a political factor here, it's really legislative; legislation involving or affecting the Federal Reserve. (*Transcripts*, July 19, 1977, tape E, 7)

Concerns about congressional threats to the Fed's position also sur-faced from time to time during the Greenspan years. In July 1991, the chairman commented on how fiscal paralysis had intensified the de-gree of scrutiny accorded to monetary policy:

So, I would argue at this particular stage with fiscal policy clearly shackled and likely to remain shackled for a while, that the spotlight is on us in a way that I don't think we've seen for a while. And I see frankly, very little benefit to moving now on lowering the [money growth] targets, although I think it's es-sential that we not stop here.... I'm not sure there's anything to be gained in the short run in signaling a tightening for '92 this far in advance. I don't think we need it. *All that will do is to galvanize some anti-Fed actions which since the banking bill is still open and under negotiation, can create an inadvertent problem for us because amendments on the floor of the House and the Senate can be particularly ill-informed and still pass.* (Transcripts, July 3, 1991, 33–34, emphasis added)

These comments by Burns and Greenspan express the view that while the committee should pursue the monetary policy that it believes is appropriate, it also needs to be mindful of the legislative environment in which it makes its decisions.

### 9.1.3 Pressure from Public Opinion

During the 1970s, as the problem of stagflation first developed and then worsened, it was clear that political pressure came not only through the filter of elected politicians but also directly from the pub-lic. In July 1974, when facing a double-digit inflation rate, Governor Charles Partee claimed that a growth rate of real output of 1.0 percent would be unacceptable even when it was recognized that the Fed was combating inflation. Yet Chicago Fed president Mayo challenged Par-tee's assessment:

[Mayo] would question Mr. Partee's judgment that a real growth rate of less than 1 percent would be unacceptable to the public. Until a few months ago he would have agreed with that statement, but it now seemed to him that a sub-stantial body of support for inflation control had developed throughout the nation, even among those who were adversely affected by anti-inflation policy. He thought the public at present would be prepared to accept a 1 per cent growth rate in GNP over the next year if that were required for better control of inflation. (*Memorandum*, July 16, 1974, 792–793)

At the February 1975 meeting in which Burns argued for resisting po-litical pressures, Philadelphia Fed president David Eastburn neverthe-less took a view that acknowledged concerns with public opinion: "While the Federal Reserve System was an independent entity, its actions were being closely observed. He [Eastburn] was concerned that there would be critical public reaction to continuation of a monetary policy that had produced very little growth in the narrow money stock over the past 6 months, a period when the economy was moving into the worst recession since the 1930's" (*Memorandum*, February 19, 1975, 222).

Pressures from the public as well as elected representatives were also felt during the Greenspan years, as the chairman noted in 1996: "We are an independent central bank in that our decisions are not subject to reversal by any other agency of government. Our existence and ability to function, however, are subject to acceptance by a public and a Congress who exhibit decidedly asymmetric propensities in favor of policy ease" (*Transcripts*, July 2–3, 1996, 82). Clearly, then, regardless of the source (the president, Congress, or the public), the Greenspan Fed faced political pressures similar to those endured by the Burns Fed. More often than not, those pressures favored easier monetary policies.

## 9.2   Electoral Cycles

The previous section makes it clear that the FOMC acknowledges the presence of political pressures. Further, at least in the early 1970s, it seems likely that political pressures were applied in a way that was electorally motivated, and the same can probably be said for the early 1990s. Even if members are not actively trying to generate a political monetary cycle, they are aware of approaching elections and how their actions might be perceived in such a context. In this section, we first look at how the electoral calendar figured in monetary policy discussions during the Burns and Greenspan years. We then take a more detailed look at President Nixon's 1972 reelection campaign.

### 9.2.1   Elections and the Monetary Policy Decision Process

The conventional wisdom is that during preelection periods, the Fed avoids taking actions that might appear to be politically motivated, leading to added policy inertia. This is the view of former Federal Reserve governor Sherman J. Maisel (1973), who served on the board in the late 1960s and early 1970s. It is a view that has also found occasional expression within FOMC meetings. Of course, if the Fed were targeting interest rates and if fiscal policy were electorally timed, such a strategy would also result in accommodative monetary policy before elections (Beck 1987). Further, the avoidance of preelection actions might be asymmetric—contractionary actions might be subject to more inertia than expansionary ones, as Richmond Fed president Alfred Broaddus hinted early in 1996: "I do think it needs to be said that it may be more difficult this year than in most other years to move the funds rate back up later if things don't go the way we want them to" (*Transcripts*, January 30–31, 1996, 57).

A number of references that we have found in the FOMC records seem to suggest a desire to appear apolitical, perhaps consistent with a tendency to avoid overt actions during preelection periods. For example, in October 1970, with congressional elections imminent, New York Fed president Alfred Hayes commented that a reduction in the discount rate would be a deliberate signal of further ease and therefore not appropriate under the circumstances. He then went on to note, "This view is reinforced by even keel considerations and *by the desirability of avoiding a discount rate change either immediately before, or immediately after, Election Day*" (*Memorandum*, October 20, 1970, 929, emphasis added). Before the 1976 elections, there were similar remarks from Minneapolis Fed president Bruce MacLaury, who said, "I think that it will be more difficult in October–November of election time to make a further adjustment downward in the M1 range than it is to do so today" (*Transcripts*, July 20, 1976, tape 2, 4). When October arrived, Kansas City Fed president Roger Guffey added, "I think we have some other tools of monetary policy that I'd like to see us use if we were perhaps not so close to November 2" (*Transcripts*, October 19, 1976, tape 8, 5). New York Fed president Paul Volcker agreed, saying, "It is premature right now, given account not only of our economic conditions but also of this time on the calendar, to give a really strong signal of easing" (*Transcripts*, October 19, 1976, tape 7, 7).

In May 1996, Broaddus suggested that the committee should do more than simply try to appear apolitical. In his comments during the monetary policy go-around, he noted that financial markets did not seem to expect tightening despite firming conditions in the real economy and went so far as to argue that the committee should actively work against perceptions of political influence over its decisions: "One explanation might be that market participants are expecting us to be somewhat more hesitant in this period of the political cycle. Partly because of this, and given the underlying inflation risks and the upside risks in the outlook for economic growth that I and others mentioned earlier, I think we should raise the funds rate today" (*Transcripts*, May 21, 1996, 33).

During Greenspan's tenure, there is evidence of an almost conscious effort by the FOMC to distance itself from its traditional reluctance to take action during election years. In November 1991, Greenspan recommended a twenty-five-basis-point reduction in the funds rate. Part of his support for a rate cut at the time depended on his belief that a subsequent firming would be feasible even in the upcoming election year, if conditions warranted:

Secondly, I think the evidence of our ability to move on the up side during an election year is fairly significant. Earlier views were that the Fed could not move under those conditions. I think what we were able to do in 1988 clearly indicates that there's a change in the tone of how money and politics run. And, if it becomes necessary to turn around, I don't see any reason why we shouldn't be able to do that. I certainly would say, and I hope, that the will of this Committee is clearly in that direction. (*Transcripts*, November 5, 1991, 28)

In 1988, the committee had increased its funds rate target in fourteen steps from 6.8125 to 8.75 percent; ten of these steps, reflecting all but the last fifty basis points of the total adjustment, had been taken prior to the election. As events unfolded in 1991 and 1992, however, the committee saw no need "to move on the up side"—it continued to ease monetary policy in the face of the sluggish recovery, lowering its funds rate target to 3.00 percent in September 1992. At the October meeting, Greenspan noted the political interpretation being given to the committee's policy course, even as he denied that politics had anything to do with these decisions: "I would like to say finally that I wish we had the luxury to sit back and do nothing until after the election, as is the conventional procedure of the Federal Open Market Committee. I don't think we have that luxury.... I do think that we should move toward ease" (*Transcripts*, October 6, 1992, 42–43). In section 9.1.1, we documented the committee's concern about appearing to give in to administration pressure during the latter half of 1992, even as it lowered its funds rate target by seventy-five basis points over a two-month period from early July to early September. The chairman's assertions at the October meeting notwithstanding, the pattern of funds rate reductions implemented by the FOMC throughout 1992 looked much like that of a standard political monetary cycle.

### 9.2.2  Nixon's Reelection Campaign
On one occasion, there was a brief FOMC discussion of the alleged 1972 political monetary cycle. This occurred in 1977, when the com-

mittee considered a request from the *New York Times* to release the 1972 *Memoranda* in advance of the usual date. Presumably, the *Times* was interested in developing a story on the political motivations of the Fed prior to the election. Burns offered the following comment: "[T]here has been some speculation to the effect that in 1972, the Federal Open Market Committee, having as its chairman a certain individual was inclined to do what it could to promote the reelection of a certain gentleman called Richard M. Nixon as President" (*Transcripts*, August 16, 1977, tape 6, 22). Burns then stated that he felt that it was inappropriate to release the minutes just to prove that his 1972 actions were honorable, as the record would demonstrate. Doing so would itself appear political given the current controversy over whether Burns would be reappointed by Carter.

In an early study using the *Memoranda* as a primary data source, Woolley (1984) examined records from 1972 in order to assess election-year political motivations. He concluded that while the Fed may not have directly sought Nixon's reelection, the desire to deflect political threats led the FOMC to keep interest rates low during the period of wage and price controls, an assessment with which Wells (1994) concurs. Thus, the Fed abetted Nixon's political aims by pursuing its own bureaucratic interests. As some of our discussion in section 9.1 suggested, our reading of the *Memoranda* also largely supports this view. We should note, however, that there is evidence of more direct political influence in 1971 than in 1972.

In early 1971, Burns explicitly cited administration displeasure with low money growth when advocating ease. Later in 1971, when money growth dropped again, the Nixon administration showed its displeasure more vehemently. In October, Nixon snubbed Burns by refusing to meet with him to discuss an appointment to the Board of Governors. In early November, he sent Burns a three-page letter advising him to "get off his tail and get the money supply flowing again" (*Haldeman Diaries*, CD-ROM, entry for November 5, 1971). At the next FOMC meeting, on November 19, Burns spoke early and advocated an easier policy, which the committee adopted. The funds rate declined by seventy-five basis points during the subsequent intermeeting period.

Moreover, with inflation becoming more of a threat as 1971 wore on, the Nixon administration decided in August of that year to impose wage and price controls. While these controls did not directly affect the Fed's options, it is likely that Nixon imposed them so that he could fight inflation without resorting to monetary or fiscal restraint. Burns and the FOMC recognized that raising interest rates when prices and wages were controlled might be politically dangerous: "So long as interest rates in general remained below the levels that had prevailed before the President's address he [Burns] did not think much pressure would build up for including them in the freeze. *The situation would be different, of course, if rates were to move back up above those levels*" (*Memorandum,* August 24, 1971, 811, emphasis added). In September 1971, New York Fed president Hayes commented on the administration's apparent disposition to keep interest rates below their precontrol levels:

For the time being this should not present the System with any problems, as long as there is a sizable cushion between current rate levels and those of August 13. However, the cushion is not so large as to give me any feeling of assurance that the Administration's rate policy will not become a serious obstacle to effective monetary policy.... We can only hope that these developments will work out in such a way that the System will not be confronted with a most difficult policy dilemma. (*Memorandum,* September 21, 1971, 980)

Eight months later, in the face of continuing inflation, Governor Andrew Brimmer noted that still tighter wage and price controls might be needed, since the administration clearly preferred not to deal with inflation by means of a tighter monetary policy that would risk an economic slowdown:

Mr. Brimmer observed that there also was a continuing problem of inflation, despite the control program that had been in effect since mid-August 1971. However, no one should have expected to see the problems of inflation and unemployment simultaneously resolved within the eight months that had elapsed since last August 15. The significant point was that the Administration had decided at that time—with the support of the Congress and the Federal Reserve—that the way to solve the problem of inflation was to apply direct controls rather than to slow the rate of economic growth and increase excess capacity. If more effective means of fighting inflation were needed they should be sought in tighter controls, perhaps along the lines the Chairman had suggested, and not through monetary policy. (*Memorandum,* April 17–18, 1972, 447–448)

The awkwardness of the Fed's position was magnified by Nixon's decision to name Burns the chairman of the Committee on Interest and Dividends (CID), the administrative unit charged with overseeing policy toward interest rates and dividends during the period of wage and price controls.[5] In July 1972, Burns discussed his role with the CID more explicitly in response to an inquiry from Brimmer about whether "constraints" on interest rates were political. Burns answered that they were not, but then qualified his statement:

> Nevertheless, the Federal Reserve System was a part of the Government. At present the Government had an incomes policy that applied to prices, to wages, and to profits; and through the Committee on Interest and Dividends, it also applied—on a voluntary basis—to dividends and interest rates.... Despite the existence of a national policy affecting prices, wages, profits, and dividends, he had considered it his duty to oppose the establishment of guidelines for interest rates. Given the framework of the Government's incomes policy, Chairman Burns continued, there was widespread opposition to higher interest rates.... [V]oices had been raised to advocate ceilings on interest rates. Fortunately, resistance to ceilings had come from the President and from the Secretary of the Treasury as well as from himself, and so far resistance had succeeded. *In the circumstances, the Federal Reserve should not be eager to raise interest rates.* (*Memorandum*, August 15, 1972, 826–827, emphasis added)

Arguably, the administration limited monetary policy options during the period of wage and price controls by the implied threat of imposing rigid controls on interest rates if the Fed behaved inappropriately. Compounding the Fed's dilemma was the fact that the White House was not the only source of pressure for monetary ease (Kettl 1986). Democrats on the House Banking Committee were developing a plan to impose mandatory interest rate ceilings. In that environment, Burns felt that interest rates could not be allowed to increase, and this led him to advocate monetary ease to his colleagues on the FOMC.

## 9.3   The FOMC and the Provision of Information

In recent years, the FOMC has moved in the direction of providing more timely information about its policy actions than it did in the past. Throughout its history, however, the committee has been cautious about what information it releases, how much information it releases, and when it releases information. FOMC members sometimes asserted that by limiting information, they were acting in society's best

---

5. The difficulties Burns faced in his simultaneous roles as Fed chairman and CID chairman are discussed by Kettl (1986) and Wells (1994). Kettl (1986) reports that Burns took the job despite the potential conflict of interest because he feared that it would otherwise go to Treasury secretary John Connally, which, in Burns's view, would have risked a revival of the pre-Accord interest rate peg.

interests—they avoided unnecessary disturbances to market expectations and outcomes. At other times, the motive seemed more clearly
related to the Fed's bureaucratic interests. By limiting information, the
FOMC could more easily deflect external pressures that might be divi-
sive within the committee. In this section, we describe key debates over
information provision that occurred during the Burns and Greenspan
years.

### 9.3.1    The Burns Years

During the Burns years, the Fed took the view that full disclosure of its
actions and intentions would be counterproductive in achieving the
results it desired. Furthermore, at that time, the Fed was subjected to
considerable outside pressure to become more open. On one front, the
Fed faced Georgetown University law student David Merrill's legal
challenge to its practice of delaying the release of the *Memorandum* for
five years after a meeting.[6] At the same time, Congress was considering passage of the Freedom of Information Act, which also threatened
some of the Fed's secretive practices. One consequence of these external threats was that the FOMC frequently had explicit discussions
about its information revelation strategies during the Burns years.

In general, it seems apparent that the FOMC usually wanted to conduct its policies in a way that did not "disturb" markets.[7] This concern
stemmed from a general view that markets are often irrational and in-
efficient. In July 1976, San Francisco Fed president John Balles noted
the market's "improper" reaction to the latest money growth figures,
saying that he thought the Fed should publish moving averages over
several weeks instead of just the last week (as if market participants
could not construct such averages for themselves): "I'd like to have us
educate the market not to place so much weight on what the very latest weekly figures show. I think they react irrationally to that. We're
getting observations that are unjustified and disturbing" (*Transcripts*,
July 20, 1976, tape 1, 16). Burns then remarked that both the market
and the Open Market Desk also tended to respond irrationally to the
latest money growth figures: "I would say the market reacts irrationally; I would also say that I think there is some tendency on the part

---

6. The Merrill lawsuit is discussed in Goodfriend (1986); Kettl (1986); and Wells (1994).
7. Goodfriend (1986) confirms this motive and lists several others. The FOMC believed
that prompt release of information would allow major traders to profit from speculation,
that open market operations would be more costly, and that orderly execution of monetary policy would be impaired.

of this committee and, because of this committee, at the desk also to react irrationally to these figures" (*Transcripts*, July 20, 1976, tape 1, 16).

In February 1976, the committee was concerned that developments in the Merrill lawsuit might force a premature revelation of the committee's policy directive. In light of this circumstance, Boston Fed president Frank Morris urged the committee to broaden the funds rate ranges it was adopting in order to limit the information content that would be revealed if the courts ruled in favor of Merrill:

> Mr. Morris added that, while he preferred stability in the funds rate over the next inter-meeting interval, he thought that the Committee should adopt the practice of setting a range for the Federal funds [rate] at least $1\frac{1}{2}$ percentage points in width because of the possibility of early publication of the specifications. . . . Accordingly, he favored a range of 4 to $5\frac{1}{2}$ per cent for the funds rate, even though the consensus might be for little if any movement in the rate. (*Memorandum*, February 17–18, 1976, 225)

In some instances, the committee's effort to limit information provision revealed a more active effort to deceive outside observers, not just an effort to be vague. In September 1977, several FOMC members, including Burns, advocated publishing a range for M1 growth with a lower limit around 3.00 percent, when they said they would be perfectly willing to see zero growth. They apparently did not want the public to know that they would tolerate such low rates of money growth (*Transcripts*, September 20, 1977, tape 7, 17–18). In another instance, in June 1977, Burns considered the choice of "money market" or "aggregates" wording for the directive (to indicate a focus on either interest rates or monetary aggregates), saying, "Well, logic is a stern master and if one respected it really, one would have to use a money market directive, but I have found it desirable at times to throw logic to the winds and to, and I see some advantage in the monetary aggregates directive because, basically, that is what we ought to be doing" (*Transcripts*, June 21, 1977, tape 4, 2). In other words, he was targeting the funds rate, but he wanted to suggest that he was targeting money instead.

It was also common for FOMC members to view the committee's money growth targets as a shield from the political attacks that often followed increases in interest rates. In August 1975, Governor Robert Holland suggested a strategy of backing off from stating interest rate targets because that would soon require them to be explicit about seeking higher rates (*Memorandum*, August 15, 1975, 970). Sixteen

months later, Minneapolis Fed president MacLaury spoke of his desire
to attach a bit more importance to the monetary aggregates:

I have certainly been among those who have viewed the greater emphasis on
the monetary aggregates as useful but perhaps in a different way than the
monetarists do. Not because I think there is great stability between any particular aggregate and the economy.... Rather it has seemed to me for a rather
political point of view dealing with the Congress, the public in general, that
the aggregates, in an admittedly oversimplified way distracted some over-
attention to interest rates and our impact upon interest rates[;] that we could
explain to the public what we were doing by reference to the aggregates in a
way that seemed to make at least structural sense. *And that therefore, when the
time came for raising interest rates we could adhere to and speak in terms of the
aggregates.* (*Transcripts*, December 20, 1976, tape 8, 2, emphasis added)

This was not the first time that MacLaury had taken such a position.
During an earlier meeting, he had said, "I think for political reasons,
it's very important that we continue to attach some significance to
these aggregates and let interest rates in effect move as we try to pursue those aggregates" (*Transcripts*, April 20, 1976, tape 7, 1). These
examples illustrate a strategy that the committee would again find
appealing in 1979, when the Fed ostensibly abandoned interest rate
targets in favor of reserve aggregates: when interest rates start getting
high, (pretend to) target money.[8]

The importance the FOMC attached to secrecy is highlighted by its
response to the Merrill lawsuit, which threatened to force the committee to release the *Memorandum* promptly after each meeting. Facing the
threat posed by Merrill, the FOMC chose simply to discontinue publication of the *Memoranda*. Although the Fed did not directly note its
motive for this action at the time, Burns left little doubt when he
reflected on it in 1977. He said, "If we had had the feeling of protection
that we could go along as we had, we would not have as a Committee
abandoned the memorandum of discussion. *We did it only as a Committee, as a reaction to the judicial proceeding that had been started*" (*Transcripts*, August 16, 1977, tape 6, 6, emphasis added).

In May 1976, just one month after the decision to eliminate the *Memoranda*, Burns instructed the staff to prepare a new "enhanced" policy
directive to be published after each meeting. The actual purpose of the

---

8. Greider (1987) argues that the FOMC's October 1979 shift from federal funds rate targeting to nonborrowed reserves targeting was intended to help divert attention from the
committee's responsibility for the high interest rates that its coming fight against inflation
would require.

enhanced directive was apparently to mollify politicians annoyed by the demise of the *Memoranda*. With the timely publication of an enhanced policy directive, Burns could argue that the committee was providing more information more promptly than before. The enhancements were of doubtful value, though. After receiving a rather short draft of the enhanced directive from his staff, Burns directed them to "produce several additional pages." Burns added that "I'm certainly not going to say that we should do anything that remotely resembles padding," but he seemed to want exactly that (*Transcripts*, May 18, 1976, tape 1, 8).

It is also apparent that the committee often selected its long-term money growth targets with an eye toward public consumption rather than legitimate long-term planning. In July 1977, Kansas City Fed president Guffey discussed long-run targets:

On the [other] hand, the cosmetic effect, if that's the right term, of continuing to move [to lower money growth targets] is very attractive, and as a result, I think we would opt for a solution that you have proposed on the M-1 alone, that is, moving the bottom $\frac{1}{2}$ percent. I don't think it's very meaningful at the moment. I think we've got to begin to focus on the shorter range of getting those aggregates down and what we do in the longer range is basically for consumption of the public and not for this Committee. So in conclusion, I guess, I would be perfectly willing to buy the cosmetic effect of moving the lower side of M-1, but leaving the remainder of the aggregates where they are for the moment, long range. (*Transcripts*, July 19, 1977, tape E, 16–17)

At the same meeting, Burns adopted a similar attitude about a different issue. Responding to Governor Philip Coldwell, who had asked why the committee should adopt a bank credit target, Burns replied, "Oh, I think it's quite important ... to have a credit figure as well as the money figure because we don't want to go completely monetarist at this Committee." Coldwell answered, "It's pure cosmetics," to which Burns responded, "Well, I think sometimes, I think they [the targets] are symbolic. Much of life is based on symbolism" (*Transcripts*, July 19, 1977, tape F, 3–4).

Although there was much agreement that limiting information to the public was desirable, there were occasional dissenting voices. As the FOMC faced increasing legal pressure, St. Louis Fed president Lawrence Roos argued that additional openness might not be such a bad thing. He therefore suggested that the committee should publish its policy directives immediately just to test whether any undesirable market reactions would occur (*Transcripts*, November 17, 1977, tape 1,

12). Minneapolis Fed president Mark Willes voiced a similar opinion, but other members were not supportive.

Limited and delayed information revelation also provided a means of deflecting criticism and political pressure that might have divided the committee and weakened its bargaining power with external clients. During the July 20, 1976, FOMC meeting, Governor Henry Wallich suggested that it might be acceptable to include comments of specific members within the published policy directive. Burns responded as follows:

I think it can be done. I think the sentiment of the Committee was that this should not be done. That would also be my view. I think when you start mentioning names, identifying positions with individuals, one is inviting a certain emphasis on differences. And remember that this is a document that is now released approximately 30 days after our meeting. And to have the differences displayed by name I think it could excite some of us unduly to extreme utterances and I think also that our critics on Capitol Hill and elsewhere would maximize and exaggerate the differences among us and the unity and the consensus that we should be striving for might well be lost in the process. (*Transcripts*, July 20, 1976, tape 2, 3)

### 9.3.2   The Greenspan Years

Occasional calls for more prompt release of the committee's policy decisions were also made during the Greenspan years. At least initially, these calls were either dismissed or ignored. In August 1988, for example, Governor Martha Seger expressed concern about the instability in the funds rate that seemed to stem from market participants trying to discern the committee's policy stance from the system's open market operations:

I can certainly accept targeting a borrowing figure. But it does concern me when the fed funds rate whips all over and then that confuses market participants. But I think the way to fix this—maybe we can discuss this issue at some future luncheon—is to release our minutes more promptly so people will know what we are up to. Then they wouldn't have to be going through all these little subtle signals trying to figure out what it is we are really doing. And, you know, if the fed funds rate goes to 9 this afternoon at 3:00, some people are going to suggest probably that it's there because we put it there. They won't know. I think that getting the information out more promptly about what our policy moves are would help to calm the markets down and would really eliminate some of this confusion. (*Transcripts*, August 16, 1988, 36)

The issue of the committee's information revelation strategies finally came to a head in 1993, when Congress was intensely pressuring the committee about detailed records of its deliberations. In October of that year, Greenspan revealed in testimony before the House Banking Committee that even after the *Memoranda* were discontinued in 1976, FOMC meetings had been audiotaped and transcribed to assist the FOMC Secretariat in preparing the "Record of Policy Actions" (now called the "Minutes") for publication in the board's annual report and the *Federal Reserve Bulletin*. The raw transcripts, he said, had been retained, but the audiotapes had been reused.

Records of the committee's deliberations on the matter of the transcripts indicate that members were predisposed to resist efforts to force the release of those records. Prior to the testimony in which their existence was revealed, Greenspan outlined the strategy he wanted to follow to protect the status quo:

With respect to the disclosure issues in the October 13 and 19 testimonies: First, on the 13th, I will cover the general principles on disclosure and accountability; that will essentially be incorporated into the text of my testimony. I will defend current disclosure policy as telling the public as much as possible without impairing the FOMC's ability to make the best possible policy. Accountability [is provided] via the minutes [we publish for each meeting] since those not dissenting agree with the majority view and should be held accountable for the results. Separate statements giving details of individual positions would serve no useful purpose. Secondly, release of videotape, audiotape, or a literal transcript would have a chilling effect on the free flow of ideas and the ability to bring confidential information to the deliberations. Third, immediate release of the directive could threaten to roil markets unnecessarily, and concern about market reaction could reduce flexibility in decisionmaking, possibly deterring the FOMC from writing needed instructions to the Desk from time to time. Moreover, the decision can't be evaluated without the minutes, which take some time to prepare. (*Transcripts*, October 5, 1993, 1)

The chairman also brought up the issue of immediate release of the operating target, but indicated his resistance to doing this on the (usual) grounds of not wanting to complicate monetary policy through announcement effects (*Transcripts*, October 5, 1993, 3).

Although the committee eventually decided to adopt its current practice of releasing edited transcripts with the same five-year lag that had previously been applied to the *Memoranda*, it was not before considering a move that paralleled the 1976 decision to discontinue the *Memoranda*. During one of the committee's deliberations on the issue, St. Louis Fed president Thomas Melzer argued that the existence of the past transcripts could be separated from what the committee did in the future, leading him to recommend that the practice of keeping raw transcripts be discontinued from then on (*Transcripts*, October 15, 1993, 14–15). Kansas City Fed president Thomas Hoenig, seconded by Richmond Fed president Broaddus, contended that such a decision would not be well received by interested politicians and so was not likely to prove a viable option (*Transcripts*, October 15, 1993, 16). On this occasion, the cause of preserving information prevailed.

In February 1994, just a few months after the existence of the transcripts became public knowledge, the committee also abandoned its long-standing practice of not releasing its policy decisions immediately after its meetings. Greenspan anticipated that the committee's first policy move since September 1992—and its first tightening move since August 1989—was in the offing and wanted to find a way to make sure that there was widespread recognition among the public at large, not just among market professionals, of what the committee was doing. He likened the possible funds rate move in this case to a change in the discount rate and argued accordingly that this similarity justified an announcement:

The question I want to raise this evening before we close is one that has been tugging at me for the last number of weeks. This really gets to the issue that when we move in this particular context, which of course will be the first time we have moved since September 1992, we are going to have to make our action very visible. It's more the equivalent of a discount rate move than the incremental federal funds rate changes that we have been embarking on for quite a long period of time. I am particularly concerned that if we choose to move tomorrow, we make certain that there is no ambiguity about our move.... One of the things that we have argued, and I would continue to argue, is that there is a distinction between a discount rate and a federal funds rate action in the sense that we don't want an announcement effect ordinarily on the funds rate.... But a federal funds rate change in this particular instance is a discount rate change, as far as the Federal Reserve System is concerned. I'm very strongly inclined to make it clear that we are doing this but to find a way to do it that does not set a precedent. (*Transcripts*, February 2–3, 1994, 29)

Comments by Greenspan's colleagues were generally supportive. There was some concern that this would become a permanent feature of the committee's operations (as it eventually would), but there was a willingness to see what the reaction to an announcement would be.

At first, press releases were issued only when a policy change was made; now, the committee issues a statement after each of its meetings, regardless of whether it has changed its policy stance. Contrary to members' long-held views, evidence suggests that this greater openness has actually improved market reactions to monetary policy decisions (Poole and Rasche 2003).

Moreover, since March 2002, the recorded vote on the monetary policy directive has been included in the FOMC statement released after each committee meeting—another departure from traditional practice. When dissenting votes are cast, reasons for dissent are given, so the positions of those specific individuals are identified. Eventually, it should be possible to study how this new procedure affects committee members' tendencies to cast dissenting votes.

## 9.4   Conclusions

Our exploration of the written records of FOMC meetings from the Burns and Greenspan eras illustrates how a multitude of political forces have shaped monetary policy. At times, the Fed has clearly been sensitive to its political environment. For example, there is little doubt that monetary policy was politicized in the period preceding Nixon's 1972 reelection, even if the motive was bureaucratic self-interest rather than a direct attempt to support the incumbent. FOMC discussions have frequently referred to the concerns of its political principals, including the president, Congress, and the public. Acknowledgments of the existence of political pressures are relatively infrequent, however, and, as often as not, are followed by assertions that such pressures should be resisted.

The Fed has also been concerned with limiting and protecting information. Limiting information sometimes reflected a sincere concern that markets would not absorb complete information in a rational and efficient way. At other times, it appeared to be a device for protecting bureaucratic autonomy. In recent years, the FOMC has adopted more open practices that appear to have contributed positively to the market's understanding of the committee's policy actions.

# 10      Time Inconsistency and the Great Inflation: Evidence from the *Memoranda* and the *Transcripts*

In the preceding chapters, we have examined FOMC policymaking during the Burns and Greenspan eras in detail.[1] Our analysis provided descriptions of policy preferences of individual committee members and investigated aspects of the aggregation of those preferences to produce collective choices. In many ways, the FOMC's institutional and economic surroundings were similar across the Burns and Greenspan years, and our analyses have reflected this. Yet an important difference has so far received little attention.

Economic outcomes were fundamentally different for the two periods. The Burns years were noteworthy for an unprecedented peacetime inflation that developed and worsened throughout the 1970s, a period that many observers now refer to as the Great Inflation. That inflation was accompanied by a severe business cycle contraction in the middle of the decade as well as persistently high unemployment rates. In contrast, inflation steadily declined under Greenspan's tenure, economic growth was robust, and unemployment trended downward.

A complete analysis of the events and policies that might account for these differences is clearly beyond the scope of this book. We nevertheless believe that evidence from the *Memoranda* and the *Transcripts* sheds light on the circumstances that gave rise to the Great Inflation as well as its subsequent decline. Further, we will argue that the theory of the time inconsistency problem provides a useful framework for understanding the behavior of inflation over the last three decades.[2]

The time inconsistency problem has been invoked to explain an inflationary bias alleged to plague central banks (Barro and Gordon 1983). The assumptions behind the reasoning are as follows. First, the

---

1. The material presented in this chapter is based on Chappell and McGregor (2004).
2. Seminal contributions on the time inconsistency problem include Kydland and Prescott (1977) and Barro and Gordon (1983).

central bank is assumed to choose policy actions on a period-by-period basis at each of its meetings; it is not constrained by rules but instead uses discretion in each period. Second, public expectations of inflation for the upcoming period are viewed as given at the time of the meeting. Third, the economy can be characterized by an expectational Phillips curve; that is, if inflation is higher than the public expects, unemployment will temporarily fall below its natural rate. Fourth, the central bank values a marginal reduction of unemployment below its natural rate, but also dislikes high inflation. Finally, it is assumed that expectations are rational.

With predetermined inflation expectations, the central bank sees an opportunity to lower unemployment via surprise money growth at each of its meetings. If expected inflation were zero, for example, the reduction in unemployment created by a money growth surprise would be "worth" the modest increase in inflation. A problem arises when public expectations are rational, however. The public, understanding the central bank's objectives, will correctly anticipate monetary stimulus, rendering the effort to reduce unemployment ineffective. Instead, the result is inflation. At the equilibrium level of inflation, the marginal output gains from unemployment reduction are balanced by the added costs of additional inflation in the current period. This is suboptimal in comparison to a zero inflation outcome, but the latter is not an equilibrium in the absence of credible precommitment.

Alan Blinder (1997, 14), a former governor of the Federal Reserve, has argued that the time inconsistency literature is largely irrelevant to present-day monetary policymaking: "Well, I can assure you that my central banker friends would not be surprised to learn that academic theories that assume that they seek to push unemployment below the natural rate then deduce that monetary policy will be too inflationary. They would doubtless reply, 'Of course. That's why we don't do it.'" Blinder goes on to say that the appropriate solution—to avoid trying to push unemployment below its natural rate—is adopted by practical central bankers "as if it were second nature" (ibid.). DeLong (1997, 265) observes that he has "found no sign in Federal Reserve deliberations in the 1970s that time-inconsistency issues—either that future central bankers would not carry out the policies to which earlier central bankers had tried to commit them, or that the private sector would fail to believe long-run commitments to a low-inflation policy—played any role in policy formation." Similarly, Mayer (1999, 8) concludes, "All in all, it would be hard to write a reasonable history of Fed policy in which time inconsistency plays a major role."

Persson and Tabellini (2000), however, argue that these criticisms miss the point, since time inconsistency analysis does not predict that the Fed would want to generate policy surprises in equilibrium. Rather, in an inflationary equilibrium, the Fed's lack of credibility would cause a more restrictive policy to produce a recession. As a consequence, the Fed would refrain from pursuing a disinflationary policy. Some empirical evidence also supports the relevance of the time inconsistency theory of monetary policy. Ireland (1999) notes that the Barro-Gordon model predicts a positive association between the natural rate of unemployment and the equilibrium inflation rate; econometric results that build on this observation "can successfully explain inflation's initial rise and subsequent fall over the past four decades" (Ireland 1999, 283).

In this chapter, we use evidence from the *Memoranda* and the *Transcripts* to argue that time inconsistency analysis does help us understand why the Fed adopted an excessively expansionary policy stance during Burns's tenure as Fed chairman. As in chapter 9, the methodological approach is anecdotal rather than analytical. As we read the transcripts of FOMC deliberations to code the data sets described in chapter 5, our intention was not to select items that would support an argument in favor of time inconsistency theory. Rather, the relevance of that theory emerged as we read the documents, and this chapter represents our attempt to organize the anecdotal evidence in a manner that reflects the logic of the theory.

Our discussion will proceed as follows. In the first section, we sketch out the basic time inconsistency model of monetary policy and highlight the features of the analysis that we will subsequently document. In the second section, we consider the individual elements of the time inconsistency story. We first examine external pressures on the FOMC to make the case that real economic activity was generally viewed as unsatisfactory during the Burns years. We then explore the committee's views on the prevailing inflation-unemployment trade-off, the short-term nature of its policy actions, and the role of expectations in equilibrium. In the third section, we tie together the various threads of our analysis to construct an explanation of why inflation arose during the 1970s and not before, and in the fourth section we discuss alternative explanations of the 1970s inflation. In the fifth section, we consider the relevance of time inconsistency theory to the Greenspan years. We then offer some concluding remarks in the sixth section, where we also question whether the current FOMC is likely to be immune to a recurrence of high inflation.

## 10.1   The Basic Time Inconsistency Model of Monetary Policy

Following the approach of Barro and Gordon (1983), assume that
the economy is characterized by an expectations-augmented Phillips
curve:

$$u_t = u_t^n - \alpha(\pi_t - \pi_t^e), \ \alpha > 0, \tag{10.1}$$

where $u_t$ is the actual rate of unemployment, $u_t^n$ is the natural rate of
unemployment, $\pi_t$ is the actual inflation rate, and $\pi_t^e$ is the expected inflation rate. Further, the natural rate of unemployment is stochastic
and determined in accordance with

$$u_t^n = \lambda \bar{u}^n + (1 - \lambda)u_{t-1}^n + \varepsilon_t, \ 0 < \lambda < 1, \tag{10.2}$$

where $\bar{u}^n$ is the constant long-run mean of the natural rate of unemployment, and $\varepsilon_t$ is a white noise disturbance. Equation (10.2) implies
that unemployment is subject to shocks that are persistent but not permanent. Further assume that the monetary authority directly controls
the inflation rate, its policy instrument. The monetary authority must
choose $\pi_t$ before observing $\varepsilon_t$, and it makes this choice to minimize the
expected value of its quadratic loss function:

$$L_t = (u_t - ku_t^n)^2 + \beta(\pi_t)^2, \ \beta > 0, \ 0 < k < 1. \tag{10.3}$$

In equation (10.3), $ku_t^n$ represents a target value for unemployment.
Because $k < 1$, the target for unemployment is always below the prevailing natural rate. The parameter $\beta$ indicates the degree of inflation
aversion.[3]

   If the monetary authority could credibly commit to a particular inflation rate and if private agents recognized this commitment, then $\pi_t^e$
would equal $\pi_t$, and equation (10.1) would imply that unemployment
would be equal to its natural rate in each period. Further, because
$u_t$ would equal $u_t^n$ regardless of the rate of inflation, optimal policy
would call for zero inflation.

---

3. In the original Barro-Gordon analysis, the monetary authority's loss function was
assumed to be identical to that of society as a whole, but the model does not require this
strong assumption. In our formulation, it is sufficient to require that the target rate of unemployment be less than the natural rate. Later contributions to the literature have noted
that politicians might appoint conservative central bankers with the express purpose of
reducing the inflationary bias produced by the time inconsistency problem (Rogoff 1985).
Cukierman (2000) has shown that if there is uncertainty about the future state of the
economy and if upward deviations of unemployment from the natural rate are penalized
more heavily than downward deviations, then the inflation bias result holds even if the
unemployment target coincides with the natural rate.

Under period-by-period discretion, however, the situation will be different. In this case, the following sequence is played out in each period: (1) private agents form rational expectations of inflation for period $t$, so that $\pi_t^e = E_{t-1}\pi_t$; (2) the monetary authority chooses the actual rate of inflation, $\pi_t$; and (3) unemployment is determined via the Phillips curve given $\pi_t$, $\pi_t^e$, and the realization of the disturbance, $\varepsilon_t$. In step (2), the monetary authority chooses $\pi_t$ by minimizing $E_{t-1}L_t$ subject to equations (10.1) and (10.2), treating expected inflation as given. Moreover, because rational private agents understand the monetary authority's decision problem and have the same information, they correctly anticipate the chosen inflation rate, so that $\pi_t = \pi_t^e$. The first-order condition for this minimization problem, together with the assumption of rational expectations, requires that $\pi_t$ be set in accordance with

$$\pi_t = \frac{\alpha}{\beta}(1 - k)E_{t-1}u_t^n, \tag{10.4}$$

where $E_{t-1}u_t^n = \lambda\bar{u}^n + (1 - \lambda)u_{t-1}^n$. Since $\pi_t = \pi_t^e$, equation (10.1) also implies that $u_t = u_t^n$ in each period, but now the inflation rate is greater than zero. Under discretion, therefore, policymakers cannot credibly commit to a policy of zero inflation.

Equation (10.4) indicates that the inflation rate varies (1) positively with the slope of the short-run Phillips curve, $\alpha$; (2) positively with the gap between the unemployment target and its natural rate;[4] and (3) inversely with the monetary authority's disutility of inflation parameter, $\beta$. In addition, the model predicts that inflation will be higher when there are adverse supply shocks (that is, when the expected natural rate of unemployment is higher). Finally, the model implies that if the monetary authority were to deviate from equilibrium by choosing a lower inflation rate ($\pi_t < \pi_t^e$), then unemployment would exceed its natural rate; in the absence of credible commitment, pursuing a disinflationary policy would cause a recession.

## 10.2    The Case for Time Inconsistency

In this section, we draw on the *Memoranda* and the *Transcripts* to document point-by-point key elements of the time inconsistency story of the 1970s inflation. We discuss (1) political and public preferences about economic performance, (2) the short- and long-run Phillips curve

---

4. A smaller value of $k$ implies a larger gap between the unemployment target and its natural rate.

trade-offs, (3) the period-by-period nature of FOMC policymaking, and (4) the role of expectations in equilibrium.

### 10.2.1 Political and Public Preferences about Economic Performance

In chapter 9, we noted that the textual record contains no evidence that the FOMC followed the dictates of any outside authority during the 1970s. We also documented, however, the committee's awareness of the views of the president, Congress, and the public. During the 1970s, the message the Fed received consistently from its external clients was that economic growth was too slow and unemployment too high. In November 1970, for example, Governor William Sherrill cited public attitudes in advocating a more expansionary policy: "If the staff's projections for 1971 were realized the nation would be paying a price, in terms of unemployment and underutilization of other resources, that was disproportionately high relative to the benefits that would be gained in the form of slower price advances. *For the battle against inflation to take that form would, in his [Sherrill's] view, be unacceptable to the country*" (*Memorandum*, November 17, 1970, 1028, emphasis added).

Later, in February 1974, the committee again discussed acceptable inflation-unemployment trade-offs. In response to a comment by New York Fed president Alfred Hayes that an unemployment rate of 5.75 percent, as projected for the second quarter of that year, was not sufficient to justify a decisive move toward ease, Governor Jeffrey Bucher responded that it was also important to consider the trade-off that Congress might consider appropriate: "Although many people now regarded a rate of unemployment in excess of 4 percent as acceptable, he [Bucher] was not convinced that Congress as a whole was prepared to accept a rate as high as 5 per cent; certainly, it would not find a 6 per cent rate acceptable" (*Memorandum*, February 20, 1974, 191). A year later, Boston Fed president Frank Morris argued that annual real growth as high as 5.00 percent was still inadequate as the economy moved into a recovery phase: "Mr. Morris observed that in his view acceptance of the staff projection led to the conclusion that the policy course being pursued by the Committee could not be defended before the Congress or the American people. *Growth in real GNP of 5 per cent over the four quarters to the second quarter of next year, as projected, was not acceptable, and that slow a recovery could not be justified in the interest of dampening inflationary pressures*" (*Memorandum*, May 20, 1975, 596, emphasis added).

In sum, the FOMC's view during the Burns years was that output and unemployment had never reached politically acceptable levels. In terms of our model, while inflation was seen as undesirable ($\beta > 0$), political pressures caused the Fed to value unemployment below its natural rate ($k < 1$).

### 10.2.2 Phillips Curve Trade-offs

The observed inflation-unemployment trade-off, or Phillips curve, had been relatively stable during the 1950s and 1960s, leading some to believe that lower unemployment could be achieved, perhaps permanently, if society was willing to tolerate a moderately higher rate of inflation. By the late 1960s, though, the Friedman-Phelps natural rate hypothesis had questioned the likelihood of a permanent trade-off between inflation and unemployment. Friedman (1968) and Phelps (1968) argued that in the long run, any attempt to exploit the Phillips curve trade-off would lead to higher inflation but no permanent reduction in unemployment (that is, unemployment would tend toward its natural rate in the long run). Their formulation underlies the Phillips curve of our model (equation [10.1]).

Although the record of FOMC deliberations does not show that members accepted the Friedman-Phelps vertical long-run Phillips curve, it is clear that they appreciated two of its key features. First, the trade-off between output and inflation was more favorable in the short run than in the long run. Second, inflationary expectations had an important effect on the outcomes that were feasible at a moment in time.

On the first point, consider Morris's remarks in July 1976:

I'd like to go back to [the] comment I wanted to make earlier on the usefulness of these alternative monetary [policy] formulations. ... [W]henever you ask an economic model to give you the economic effects of the more expansionary policy over a fairly short period of time, you're up against the fact that the lags in the impact of monetary policy are much shorter on production than they are on prices and I think every sheet of this kind that I have seen in the past eight years around this table suggested that a more expansionary policy would produce benefits in greater real growth and very little price effects and I think that reflects the fact that the time horizon for this kind of exercise has got to be longer to be useful to the Committee. (*Transcripts*, "Longer-Run Targets," July 20, 1976, tape 1, 6–7)

On the second point, the role of expectational inertia in sustaining inflation was clearly recognized as a complicating factor when committee members considered efforts to slow the rate of price advances.

In December 1970, Kansas City Fed president George Clay stated that "the current inflationary episode had proceeded so far and had become so involved in the wage-cost structure that there was serious doubt that the inflation could be curbed by any feasible monetary-fiscal policy mix.... Moreover, it had been and continued to be necessary for public economic policy to provide some stimulus to the economy" (*Memorandum*, December 15, 1970, 1125). Governor Charles Partee best stated the committee's view, saying, "We certainly know that there's a built-in inflation rate of some considerable size resulting from the cost increases and the labor contracts [that] *have been negotiated and will pay off regardless* in this period to come" (*Transcripts*, February 28, 1978, tape 4, 10, emphasis added). Both of these comments not only illustrate recognition of the role of expectations in shifting the available Phillips curve trade-off but also make it clear that these expectations were essentially regarded as predetermined at the time of a meeting. It was common for committee members to speak of the inflationary inertia as a cost-push phenomenon, emphasizing its exogeneity (as well as their lack of culpability) when advocating more stimulus.

Some committee members explicitly adopted the view that the long-run Phillips curve might be vertical or nearly so. As early as May 1971, for example, St. Louis Fed president Darryl Francis noted that money growth and unemployment seemed to be unrelated over several extended episodes in the two previous decades:

In each case, Mr. Francis continued, the rate of growth in money was accelerated in order to overcome weakness in the economy. Despite those progressively more stimulative monetary actions, the rate of unemployment had averaged about the same whether the trend growth of money was 6 per cent, 3.5 per cent, or 1.5 per cent. The trend growth had had its chief impact on prices, whereas fluctuations around the trend had had the greatest impact on production and employment. (*Memorandum*, May 11, 1971, 476)

A month later, his comments again described the vertical long-run Phillips curve:

Mr. Francis said that such a slower growth in money would probably mean a less rapid recovery of production and employment, but one which was more likely to be sustained. Production and employment had risen at relatively rapid rates from 1962 to 1964 with a moderate 3.4 per cent average annual rate of growth of money. One might also observe that average unemployment since early 1967, when the growth rate of money had averaged more than 6 per cent, had been about the same as in the 1953–62 period when money had grown at an average 1.7 per cent rate. Production and employment benefits gained by accelerating money upward from a previous trend had always been temporary. (*Memorandum*, June 8, 1971, 590–591)

In chapter 6, we noted that representatives of the St. Louis Fed have traditionally represented a monetarist perspective that was distinctly different from the mainstream committee view. Nevertheless, the central point that long- and short-run Phillips curves offered different trade-offs seems to have been widely appreciated.

In sum, the FOMC recognized Phillips curve constraints much like those assumed by time inconsistency theory. In the short run, the costs (in terms of output and employment) of reducing inflation seemed high. In the long run, ingrained inflationary expectations permitted high inflation and high unemployment to coexist. Furthermore, from the committee's perspective, expectations-induced cost increases appeared to be exogenous at any single policy meeting. Therefore, even though the equilibrium inflation rate was high, the actions of reasonable policymakers sustained it.

### 10.2.3   Period-by-Period Policymaking

During the 1970s, FOMC members clearly perceived an unhealthy tension between their focus on policies to be selected for the next period and the longer-run consequences of those policies. As noted in the preceding section, Morris once complained that the policy alternatives presented to the committee were based on a time horizon that was too short—a longer planning horizon was needed to show the eventual inflationary effect of a more stimulative policy. Burns's response to Morris neatly summarized the committee's dilemma: "Let me just make a comment, [that] to do what we can in the way of longer run objectives, I think is salutary.... But we have to do something very specific today. Mainly to set monetary growth ranges for the next 12 months for the interval between the second quarter of this year and the second quarter of next year" (*Transcripts*, "Longer-Run Targets," July 20, 1976, tape 1, 7). In other words, the long run may be important, but it is not relevant to the subject of the committee's decision to be made today.[5]

---

5. This point is also made by Lucas (1980, 208) in his assessment of rules versus discretion: "In the current system of discretionary economic management, no one or no small group ... is in a position to influence the economy in any significant way toward a regime of fixed, non-reactive policy rules. They are simply reacting, sometimes well, sometimes badly, to current difficulties, with no more capability of affecting policy five years hence than of affecting what happened five years before."

In October 1977, San Francisco Fed president John Balles commented that even hitting the twelve-month targets was problematic. He noted that "the Committee doesn't seem to have any systematic way of getting from here to there in terms of the two-month range versus the twelve-month range" (*Transcripts*, October 17, 1977, tape 8, 10). St. Louis Fed president Lawrence Roos summed up his experience on the committee in this fashion: "I liken what we have done in the last year sort of to the alcoholic who should do something but he takes a little drink this time and a little one [next time] and he's always going to do something down the road.... We've set ranges until we're blue in the face.... [W]e're just deluding ourselves if we think that we are really doing anything to correct the excessive growth of the money supply" (*Transcripts*, January 17, 1978, tape 6, 15–16). Correcting the excessive money growth might have risked a recession, though, and we have seen previously that political pressures and public opinion during the 1970s weighed against taking such risks. Thus, FOMC members may have been obliged to pursue short-term objectives even when they appreciated the risk for unpleasant longer-run consequences.

### 10.2.4   Expectations and Equilibrium

The time inconsistency model is closed with an assumption of rational expectations. Although the committee never seriously discussed the rational expectations hypothesis during the Burns era, it would be safe to assume that it was not a highly regarded notion. Despite this, it is useful as an assumption to make about *equilibrium*—in equilibrium, expectations about both inflation and policymaker actions should become correct. Furthermore, the strict rational expectations assumption is not essential for the key result regarding an inflationary bias. Nordhaus's 1975 article on political business cycles also included an analysis of inflation that used a framework similar to that of Barro and Gordon (1983), but with adaptive rather than rational expectations assumed.[6]

FOMC members tended to view the public's expectations as largely inertial, but they also felt that financial markets irrationally overreacted to perceived policy changes.[7] Because of this, the committee was sensitive to how its policy decisions might be interpreted. At times, they

---

6. In the Nordhaus model, adaptively formed inflation expectations converge to the equilibrium inflation rate in the long run.

7. In chapter 9, in an extended discussion of the FOMC's views about revelation of information, we documented that many members were skeptical of markets' abilities to absorb information efficiently.

hoped to influence how expectations would change as their policy actions were revealed. In October 1974, for example, as the economy drifted into recession, the committee's directive called for continued reductions in the federal funds rate. At the meeting, several members expressly argued that the easing should be carried out in a subtle fashion that would minimize changes in expectations. Dallas Fed president Philip Coldwell supported the easing, but opposed a discount rate change, noting that "in continuation of the gradual approach ... the System should not take any *overt* actions to ease at this time" (*Memorandum*, October 14–15, 1974, 1133, emphasis added). Burns maintained that "any easing should be undertaken very cautiously" (*Memorandum*, October 14–15, 1974, 1124). Atlanta Fed president Monroe Kimbrel "hoped that the System would not give the impression that it had abandoned its role in fighting inflation" (*Memorandum*, October 14–15, 1974, 1136), while New York Fed president Hayes added that "[i]t was of crucial importance that the system not undermine the belief that it meant business about combating inflation" (*Memorandum*, October 14–15, 1974, 1127–1128).

While these remarks may reflect a sincere desire to avoid "irrational overreactions," it is also apparent that the committee realized that the benefits from monetary stimulus would be stronger if the stimulus could be implemented without aggravating inflation expectations. Such motives are consistent with those attributed to policymakers in time inconsistency theory, even if the rational expectations assumption ultimately renders them futile.

## 10.3   The Time Inconsistency Explanation of Inflation

Thus far, we have argued that the Burns era FOMC faced an environment that conforms to the theoretical setting for the time inconsistency problem and that the inflation of that era is compatible with its predicted equilibrium. Specifically, we have argued that FOMC documents show that policymakers desired unemployment lower than the natural rate, that they perceived an economy that could be characterized by an expectational Phillips curve, and that policy choices were made on a period-by-period basis without credible precommitment. Further, the FOMC believed that price expectations were essentially predetermined at the time of a policy meeting, but also knew that these expectations contributed to inflationary momentum over longer horizons. These are key ingredients in the theory of the time inconsistency problem. We have also noted that members occasionally voiced frustration with their inability to escape what appeared to be a suboptimal inflationary outcome.

An obvious question arises, however: Why was inflation high during the Burns years compared to other periods? Mayer (1999, 8) contends that if the time inconsistency problem is to provide a convincing explanation for the Great Inflation, one must claim that the assumptions of the theory fit that period more closely than other periods. As in many economic models, predictions of time inconsistency theory can be interpreted as comparative static results. The equilibrium inflation rate depends on the parameters of the model, and when those parameters change, the model predicts changes in inflation as well. Mayer's observation that inflation was higher during the Burns years than other times is not a refutation of the theory; rather, it requires us to ask if there is a comparative static interpretation of the emergence of inflation that is consistent with the model's predictions. In this section, we argue that this is the case.

Recall equation (10.4), which provides the equilibrium inflation rate in our model:

$$\pi_t = \frac{\alpha}{\beta}(1 - k)E_{t-1}u_t^n. \tag{10.4}$$

According to (10.4), the economy's equilibrium inflation rate depends on the short-run Phillips curve trade-off (parameter $\alpha$), the monetary authority's aversion to inflation versus output (parameter $\beta$), the gap between target and natural rates of unemployment (determined by the parameter $k$), and the expected value of the natural rate of unemployment. In our view, it is plausible that changes in parameters and the natural rate of unemployment led to higher equilibrium inflation rates in the 1970s.

First, consider the preferences of policymakers. Nixon blamed his 1960 presidential election loss on a stagnating economy and was determined that there should be no repetition in 1972.[8] One reason he imposed wage and price controls in 1971 was so that he could fight

---

8. In a 1962 book, Nixon described his view of the principal factors that cost him the 1960 election as well as the importance of a sound economy at election time. In 1954 and 1958, economic slumps that bottomed out in October had, from Nixon's perspective, cost Republicans dearly in those midterm elections. Similarly, an increase of 452,000 in the jobless rolls in October 1960 seemed to Nixon to have been decisive: "All the speeches, television broadcasts, and precinct work in the world could not counteract that one hard fact" (1962, 310–311).

inflation without imposing monetary or fiscal restraint that might lead to recession. This policy, along with Nixon's decision to name Burns as chairman of the Committee on Interest and Dividends, effectively obliged the FOMC to pursue an accommodative policy or risk losing control of its principal policy instrument.[9] Nixon's obsession with ensuring rapid output growth and high employment in 1972, when he would be facing reelection, led him to take extraordinary actions that amounted to imposing altered preferences on the Fed. These preference changes plausibly took the form of a lower value for $k$, which would imply a lower unemployment rate target, and a lower value for $\beta$, the relative concern for inflation versus output. Either of these shifts would lead to a prediction of higher equilibrium inflation.

While a politically induced change of preferences seems plausible in this case, using preference changes to explain varying outcomes is often a last resort for economists. Because preferences are not directly observed, explanations based on preference changes are difficult to refute, even when incorrect. We therefore turn to a second comparative static argument, this one based on supply shocks ($\varepsilon_t$) that result in persistent shifts in the natural rate of unemployment.

Our premise is that the natural rate of unemployment rose during the 1970s. Economists are largely in agreement with this assessment. For example, Gordon (1981) estimated that the natural rate of unemployment rose from 4.7 to 5.4 percent from the mid-1960s to the mid-1970s. Evidence from committee deliberations suggests that members recognized that such changes had occurred. For instance, in July 1977, Chicago Fed president Robert Mayo observed, "Even the goal of 6 percent unemployment seems difficult to attain these days" (*Transcripts*, July 19, 1977, tape B, 4). Later in the same meeting, this issue came up again, along with a reference to what the politicians might find acceptable (*Transcripts*, July 19, 1977, tape B, 8–9):

[Staff economist Steven] *Zeisel:* I think in terms of our reference toward unemployment, I think one has to, as you know, recognize structural changes that have tended to occur in the labor market [that have] tended to bias up the unemployment rate and in addition we've just been through a period of enormous growth in the labor force which was very largely made up of women who tend to have high frictional rates of unemployment. I think the $6\frac{1}{4}$ per cent rate, really, for comparison with past periods, has to be adjusted down somewhat.

---

9. For additional discussion of Nixon's strategies, see Woolley (1984) and chapter 9 of this book.

[Governor Charles] *Partee:* You mean $6\frac{1}{4}$ might be a pretty good rate of unemployment?
*Zeisel:* Well $6\frac{1}{4}$ by capacity, yes.
*Partee:* Although I haven't heard anything here in the city that would suggest acceptance of that.

This exchange reveals that the FOMC had recognized an exogenous upward shift in the natural rate of unemployment, which, according to our model, leads to higher inflation.[10] The exchange also confirms our earlier suggestion that the gap between the natural rate and the politically determined target may have widened. A wider gap (smaller $k$) between natural and target rates of unemployment also leads to a prediction that equilibrium inflation should rise. Thus, the rise of inflation during the Burns era appears to be compatible with the comparative static implications of time inconsistency theory. Further, the subsequent fall of inflation in the 1980s could reflect a moderation of political preferences and a reversal of demographic trends affecting natural rates. The Volcker disinflation occurred after the election of Ronald Reagan, who, at least initially, appeared to be more inflation averse than his predecessors. In addition, Gordon (1997) estimates that the natural rate of unemployment declined from around 6.5 percent during the early 1980s to about 5.6 percent by 1996. Time inconsistency theory predicts that this would lower the equilibrium inflation rate.

### 10.4   Alternative Explanations for the Great Inflation

We have argued that contemporaneous accounts of FOMC policy discussions support the view that time inconsistency theory provides a plausible explanation for the emergence of inflation during the Burns era. In this section, we will briefly explore two competing explanations. The first of these emphasizes the importance of mistakes and misperceptions; the second stresses the role of exogenous shocks to food and energy prices.

Mayer (1999) notes that forecasting errors may have led to policy mistakes and subsequent inflation during the 1970s. He argues that the Burns era FOMC consistently underpredicted the inflation rate and overpredicted the unemployment rate, leading it to advocate more

---

10. Later in the same year, on September 20, the committee talked at length about the full-employment unemployment rate. In particular, there was some discussion of a *Wall Street Journal* article by Herbert Stein, in which Stein had suggested that the full-employment unemployment rate might be as high as 7.0 percent.

expansionary policies than it otherwise would have. Similarly, Orphanides (2002, 7) finds that policy choices in the 1970s "were consistent with application of a 'modern' systematic, activist, forward-looking approach to policy." Those policies produced poor outcomes because of policymaker misperceptions, specifically misperceptions about the natural rate of unemployment. Given these findings, we cannot dismiss the possibility that policy mistakes played a role in the increase in inflation in the 1970s. However, we can offer two arguments against the "mistakes" hypothesis.

First, while forecasts and perceptions could not always be perfectly accurate, FOMC records also make it clear that the committee realized that its actions risked exacerbating, or at least sustaining, inflation. As the discussion in the preceding section revealed, by 1977 the staff was suggesting that 6.25 percent was a "pretty good rate of unemployment," even if it was a rate that committee members thought was politically unacceptable. Members viewed the trade-offs that they confronted as unpalatable choices, but they frequently chose to favor short-run output concerns over longer-term inflation consequences. Second, if mistakes were made, their consequences were eventually revealed. If the rise of inflation was a consequence of mistakes, why were the mistakes not corrected more quickly when inflation was observed? The fact that the committee persistently kept the federal funds rate low in the face of repeated money growth overshoots and high inflation rates suggests that the committee could not bring itself to endure the consequences of producing lower inflation. Explanations relying on mistakes to account for such large and persistent accelerations of inflation are, at best, incomplete.

The second alternative explanation for the emergence of inflation during the 1970s stresses exogenous shocks to food and energy prices. Conventional wisdom attributes much of the period's inflation to supply shocks, and there is little doubt that such shocks complicated the FOMC's policymaking task. Supply shocks do not necessarily produce persistent inflations, however. Consider the comments of current Federal Reserve governor Ben Bernanke (2003a), who argues against a significant role for oil prices in the emergence of the Great Inflation:

My reading of the evidence suggests that the role the conventional wisdom has attributed to oil price increases in the stagflation of the 1970s has been overstated, for two reasons. First, the large increases in oil prices that occurred in this period would not have been possible in an environment that was not already highly inflationary because of previous monetary expansion. . . .

Second, without Fed accommodation, higher oil prices abroad would not have translated into domestic inflation to any significant degree.

In the FOMC's meeting in August 1975, oil prices and inflation were discussed at some length. In his introductory briefing, Fed staff economist Lyle Gramley suggested that the committee should accommodate exogenously higher food and energy prices with more rapid money growth, even though real output growth was expected to be robust: "Price increases of these dimensions, coming at a time of a rebound of real GNP growth to the 7 to 8 percent range, would ... put inordinate strains on financial markets if growth rates of the monetary aggregates were held to the midpoints of the current target ranges. Our GNP projection assumes, therefore, that growth rates of the major aggregates would be permitted to drift toward the upper end of the current ranges" (*Memorandum*, August 19, 1975, 923). Later in the meeting, Gramley argued that because other prices were downwardly rigid, accommodation of the food and energy price increases was necessary to maintain real growth:

Given the demand and supply conditions for [foods and energy], an adjustment in relative prices had to take place, and because of the downward inflexibility of most prices, it was just about impossible to get the adjustment in relative prices without a rise in the general level of prices. Thus, if policy did not accommodate the price increases for foods and energy by permitting a higher rate of monetary expansion, the rate of growth in real GNP would be reduced. (*Memorandum*, August 19, 1975, 933)

Philadelphia Fed president David Eastburn objected to Gramley's view, arguing that it was difficult to distinguish exogenous and endogenous price changes:

Mr. Eastburn commented that he was concerned by the distinction that had been made between exogenous and endogenous price movements and, specifically by the notion that the increases in prices of foods and fuels were exogenous and had to be accommodated. He had difficulty in distinguishing between the effects of those increases and the increases in steel, aluminum, and autos, and he felt that an accommodative posture too easily could lead to acceptance of inflation. (*Memorandum*, August 19, 1975, 933)

Burns then reinforced Eastburn's response: "Price increases were always occurring because of factors that might be classified as exogenous, and if policy always accommodated such increases, it would be validating a never-ending inflationary trend" (*Memorandum*, August

19, 1975, 934). In this exchange, Burns and Eastburn clearly anticipated Bernanke's point that a supply shock requires monetary accommodation to produce inflation. Despite the anti-inflation rhetoric expressed during this meeting, Burns and the FOMC ultimately chose to leave the funds rate target unchanged, effectively adopting a policy of accommodation.

This discussion suggests that supply shocks were relevant to the inflationary process, but in a way that is compatible with the theory of the time inconsistency problem. If the FOMC had consistently followed a Friedman-type constant money growth rule during the 1970s, inflation would not have accelerated as it did. The time inconsistency theory, however, implies that unfavorable shocks to natural rates *will* affect monetary policy and the equilibrium rate of inflation. When the equilibrium inflation rate rises, inflation expectations rise as well. Changing expectations, in turn, are reflected in wages and prices, and policymakers see what they perceive to be a cost-push phenomenon. In the midst of this cost-push inflation, policymakers recognize that failure to accommodate will precipitate recession. As a result, they choose to "ratify" the higher equilibrium inflation rate, as they apparently did in August 1975. It is precisely this comparative static result that lies at the heart of both Ireland's (1999) econometric support for time inconsistency theory and our argument in section 10.3.

## 10.5  Time Inconsistency Theory and the Greenspan Years

In this section, we will reconsider the time inconsistency theory in light of the experience of the Greenspan years. We will argue that, despite the improvement in macroeconomic performance, and despite claims that central bankers have learned from past mistakes, the time inconsistency theory still has relevance. Our argument proceeds in three steps. First, we note that the economy benefited from favorable supply shocks during the Greenspan era. As our earlier discussion indicates, this does produce a less inflationary time consistent equilibrium. Second, FOMC members still exhibited a willingness to risk higher inflation, just as they had during the Burns era; during the Greenspan years, the gambles had more favorable outcomes. Third, as in the Burns years, we find that political pressures, attractive short-run trade-offs, and discretionary policymaking continued to characterize the policymaking equilibrium.

### 10.5.1   Favorable Supply Shocks

The favorable supply shocks that occurred in the 1990s have been widely recognized. In 1995, Greenspan himself noted that "breaking the back of the inflationary surge last year and early this year was a lot easier in retrospect than it should have been" (*Transcripts*, December 19, 1995, 38). He had previously observed that the absence of inflationary pressure was a result of technological change that produced "a very significant increase in the sense of job insecurity" and an associated "trade-off between job insecurity and wage increases" (*Transcripts*, December 19, 1995, 36). Essentially, technological changes left workers unsure of their job security, and this made them less inclined to demand inflationary wage increases. He went on to argue that technological changes reduced inflation prospects in other ways:

> I think the accelerated capital turnover and the advancing technology are having, in addition to the labor market effect, a fairly pronounced impact on costs for different reasons. Basically, the downsizing of products as a consequence of computer chip technologies has created, as you are all aware, a significant decline in implicit transportation costs. We are producing very small products that are cheaper to move.... More importantly—and this is really a relatively recent phenomenon—is the dramatic effect of telecommunications technology in reducing the cost of communications....
> ... What we are now seeing is a tremendous move toward the proliferation of outsourcing, not only in the immediate area but ever increasingly around the globe. What one would expect to see as this occurs—and indeed it is happening—is the combination of rising capital efficiency and falling nominal unit labor costs. In fact, that is happening by every measure we can look at. (*Transcripts*, December 19, 1995, 36–37)

Greenspan acknowledged that the phenomenon he was describing was "the statistical equivalent of a falling NAIRU" (*Transcripts*, December 19, 1995, 39), or in the context of our Phillips curve equation (10.2), a fortuitous deflationary supply shock. Greenspan went on to emphasize that if what he was arguing was correct, the committee was "looking at a significantly different set of inflation pressures in the world economy" (*Transcripts*, December 19, 1995, 39).

### 10.5.2   Gambling on Inflation

Not all of Greenspan's colleagues were convinced that an altered economic structure would permit a continuation of rapid noninflationary growth. In September 1996, for example, San Francisco Fed president Robert Parry contended that the committee needed to be sure that its federal funds rate target was in line with the higher equilibrium real interest rate that was justified by stronger investment demand (*Transcripts*, September 24, 1996, 33). Later in the same meeting, Governors Laurence Meyer and Janet Yellen reinforced Parry's point. Meyer stated, "I believe that increases in utilization rates should in general be followed by increases in short-term interest rates. That is, procyclicality in short-term interest rates is one of the most important rules of prudent monetary policy" (*Transcripts*, September 24, 1996, 37). Yellen said that "a very solid case can also be made for raising the federal funds rate at least modestly ... on the grounds that the unemployment rate has notched down further, the decline in labor market slack is palpable, and the odds of a rise in the inflation rate have increased" (*Transcripts*, September 24, 1996, 39). Interestingly, though, at that September 1996 meeting, both Meyer and Yellen decided that there were enough uncertainties in the outlook to justify supporting Greenspan's proposal for no change in policy in the formal vote (Parry was not in the voting rotation).

While the arguments of Meyer and Yellen demonstrate a concern for inflation, they also illustrate another phenomenon. Despite an acknowledged risk of inflation, these members were willing to risk higher inflation to sustain the prevailing expansion. Even Greenspan recognized that this was implicit in his recommendation: "Having said all that, I fully acknowledge that we have a very tight labor market situation at this stage. I think identifying the current situation as an inflationary zone, as some have argued, is a proper judgment at this point. But it is a zone, not a breakthrough, and I would therefore conclude and hope, as I did last time, that we can stay at [policy alternative] 'B,' no change" (*Transcripts*, September 24, 1996, 31). In hindsight, Greenspan's recommendation seems to have been the correct one. When Burns era policymakers had chosen to take similar risks, however, the outcomes had been less favorable.

### 10.5.3  The Time Consistent Equilibrium

Under Greenspan, the FOMC continues to operate in a discretionary environment, choosing funds rate targets on a meeting-by-meeting basis, without rule-based restrictions or long-run constraints. Political pressures continue to exert their force in the direction of ease. As Greenspan once noted, "Our existence and ability to function ... are subject to acceptance by a public and a Congress who exhibit decidedly asymmetric propensities in favor of policy ease" (*Transcripts*, July 2–3, 1996, 82).

In 1993, Governor Wayne Angell described his concerns about FOMC choice procedures in a way that almost offers a textbook illustration of the time inconsistency problem:

> Mr. Chairman, I agree with your prescription. I am very tempted, of course, to believe that we may be falling behind in regard to maintaining price level targeting by targeting the fed funds rate at 3 percent.... Certainly, there's difficulty in targeting the fed funds rate.... Also, targeting nominal GDP poses real political dangers for us because it's just so difficult to go before the Congress and explain why we like $5\frac{1}{2}$ percent nominal GDP better than $6\frac{1}{2}$ percent when there's clearly a relationship between GDP and the unemployment rate. The unemployment rate at $6\frac{1}{2}$ percent GDP would be more desirable than the one at $5\frac{1}{2}$ percent.... I'm inclined to believe that we ought to be thinking about tightening at this stage. But I just don't have the stomach for doing it, Mr. Chairman; I lack the courage to be what I think would be seen as somewhat rash. And it was that prediction of lack of courage on my part and your part that caused me some meetings ago to suggest that at some point in time we might find ourselves with the need for a very large-scale move. (*Transcripts*, February 2–3, 1993, 55)

Angell's comments not only recognize the political pressure to exploit the short-run Phillips curve trade-off; they also explicitly acknowledge his rational foresight in recognizing unfortunate characteristics of the time consistent equilibrium.

## 10.6   Conclusions

We have used the texts of the *Memoranda* and the *Transcripts* to support an argument favoring time inconsistency theory as an explanation for the emergence of inflation during the 1970s. Our discussion documents the applicability of the assumptions of the theory and also finds that its comparative static predictions are consistent with the subsequent fall of inflation during the 1980s and 1990s.

Members of the Greenspan FOMC undoubtedly learned from the experience of the 1970s. They often acknowledged that Burns era policies had played a role in the inflation of that period, and they were wary of repeating that experience. Their remarks frequently indicate a heightened awareness of the importance of achieving and maintaining price stability.

Yet we have also argued that policymaking institutions continue to conform to the assumptions of time inconsistency theory. Policymaking is discretionary; a short-run trade-off between unemployment and inflation presumably exists; and political pressure usually favors monetary ease. The Greenspan years have been characterized by favorable supply shocks in the form of rapid productivity growth, and Greenspan himself has shown what seems to be an uncanny ability to make good policy choices. Less favorable shocks, similar to those that plagued the 1970s, could occur again, however, and Greenspan cannot permanently chair the FOMC. While Blinder (1997) may be correct when he claims that the time inconsistency problem is no longer relevant, there is a less sanguine possibility. In the Greenspan era, the time consistent equilibrium has been more pleasant than the one prevailing during the 1970s, not just because the Fed is more enlightened, but also because of a fortunate confluence of exogenous economic and political forces.

# 11        Conclusions

If political and economic pressures affect the FOMC's decisions, they must first affect the preferences and choices of its individual members. Because individual policymakers differ from one another, a careful description of individual preferences and decisions is an essential step in describing how collective choices are made. In this book, we have explored how the policy choices of the FOMC are related to the underlying preferences of its members.

The book makes four major contributions. First, we have developed econometric techniques that permit better description of the preferences of individual FOMC policymakers via the estimation of monetary policy reaction functions. Second, we have developed original data sets that provide a richer characterization of preferences than those previously available in voting records. Third, we have used the original data and our econometric methods to make inferences about substantive issues associated with the making of monetary policy decisions. Finally, we have described the content of available records of FOMC deliberations in anecdotal as well as analytical fashion. In this chapter, we summarize the major findings of the book in each of these areas and then consider related opportunities for further research and policy implications.

## 11.1   Summary of Contributions and Results

The book's content has been organized in part according to the nature of the data employed. Chapter 4 uses FOMC voting records covering the 1966–1996 period. Chapters 5–8 analyze more detailed original data sets derived from the *Memoranda of Discussion* and *FOMC Transcripts* for the 1970–1978 period when Arthur Burns chaired the committee and the 1987–1996 portion of Alan Greenspan's tenure.

Chapters 9 and 10 also use these textual records, but our discussions there rely on anecdotal rather than quantitative evidence.

### 11.1.1  Analysis of FOMC Voting Records

We began our investigation in chapter 4 with analyses of dissent voting patterns within the FOMC. By exploring voting records, we followed the example of much of the existing literature that has attempted to characterize the preferences of individual monetary policy decision makers. In contrast to previous studies, however, we developed methods for using the voting data to estimate policy reaction function parameters for individual FOMC members. Reaction functions explain the setting of a policy instrument (for instance, the federal funds rate) as a function of prevailing or forecasted macroeconomic conditions. Our method is notable because individuals' desired interest rates are not directly observed; rather, our method relies only on discrete voting choices.

Several findings from the FOMC voting record are noteworthy. First, our reaction function estimates documented the considerable diversity in committee members' policy preferences over the 1966–1996 period. We produced a ranking of eighty-three individuals ranging from easiest to tightest and highlighted differences across members. The results also confirmed that there are systematic differences between governors and Reserve Bank presidents, with governors, on average, favoring more expansionary monetary policy than their bank president colleagues.

We then explored the influence of partisan and electoral pressures on the monetary policy voting behavior of FOMC members. Our results showed that once one controls for the state of the economy and the prevailing stance of monetary policy, both partisan ideologies and partisan loyalties played important roles in the voting decisions of FOMC members. Specifically, we found that individuals appointed by Democratic and Republican presidents exhibited preferences in their FOMC voting behavior consistent with the traditional reputations of the Democrats for favoring monetary ease and the Republicans for favoring monetary tightness. As elections have approached, though, governors have been willing to depart from their customary partisan ideologies in pursuit of electoral success for their respective parties. While the traditional political business cycle model predicts that policymakers will adopt an accommodative policy stance prior to an election, our results showed a more subtle but plausible result: the incentive for a particular FOMC member to support preelection stimulus depends on whether that member was appointed by a president of the incumbent party or the opposition.

### 11.1.2  Analysis of Data Derived from Records of FOMC Deliberations

Because dissenting votes are infrequent, the voting record is limited in its ability to reveal differences across individuals. Recognizing this, chapters 5–8 investigated more detailed data derived from the *Memoranda* and the *Transcripts* that describe committee deliberations held during the 1970–1978 and 1987–1996 periods. The first of these intervals corresponds to the Burns chairmanship, while the second corresponds to the portion of Greenspan's tenure for which records are currently available. Chapter 5 explained the methods we employed to code individual FOMC members' preferences based on the statements attributed to them at meetings. We coded individuals' numerical federal funds rate targets in about 80 percent of all member-meeting observations for the Burns years and about 92 percent of all such observations for the Greenspan years; in the remaining cases for both periods, we coded qualitative indications of preferences.

Chapter 6 introduced an econometric method for estimating individuals' monetary policy reaction functions using a sample consisting of both continuous (explicitly stated desired federal funds rates) and discrete (leaning positions) indications of preferences. We applied this method to the data describing monetary policy preferences of Burns and Greenspan era FOMC members. Reaction function estimates were compared across individuals, emphasizing differences in theoretical perspectives. In a number of instances, differences in policy perspectives revealed by our reaction function estimates could be verified from external sources. For the Burns era, the reaction functions of monetarist presidents from the Federal Reserve Bank of St. Louis showed more concern with money growth and less concern with federal funds rate stability than other members of the committee who were more traditionally Keynesian. During the Greenspan era, traditional monetarism fell into decline, as the monetary aggregates were acknowledged to be unsatisfactory guides to policy. Yet the monetarist tradition was preserved by a group of members who were suspicious of fine-tuning and who argued that price stability should be the FOMC's primary objective.

In chapter 7, we presented a technique for using the results of individual reaction function estimations to impute desired funds rate targets for individuals who failed to directly state their target preferences at particular meetings. We then used both directly stated and imputed funds rate targets to construct complete preference profiles (that is, listings of all members' desired interest rates) for all FOMC meetings held during our Burns and Greenspan sample periods. These data sets, which are presented in appendixes 4 and 5, are themselves important products of our research.

In the remainder of chapter 7, we used the Burns era preference profiles to investigate the aggregation of preferences that produces committee choices. The analysis produced quantitative evidence about several issues that had not previously been addressed in the literature. First, we substantiated the claim that the chairman carries greater weight within the FOMC than rank-and-file members; specifically, we estimated a voting weight of roughly 50 percent for Burns. Additional results showed that the chairman directly influenced the stated preferences of other committee members. Although we confirmed the view that Burns wielded enhanced power, we were also able to refute the chairman-as-dictator view, since measures of the overall committee sentiment (median or mean desired funds rates) were significant determinants of policy outcomes. Further, we rejected the hypothesis that nonvoting members influenced committee choices, but we were unable to reject the hypothesis that governors and Reserve Bank presidents were equally powerful. Finally, we found support for Blinder's hypothesis that committee decisions should exhibit more inertia than those of an individual decision maker.

Chapter 8 presented econometric evidence that described the choices made by the FOMC during the Greenspan years of 1987–1996. In many ways, the FOMC operated in a similar fashion under Burns and Greenspan, but there were subtle differences as well. These differences were reflected in the data we collected to describe the preferences of individual committee members. Because Greenspan's proposed policy was almost always adopted, and because the median voter preference and Greenspan's preference almost always coincided, we could not directly use econometric procedures to estimate the relative power shares of the chairman and the committee. Nevertheless, we were able to present evidence of Greenspan's influence on the stated policy positions of rank-and-file committee members. Although it is difficult to show conclusively that the preferences of other committee members had an impact on chosen policies, there are at least suggestions that Greenspan's proposals were crafted with knowledge of what other members might find acceptable. Thus, it would be inappropriate to conclude that Greenspan is, in effect, a dictator.

### 11.1.3 An Anecdotal Approach

To create the data sets employed in chapters 5–8, we read documents describing the policy go-around discussions at each FOMC meeting held during the Burns and Greenspan eras. Although we have captured much of the information from these records in our codings, the documents are also rich in anecdotal content that is not easily quantified. Chapters 9 and 10 provided a sense of the anecdotal content of meeting records while focusing on specific questions of interest to scholars of monetary policymaking. In chapter 9, we investigated political pressures exerted on the FOMC during the Burns and Greenspan eras. Although the Fed has always taken pride in its independence, our discussion in chapter 9 made it clear that members were aware of pressures from the public and politicians, and that policy was made in a context that encompassed expected reactions from Congress and the president. Although the Fed has moved toward greater openness in recent years, meeting records show that it has continued to limit information about its decisions in order to deflect external criticism that might lead to internal division.

In chapter 10, we explored anecdotal evidence related to the theory of the time inconsistency problem as an explanation for an inflationary bias in monetary policy. We made the argument that the key assumptions of the time inconsistency problem accurately described the Burns era policymaking environment. Specifically, the committee perceived a Phillips curve trade-off and political pressures that made it difficult to adopt anti-inflationary policies at any moment in time. In addition, the tendency toward expansionary policy was exacerbated by a short-run planning horizon and a discretionary approach to policymaking in each of a sequence of meetings. We also explained how the comparative static predictions of the time inconsistency model are consistent with both the rise of inflation during the 1970s and its subsequent fall during the 1980s and 1990s.

### 11.2 Opportunities for Future Research

There are a number of directions available for future research on committee decision making on monetary policy issues. Much of our analysis has been directed at describing how the preferences of individual policymakers differ, but our characterization of differences has remained limited. For example, the reaction function specifications of chapter 7 permitted individual coefficients to differ across members, but did not tailor the selection of explanatory variables to individuals. If records of FOMC meetings suggest that one member responds to commodity inflation, another to the spread between long-term and short-term interest rates, and another to the gap between actual and potential output, then reaction function specifications could be modified to reflect such differences.

The role of regional representation in central bank decision-making procedures is also potentially important; both the Federal Reserve and the European Central Bank are designed to ensure that regional interests are represented in the policymaking process. Although Laney (1990) and Meade and Sheets (2002) find that FOMC members are especially responsive to economic conditions in the regions they represent, their results are based on voting patterns rather than detailed evidence from transcripts. Given the limitations of voting data, the data sets we have constructed should permit more conclusive tests of the hypothesis that FOMC members respond to regional as well as national economic conditions.

Our study of committee decision making suggests that both the chairman and other members of the FOMC influence outcomes, but questions regarding preference aggregation remain. The resolution of majoritarian and consensual pressures may be more complex than our simple models have been able to capture. For example, while the committee may reach out to some members with outlying preferences to encourage consensus, it is widely believed that those with more extreme views have little influence. Determining when an extreme member crosses the line from relevance to irrelevance is a subtle issue. Further, while our work also confirms that the chairman has disproportionate power in FOMC decision making, questions remain regarding the specific strategies that are most significant in securing that power. For example, transcripts of committee deliberations do not reveal the chairman's role in building coalitions, nor do they fully expose the extent to which member preferences influence proposals made by the chairman.

Finally, application of our methods to other central banks would be of interest. Currently, the Federal Reserve appears to be unique in providing transcripts of policymaking deliberations; however, several central banks, including both the Bank of Japan and the

Bank of England, make dissent voting records public in a timely fashion.

## 11.3   Implications for Central Banking Institutions

There can be little doubt that the beliefs and preferences of individual policymakers are critical in explaining policy outcomes. Romer and Romer (2004) have argued that over the Fed's history, the most important determinant of the quality of monetary policy has been the character of policymakers' beliefs about how the economy works and what monetary policy can accomplish.[1] This book has provided added confirmation for the importance of individuals by documenting the existence of diverse views within the FOMC as well as the links between individuals' preferences and committee choices.

The institutional rules and practices that govern how policymakers are selected and how their preferences are aggregated to produce choices are also important, and a number of institutional and procedural changes have been suggested for improving the quality of monetary policymaking. Some politicians have called for increased political oversight and accountability; many academic economists have argued in favor of increased central bank independence. More recently, increased policymaking transparency has been promoted, often in connection with the adoption of a more explicit inflation-targeting mandate. And as the end of the Greenspan era approaches, many observers ask how the successes of his regime can be embodied in the FOMC's institutional memory rather than lost with his departure.

This book was not intended to resolve these issues, but it does suggest some observations. First, our evidence confirms that FOMC policy decisions are, at least occasionally, responsive to politically communicated pressures. This has not prevented the Federal Reserve from achieving some degree of price stability over time, at least in comparison to many other central banks. Yet there is little reason to believe

---

1. For example, Romer and Romer (2004) note that in the 1930s, policymakers were skeptical about the ability of expansionary monetary policy to spur recovery; their resulting failure to act prolonged the Depression. Meltzer (2003) also argues that the failure of monetary policy in the 1930s followed directly from the incorrect economic beliefs of policymakers. Meltzer observes (282) that "the main reason for the failure of monetary policy in the depression was the reliance on an inappropriate set of beliefs about speculative excesses and real bills." He adds (196) that "many of the principals responsible for policy in the 1920s, and during 1929 to 1933, were weak men with little knowledge of central banking and not much interest in developing their knowledge."

that the central bank's performance would be improved by expanding the scope of political influence over its monetary policy decisions.

Indeed, based on our results, one might expect the political dimensions of monetary policy to become *more* apparent over the coming years. Despite the long terms that Federal Reserve governors can serve, many now tend not to complete their terms. This increases the rate of partisan turnover in board positions and reduces the number of out-party appointees whose actions might thwart electorally timed monetary ease promoted by in-party appointees. In addition, the president's influence might also be enhanced when new members assume partial terms with an opportunity for reappointment. Such members might be more likely to consider whether policy positions they advocate would please the president.

Arguments for increased transparency in monetary policymaking have received increasing support from academics in recent years.[2] In many cases, proposals for transparency have been coupled with plans to adopt inflation targets. The rationale for this combination is that when a central bank is committed to an inflation targeting strategy, openness about its reasoning for specific short-term actions may permit the bank to maintain credibility as it flexibly responds to short-term shocks. Current Fed governor Ben Bernanke has offered a variant of the inflation targeting scheme, asserting that the FOMC might benefit from simply announcing its perception of the "optimal long-run inflation rate" (OLIR), the rate that "would have been judged by the Committee to be the one under which the economy operates best in the long run" (Bernanke 2003b). The announced OLIR would not be a binding target; rather, it would simply be a communication of a committee perception.

Although support for the concept of transparency is widespread, the analysis undertaken in this book suggests that implementing policies to promote goal transparency could be difficult. Bernanke's proposal for reporting the FOMC's OLIR seems to be a minimal extension of current practice, but it does require that the committee agree on a number. Bernanke (2003b) notes that FOMC members' expressed preferences for long-run inflation rates "have ranged considerably, from less than 1 percent to 2.5 percent or more." Variation across members does not preclude choice—the committee can adopt long-run as well

---

2. Posen (2002, 1) says that transparency "is now an accepted broad goal to which all central banks pay at least lip service."

as short-term targets. But any long-run objective, even if it reflects the sincere views of current members, will not determine future policy choices. The composition of the FOMC will be different in the future, and market participants who predict long-run inflation rates must acknowledge this.[3] At the very least, the prospect of the replacement of a chairman might change public expectations about the FOMC's long-term objectives.

The role of the chairman could also be altered by institutional change. Currently, it is acknowledged that the chairman has more power than other committee members, even if the explicit arrangements that support an enhanced role are based on tradition. There are both costs and benefits evident in the elevated status of the chairman. As the preceding discussion notes, credibility of longer-term committee objectives may be undermined when a chairman is both powerful and likely to be replaced in the near term. The chairman's power might produce benefits in other ways, however. Blinder (1998, 20–21) contends that one important and beneficial consequence of the elevated role of the chairman is a reduction of inertial tendencies associated with committee decision making.

A general conclusion is that realistic appraisals of proposals to alter monetary policy institutions require consideration of the collective choice aspects of decision making. To understand the process that generates monetary policy choices, one should begin by studying the choices made by individual policymakers in a committee setting. This book—with its emphasis on individuals, the factors that shape their policy preferences, and the mechanisms by which those preferences are translated into a committee decision—has taken a step in that direction.

---

3. Further, as we discussed in chapter 10, the time inconsistency problem can produce an equilibrium in which a sequence of short-term choices does not produce the desired long-run equilibrium (Barro and Gordon 1983).

# Appendix 1
# Voting Data

**Table A1.1**
Data on the FOMC voting record, 1966–1996

| FOMC member | Total votes | Dissents for ease | Dissents for tightness |
|---|---|---|---|
| *Chairmen* | | | |
| Arthur Burns | 99 | 0 | 0 |
| Alan Greenspan | 76 | 0 | 0 |
| William McChesney Martin | 62 | 0 | 0 |
| G. William Miller | 15 | 0 | 0 |
| Paul Volcker | 68 | 0 | 0 |
| *Republican-appointed governors* | | | |
| Wayne Angell | 64 | 1 | 7 |
| Canby Balderston | 2 | 0 | 0 |
| Jeffrey Bucher | 40 | 4 | 0 |
| Philip Coldwell | 61 | 3 | 5 |
| Stephen Gardner | 28 | 0 | 0 |
| Robert Heller | 22 | 0 | 0 |
| Robert Holland | 34 | 1 | 0 |
| Philip Jackson | 39 | 0 | 1 |
| Manuel Johnson | 35 | 1 | 0 |
| Edward Kelley | 76 | 1 | 1 |
| John LaWare | 53 | 0 | 6 |
| David Lilly | 20 | 1 | 0 |
| Lawrence Lindsey | 41 | 2 | 2 |
| Preston Martin | 31 | 5 | 0 |
| David Mullins | 29 | 0 | 0 |
| Charles Partee | 95 | 5 | 0 |
| Susan Phillips | 41 | 0 | 0 |
| Martha Seger | 54 | 16 | 0 |
| John Sheehan | 38 | 2 | 0 |
| Charles Shepardson | 18 | 0 | 2 |
| Henry Wallich | 122 | 2 | 24 |

**Table A1.1**
(continued)

| FOMC member | Total votes | Dissents for ease | Dissents for tightness |
|---|---|---|---|
| *Democratic-appointed governors* | | | |
| Alan Blinder | 13 | 0 | 0 |
| Andrew Brimmer | 112 | 0 | 2 |
| Dewey Daane | 100 | 0 | 2 |
| Lyle Gramley | 39 | 0 | 3 |
| Sherman Maisel | 90 | 6 | 0 |
| Laurence Meyer | 5 | 0 | 0 |
| George Mitchell | 125 | 4 | 0 |
| Emmett Rice | 63 | 4 | 0 |
| Alice Rivlin | 5 | 0 | 0 |
| J. L. Robertson | 98 | 0 | 1 |
| Frederick Schultz | 24 | 0 | 0 |
| William Sherrill | 63 | 0 | 0 |
| Nancy Teeters | 50 | 9 | 0 |
| Janet Yellen | 20 | 0 | 0 |
| *Atlanta* | | | |
| Malcolm Bryan | 37 | 0 | 0 |
| William Ford | 8 | 0 | 5 |
| Robert Forrestal | 32 | 0 | 0 |
| Monroe Kimbrel | 64 | 1 | 4 |
| Harold Patterson | 5 | 0 | 0 |
| *Boston* | | | |
| George Ellis | 11 | 0 | 0 |
| Cathy Minehan | 8 | 0 | 0 |
| Frank Morris | 72 | 4 | 4 |
| Richard Syron | 15 | 0 | 0 |
| *Chicago* | | | |
| Silas Keehn | 55 | 0 | 0 |
| Robert Mayo | 63 | 0 | 0 |
| Michael Moskow | 8 | 0 | 0 |
| Charles Scanlon | 32 | 0 | 2 |
| *Cleveland* | | | |
| Braddock Hickman | 41 | 0 | 3 |
| Karen Horn | 19 | 1 | 0 |
| Lee Hoskins | 16 | 0 | 7 |
| Jerry Jordan | 23 | 2 | 1 |
| Willis Winn | 59 | 0 | 5 |
| William Hendricks* | 1 | 0 | 0 |
| *Dallas* | | | |
| Ernest Baughman | 24 | 0 | 1 |
| Robert Boykin | 32 | 0 | 5 |
| Philip Coldwell | 27 | 0 | 3 |

**Table A1.1**
(continued)

| FOMC member | Total votes | Dissents for ease | Dissents for tightness |
|---|---|---|---|
| Watrous Irons | 15 | 0 | 2 |
| Robert McTeer | 16 | 0 | 0 |
| *Kansas City* | | | |
| George Clay | 55 | 0 | 2 |
| Roger Guffey | 46 | 1 | 3 |
| Thomas Hoenig | 16 | 0 | 1 |
| *Minneapolis* | | | |
| Gerald Corrigan | 15 | 0 | 0 |
| Hugh Galusha | 18 | 0 | 0 |
| Bruce MacLaury | 24 | 0 | 1 |
| Gary Stern | 32 | 0 | 3 |
| Mark Willes | 11 | 0 | 6 |
| *New York* | | | |
| Gerald Corrigan | 66 | 0 | 0 |
| Alfred Hayes | 103 | 0 | 16 |
| William McDonough | 28 | 0 | 0 |
| Anthony Solomon | 38 | 1 | 1 |
| Paul Volcker | 45 | 0 | 3 |
| Richard Debs* | 6 | 0 | 0 |
| James Oltman* | 1 | 0 | 0 |
| Thomas Timlen* | 9 | 0 | 0 |
| William Treiber* | 20 | 0 | 1 |
| *Philadelphia* | | | |
| Edward Boehne | 47 | 1 | 0 |
| Karl Bopp | 29 | 0 | 0 |
| David Eastburn | 35 | 3 | 0 |
| *Richmond* | | | |
| Robert Black | 67 | 0 | 12 |
| Alfred Broaddus | 8 | 0 | 3 |
| Aubrey Heflin | 11 | 0 | 0 |
| Edward Wayne | 16 | 0 | 0 |
| *Saint Louis* | | | |
| Darryl Francis | 35 | 1 | 11 |
| Thomas Melzer | 31 | 1 | 8 |
| Theodore Roberts | 8 | 0 | 0 |
| Lawrence Roos | 22 | 1 | 4 |
| *San Francisco* | | | |
| John Balles | 48 | 1 | 2 |
| Robert Parry | 25 | 0 | 2 |
| Eliot Swan | 29 | 0 | 0 |

*Indicates that the individual was a vice president

**Table A1.2**
Dissent voting by party during the first two years and last two years of election cycles, 1966–1996

|  | First two years | Last two years | Totals |
|---|---|---|---|
| **Governors** | | | |
| *Total dissents* | 59 | 64 | 123 |
| Democrats | 18 | 13 | 31 |
| Republicans | 41 | 51 | 92 |
| *Ease dissents* | 34 | 33 | 67 |
| Democrats | 14 | 9 | 23 |
| Republicans | 20 | 24 | 44 |
| *Tightness dissents* | 25 | 31 | 56 |
| Democrats | 4 | 4 | 8 |
| Republicans | 21 | 27 | 48 |
| *Total in-party dissents* | 31 | 38 | 69 |
| Democrats | 4 | 5 | 9 |
| Republicans | 27 | 33 | 60 |
| *In-party ease dissents* | 18 | 26 | 44 |
| Democrats | 2 | 5 | 7 |
| Republicans | 16 | 21 | 37 |
| *In-party tightness dissents* | 13 | 12 | 25 |
| Democrats | 2 | 0 | 2 |
| Republicans | 11 | 12 | 23 |
| *Total out-party dissents* | 28 | 26 | 54 |
| Democrats | 14 | 8 | 22 |
| Republicans | 14 | 18 | 32 |
| *Out-party ease dissents* | 16 | 7 | 23 |
| Democrats | 12 | 4 | 16 |
| Republicans | 4 | 3 | 7 |
| *Out-party tightness dissents* | 12 | 19 | 31 |
| Democrats | 2 | 4 | 6 |
| Republicans | 10 | 15 | 25 |
| **Reserve Bank presidents** | | | |
| *Total dissents* | 72 | 67 | 139 |
| *Ease dissents* | 7 | 11 | 18 |
| *Tightness dissents* | 65 | 56 | 121 |

*Note:* In-party governors are Democratic (Republican) appointees serving under Democratic (Republican) presidents; out-party governors are Democratic (Republican) appointees serving under Republican (Democratic) presidents.

# Appendix 2
# Estimation of Individual Reaction Functions Using Dissent Voting Data

This appendix describes several aspects of the procedure employed in chapter 4 to estimate individual reaction function parameters. We will first show that model restrictions imply that the variance of the probit model error term, $v_{it}$, is identified. This means that the scale of the probit model's underlying latent propensity can be expressed in interest rate units and permits us to interpret our estimations as conventional reaction functions. We will then discuss procedures employed in the estimation.

Regarding the identification issue, recall that the error terms appearing in the reduced-form conditions (4.5) and (4.6) are

$$u_t = \gamma e_{0t} + (1 - \gamma)\bar{e}_t$$

and

$$v_{it} = \gamma e_{0t} + (1 - \gamma)\bar{e}_t - e_{it}.$$

Variances of these error terms are given by

$$\sigma_u^2 = \gamma^2 \sigma^2 + (1 - \gamma)^2 \left[ \frac{\sigma^2}{N} + \frac{N - 1}{N} \rho \sigma^2 \right] + 2\gamma(1 - \gamma)\rho\sigma^2 \tag{A.2.1}$$

and

$$\sigma_v^2 = \sigma^2(1 + \gamma^2 - 2\rho\gamma^2) + [(1 - \gamma)^2 - 2(1 - \gamma)] \left[ \frac{\sigma^2}{N} + \frac{N - 1}{N} \rho\sigma^2 \right]. \tag{A.2.2}$$

Equation (A.2.1) can be solved for $\sigma^2$ and the resulting expression substituted into (A.2.2) so that $\sigma_v^2$ is expressed as a function of $\sigma_u^2, N, \rho$, and $\gamma$. An estimate of $\sigma_u^2$ can be obtained from the OLS regression estimating (4.5); $N$ is observable; and, as we discuss below, values for $\rho$ and $\gamma$ can be obtained from external sources. Consequently, (A.2.2) determines a value for $\sigma_v^2$, and no normalization is required for identification.

To estimate the model, we first estimate equation (4.5) by OLS and the ordered probit model (4.6) by the maximum likelihood method. By imposing cross-equation restrictions and using estimates of $\gamma$ and $\rho$ obtained from external sources, we are able to identify all of the remaining model parameters. Specifically, we first obtain estimates of $\lambda$ and $\alpha_k, k = 1, \ldots, K$, from the ordered probit model (4.6), initially employing an arbitrary value for $\sigma_u^2$ (hence an arbitrary value for $\sigma_v^2$) to determine the scale of the underlying latent propensity in the probit model. We then incorporate estimates of the $\alpha_k$s into an OLS estimation of (4.5), obtaining estimates of the $\beta_j$s and $\sigma_u^2$. Given those estimates, we correctly recalibrate the scale of the latent propensity and the estimated $\alpha_k$s in conditions (4.6) and $(1 - \gamma)$ in equation (4.5).

We now return to the issue of obtaining values of $\gamma$ and $\rho$. In principle, these parameters can also be estimated with the available voting data, but in practice estimates tend to be imprecise and unstable. In later chapters, using richer data sets and alternative econometric models, we obtain estimates of similar parameters that we believe are more reliable. Specifically, chapter 7 reports a voting weight for Burns that was close to 0.50. In addition, individual reaction function estimations like those reported in chapter 6 can be used to estimate error term correlations across individuals. In that chapter, we obtained correlation coefficients between individual and committee reaction function errors for Burns and Greenspan era FOMC members. Averaging these correlation coefficients yields a result close to 0.70. To carry out the estimations reported in chapter 4, we therefore imposed the values $\gamma = 0.50$ and $\rho = 0.70$. As a practical matter, only the scale of the probit model depends on these choices. Significance levels associated with all coefficients and all tests of hypothesis are invariant to the normalization.

An additional econometric caveat should be noted: the reduced-form probit model error terms, the $v_{it}$, are correlated across members at time $t$. As a consequence, the statistical properties of the reported estimates are uncertain. To investigate these properties, we evaluated our technique with a Monte Carlo study (Chappell and McGregor 2000). Our coefficient estimates appear to be consistent and reported standard errors are close to "true" standard errors calculated in the Monte Carlo experiments. On average, true Monte Carlo standard errors exceed our reported standard errors by 0.43 percent.

# Appendix 3
## Estimation of Individual Reaction Functions Using Data from the *Memoranda* and the *Transcripts*

This appendix provides details on the estimation of reaction functions for individual FOMC members using the data derived from the *Memoranda* and the *Transcripts*. These techniques are employed in chapters 6, 7, and 8. In section A3.1, we derive the likelihood function for a single-equation estimator for the individual reaction function model. In section A3.2, we describe an extension of that model to permit estimation of a two-equation model in which an individual's reaction function is jointly estimated with an "aggregate" committee reaction function. This method is useful when one wishes to test for parameter differences between an individual and the committee. In section A3.3, we explain how estimates of the model can be used to impute desired funds rate targets for committee members who did not directly state them.

### A3.1 The Likelihood Function for the Individual Reaction Function Model

In this section, we derive the likelihood function for the individual reaction function model. Recall that our model, initially presented in chapter 6, assumes that each individual committee member $i$ has a reaction function of the form

$$R_{it}^* = X_t \beta_i + e_{it}, \qquad e_{it} \sim N(0, \sigma_i). \tag{6.1}$$

In this equation, $R_{it}^*$ may or may not be observed. When $R_{it}^*$ is not observed, we instead observe leaning positions relative to a benchmark rate, $\tilde{R}_{it}$. Leaning positions are assumed to be generated according to the following conditions:

if $R_{it}^* - \tilde{R}_{it} > \lambda_i$, then $V_{it} = 1$     (member $i$ leans for tightness);     (6.2.a)

if $R_{it}^* - \tilde{R}_{it} < -\lambda_i$, then $V_{it} = -1$     (member $i$ leans for ease);     (6.2.b)

if $-\lambda_i \leq R_{it}^* - \tilde{R}_{it} \leq \lambda_i$, then $V_{it} = 0$     (member $i$ assents).     (6.2.c)

We now derive the likelihood functions for observations falling into each of four categories: (1) $R_{it}^*$ is not observed and member $i$ leans for tightness, (2) $R_{it}^*$ is not observed and member $i$ leans for ease, (3) $R_{it}^*$ is not observed and member $i$ assents, and (4) $R_{it}^*$ is observed.

## Case 1    $R_{it}^*$ is Not Observed and Member $i$ Leans toward Tightness

Because $V_{it} = 1$, we know that $R_{it}^* - \tilde{R}_{it} > \lambda_i$, or equivalently, that $e_{it} > a_{it}$, where $a_{it} = \lambda_i + \tilde{R}_{it} - \mathbf{X}_t\boldsymbol{\beta}_i$. The likelihood for the observation is given by the probability that we observe this case given the parameter values:

$$L_{I,it} = \text{Prob}(e_{it} > a_{it})$$

$$= 1 - F\left(\frac{a_{it}}{\sigma_i}\right),$$

where $F(\cdot)$ is the standard normal cumulative distribution function.

## Case 2    $R_{it}^*$ is Not Observed and Member $i$ Leans toward Ease

Because $V_{it} = -1$, we know that $R_{it}^* - \tilde{R}_{it} < -\lambda_i$, or equivalently, that $e_{it} < b_{it}$, where $b_{it} = -\lambda_i + \tilde{R}_{it} - \mathbf{X}_t\boldsymbol{\beta}_i$. The likelihood for this observation is given by

$$L_{II,it} = \text{Prob}(e_{it} < b_{it})$$

$$= F\left(\frac{b_{it}}{\sigma_i}\right).$$

## Case 3    $R_{it}^*$ is Not Observed and Member $i$ Assents

Because $V_{it} = 0$, we know that $-\lambda_i \le R_{it}^* - \tilde{R}_{it} \le \lambda_i$, or equivalently, that $b_{it} \le e_{it} \le a_{it}$. The likelihood for this observation is given by

$$L_{III,it} = \text{Prob}(b_{it} \le e_{it} \le a_{it})$$

$$= F\left(\frac{a_{it}}{\sigma_i}\right) - F\left(\frac{b_{it}}{\sigma_i}\right).$$

## Case 4    $R_{it}^*$ is Observed

In this case, the likelihood function for observation $t$ is identical to that for an OLS regression:

$$L_{IV,it} = \frac{1}{\sqrt{2\pi}\sigma_i} \exp\left[-\left(\frac{1}{2}\right)\left(\frac{R_{it}^* - \mathbf{X}_t\boldsymbol{\beta}_i}{\sigma_i}\right)^2\right].$$

The likelihood function for the sample of observations $t = 1, \ldots, T$ for member $i$ is given by

$$L_i = \prod_{t=1}^{T}(D_{I,it}L_{I,it} + D_{II,it}L_{II,it} + D_{III,it}L_{III,it} + D_{IV,it}L_{IV,it}),$$

where the variables $D_I, D_{II}, D_{III}$, and $D_{IV}$ are dummy variables equal to one for the indicated case and otherwise equal to zero.

## A3.2    Joint Estimation of Individual and Committee Reaction Functions

In this section, we describe a procedure for jointly estimating an individual FOMC member's reaction function and an aggregate committee reaction function. The implied model is analogous to the "seemingly unrelated regressions" extension of OLS. We again assume that the individual reaction function model can be described by equation (6.1) and conditions (6.2). In addition, we assume that the committee has a reaction function of the form

$$\bar{R}_t = \mathbf{X}_t\boldsymbol{\beta} + u_t. \tag{6.4}$$

In this equation, $\bar{R}_t$ is the committee's adopted funds rate, and the elements of $\boldsymbol{\beta}$ are committee reaction function parameters.

We assume that the individual and committee reaction function error terms, $e_{it}$ and $u_t$, have a bivariate normal distribution with joint density $g_{u,e}(u_t, e_{it})$. Means of $u_t$ and $e_{it}$ are zero; variances are $\sigma_u^2$ and $\sigma_e^2$; and the covariance is $\sigma_{ue}$.

The correlation coefficient for the error terms is therefore $\rho = \dfrac{\sigma_{ue}}{\sigma_u \sigma_e}$. It is useful to note that the joint density can be written as the product of marginal and conditional densities:

$$g_{u,e}(u_t, e_{it}) = g_u(u_t)g_{e|u}(e_{it}|u_t).$$

We next describe the form of the likelihood function for observations falling into each of four possible categories.

### Case 1    $R_{it}^*$ is Not Observed and Member $i$ Leans toward Tightness

Because $V_{it} = 1$, we know that $R_{it}^* - \tilde{R}_{it} > \lambda_i$, or equivalently, that $e_{it} > a_{it}$, where $a_{it} = \lambda_i + \tilde{R}_{it} - \mathbf{X}_t\boldsymbol{\beta}_i$. The likelihood for the observation is given by

$$L_{I,it} = \int_{a_{it}}^{\infty} g_{u,e}(\bar{R}_t - \mathbf{X}_t\boldsymbol{\beta}, e_{it})\, de_{it} = g_u(\bar{R}_t - \mathbf{X}_t\boldsymbol{\beta})\int_{a_{it}}^{\infty} g_{e|u}(e_{it})\, de_{it}$$

$$= g_u(\bar{R}_t - \mathbf{X}_t\boldsymbol{\beta})\int_{-\infty}^{-a_{it}} g_{e|u}(e_{it})\, de_{it},$$

where $g_u$ is the marginal distribution with mean zero and variance $\sigma_u^2$, and $g_{e|u}$ is the conditional density of $e_{it}$ given $u_t$ with mean

$$\mu_{e|u} = \rho\left(\frac{\sigma_e}{\sigma_u}\right)u_t$$

and standard deviation

$$\sigma_{e|u} = \sigma_e(1 - \rho^2)^{0.5}.$$

It then follows that

$$g_u(\bar{R}_t - \mathbf{X}_t\boldsymbol{\beta})\int_{a_{it}}^{\infty} g_{e|u}(e_{it})\, de_{it} = f\left(\frac{\bar{R}_t - \mathbf{X}_t\boldsymbol{\beta}}{\sigma_u}\right)F\left(\frac{-a_{it} - \mu_{e|u}}{\sigma_{e|u}}\right),$$

where $f(\cdot)$ is the standard normal density function, and $F(\cdot)$ is the standard normal distribution function.

### Case 2    $R_{it}^*$ is Not Observed and Member $i$ Leans toward Ease

Because $V_{it} = -1$, we know that $R_{it}^* - \tilde{R}_{it} < -\lambda_i$, or equivalently, that $e_{it} < b_{it}$, where $b_{it} = -\lambda_i + \tilde{R}_{it} - \mathbf{X}_t\boldsymbol{\beta}_i$. The likelihood for this observation is given by

$$L_{II,\,it} = \int_{-\infty}^{b_{it}} g_{u,\,e}(\bar{R}_t - \mathbf{X}_t\boldsymbol{\beta}, e_{it})\, de_{it} = g_u(\bar{R}_t - \mathbf{X}_t\boldsymbol{\beta}) \int_{-\infty}^{b_{it}} g_{e|u}(e_{it})\, de_{it}$$

$$= f\left(\frac{\bar{R}_t - \mathbf{X}_t\boldsymbol{\beta}}{\sigma_u}\right) F\left(\frac{b_{it} - \mu_{e|u}}{\sigma_{e|u}}\right).$$

### Case 3   $R_{it}^*$ is Not Observed and Member $i$ Assents

Because $V_{it} = 0$, we know that $-\lambda_i \leq R_{it}^* - \tilde{R}_{it} \leq \lambda_i$, or equivalently, that $b_{it} \leq e_{it} \leq a_{it}$. The likelihood for this observation is given by

$$L_{III,\,it} = \int_{b_{it}}^{a_{it}} g_{u,\,e}(\bar{R}_t - \mathbf{X}_t\boldsymbol{\beta}, e_{it})\, de_{it} = g_u(\bar{R}_t - \mathbf{X}_t\boldsymbol{\beta}) \int_{b_{it}}^{a_{it}} g_{e|u}(e_{it})\, de_{it}$$

$$= f\left(\frac{\bar{R}_t - \mathbf{X}_t\boldsymbol{\beta}}{\sigma_u}\right)\left[F\left(\frac{a_{it} - \mu_{e|u}}{\sigma_{e|u}}\right) - F\left(\frac{b_{it} - \mu_{e|u}}{\sigma_{e|u}}\right)\right].$$

### Case 4   $R_{it}^*$ is Observed

In this case, the likelihood function for observation $t$ is identical to that for the seemingly unrelated regressions model:

$$L_{IV,\,it} = g_{u,\,e}(\bar{R}_t - \mathbf{X}_t\boldsymbol{\beta}, R_{it}^* - \mathbf{X}_t\boldsymbol{\beta}_i).$$

Each observation falls into one of the four categories described above. The likelihood function for the sample of observations $t = 1, \ldots, T$ for member $i$ is then given by

$$L_i = \prod_{t=1}^{T}(D_{I,\,it}L_{I,\,it} + D_{II,\,it}L_{II,\,it} + D_{III,\,it}L_{III,\,it} + D_{IV,\,it}L_{IV,\,it}),$$

where the variables $D_I, D_{II}, D_{III}$, and $D_{IV}$ are dummy variables equal to one for the indicated case and otherwise equal to zero.

### A3.3   Imputing Desired Interest Rates

In this section, we describe how we impute values for an individual's desired interest rate in cases where the desired interest rate is not directly observed, making use of the information coded into leaning positions. We will consider three cases corresponding to the three possible qualitative categorizations of members' leaning positions. We again assume that the individual reaction function model can be described by equation (6.1) and conditions (6.2); in this section, however, we adopt a convenient notational change. Specifically, we let

$$e_{it} = \sigma_i \varepsilon_{it},$$

where $\sigma_i$ is a constant and $\varepsilon_{it}$ is standard normal; that is, $\varepsilon_{it} \sim N(0, 1)$. With this notational change, equation (6.1), the individual reaction function, can be written as

$$R_{it}^* = \mathbf{X}_t\boldsymbol{\beta}_i + \sigma_i \varepsilon_{it}. \tag{A.3.1}$$

## Case 1    Member *i* Leans toward Tightness

For given values of the exogenous variables and the parameters of the reaction function, taking expected values on each side of (A.3.1) yields

$$E(R_{it}^*) = \mathbf{X}_t\boldsymbol{\beta}_i + \sigma_i E(\varepsilon_{it}). \tag{A.3.2}$$

Because we have observed a lean toward tightness, we know that $R_{it}^* - \tilde{R}_{it} > \lambda_i$, or, equivalently, that $\varepsilon_{it} > \tilde{a}_{it}$, where

$$\tilde{a}_{it} = \frac{\lambda_i + \tilde{R}_{it} - \mathbf{X}_t\boldsymbol{\beta}_i}{\sigma_i}.$$

Applying Bayes rule, the expected value of $\varepsilon_{it}$ is given by

$$E(\varepsilon_{it}) = \frac{\int_{\tilde{a}_{it}}^{\infty} xf(x)\,dx}{1 - F(\tilde{a}_{it})}. \tag{A.3.3}$$

For a normal density, $f'(x) = -xf(x)$, so

$$\int_{\tilde{a}_{it}}^{\infty} xf(x)\,dx = -\int_{\tilde{a}_{it}}^{\infty} f'(x)\,dx$$
$$= -[f(x)]_{\tilde{a}_{it}}^{\infty}$$
$$= f(\tilde{a}_{it}).$$

Substituting this result into (A.3.3), we obtain

$$F(\varepsilon_{it}) = \frac{f(\tilde{a}_{it})}{1 - F(\tilde{a}_{it})}.$$

Then, substituting into (A.3.2) yields

$$E(R_{it}^*) = \mathbf{X}_t\boldsymbol{\beta}_i + \sigma_i \frac{f(\tilde{a}_{it})}{1 - F(\tilde{a}_{it})}.$$

## Case 2    Member *i* Leans toward Ease

Again, we have

$$E(R_{it}^*) = \mathbf{X}_t\boldsymbol{\beta}_i + \sigma_i E(\varepsilon_{it}). \tag{A.3.2}$$

Because we have observed a lean toward ease, we know that $R_{it}^* - \tilde{R}_{it} < -\lambda_i$, or, equivalently, that $\varepsilon_{it} < \tilde{b}_{it}$, where

$$\tilde{b}_{it} = \frac{-\lambda_i + \tilde{R}_{it} - \mathbf{X}_t\boldsymbol{\beta}_i}{\sigma_i}.$$

Applying Bayes rule, the expected value of $\varepsilon_{it}$ is given by

$$E(\varepsilon_{it}) = \frac{\int_{-\infty}^{\tilde{b}_{it}} xf(x)\,dx}{F(\tilde{b}_{it})}.$$

Using the condition $f'(x) = -xf(x)$ and integrating yields

$$E(\varepsilon_{it}) = -\frac{f(\tilde{b}_{it})}{F(\tilde{b}_{it})}.$$

Finally, substituting into (A.3.2), we obtain

$$E(R_{it}^*) = \mathbf{X}_t\boldsymbol{\beta}_i - \sigma_i \frac{f(\tilde{b}_{it})}{F(\tilde{b}_{it})}.$$

## Case 3   Member $i$ Assents

Once again, we have

$$E(R_{it}^*) = \mathbf{X}_t\boldsymbol{\beta}_i + \sigma_i E(\varepsilon_{it}). \tag{A.3.2}$$

Because member $i$ assents, we know that $-\lambda_i \leq R_{it}^* - \tilde{R}_{it} \leq \lambda_i$, or equivalently, that $\tilde{b}_{it} \leq \varepsilon_{it} \leq \tilde{a}_{it}$. Again applying Bayes rule, the expected value of $\varepsilon_{it}$ is given by

$$E(\varepsilon_{it}) = \frac{\int_{\tilde{b}_{it}}^{\tilde{a}_{it}} xf(x)\,dx}{F(\tilde{a}_{it}) - F(\tilde{b}_{it})}.$$

Then employing the condition $f'(x) = -xf(x)$ and integrating, we obtain

$$E(\varepsilon_{it}) = \frac{f(\tilde{b}_{it}) - f(\tilde{a}_{it})}{F(\tilde{a}_{it}) - F(\tilde{b}_{it})}.$$

Finally, substituting into (A.3.2), the expected value of $R_{it}^*$ is given by

$$E(R_{it}^*) = \mathbf{X}_t\boldsymbol{\beta}_i + \sigma_i \frac{f(\tilde{b}_{it}) - f(\tilde{a}_{it})}{F(\tilde{a}_{it}) - F(\tilde{b}_{it})}.$$

# Appendix 4
# Burns Era Preference
# Profiles by Meeting

| February 10, 1970 (99) | | March 10, 1970 (99) | |
|---|---|---|---|
| *Individual voters' desired funds rates* | | | |
| Maisel | 8.125 | Daane | 7.500 |
| Mitchell | 8.500 | Swan | 7.500 |
| Sherrill | 8.500 | Burns | 7.702 A |
| Daane | 8.542 A | Hickman | 7.735 A |
| Burns | 8.564 A | Robertson | 7.794 A |
| Bopp | 9.000 | Brimmer | 8.250 |
| Brimmer | 9.000 | Hayes | 8.250 |
| Clay | 9.000 | Heflin | 8.250 |
| Hayes | 9.000 | Kimbrel | 8.250 |
| Robertson | 9.000 | Maisel | 8.250 |
| Scanlon | 9.000 | Mitchell | 8.250 |
| Coldwell | 9.125 | Sherrill | 8.250 |
| *Individual alternates' desired funds rates* | | | |
| Hickman | 8.000 | Galusha | 7.500 |
| Black | 8.328 LE | Morris | 7.500 |
| Morris | 8.497 A | Baughman | 7.732 A |
| Galusha | 8.498 A | Clay | 8.250 |
| Francis | 9.000 | Coldwell | 8.250 |
| Kimbrel | 9.000 | Eastburn | 8.250 |
| Swan | 9.000 | Lewis | 8.250 |
| *Summary statistics* | | | |
| Target funds rate | 8.500 | Target funds rate | 8.250 |
| Staff proposal | 8.500 | Staff proposal | 7.750 |
| Premeeting funds rate | 9.143 | Premeeting funds rate | 7.857 |
| Number (voters) | 12 | Number (voters) | 12 |
| Mean (voters) | 8.780 | Mean (voters) | 7.998 |
| Median (voters) | 9.000 | Median (voters) | 8.250 |
| Number (alternates) | 7 | Number (alternates) | 7 |
| Mean (alternates) | 8.618 | Mean (alternates) | 7.962 |
| Median (alternates) | 8.498 | Median (alternates) | 8.250 |
| Number (all) | 19 | Number (all) | 19 |
| Mean (all) | 8.720 | Mean (all) | 7.985 |
| Median (all) | 9.000 | Median (all) | 8.250 |

| April 7, 1970 (99, 63) | | May 5, 1970 (99) | |
|---|---|---|---|
| *Individual voters' desired funds rates* | | | |
| Maisel | 7.707 LE | Daane | 7.942 LE |
| Hayes | 7.750 | Maisel | 7.984 LE |
| Brimmer | 8.000 | Burns | 8.249 A |
| Burns | 8.000 | Heflin | 8.250 |
| Daane | 8.000 | Hickman | 8.250 |
| Heflin | 8.000 | Mitchell | 8.250 |
| Hickman | 8.000 | Robertson | 8.250 |
| Mitchell | 8.000 | Sherrill | 8.250 |
| Sherrill | 8.000 | Hayes | 8.305 |
| Swan | 8.016 A | Swan | 8.461 A |
| Francis | 8.033 A | Francis | 8.656 LT |
| Robertson | 8.271 LT | Brimmer | 8.660 LT |
| *Individual alternates' desired funds rates* | | | |
| Galusha | 7.659 LE | Morris | 7.988 LE |
| Baughman | 8.000 | Baughman | 8.250 |
| Clay | 8.000 | Coldwell | 8.250 |
| Eastburn | 8.000 | Eastburn | 8.250 |
| Kimbrel | 8.000 | Galusha | 8.250 |
| Morris | 8.000 | Clay | 8.626 LT |
| Coldwell | 8.020 A | Kimbrel | 8.641 LT |
| *Summary statistics* | | | |
| Target funds rate | 8.000 | Target funds rate | 8.250 |
| Staff proposal | 8.000 | Staff proposal | 8.250 |
| Premeeting funds rate | 7.750 | Premeeting funds rate | 8.500 |
| Number (voters) | 12 | Number (voters) | 12 |
| Mean (voters) | 7.981 | Mean (voters) | 8.292 |
| Median (voters) | 8.000 | Median (voters) | 8.250 |
| Number (alternates) | 7 | Number (alternates) | 7 |
| Mean (alternates) | 7.954 | Mean (alternates) | 8.322 |
| Median (alternates) | 8.000 | Median (alternates) | 8.250 |
| Number (all) | 19 | Number (all) | 19 |
| Mean (all) | 7.971 | Mean (all) | 8.303 |
| Median (all) | 8.000 | Median (all) | 8.250 |

| May 26, 1970 (99) | | June 23, 1970 (99, 63) | |
|---|---|---|---|
| *Individual voters' desired funds rates* | | | |
| Daane | 7.933 LE | Maisel | 7.500 |
| Hickman | 8.026 LE | Robertson | 7.593 LE |
| Burns | 8.238 A | Hickman | 7.809 A |
| Maisel | 8.250 | Brimmer | 7.813 |
| Brimmer | 8.500 | Burns | 7.813 |
| Francis | 8.500 | Daane | 7.813 |
| Hayes | 8.500 | Heflin | 7.813 |
| Mitchell | 8.500 | Mitchell | 7.813 |
| Morris | 8.500 | Sherrill | 7.813 |
| Robertson | 8.500 | Swan | 7.813 |
| Sherrill | 8.500 | Treiber | 7.813 |
| Swan | 8.500 | Francis | 8.000 |
| *Individual alternates' desired funds rates* | | | |
| Baughman | 8.500 | Strohman | 7.500 |
| Black | 8.500 | Baughman | 7.813 |
| Coldwell | 8.500 | Coldwell | 7.813 |
| Eastburn | 8.500 | Kimbrel | 7.874 A |
| Galusha | 8.500 | Clay | 8.000 |
| Kimbrel | 8.500 | Morris | 8.000 |
| Tow | 8.500 | Eastburn | 8.191 LT |
| *Summary statistics* | | | |
| Target funds rate | 8.500 | Target funds rate | 7.813 |
| Staff proposal | 8.375 | Staff proposal | 7.813 |
| Premeeting funds rate | 7.679 | Premeeting funds rate | 7.518 |
| Number (voters) | 12 | Number (voters) | 12 |
| Mean (voters) | 8.371 | Mean (voters) | 7.783 |
| Median (voters) | 8.500 | Median (voters) | 7.813 |
| Number (alternates) | 7 | Number (alternates) | 7 |
| Mean (alternates) | 8.500 | Mean (alternates) | 7.884 |
| Median (alternates) | 8.500 | Median (alternates) | 7.874 |
| Number (all) | 19 | Number (all) | 19 |
| Mean (all) | 8.418 | Mean (all) | 7.821 |
| Median (all) | 8.500 | Median (all) | 7.813 |

| July 21, 1970 (99) | | August 18, 1970 (99) | |
|---|---|---|---|
| *Individual voters' desired funds rates* | | | |
| Burns | 7.199 LE | Burns | 6.087 LE |
| Brimmer | 7.500 | Maisel | 6.250 |
| Daane | 7.500 | Daane | 6.500 |
| Francis | 7.500 | Heflin | 6.500 |
| Heflin | 7.500 | Mitchell | 6.500 |
| Hickman | 7.500 | Sherrill | 6.500 |
| Maisel | 7.500 | Brimmer | 6.625 |
| Robertson | 7.500 | Francis | 6.625 |
| Sherrill | 7.500 | Hayes | 6.625 |
| Swan | 7.500 | Hickman | 6.625 |
| Treiber | 7.500 | Robertson | 6.625 |
| | | Swan | 6.625 |
| *Individual alternates' desired funds rates* | | | |
| Baughman | 7.500 | Mayo | 6.094 LE |
| Clay | 7.500 | Coldwell | 6.448 A |
| Coldwell | 7.500 | Kimbrel | 6.467 A |
| Eastburn | 7.500 | Galusha | 6.500 |
| Galusha | 7.500 | Morris | 6.500 |
| Kimbrel | 7.500 | Melnicoff | 6.625 |
| Morris | 7.500 | Clay | 6.724 LT |
| *Summary statistics* | | | |
| Target funds rate | 7.500 | Target funds rate | 6.500 |
| Staff proposal | 7.500 | Staff proposal | 6.375 |
| Premeeting funds rate | 7.518 | Premeeting funds rate | 6.696 |
| Number (voters) | 11 | Number (voters) | 12 |
| Mean (voters) | 7.473 | Mean (voters) | 6.507 |
| Median (voters) | 7.500 | Median (voters) | 6.563 |
| Number (alternates) | 7 | Number (alternates) | 7 |
| Mean (alternates) | 7.500 | Mean (alternates) | 6.480 |
| Median (alternates) | 7.500 | Median (alternates) | 6.500 |
| Number (all) | 18 | Number (all) | 19 |
| Mean (all) | 7.483 | Mean (all) | 6.497 |
| Median (all) | 7.500 | Median (all) | 6.500 |

| September 15, 1970 (99, 63) | | October 20, 1970 (99, 63) | |
| --- | --- | --- | --- |
| *Individual voters' desired funds rates* | | | |
| Sherrill | 6.000 | Maisel | 5.875 |
| Maisel | 6.124 A | Sherrill | 5.875 |
| Brimmer | 6.313 | Morris | 5.974 LE |
| Burns | 6.313 | Brimmer | 6.250 |
| Daane | 6.313 | Burns | 6.250 |
| Francis | 6.313 | Francis | 6.250 |
| Hayes | 6.313 | Hayes | 6.250 |
| Heflin | 6.313 | Hickman | 6.250 |
| Hickman | 6.313 | Mitchell | 6.250 |
| Robertson | 6.313 | Robertson | 6.250 |
| Swan | 6.313 | Swan | 6.250 |
| | | | |
| *Individual alternates' desired funds rates* | | | |
| Galusha | 6.000 | Mayo | 5.951 LE |
| Mayo | 6.000 | Galusha | 6.001 LE |
| Morris | 6.000 | Black | 6.250 |
| Clay | 6.313 | Clay | 6.250 |
| Coldwell | 6.313 | Coldwell | 6.250 |
| Eastburn | 6.313 | Eastburn | 6.250 |
| Kimbrel | 6.313 | Kimbrel | 6.250 |
| *Summary statistics* | | | |
| Target funds rate | 6.313 | Target funds rate | 6.250 |
| Staff proposal | 6.125 | Staff proposal | 6.250 |
| Premeeting funds rate | 6.625 | Premeeting funds rate | 6.250 |
| Number (voters) | 11 | Number (voters) | 11 |
| Mean (voters) | 6.267 | Mean (voters) | 6.157 |
| Median (voters) | 6.313 | Median (voters) | 6.250 |
| Number (alternates) | 7 | Number (alternates) | 7 |
| Mean (alternates) | 6.179 | Mean (alternates) | 6.172 |
| Median (alternates) | 6.313 | Median (alternates) | 6.250 |
| Number (all) | 18 | Number (all) | 18 |
| Mean (all) | 6.233 | Mean (all) | 6.163 |
| Median (all) | 6.313 | Median (all) | 6.250 |

| November 17, 1970 (99) | | December 15, 1970 (99) | |
|---|---|---|---|
| *Individual voters' desired funds rates* | | | |
| Burns | 4.974 A | Maisel | 4.500 |
| Maisel | 5.000 | Mayo | 4.500 |
| Sherrill | 5.000 | Burns | 4.866 A |
| Heflin | 5.370 LT | Mitchell | 5.000 |
| Brimmer | 5.375 | Robertson | 5.000 |
| Daane | 5.375 | Sherrill | 5.000 |
| Francis | 5.375 | Swan | 5.000 |
| Hickman | 5.375 | Brimmer | 5.125 |
| Mitchell | 5.375 | Daane | 5.125 |
| Robertson | 5.375 | Hayes | 5.125 |
| Swan | 5.375 | Heflin | 5.136 LT |
| Hayes | 5.750 | Francis | 5.250 |
| *Individual alternates' desired funds rates* | | | |
| Mayo | 4.500 | Galusha | 4.500 |
| Morris | 4.500 | Morris | 4.500 |
| Galusha | 5.000 | Coldwell | 5.000 |
| Clay | 5.375 | Eastburn | 5.000 |
| Coldwell | 5.375 | Kimbrel | 5.000 |
| Eastburn | 5.375 | MacDonald | 5.000 |
| Fossum | 5.375 | Clay | 5.245 LT |
| *Summary statistics* | | | |
| Target funds rate | 5.375 | Target funds rate | 5.000 |
| Staff proposal | 4.875 | Staff proposal | 4.938 |
| Premeeting funds rate | 5.643 | Premeeting funds rate | 4.732 |
| Number (voters) | 12 | Number (voters) | 12 |
| Mean (voters) | 5.310 | Mean (voters) | 4.969 |
| Median (voters) | 5.375 | Median (voters) | 5.000 |
| Number (alternates) | 7 | Number (alternates) | 7 |
| Mean (alternates) | 5.071 | Mean (alternates) | 4.892 |
| Median (alternates) | 5.375 | Median (alternates) | 5.000 |
| Number (all) | 19 | Number (all) | 19 |
| Mean (all) | 5.222 | Mean (all) | 4.941 |
| Median (all) | 5.375 | Median (all) | 5.000 |

| January 12, 1971 (99) | | February 9, 1971 (99, 63) | |
|---|---|---|---|
| *Individual voters' desired funds rates* | | | |
| Maisel | 4.125 | Maisel | 3.250 |
| Mitchell | 4.250 | Mayo | 3.250 |
| Daane | 4.375 | Sherrill | 3.250 |
| Heflin | 4.375 | Burns | 3.625 |
| Treiber | 4.375 | Brimmer | 3.875 |
| Burns | 4.376 A | Daane | 3.875 |
| Mayo | 4.389 A | Hayes | 3.875 |
| Robertson | 4.389 A | Heflin | 3.875 |
| Brimmer | 4.500 | Mitchell | 3.875 |
| Swan | 4.800 LT | Robertson | 3.875 |
| Francis | 5.375 | Swan | 3.875 |
| | | Francis | 3.950 LT |
| *Individual alternates' desired funds rates* | | | |
| Morris | 4.121 LE | MacDonald | 3.250 |
| Coldwell | 4.250 | Morris | 3.250 |
| Galusha | 4.375 | Strohman | 3.250 |
| MacDonald | 4.375 | Clay | 3.875 |
| Kimbrel | 4.761 LT | Coldwell | 3.875 |
| Clay | 5.375 | Eastburn | 3.875 |
| Eastburn | 5.375 | Kimbrel | 3.875 |
| *Summary statistics* | | | |
| Target funds rate | 4.250 | Target funds rate | 3.625 |
| Staff proposal | 4.375 | Staff proposal | 3.250 |
| Premeeting funds rate | 4.518 | Premeeting funds rate | 3.911 |
| Number (voters) | 11 | Number (voters) | 12 |
| Mean (voters) | 4.484 | Mean (voters) | 3.704 |
| Median (voters) | 4.376 | Median (voters) | 3.875 |
| Number (alternates) | 7 | Number (alternates) | 7 |
| Mean (alternates) | 4.662 | Mean (alternates) | 3.607 |
| Median (alternates) | 4.375 | Median (alternates) | 3.875 |
| Number (all) | 18 | Number (all) | 19 |
| Mean (all) | 4.553 | Mean (all) | 3.668 |
| Median (all) | 4.376 | Median (all) | 3.875 |

| March 9, 1971 (99) | | April 6, 1971 (99, 63) | |
|---|---|---|---|
| *Individual voters' desired funds rates* | | | |
| Daane | 3.500 | Morris | 3.875 |
| Maisel | 3.500 | Burns | 4.000 |
| Mitchell | 3.500 | Daane | 4.000 |
| Morris | 3.500 | Maisel | 4.000 |
| Robertson | 3.500 | Mayo | 4.000 |
| Sherrill | 3.500 | Sherrill | 4.000 |
| Burns | 3.538 LE | Brimmer | 4.375 |
| Mayo | 3.625 | Clay | 4.375 |
| Hayes | 3.750 | Robertson | 4.375 |
| Brimmer | 4.185 LT | Hayes | 4.500 |
| Kimbrel | 4.227 LT | Kimbrel | 4.750 |
| Clay | 4.500 | | |
| *Individual alternates' desired funds rates* | | | |
| Coldwell | 3.500 | Strohman | 3.750 |
| Strohman | 3.500 | Coldwell | 4.000 |
| Heflin | 3.514 LE | Heflin | 4.000 |
| Swan | 3.625 | MacDonald | 4.000 |
| Eastburn | 4.000 | Swan | 4.000 |
| MacDonald | 4.000 | Melnicoff | 4.281 A |
| Francis | 4.575 LT | Francis | 4.989 LT |
| *Summary statistics* | | | |
| Target funds rate | 3.500 | Target funds rate | 4.000 |
| Staff proposal | 3.875 | Staff proposal | 4.250 |
| Premeeting funds rate | 3.321 | Premeeting funds rate | 4.089 |
| Number (voters) | 12 | Number (voters) | 11 |
| Mean (voters) | 3.735 | Mean (voters) | 4.205 |
| Median (voters) | 3.519 | Median (voters) | 4.000 |
| Number (alternates) | 7 | Number (alternates) | 7 |
| Mean (alternates) | 3.816 | Mean (alternates) | 4.146 |
| Median (alternates) | 3.625 | Median (alternates) | 4.000 |
| Number (all) | 19 | Number (all) | 18 |
| Mean (all) | 3.765 | Mean (all) | 4.182 |
| Median (all) | 3.538 | Median (all) | 4.000 |

| May 11, 1971 (99) | | June 8, 1971 (99, 63) | |
|---|---|---|---|
| *Individual voters' desired funds rates* | | | |
| Maisel | 4.250 | Maisel | 4.769 LE |
| Morris | 4.250 | Sherrill | 4.813 LE |
| Sherrill | 4.355 LE | Daane | 5.220 A |
| Brimmer | 4.435 LE | Brimmer | 5.250 |
| Burns | 4.453 LE | Burns | 5.250 |
| Mayo | 4.500 | Clay | 5.250 |
| Mitchell | 4.500 | Kimbrel | 5.250 |
| Clay | 4.750 | Mayo | 5.250 |
| Daane | 4.750 | Morris | 5.250 |
| Hayes | 4.750 | Robertson | 5.250 |
| Robertson | 4.750 | Treiber | 5.489 LT |
| Kimbrel | 5.149 LT | Mitchell | 6.000 |
| *Individual alternates' desired funds rates* | | | |
| Heflin | 4.500 | Strohman | 4.884 LE |
| Coldwell | 4.750 | Heflin | 4.906 |
| MacDonald | 4.750 | MacDonald | 4.940 LE |
| Strohman | 4.750 | Coldwell | 5.250 |
| Swan | 4.750 | Swan | 5.250 |
| Eastburn | 5.231 LT | Eastburn | 6.000 |
| Francis | 5.600 LT | Francis | 6.054 LT |
| *Summary statistics* | | | |
| Target funds rate | 4.500 | Target funds rate | 5.250 |
| Staff proposal | 4.750 | Staff proposal | 5.250 |
| Premeeting funds rate | 4.661 | Premeeting funds rate | 4.732 |
| Number (voters) | 12 | Number (voters) | 12 |
| Mean (voters) | 4.574 | Mean (voters) | 5.253 |
| Median (voters) | 4.500 | Median (voters) | 5.250 |
| Number (alternates) | 7 | Number (alternates) | 7 |
| Mean (alternates) | 4.904 | Mean (alternates) | 5.326 |
| Median (alternates) | 4.750 | Median (alternates) | 5.250 |
| Number (all) | 19 | Number (all) | 19 |
| Mean (all) | 4.696 | Mean (all) | 5.280 |
| Median (all) | 4.750 | Median (all) | 5.250 |

| June 29, 1971 (99, 63) | | July 27, 1971 (99) | |
|---|---|---|---|
| *Individual voters' desired funds rates* | | | |
| Maisel | 4.853 LE | Hayes | 5.470 LE |
| Morris | 5.125 | Brimmer | 5.500 |
| Mayo | 5.236 A | Clay | 5.500 |
| Brimmer | 5.250 | Maisel | 5.500 |
| Burns | 5.250 | Mitchell | 5.500 |
| Clay | 5.250 | Morris | 5.500 |
| Mitchell | 5.250 | Sherrill | 5.500 |
| Robertson | 5.250 | Daane | 5.625 |
| Daane | 5.265 A | Mayo | 5.625 |
| Coldwell | 5.375 | Burns | 5.682 A |
| Hayes | 5.547 LT | Kimbrel | 5.750 |
| Sherrill | 5.555 LT | Robertson | 5.750 |
| *Individual alternates' desired funds rates* | | | |
| Strohman | 5.000 | Heflin | 5.500 |
| Fossum | 5.250 | MacDonald | 5.500 |
| Heflin | 5.250 | MacLaury | 5.500 |
| MacDonald | 5.250 | Coldwell | 5.750 |
| Melnicoff | 5.250 | Eastburn | 5.750 |
| Swan | 5.250 | Swan | 5.853 A |
| Francis | 6.023 LT | Francis | 6.408 LT |
| *Summary statistics* | | | |
| Target funds rate | 5.250 | Target funds rate | 5.563 |
| Staff proposal | 5.250 | Staff proposal | 5.750 |
| Premeeting funds rate | 5.107 | Premeeting funds rate | 5.393 |
| Number (voters) | 12 | Number (voters) | 12 |
| Mean (voters) | 5.267 | Mean (voters) | 5.575 |
| Median (voters) | 5.250 | Median (voters) | 5.500 |
| Number (alternates) | 7 | Number (alternates) | 7 |
| Mean (alternates) | 5.325 | Mean (alternates) | 5.752 |
| Median (alternates) | 5.250 | Median (alternates) | 5.750 |
| Number (all) | 19 | Number (all) | 19 |
| Mean (all) | 5.288 | Mean (all) | 5.640 |
| Median (all) | 5.250 | Median (all) | 5.500 |

| August 24, 1971 (99) | | September 21, 1971 (99, 63) | |
|---|---|---|---|
| *Individual voters' desired funds rates* | | | |
| Robertson | 4.750 | Maisel | 4.750 |
| Burns | 4.872 A | Morris | 5.000 |
| Maisel | 5.000 | Sherrill | 5.000 |
| Mitchell | 5.169 LT | Robertson | 5.071 A |
| Clay | 5.375 | Brimmer | 5.116 A |
| Mayo | 5.375 | Daane | 5.125 |
| Sherrill | 5.375 | Mayo | 5.125 |
| Hayes | 5.500 | Mitchell | 5.125 |
| Brimmer | 5.563 | Burns | 5.313 |
| Daane | 5.563 | Clay | 5.313 |
| Kimbrel | 5.563 | Hayes | 5.313 |
| Morris | 5.563 | Kimbrel | 5.313 |
| *Individual alternates' desired funds rates* | | | |
| MacLaury | 5.016 LT | Coldwell | 5.000 |
| Coldwell | 5.375 | MacLaury | 5.000 |
| Swan | 5.375 | Swan | 5.000 |
| Eastburn | 5.563 | Heflin | 5.083 A |
| Francis | 5.563 | Winn | 5.110 A |
| Heflin | 5.563 | Eastburn | 5.313 |
| MacDonald | 5.563 | Francis | 5.313 |
| *Summary statistics* | | | |
| Target funds rate | 5.375 | Target funds rate | 5.313 |
| Staff proposal | 4.750 | Staff proposal | 5.063 |
| Premeeting funds rate | 5.518 | Premeeting funds rate | 5.384 |
| Number (voters) | 12 | Number (voters) | 12 |
| Mean (voters) | 5.305 | Mean (voters) | 5.130 |
| Median (voters) | 5.375 | Median (voters) | 5.125 |
| Number (alternates) | 7 | Number (alternates) | 7 |
| Mean (alternates) | 5.431 | Mean (alternates) | 5.117 |
| Median (alternates) | 5.563 | Median (alternates) | 5.083 |
| Number (all) | 19 | Number (all) | 19 |
| Mean (all) | 5.352 | Mean (all) | 5.125 |
| Median (all) | 5.375 | Median (all) | 5.116 |

| October 19, 1971 (99) | | November 16, 1971 (99, 63) | |
|---|---|---|---|
| *Individual voters' desired funds rates* | | | |
| Maisel | 4.750 | Maisel | 4.377 A |
| Mitchell | 4.750 | Daane | 4.421 A |
| Morris | 4.750 | Kimbrel | 4.438 |
| Robertson | 4.750 | Brimmer | 4.563 |
| Hayes | 4.816 A | Burns | 4.563 |
| Burns | 4.823 A | Morris | 4.563 |
| Mayo | 5.063 | Robertson | 4.563 |
| Clay | 5.118 LT | Mayo | 4.625 |
| Brimmer | 5.188 | Clay | 4.688 |
| Kimbrel | 5.188 | Hayes | 4.806 LT |
| Sherrill | 5.188 | Mitchell | 4.868 |
| | | | |
| *Individual alternates' desired funds rates* | | | |
| MacLaury | 4.961 LT | Eastburn | 4.563 |
| Swan | 5.063 | Heflin | 4.563 |
| Coldwell | 5.125 | MacLaury | 4.563 |
| Black | 5.188 | Swan | 4.563 |
| Eastburn | 5.188 | Coldwell | 4.625 |
| Francis | 5.188 | Winn | 4.625 |
| Winn | 5.188 | Leonard | 4.688 |
| *Summary statistics* | | | |
| Target funds rate | 5.063 | Target funds rate | 4.563 |
| Staff proposal | 4.750 | Staff proposal | 4.375 |
| Premeeting funds rate | 5.286 | Premeeting funds rate | 4.857 |
| Number (voters) | 11 | Number (voters) | 11 |
| Mean (voters) | 4.944 | Mean (voters) | 4.588 |
| Median (voters) | 4.823 | Median (voters) | 4.563 |
| Number (alternates) | 7 | Number (alternates) | 7 |
| Mean (alternates) | 5.128 | Mean (alternates) | 4.598 |
| Median (alternates) | 5.188 | Median (alternates) | 4.563 |
| Number (all) | 18 | Number (all) | 18 |
| Mean (all) | 5.016 | Mean (all) | 4.592 |
| Median (all) | 5.090 | Median (all) | 4.563 |

| December 14, 1971 (99) | | January 11, 1972 (99) | |
|---|---|---|---|
| *Individual voters' desired funds rates* | | | |
| Mitchell | 3.813 | Sheehan | 2.781 LE |
| Daane | 4.007 LE | Morris | 2.918 LE |
| Maisel | 4.051 LE | Clay | 3.125 |
| Morris | 4.313 | Robertson | 3.125 |
| Robertson | 4.313 | Mitchell | 3.167 A |
| Burns | 4.320 A | Daane | 3.206 A |
| Brimmer | 4.361 A | Burns | 3.208 A |
| Clay | 4.375 | Brimmer | 3.209 A |
| Mayo | 4.375 | Kimbrel | 3.500 |
| Kimbrel | 4.438 | Maisel | 3.500 |
| Hayes | 4.500 | Mayo | 3.500 |
| | | Hayes | 3.625 |
| *Individual alternates' desired funds rates* | | | |
| Coldwell | 4.313 | MacDonald | 2.877 LE |
| MacLaury | 4.313 | MacLaury | 2.982 LE |
| Winn | 4.313 | Coldwell | 3.125 |
| Heflin | 4.316 A | Swan | 3.125 |
| Swan | 4.438 | Willes | 3.125 |
| Eastburn | 4.813 | Heflin | 3.313 |
| Francis | 4.813 | Francis | 3.500 |
| *Summary statistics* | | | |
| Target funds rate | 4.188 | Target funds rate | 3.125 |
| Staff proposal | 4.313 | Staff proposal | 3.125 |
| Premeeting funds rate | 4.536 | Premeeting funds rate | 3.786 |
| Number (voters) | 11 | Number (voters) | 12 |
| Mean (voters) | 4.260 | Mean (voters) | 3.239 |
| Median (voters) | 4.320 | Median (voters) | 3.207 |
| Number (alternates) | 7 | Number (alternates) | 7 |
| Mean (alternates) | 4.474 | Mean (alternates) | 3.149 |
| Median (alternates) | 4.316 | Median (alternates) | 3.125 |
| Number (all) | 18 | Number (all) | 19 |
| Mean (all) | 4.343 | Mean (all) | 3.206 |
| Median (all) | 4.318 | Median (all) | 3.167 |

| February 15, 1972 (99, 63, 43) | | March 21, 1972 (99) | |
|---|---|---|---|
| *Individual voters' desired funds rates* | | | |
| Mitchell | 3.149 LE | Sheehan | 4.000 |
| Sheehan | 3.151 LE | Burns | 4.063 A |
| Burns | 3.250 | Brimmer | 4.125 |
| Mayo | 3.375 | Daane | 4.125 |
| Brimmer | 3.500 | MacLaury | 4.125 |
| Clay | 3.500 | Maisel | 4.125 |
| Daane | 3.500 | Mitchell | 4.125 |
| Hayes | 3.500 | Robertson | 4.125 |
| Maisel | 3.500 | Winn | 4.250 |
| Morris | 3.500 | Hayes | 4.445 LT |
| Robertson | 3.500 | Coldwell | 4.447 LT |
| Kimbrel | 3.879 LT | Eastburn | 4.500 |
| *Individual alternates' desired funds rates* | | | |
| Heflin | 3.500 | Heflin | 3.750 |
| Swan | 3.500 | Clay | 4.125 |
| Winn | 3.561 A | Morris | 4.125 |
| MacLaury | 3.625 | Mayo | 4.250 |
| Eastburn | 3.750 | Swan | 4.250 |
| Coldwell | 3.821 LT | Kimbrel | 4.509 LT |
| Francis | 4.500 | Francis | 5.000 |
| *Summary statistics* | | | |
| Target funds rate | 3.375 | Target funds rate | 4.125 |
| Staff proposal | 3.500 | Staff proposal | 4.125 |
| Premeeting funds rate | 3.321 | Premeeting funds rate | 3.911 |
| Number (voters) | 12 | Number (voters) | 12 |
| Mean (voters) | 3.442 | Mean (voters) | 4.205 |
| Median (voters) | 3.500 | Median (voters) | 4.125 |
| Number (alternates) | 7 | Number (alternates) | 7 |
| Mean (alternates) | 3.751 | Mean (alternates) | 4.287 |
| Median (alternates) | 3.625 | Median (alternates) | 4.250 |
| Number (all) | 19 | Number (all) | 19 |
| Mean (all) | 3.556 | Mean (all) | 4.235 |
| Median (all) | 3.500 | Median (all) | 4.125 |

| April 17, 1972 (99) | | May 23, 1972 (99, 63) | |
|---|---|---|---|
| *Individual voters' desired funds rates* | | | |
| Maisel | 4.125 | Sheehan | 4.485 LE |
| Sheehan | 4.186 LE | Brimmer | 4.508 LE |
| Mitchell | 4.250 | Burns | 4.625 |
| Burns | 4.298 LE | MacLaury | 4.750 |
| Brimmer | 4.500 | Daane | 4.875 |
| Hayes | 4.500 | Eastburn | 4.875 |
| Daane | 4.593 A | Hayes | 4.875 |
| Coldwell | 4.625 | Mitchell | 4.875 |
| MacLaury | 4.625 | Winn | 4.875 |
| Robertson | 4.850 LT | Coldwell | 5.176 LT |
| Winn | 5.021 LT | | |
| Eastburn | 5.076 LT | | |
| *Individual alternates' desired funds rates* | | | |
| Swan | 4.499 A | Black | 4.625 |
| Heflin | 4.500 | Merritt | 4.750 |
| Morris | 4.500 | Kimbrel | 4.875 |
| Kimbrel | 4.685 A | Mayo | 4.875 |
| Mayo | 4.750 | Morris | 4.875 |
| Clay | 5.000 | Clay | 5.000 |
| Francis | 5.261 LT | Leonard | 5.375 |
| *Summary statistics* | | | |
| Target funds rate | 4.500 | Target funds rate | 4.875 |
| Staff proposal | 4.625 | Staff proposal | 4.875 |
| Premeeting funds rate | 4.134 | Premeeting funds rate | 4.304 |
| Number (voters) | 12 | Number (voters) | 10 |
| Mean (voters) | 4.554 | Mean (voters) | 4.792 |
| Median (voters) | 4.546 | Median (voters) | 4.875 |
| Number (alternates) | 7 | Number (alternates) | 7 |
| Mean (alternates) | 4.742 | Mean (alternates) | 4.911 |
| Median (alternates) | 4.685 | Median (alternates) | 4.875 |
| Number (all) | 19 | Number (all) | 17 |
| Mean (all) | 4.623 | Mean (all) | 4.841 |
| Median (all) | 4.593 | Median (all) | 4.875 |

| June 19, 1972 (99, 63, 43) | | July 18, 1972 (99, 63, 43) | |
|---|---|---|---|
| *Individual voters' desired funds rates* | | | |
| Sheehan | 4.729 A | Brimmer | 4.750 |
| Burns | 4.750 | Burns | 4.750 |
| Coldwell | 4.750 | Daane | 4.750 |
| Eastburn | 4.750 | Robertson | 4.750 |
| Mitchell | 4.750 | Sheehan | 4.750 |
| Bucher | 4.764 A | Bucher | 4.772 A |
| Winn | 4.801 A | Eastburn | 4.783 A |
| Brimmer | 4.875 | Winn | 4.798 A |
| Daane | 4.875 | MacLaury | 4.875 |
| MacLaury | 4.875 | Hayes | 5.000 |
| Treiber | 4.875 | Coldwell | 5.073 LT |
| Robertson | 4.978 LT | | |
| *Individual alternates' desired funds rates* | | | |
| Heflin | 4.446 LE | Heflin | 4.750 |
| Mayo | 4.750 | Mayo | 4.875 |
| Morris | 4.993 LT | Kimbrel | 5.109 LT |
| Francis | 5.250 | Leonard | 5.250 |
| Kimbrel | 5.250 | | |
| *Summary statistics* | | | |
| Target funds rate | 4.750 | Target funds rate | 4.750 |
| Staff proposal | 4.750 | Staff proposal | 4.750 |
| Premeeting funds rate | 4.393 | Premeeting funds rate | 4.518 |
| Number (voters) | 12 | Number (voters) | 11 |
| Mean (voters) | 4.814 | Mean (voters) | 4.823 |
| Median (voters) | 4.782 | Median (voters) | 4.772 |
| Number (alternates) | 5 | Number (alternates) | 4 |
| Mean (alternates) | 4.938 | Mean (alternates) | 4.996 |
| Median (alternates) | 4.993 | Median (alternates) | 4.992 |
| Number (all) | 17 | Number (all) | 15 |
| Mean (all) | 4.851 | Mean (all) | 4.869 |
| Median (all) | 4.801 | Median (all) | 4.783 |

| August 15, 1972 (99) | | September 19, 1972 (99) | |
|---|---|---|---|
| *Individual voters' desired funds rates* | | | |
| Bucher | 4.750 | Burns | 4.928 LE |
| Daane | 4.750 | Sheehan | 5.063 |
| Mitchell | 4.750 | Bucher | 5.125 |
| Sheehan | 4.875 | Daane | 5.125 |
| Burns | 4.924 LE | Mitchell | 5.234 A |
| Brimmer | 5.000 | Coldwell | 5.265 A |
| MacLaury | 5.000 | Brimmer | 5.375 |
| Winn | 5.000 | Eastburn | 5.375 |
| Coldwell | 5.125 | Hayes | 5.375 |
| Eastburn | 5.125 | MacLaury | 5.375 |
| Robertson | 5.245 A | Robertson | 5.375 |
| Hayes | 5.250 | Winn | 5.375 |
| *Individual alternates' desired funds rates* | | | |
| Heflin | 4.750 | Heflin | 4.965 LE |
| Merritt | 5.000 | Merritt | 5.125 |
| Morris | 5.000 | Mayo | 5.250 |
| Kimbrel | 5.125 | Kimbrel | 5.305 A |
| Francis | 5.250 | Clay | 5.375 |
| Mayo | 5.250 | Morris | 5.375 |
| Clay | 5.375 | Francis | 5.875 |
| *Summary statistics* | | | |
| Target funds rate | 4.875 | Target funds rate | 5.063 |
| Staff proposal | 5.250 | Staff proposal | 5.250 |
| Premeeting funds rate | 4.804 | Premeeting funds rate | 4.831 |
| Number (voters) | 12 | Number (voters) | 12 |
| Mean (voters) | 4.983 | Mean (voters) | 5.249 |
| Median (voters) | 5.000 | Median (voters) | 5.320 |
| Number (alternates) | 7 | Number (alternates) | 7 |
| Mean (alternates) | 5.107 | Mean (alternates) | 5.324 |
| Median (alternates) | 5.125 | Median (alternates) | 5.305 |
| Number (all) | 19 | Number (all) | 19 |
| Mean (all) | 5.029 | Mean (all) | 5.277 |
| Median (all) | 5.000 | Median (all) | 5.305 |

| October 17, 1972 (99, 63, 43) | | November 20, 1972 (99, 63) | |
|---|---|---|---|
| *Individual voters' desired funds rates* | | | |
| Daane | 5.041 LE | Brimmer | 5.125 |
| Burns | 5.125 | Bucher | 5.125 |
| Robertson | 5.125 | Burns | 5.125 |
| Hayes | 5.250 | Daane | 5.125 |
| Bucher | 5.306 A | Eastburn | 5.125 |
| Sheehan | 5.346 A | Francis | 5.125 |
| Mitchell | 5.359 A | Hayes | 5.125 |
| Brimmer | 5.361 A | MacLaury | 5.125 |
| MacLaury | 5.375 A | Robertson | 5.125 |
| Coldwell | 5.396 A | Sheehan | 5.125 |
| Eastburn | 5.414 A | Winn | 5.125 |
| Winn | 5.431 A | Mitchell | 5.250 |
| *Individual alternates' desired funds rates* | | | |
| No alternates spoke in the policy | | Heflin | 5.125 |
| go-around. | | Mayo | 5.250 |
| | | Morris | 5.250 |
| | | Plant | 5.313 |
| | | Balles | 5.405 LT |
| | | Clay | 5.415 LT |
| | | Kimbrel | 5.469 LT |
| *Summary statistics* | | | |
| Target funds rate | 5.125 | Target funds rate | 5.125 |
| Staff proposal | 5.375 | Staff proposal | 5.125 |
| Premeeting funds rate | 4.965 | Premeeting funds rate | 4.697 |
| Number (voters) | 12 | Number (voters) | 12 |
| Mean (voters) | 5.294 | Mean (voters) | 5.135 |
| Median (voters) | 5.352 | Median (voters) | 5.125 |
| Number (alternates) | 0 | Number (alternates) | 7 |
| Mean (alternates) | | Mean (alternates) | 5.318 |
| Median (alternates) | | Median (alternates) | 5.313 |
| Number (all) | 12 | Number (all) | 19 |
| Mean (all) | 5.294 | Mean (all) | 5.203 |
| Median (all) | 5.352 | Median (all) | 5.125 |

| December 19, 1972 (99, 63, 43) | | January 16, 1973 (99) | |
|---|---|---|---|
| *Individual voters' desired funds rates* | | | |
| Sheehan | 5.476 A | Sheehan | 5.535 LE |
| Daane | 5.499 A | Mitchell | 5.591 LE |
| Burns | 5.500 | Burns | 5.872 A |
| Coldwell | 5.500 | Bucher | 5.930 A |
| Hayes | 5.500 | Daane | 5.933 |
| Mitchell | 5.502 A | Coldwell | 5.985 A |
| MacLaury | 5.505 A | Winn | 6.036 A |
| Robertson | 5.516 A | Brimmer | 6.125 |
| Brimmer | 5.518 A | Treiber | 6.125 |
| Bucher | 5.531 A | MacLaury | 6.139 LT |
| Eastburn | 5.537 A | Robertson | 6.194 LT |
| Winn | 5.571 A | Eastburn | 6.375 |
| *Individual alternates' desired funds rates* | | | |
| Heflin | 5.500 | Mayo | 5.938 |
| Morris | 5.505 A | Balles | 5.955 A |
| Clay | 5.509 A | Heflin | 6.000 |
| Balles | 5.509 A | Morris | 6.250 |
| Mayo | 5.513 A | | |
| Kimbrel | 5.573 A | | |
| Francis | 5.583 A | | |
| *Summary statistics* | | | |
| Target funds rate | 5.500 | Target funds rate | 6.063 |
| Staff proposal | 5.500 | Staff proposal | 5.938 |
| Premeeting funds rate | 5.429 | Premeeting funds rate | 5.696 |
| Number (voters) | 12 | Number (voters) | 12 |
| Mean (voters) | 5.513 | Mean (voters) | 5.987 |
| Median (voters) | 5.504 | Median (voters) | 6.010 |
| Number (alternates) | 7 | Number (alternates) | 4 |
| Mean (alternates) | 5.528 | Mean (alternates) | 6.036 |
| Median (alternates) | 5.509 | Median (alternates) | 5.978 |
| Number (all) | 19 | Number (all) | 16 |
| Mean (all) | 5.518 | Mean (all) | 5.999 |
| Median (all) | 5.509 | Median (all) | 5.992 |

| February 13, 1973 (99) | | March 19, 1973 (99, 63, 43) | |
|---|---|---|---|
| *Individual voters' desired funds rates* | | | |
| Burns | 6.207 A | Bucher | 7.000 |
| Mitchell | 6.252 A | Burns | 7.000 |
| Sheehan | 6.313 | Daane | 7.000 |
| Winn | 6.358 A | Morris | 7.000 |
| Brimmer | 6.375 | Sheehan | 7.000 |
| Bucher | 6.375 | Mitchell | 7.014 A |
| Coldwell | 6.375 | Robertson | 7.035 A |
| Hayes | 6.375 | Brimmer | 7.125 |
| MacLaury | 6.375 | Francis | 7.125 |
| Robertson | 6.527 LT | Balles | 7.250 |
| Eastburn | 6.706 LT | Hayes | 7.250 |
| | | Mayo | 7.250 |
| *Individual alternates' desired funds rates* | | | |
| Black | 6.250 | Black | 7.125 |
| Mayo | 6.250 | Kimbrel | 7.125 |
| Morris | 6.250 | MacLaury | 7.125 |
| Balles | 6.375 | Coldwell | 7.250 |
| Kimbrel | 6.375 | | |
| Francis | 6.500 | | |
| Clay | 6.606 LT | | |
| *Summary statistics* | | | |
| Target funds rate | 6.375 | Target funds rate | 7.125 |
| Staff proposal | 6.250 | Staff proposal | 7.000 |
| Premeeting funds rate | 6.188 | Premeeting funds rate | 7.214 |
| Number (voters) | 11 | Number (voters) | 12 |
| Mean (voters) | 6.385 | Mean (voters) | 7.087 |
| Median (voters) | 6.375 | Median (voters) | 7.025 |
| Number (alternates) | 7 | Number (alternates) | 4 |
| Mean (alternates) | 6.372 | Mean (alternates) | 7.156 |
| Median (alternates) | 6.375 | Median (alternates) | 7.125 |
| Number (all) | 18 | Number (all) | 16 |
| Mean (all) | 6.380 | Mean (all) | 7.105 |
| Median (all) | 6.375 | Median (all) | 7.125 |

| April 17, 1973 (99) | | May 15, 1973 (99, 63) | |
|---|---|---|---|
| *Individual voters' desired funds rates* | | | |
| Burns | 6.913 A | Burns | 7.563 |
| Morris | 7.000 | Balles | 7.625 |
| Sheehan | 7.000 | Brimmer | 7.625 |
| Winn | 7.045 A | Bucher | 7.625 |
| Bucher | 7.125 | Daane | 7.625 |
| Balles | 7.245 LT | Morris | 7.625 |
| Daane | 7.250 | Sheehan | 7.625 |
| Robertson | 7.250 | Francis | 7.875 |
| Mitchell | 7.330 LT | Hayes | 7.875 |
| Brimmer | 7.331 LT | Mayo | 7.875 |
| Hayes | 7.375 | | |
| Francis | 7.500 | | |
| *Individual alternates' desired funds rates* | | | |
| Black | 7.125 | Black | 7.625 |
| Coldwell | 7.250 | Clay | 7.625 |
| MacLaury | 7.250 | Eastburn | 7.625 |
| Kimbrel | 7.375 | MacLaury | 7.625 |
| | | Winn | 7.625 |
| | | Kimbrel | 7.750 |
| | | Coldwell | 7.875 |
| *Summary statistics* | | | |
| Target funds rate | 7.188 | Target funds rate | 7.563 |
| Staff proposal | 7.000 | Staff proposal | 7.625 |
| Premeeting funds rate | 6.750 | Premeeting funds rate | 7.723 |
| Number (voters) | 12 | Number (voters) | 10 |
| Mean (voters) | 7.197 | Mean (voters) | 7.694 |
| Median (voters) | 7.248 | Median (voters) | 7.625 |
| Number (alternates) | 4 | Number (alternates) | 7 |
| Mean (alternates) | 7.250 | Mean (alternates) | 7.679 |
| Median (alternates) | 7.250 | Median (alternates) | 7.625 |
| Number (all) | 16 | Number (all) | 17 |
| Mean (all) | 7.210 | Mean (all) | 7.688 |
| Median (all) | 7.250 | Median (all) | 7.625 |

| June 18, 1973 (99) | | July 17, 1973 (99, 63, 43) | |
|---|---|---|---|
| *Individual voters' desired funds rates* | | | |
| Sheehan | 7.750 | Bucher | 9.250 |
| Bucher | 8.000 | Sheehan | 9.250 |
| Mayo | 8.000 | Brimmer | 9.750 |
| Holland | 8.253 LE | Daane | 9.750 |
| Burns | 8.422 A | Holland | 9.750 |
| Daane | 8.467 A | Mayo | 9.750 |
| Brimmer | 8.479 A | Morris | 9.750 |
| Mitchell | 8.481 A | Balles | 9.754 A |
| Clay | 8.500 | Burns | 10.000 |
| Francis | 8.500 | Hayes | 10.000 |
| Debs | 8.625 | Francis | 10.125 LT |
| Morris | 8.750 | | |
| *Individual alternates' desired funds rates* | | | |
| Eastburn | 8.183 LE | MacLaury | 9.250 |
| Black | 8.375 | Willes | 9.529 LE |
| Kimbrel | 8.500 | Black | 9.750 |
| Coldwell | 8.518 A | Clay | 9.750 |
| Winn | 8.560 A | Winn | 9.750 |
| MacLaury | 8.750 | Kimbrel | 9.801 A |
| | | Coldwell | 10.000 |
| *Summary statistics* | | | |
| Target funds rate | 8.500 | Target funds rate | 9.750 |
| Staff proposal | 8.500 | Staff proposal | 9.750 |
| Premeeting funds rate | 8.259 | Premeeting funds rate | 9.723 |
| Number (voters) | 12 | Number (voters) | 11 |
| Mean (voters) | 8.352 | Mean (voters) | 9.739 |
| Median (voters) | 8.473 | Median (voters) | 9.750 |
| Number (alternates) | 6 | Number (alternates) | 7 |
| Mean (alternates) | 8.481 | Mean (alternates) | 9.690 |
| Median (alternates) | 8.509 | Median (alternates) | 9.750 |
| Number (all) | 18 | Number (all) | 18 |
| Mean (all) | 8.395 | Mean (all) | 9.720 |
| Median (all) | 8.480 | Median (all) | 9.750 |

| August 21, 1973 (99, 63) | | September 18, 1973 (99, 63, 43) | |
|---|---|---|---|
| *Individual voters' desired funds rates* | | | |
| Mayo | 10.000 | Balles | 9.750 |
| Sheehan | 10.077 LE | Bucher | 9.750 |
| Bucher | 10.202 A | Sheehan | 9.750 |
| Morris | 10.250 | Francis | 9.771 LE |
| Daane | 10.484 A | Morris | 9.875 |
| Balles | 10.500 | Holland | 9.940 LE |
| Brimmer | 10.500 | Mayo | 10.135 A |
| Burns | 10.500 | Mitchell | 10.152 A |
| Francis | 10.500 | Daane | 10.188 A |
| Holland | 10.500 | Burns | 10.250 |
| Hayes | 10.504 A | Debs | 10.750 |
| | | | |
| *Individual alternates' desired funds rates* | | | |
| MacLaury | 10.000 | Clay | 10.125 |
| Black | 10.500 | Eastburn | 10.125 |
| Clay | 10.500 | Coldwell | 10.250 |
| Kimbrel | 10.500 | MacLaury | 10.250 |
| Winn | 10.500 | Black | 10.500 |
| Eastburn | 10.514 A | Fossum | 10.500 |
| Coldwell | 10.527 A | Winn | 10.500 |
| *Summary statistics* | | | |
| Target funds rate | 10.500 | Target funds rate | 10.250 |
| Staff proposal | 10.500 | Staff proposal | 10.125 |
| Premeeting funds rate | 10.359 | Premeeting funds rate | 10.740 |
| Number (voters) | 11 | Number (voters) | 11 |
| Mean (voters) | 10.365 | Mean (voters) | 10.028 |
| Median (voters) | 10.500 | Median (voters) | 9.940 |
| Number (alternates) | 7 | Number (alternates) | 7 |
| Mean (alternates) | 10.434 | Mean (alternates) | 10.321 |
| Median (alternates) | 10.500 | Median (alternates) | 10.250 |
| Number (all) | 18 | Number (all) | 18 |
| Mean (all) | 10.392 | Mean (all) | 10.142 |
| Median (all) | 10.500 | Median (all) | 10.143 |

| October 16, 1973 (99) | | November 19, 1973 (99, 63, 43) | |
|---|---|---|---|
| *Individual voters' desired funds rates* | | | |
| Balles | 9.000 | Morris | 9.500 |
| Morris | 9.000 | Sheehan | 9.590 LE |
| Sheehan | 9.000 | Balles | 9.625 |
| Francis | 9.107 LE | Bucher | 9.625 |
| Burns | 9.432 A | Mayo | 9.625 |
| Bucher | 9.500 | Burns | 9.750 |
| Mayo | 9.500 | Brimmer | 10.000 |
| Mitchell | 9.500 | Daane | 10.000 |
| Brimmer | 9.625 | Francis | 10.000 |
| Holland | 9.625 | Hayes | 10.000 |
| Daane | 9.793 LT | Holland | 10.000 |
| Hayes | 9.802 LT | Mitchell | 10.000 |
| *Individual alternates' desired funds rates* | | | |
| Eastburn | 9.123 LE | MacLaury | 9.625 |
| Clay | 9.500 | Black | 10.000 |
| Kimbrel | 9.500 | Clay | 10.000 |
| Winn | 9.500 | Eastburn | 10.000 |
| Black | 9.625 | Kimbrel | 10.000 |
| Coldwell | 9.750 | Plant | 10.000 |
| Strohman | 9.750 | Winn | 10.000 |
| *Summary statistics* | | | |
| Target funds rate | 9.750 | Target funds rate | 9.750 |
| Staff proposal | 9.500 | Staff proposal | 10.000 |
| Premeeting funds rate | 9.449 | Premeeting funds rate | 10.254 |
| Number (voters) | 12 | Number (voters) | 12 |
| Mean (voters) | 9.407 | Mean (voters) | 9.810 |
| Median (voters) | 9.500 | Median (voters) | 9.875 |
| Number (alternates) | 7 | Number (alternates) | 7 |
| Mean (alternates) | 9.535 | Mean (alternates) | 9.946 |
| Median (alternates) | 9.500 | Median (alternates) | 10.000 |
| Number (all) | 19 | Number (all) | 19 |
| Mean (all) | 9.454 | Mean (all) | 9.860 |
| Median (all) | 9.500 | Median (all) | 10.000 |

| December 17, 1973 (99, 63, 43) | | January 21, 1974 (99) | |
|---|---|---|---|
| *Individual voters' desired funds rates* | | | |
| Bucher | 9.000 | Bucher | 9.000 |
| Morris | 9.000 | Morris | 9.000 |
| Sheehan | 9.216 LE | Sheehan | 9.125 |
| Mitchell | 9.292 LE | Holland | 9.375 |
| Daane | 9.321 LE | Mayo | 9.500 |
| Balles | 9.374 LE | Burns | 9.701 A |
| Brimmer | 9.375 | Mitchell | 9.736 A |
| Burns | 9.375 | Daane | 9.738 A |
| Mayo | 9.625 | Balles | 9.750 |
| Holland | 9.639 A | Brimmer | 9.750 |
| Francis | 9.664 A | Hayes | 9.750 |
| Hayes | 10.000 | Francis | 10.199 LT |
| *Individual alternates' desired funds rates* | | | |
| MacLaury | 9.250 | Black | 9.250 |
| Eastburn | 9.305 LE | Coldwell | 9.375 |
| Winn | 9.375 | MacLaury | 9.625 |
| Black | 9.436 LE | Eastburn | 9.750 |
| Clay | 9.625 | Kimbrel | 9.750 |
| Coldwell | 9.625 | Winn | 9.827 A |
| Kimbrel | 9.625 | Clay | 10.250 |
| *Summary statistics* | | | |
| Target funds rate | 9.375 | Target funds rate | 9.375 |
| Staff proposal | 9.625 | Staff proposal | 9.750 |
| Premeeting funds rate | 9.933 | Premeeting funds rate | 9.719 |
| Number (voters) | 12 | Number (voters) | 12 |
| Mean (voters) | 9.407 | Mean (voters) | 9.552 |
| Median (voters) | 9.374 | Median (voters) | 9.718 |
| Number (alternates) | 7 | Number (alternates) | 7 |
| Mean (alternates) | 9.463 | Mean (alternates) | 9.690 |
| Median (alternates) | 9.436 | Median (alternates) | 9.750 |
| Number (all) | 19 | Number (all) | 19 |
| Mean (all) | 9.427 | Mean (all) | 9.603 |
| Median (all) | 9.375 | Median (all) | 9.736 |

| February 20, 1974 (99) | | March 18, 1974 (99) | |
| --- | --- | --- | --- |
| *Individual voters' desired funds rates* | | | |
| Morris | 8.125 | Bucher | 9.000 |
| Bucher | 8.500 | Black | 9.500 |
| Sheehan | 8.500 | Mitchell | 9.568 LE |
| Mayo | 8.625 | Burns | 9.607 LE |
| Burns | 8.856 A | Holland | 9.750 |
| Brimmer | 8.875 | Brimmer | 10.000 |
| Holland | 8.875 | Clay | 10.000 |
| Mitchell | 8.875 | Hayes | 10.000 |
| Daane | 8.878 A | Sheehan | 10.000 |
| Hayes | 9.000 | Kimbrel | 10.625 |
| Balles | 9.110 LT | Wallich | 10.625 |
| Francis | 9.375 | Winn | 10.625 |
| *Individual alternates' desired funds rates* | | | |
| Black | 8.750 | Morris | 9.000 |
| Eastburn | 8.750 | MacLaury | 9.375 |
| MacLaury | 8.750 | Mayo | 9.750 |
| Coldwell | 9.000 | Coldwell | 10.000 |
| Kimbrel | 9.000 | Balles | 10.208 LT |
| Winn | 9.276 LT | Eastburn | 10.276 LT |
| Clay | 9.375 | Francis | 10.625 |
| *Summary statistics* | | | |
| Target funds rate | 8.875 | Target funds rate | 9.750 |
| Staff proposal | 8.875 | Staff proposal | 10.000 |
| Premeeting funds rate | 9.051 | Premeeting funds rate | 9.241 |
| Number (voters) | 12 | Number (voters) | 12 |
| Mean (voters) | 8.799 | Mean (voters) | 9.942 |
| Median (voters) | 8.875 | Median (voters) | 10.000 |
| Number (alternates) | 7 | Number (alternates) | 7 |
| Mean (alternates) | 8.986 | Mean (alternates) | 9.891 |
| Median (alternates) | 9.000 | Median (alternates) | 10.000 |
| Number (all) | 19 | Number (all) | 19 |
| Mean (all) | 8.868 | Mean (all) | 9.923 |
| Median (all) | 8.875 | Median (all) | 10.000 |

| April 15, 1974 (99, 63) | | May 21, 1974 (99, 63, 43) | |
| --- | --- | --- | --- |
| *Individual voters' desired funds rates* | | | |
| Bucher | 9.299 LE | Brimmer | 10.750 |
| Holland | 10.000 | Black | 10.875 |
| Mitchell | 10.000 | Holland | 11.000 |
| Winn | 10.050 A | Bucher | 11.250 |
| Black | 10.250 | Burns | 11.250 |
| Burns | 10.250 | Sheehan | 11.250 |
| Hayes | 10.250 | Hayes | 11.375 |
| Wallich | 10.250 | Mitchell | 11.566 LE |
| Sheehan | 10.375 | Wallich | 11.835 LE |
| Clay | 10.500 | Kimbrel | 11.977 A |
| Brimmer | 10.625 | Winn | 12.007 A |
| Kimbrel | 10.625 | Clay | 12.500 |
| *Individual alternates' desired funds rates* | | | |
| Mayo | 10.000 | Mayo | 11.000 |
| MacLaury | 10.154 LT | Coldwell | 11.250 |
| Williams | 10.220 LT | MacLaury | 11.250 |
| Morris | 10.250 | Morris | 11.250 |
| Eastburn | 10.500 | Balles | 11.997 A |
| Leonard | 10.500 | Willes | 12.002 A |
| Coldwell | 10.625 | Francis | 12.006 A |
| *Summary statistics* | | | |
| Target funds rate | 10.250 | Target funds rate | 11.250 |
| Staff proposal | 10.000 | Staff proposal | 12.000 |
| Premeeting funds rate | 10.211 | Premeeting funds rate | 11.366 |
| Number (voters) | 12 | Number (voters) | 12 |
| Mean (voters) | 10.206 | Mean (voters) | 11.470 |
| Median (voters) | 10.250 | Median (voters) | 11.313 |
| Number (alternates) | 7 | Number (alternates) | 7 |
| Mean (alternates) | 10.321 | Mean (alternates) | 11.536 |
| Median (alternates) | 10.250 | Median (alternates) | 11.250 |
| Number (all) | 19 | Number (all) | 19 |
| Mean (all) | 10.249 | Mean (all) | 11.494 |
| Median (all) | 10.250 | Median (all) | 11.250 |

| June 18, 1974 (99, 63, 43) | | July 16, 1974 (99, 63, 43) | |
| --- | --- | --- | --- |
| *Individual voters' desired funds rates* | | | |
| Sheehan | 11.481 A | Bucher | 11.000 |
| Bucher | 11.500 | Sheehan | 11.593 LE |
| Burns | 11.500 | Black | 12.250 |
| Holland | 11.500 | Burns | 12.250 |
| Mitchell | 11.500 | Hayes | 12.250 |
| Winn | 11.597 A | Holland | 12.250 |
| Black | 11.750 | Kimbrel | 12.250 |
| Brimmer | 11.750 | Mitchell | 12.250 |
| Debs | 11.750 | Wallich | 12.250 |
| Kimbrel | 11.750 | Winn | 12.250 |
| Wallich | 12.000 | Clay | 12.750 |
| Clay | 12.250 | | |
| *Individual alternates' desired funds rates* | | | |
| Coldwell | 11.375 | Francis | 11.974 A |
| MacLaury | 11.375 | Mayo | 12.000 |
| Morris | 11.500 | Morris | 12.000 |
| Mayo | 11.625 | Van Nice | 12.000 |
| Balles | 11.750 | Balles | 12.250 |
| Leonard | 11.867 LT | Eastburn | 12.363 LT |
| Eastburn | 11.875 | Coldwell | 12.500 |
| *Summary statistics* | | | |
| Target funds rate | 11.750 | Target funds rate | 12.250 |
| Staff proposal | 11.500 | Staff proposal | 12.000 |
| Premeeting funds rate | 12.014 | Premeeting funds rate | 13.374 |
| Number (voters) | 12 | Number (voters) | 11 |
| Mean (voters) | 11.694 | Mean (voters) | 12.122 |
| Median (voters) | 11.674 | Median (voters) | 12.250 |
| Number (alternates) | 7 | Number (alternates) | 7 |
| Mean (alternates) | 11.624 | Mean (alternates) | 12.155 |
| Median (alternates) | 11.625 | Median (alternates) | 12.000 |
| Number (all) | 19 | Number (all) | 18 |
| Mean (all) | 11.668 | Mean (all) | 12.135 |
| Median (all) | 11.625 | Median (all) | 12.250 |

| August 20, 1974 (99, 63, 43) | | September 10, 1974 (99, 63, 43) | |
|---|---|---|---|
| *Individual voters' desired funds rates* | | | |
| Bucher | 11.053 LE | Clay | 10.808 LE |
| Holland | 11.750 | Bucher | 10.875 |
| Mitchell | 11.750 | Wallich | 11.000 |
| Winn | 11.811 A | Mitchell | 11.003 A |
| Black | 12.000 | Black | 11.250 |
| Burns | 12.000 | Burns | 11.250 |
| Clay | 12.000 | Holland | 11.250 |
| Kimbrel | 12.000 | Sheehan | 11.250 |
| Sheehan | 12.000 | Winn | 11.375 |
| Wallich | 12.000 | Kimbrel | 11.500 |
| Hayes | 12.250 | Hayes | 11.750 |
| | | | |
| *Individual alternates' desired funds rates* | | | |
| Eastburn | 10.750 | Balles | 11.000 |
| MacLaury | 11.500 | Eastburn | 11.000 |
| Leonard | 11.750 | MacLaury | 11.000 |
| Morris | 11.750 | Mayo | 11.000 |
| Balles | 12.000 | Morris | 11.000 |
| | | Francis | 11.028 A |
| | | Coldwell | 11.500 |
| | | | |
| *Summary statistics* | | | |
| Target funds rate | 12.000 | Target funds rate | 11.250 |
| Staff proposal | 11.750 | Staff proposal | 11.000 |
| Premeeting funds rate | 12.224 | Premeeting funds rate | 11.640 |
| Number (voters) | 11 | Number (voters) | 11 |
| Mean (voters) | 11.874 | Mean (voters) | 11.210 |
| Median (voters) | 12.000 | Median (voters) | 11.250 |
| Number (alternates) | 5 | Number (alternates) | 7 |
| Mean (alternates) | 11.550 | Mean (alternates) | 11.075 |
| Median (alternates) | 11.750 | Median (alternates) | 11.000 |
| Number (all) | 16 | Number (all) | 18 |
| Mean (all) | 11.773 | Mean (all) | 11.158 |
| Median (all) | 11.906 | Median (all) | 11.015 |

| October 14, 1974 (99, 63) | | November 19, 1974 (99, 63, 43) | |
|---|---|---|---|
| *Individual voters' desired funds rates* | | | |
| Wallich | 9.500 | Bucher | 9.000 |
| Holland | 9.625 | Holland | 9.188 |
| Black | 9.750 | Black | 9.250 |
| Bucher | 9.750 | Burns | 9.250 |
| Burns | 9.750 | Coldwell | 9.250 |
| Sheehan | 9.750 | Hayes | 9.250 |
| Winn | 9.750 | Mitchell | 9.250 |
| Kimbrel | 9.875 | Sheehan | 9.250 |
| Clay | 10.000 | Wallich | 9.250 |
| Mitchell | 10.000 | Winn | 9.250 |
| Hayes | 10.500 | Clay | 9.256 A |
| | | Kimbrel | 9.500 |
| *Individual alternates' desired funds rates* | | | |
| Mayo | 9.359 LE | Morris | 8.500 |
| MacLaury | 9.375 | Eastburn | 9.000 |
| Morris | 9.375 | MacLaury | 9.000 |
| Coldwell | 9.750 | Mayo | 9.000 |
| Eastburn | 9.750 | Balles | 9.250 |
| Leonard | 9.750 | Francis | 9.250 |
| Williams | 9.750 | Plant | 9.250 |
| *Summary statistics* | | | |
| Target funds rate | 9.750 | Target funds rate | 9.250 |
| Staff proposal | 9.750 | Staff proposal | 9.250 |
| Premeeting funds rate | 9.964 | Premeeting funds rate | 9.200 |
| Number (voters) | 11 | Number (voters) | 12 |
| Mean (voters) | 9.841 | Mean (voters) | 9.245 |
| Median (voters) | 9.750 | Median (voters) | 9.250 |
| Number (alternates) | 7 | Number (alternates) | 7 |
| Mean (alternates) | 9.587 | Mean (alternates) | 9.036 |
| Median (alternates) | 9.750 | Median (alternates) | 9.000 |
| Number (all) | 18 | Number (all) | 19 |
| Mean (all) | 9.742 | Mean (all) | 9.168 |
| Median (all) | 9.750 | Median (all) | 9.250 |

| December 16, 1974 (99, 63) | | January 20, 1975 (99) | |
|---|---|---|---|
| *Individual voters' desired funds rates* | | | |
| Mitchell | 7.788 LE | Sheehan | 6.000 |
| Bucher | 8.000 | Bucher | 6.170 LE |
| Coldwell | 8.000 | Winn | 6.474 LE |
| Wallich | 8.000 | Clay | 6.500 |
| Winn | 8.210 A | Mitchell | 6.506 LE |
| Black | 8.250 | Wallich | 6.677 LE |
| Burns | 8.250 | Black | 6.750 |
| Holland | 8.250 | Holland | 6.750 |
| Kimbrel | 8.250 | Kimbrel | 6.750 |
| Sheehan | 8.250 | Coldwell | 6.813 |
| Hayes | 8.500 | Debs | 6.875 |
| Clay | 8.750 | Burns | 6.883 A |
| *Individual alternates' desired funds rates* | | | |
| Morris | 7.375 | Balles | 6.000 |
| Mayo | 7.814 LE | Eastburn | 6.000 |
| Balles | 7.847 LE | Morris | 6.000 |
| Eastburn | 8.000 | MacLaury | 6.250 |
| MacLaury | 8.000 | Mayo | 6.750 |
| Baughman | 8.375 | Baughman | 6.875 |
| Francis | 8.750 | Francis | 7.250 |
| *Summary statistics* | | | |
| Target funds rate | 8.250 | Target funds rate | 6.875 |
| Staff proposal | 8.125 | Staff proposal | 6.875 |
| Premeeting funds rate | 8.789 | Premeeting funds rate | 7.053 |
| Number (voters) | 12 | Number (voters) | 12 |
| Mean (voters) | 8.208 | Mean (voters) | 6.596 |
| Median (voters) | 8.250 | Median (voters) | 6.714 |
| Number (alternates) | 7 | Number (alternates) | 7 |
| Mean (alternates) | 8.023 | Mean (alternates) | 6.446 |
| Median (alternates) | 8.000 | Median (alternates) | 6.250 |
| Number (all) | 19 | Number (all) | 19 |
| Mean (all) | 8.140 | Mean (all) | 6.541 |
| Median (all) | 8.210 | Median (all) | 6.677 |

| February 19, 1975 (99) | | March 18, 1975 (99, 63, 43) | |
|---|---|---|---|
| *Individual voters' desired funds rates* | | | |
| Bucher | 5.250 | Bucher | 4.500 |
| Winn | 5.250 | Sheehan | 4.500 |
| Clay | 5.500 | Coldwell | 4.875 |
| Coldwell | 5.500 | Baughman | 5.000 |
| Burns | 5.718 A | Eastburn | 5.000 |
| Black | 5.750 | MacLaury | 5.250 |
| Holland | 5.750 | Mayo | 5.250 |
| Mitchell | 5.750 | Mitchell | 5.250 |
| Hayes | 6.000 | Holland | 5.375 |
| Kimbrel | 6.000 | Burns | 5.500 |
| Wallich | 6.000 | Hayes | 5.500 |
| | | Wallich | 5.500 |
| *Individual alternates' desired funds rates* | | | |
| Balles | 4.500 | Balles | 5.000 |
| Eastburn | 4.500 | Morris | 5.000 |
| Morris | 4.875 | Winn | 5.375 |
| MacLaury | 5.000 | Black | 5.500 |
| Baughman | 5.250 | Kimbrel | 5.500 |
| Mayo | 5.250 | Clay | 5.625 |
| Francis | 6.107 LT | Francis | 5.833 A |
| *Summary statistics* | | | |
| Target funds rate | 5.750 | Target funds rate | 5.250 |
| Staff proposal | 5.625 | Staff proposal | 5.750 |
| Premeeting funds rate | 6.296 | Premeeting funds rate | 5.240 |
| Number (voters) | 11 | Number (voters) | 12 |
| Mean (voters) | 5.679 | Mean (voters) | 5.125 |
| Median (voters) | 5.750 | Median (voters) | 5.250 |
| Number (alternates) | 7 | Number (alternates) | 7 |
| Mean (alternates) | 5.069 | Mean (alternates) | 5.405 |
| Median (alternates) | 5.000 | Median (alternates) | 5.500 |
| Number (all) | 18 | Number (all) | 19 |
| Mean (all) | 5.442 | Mean (all) | 5.228 |
| Median (all) | 5.500 | Median (all) | 5.250 |

| April 14, 1975 (99) | | May 20, 1975 (99) | |
|---|---|---|---|
| *Individual voters' desired funds rates* | | | |
| Bucher | 4.500 | Eastburn | 4.750 |
| Eastburn | 5.125 | Bucher | 4.875 |
| Holland‎ | 5.125 | Mayo | 4.875 |
| Baughman | 5.250 | Baughman | 5.000 |
| Coldwell | 5.250 | Coldwell | 5.000 |
| Mayo | 5.250 | Mitchell | 5.000 |
| Hayes | 5.375 | Hayes | 5.125 |
| Mitchell | 5.375 | Holland | 5.125 |
| MacLaury | 5.500 | MacLaury | 5.125 |
| Burns | 5.899 A | Burns | 5.240 A |
| Wallich | 6.000 | Wallich | 5.251 A |
| | | | |
| *Individual alternates' desired funds rates* | | | |
| Balles | 5.250 | Balles | 4.875 |
| Black | 5.250 | Morris | 4.875 |
| Morris | 5.250 | Black | 5.000 |
| Winn | 5.499 LE | Kimbrel | 5.000 |
| Clay | 5.750 | Clay | 5.125 |
| Kimbrel | 6.000 | Winn | 5.125 |
| Francis | 6.019 A | Francis | 5.744 LT |
| *Summary statistics* | | | |
| Target funds rate | 5.250 | Target funds rate | 5.000 |
| Staff proposal | 6.000 | Staff proposal | 5.250 |
| Premeeting funds rate | 5.321 | Premeeting funds rate | 5.084 |
| Number (voters) | 11 | Number (voters) | 11 |
| Mean (voters) | 5.332 | Mean (voters) | 5.033 |
| Median (voters) | 5.250 | Median (voters) | 5.000 |
| Number (alternates) | 7 | Number (alternates) | 7 |
| Mean (alternates) | 5.574 | Mean (alternates) | 5.106 |
| Median (alternates) | 5.499 | Median (alternates) | 5.000 |
| Number (all) | 18 | Number (all) | 18 |
| Mean (all) | 5.426 | Mean (all) | 5.062 |
| Median (all) | 5.313 | Median (all) | 5.000 |

| June 16, 1975 (99) | | July 15, 1975 (99, 63) | |
|---|---|---|---|
| *Individual voters' desired funds rates* | | | |
| Bucher | 5.000 | Bucher | 5.750 |
| Eastburn | 5.250 | Jackson | 5.842 A |
| Coldwell | 5.375 | Holland | 5.875 |
| Holland | 5.438 | Baughman | 5.971 A |
| Debs | 5.500 | MacLaury | 5.988 A |
| MacLaury | 5.500 | Eastburn | 6.000 |
| Mayo | 5.500 | Mayo | 6.000 |
| Mitchell | 5.500 | Burns | 6.125 |
| Baughman | 5.750 | Coldwell | 6.125 |
| Burns | 5.886 A | Debs | 6.250 |
| Wallich | 6.000 | Wallich | 6.250 |
| | | | |
| *Individual alternates' desired funds rates* | | | |
| Balles | 5.250 | Black | 5.750 |
| Morris | 5.250 | Balles | 6.000 |
| Black | 5.500 | Clay | 6.000 |
| Kimbrel | 5.500 | Morris | 6.000 |
| Winn | 5.500 | Kimbrel | 6.250 |
| Clay | 5.750 | Leonard | 6.250 |
| Francis | 6.472 LT | | |
| *Summary statistics* | | | |
| Target funds rate | 5.500 | Target funds rate | 6.125 |
| Staff proposal | 6.000 | Staff proposal | 6.000 |
| Premeeting funds rate | 5.154 | Premeeting funds rate | 5.784 |
| Number (voters) | 11 | Number (voters) | 11 |
| Mean (voters) | 5.518 | Mean (voters) | 6.016 |
| Median (voters) | 5.500 | Median (voters) | 6.000 |
| Number (alternates) | 7 | Number (alternates) | 6 |
| Mean (alternates) | 5.603 | Mean (alternates) | 6.042 |
| Median (alternates) | 5.500 | Median (alternates) | 6.000 |
| Number (all) | 18 | Number (all) | 17 |
| Mean (all) | 5.551 | Mean (all) | 6.025 |
| Median (all) | 5.500 | Median (all) | 6.000 |

| August 19, 1975 (99, 63, 43) | | September 16, 1975 (99, 63, 43) | |
| --- | --- | --- | --- |
| *Individual voters' desired funds rates* | | | |
| Mayo | 6.125 | Coldwell | 6.250 |
| Mitchell | 6.125 | Bucher | 6.375 |
| Burns | 6.188 | Holland | 6.375 |
| Holland | 6.188 | Mayo | 6.375 |
| Coldwell | 6.250 | Volcker | 6.375 |
| Volcker | 6.250 | Eastburn | 6.500 |
| Bucher | 6.375 | Jackson | 6.500 |
| Jackson | 6.404 LE | MacLaury | 6.500 |
| Wallich | 6.625 | Mitchell | 6.500 |
| Baughman | 6.744 A | Burns | 6.625 |
| Eastburn | 6.750 | Wallich | 6.750 |
| MacLaury | 6.750 | Baughman | 6.754 A |
| *Individual alternates' desired funds rates* | | | |
| Morris | 6.125 | Balles | 6.375 |
| Leonard | 6.188 | Morris | 6.375 |
| Balles | 6.375 | Kimbrel | 6.625 |
| Kimbrel | 6.375 | Winn | 6.641 A |
| | | Black | 6.722 A |
| | | Clay | 6.750 |
| | | Francis | 7.250 |
| *Summary statistics* | | | |
| Target funds rate | 6.375 | Target funds rate | 6.500 |
| Staff proposal | 6.750 | Staff proposal | 6.750 |
| Premeeting funds rate | 6.080 | Premeeting funds rate | 6.241 |
| Number (voters) | 12 | Number (voters) | 12 |
| Mean (voters) | 6.398 | Mean (voters) | 6.490 |
| Median (voters) | 6.313 | Median (voters) | 6.500 |
| Number (alternates) | 4 | Number (alternates) | 7 |
| Mean (alternates) | 6.266 | Mean (alternates) | 6.677 |
| Median (alternates) | 6.281 | Median (alternates) | 6.641 |
| Number (all) | 16 | Number (all) | 19 |
| Mean (all) | 6.365 | Mean (all) | 6.559 |
| Median (all) | 6.313 | Median (all) | 6.500 |

| October 21, 1975 (99, 63, 43) | | November 18, 1975 (99, 63) | |
|---|---|---|---|
| *Individual voters' desired funds rates* | | | |
| Coldwell | 5.500 | Eastburn | 4.750 |
| Eastburn | 5.500 | Wallich | 4.750 |
| Mayo | 5.500 | Baughman | 4.978 LE |
| Wallich | 5.500 | Coldwell | 5.000 |
| Holland | 5.750 | MacLaury | 5.000 |
| Jackson | 5.750 | Mitchell | 5.000 |
| MacLaury | 5.750 | Bucher | 5.125 |
| Mitchell | 5.750 | Burns | 5.125 |
| Baughman | 5.875 | Mayo | 5.125 |
| Burns | 5.875 | Holland | 5.250 |
| Volcker | 5.875 | Jackson | 5.250 |
| | | Volcker | 5.250 |
| *Individual alternates' desired funds rates* | | | |
| Balles | 5.500 | Williams | 4.750 |
| Leonard | 5.500 | Leonard | 4.880 LE |
| Morris | 5.500 | Black | 5.250 |
| Black | 5.750 | Clay | 5.250 |
| Kimbrel | 5.750 | Kimbrel | 5.250 |
| | | Morris | 5.250 |
| *Summary statistics* | | | |
| Target funds rate | 5.750 | Target funds rate | 5.000 |
| Staff proposal | 5.750 | Staff proposal | 5.250 |
| Premeeting funds rate | 5.757 | Premeeting funds rate | 5.230 |
| Number (voters) | 11 | Number (voters) | 12 |
| Mean (voters) | 5.693 | Mean (voters) | 5.050 |
| Median (voters) | 5.750 | Median (voters) | 5.063 |
| Number (alternates) | 5 | Number (alternates) | 6 |
| Mean (alternates) | 5.600 | Mean (alternates) | 5.105 |
| Median (alternates) | 5.500 | Median (alternates) | 5.250 |
| Number (all) | 16 | Number (all) | 18 |
| Mean (all) | 5.664 | Mean (all) | 5.069 |
| Median (all) | 5.750 | Median (all) | 5.125 |

| December 16, 1975 (99, 63, 43) | | January 20, 1976 (99) | |
|---|---|---|---|
| *Individual voters' desired funds rates* | | | |
| Baughman | 4.987 LE | Coldwell | 4.625 |
| Coldwell | 5.000 | Mitchell | 4.625 |
| Jackson | 5.000 | Partee | 4.625 |
| MacLaury | 5.000 | Volcker | 4.764 LE |
| Mitchell | 5.200 A | Jackson | 4.767 A |
| Eastburn | 5.211 A | Baughman | 4.782 A |
| Burns | 5.250 | Mayo | 4.829 A |
| Holland | 5.250 | Eastburn | 4.833 A |
| Mayo | 5.250 | Burns | 4.860 A |
| Volcker | 5.250 | MacLaury | 4.863 A |
| Wallich | 5.250 | Holland | 4.865 A |
| | | Wallich | 4.875 A |
| *Individual alternates' desired funds rates* | | | |
| Balles | 5.000 | No alternates spoke in the policy | |
| Winn | 5.000 | go-around. | |
| Black | 5.250 | | |
| Clay | 5.250 | | |
| Francis | 5.250 | | |
| Kimbrel | 5.250 | | |
| Morris | 5.250 | | |
| *Summary statistics* | | | |
| Target funds rate | 5.000 | Target funds rate | 4.625 |
| Staff proposal | 5.250 | Staff proposal | 4.875 |
| Premeeting funds rate | 5.196 | Premeeting funds rate | 4.803 |
| Number (voters) | 11 | Number (voters) | 12 |
| Mean (voters) | 5.150 | Mean (voters) | 4.776 |
| Median (voters) | 5.211 | Median (voters) | 4.805 |
| Number (alternates) | 7 | Number (alternates) | 0 |
| Mean (alternates) | 5.179 | Mean (alternates) | |
| Median (alternates) | 5.250 | Median (alternates) | |
| Number (all) | 18 | Number (all) | 12 |
| Mean (all) | 5.161 | Mean (all) | 4.776 |
| Median (all) | 5.250 | Median (all) | 4.805 |

| February 17, 1976 (99, 63) | | March 15, 1976 (99) | |
|---|---|---|---|
| *Individual voters' desired funds rates* | | | |
| Eastburn | 4.500 | Burns | 4.457 LE |
| Baughman | 4.750 | Winn | 4.668 A |
| Burns | 4.750 | Balles | 4.750 |
| Coldwell | 4.750 | Coldwell | 4.750 |
| Holland | 4.750 | Gardner | 4.750 |
| Jackson | 4.750 | Jackson | 4.750 |
| Mayo | 4.750 | Partee | 4.750 |
| Partee | 4.750 | Holland | 4.765 A |
| Volcker | 4.750 | Black | 4.875 |
| MacLaury | 4.875 | Volcker | 4.875 |
| Wallich | 4.875 | Wallich | 4.875 |
| | | Kimbrel | 5.000 |
| *Individual alternates' desired funds rates* | | | |
| Balles | 4.404 LE | Baughman | 4.750 |
| Black | 4.750 | Eastburn | 4.750 |
| Clay | 4.750 | Mayo | 4.750 |
| Morris | 4.750 | Morris | 4.750 |
| Winn | 4.750 | Guffey | 5.000 |
| Kimbrel | 5.000 | | |
| *Summary statistics* | | | |
| Target funds rate | 4.750 | Target funds rate | 4.750 |
| Staff proposal | 4.750 | Staff proposal | 4.750 |
| Premeeting funds rate | 4.760 | Premeeting funds rate | 4.769 |
| Number (voters) | 11 | Number (voters) | 12 |
| Mean (voters) | 4.750 | Mean (voters) | 4.772 |
| Median (voters) | 4.750 | Median (voters) | 4.750 |
| Number (alternates) | 6 | Number (alternates) | 5 |
| Mean (alternates) | 4.734 | Mean (alternates) | 4.800 |
| Median (alternates) | 4.750 | Median (alternates) | 4.750 |
| Number (all) | 17 | Number (all) | 17 |
| Mean (all) | 4.744 | Mean (all) | 4.780 |
| Median (all) | 4.750 | Median (all) | 4.750 |

| April 20, 1976 (99, 63, 43) | | May 18, 1976 (99, 63, 43) | |
|---|---|---|---|
| *Individual voters' desired funds rates* | | | |
| Partee | 4.736 A | Coldwell | 5.125 |
| Black | 4.750 | Black | 5.375 |
| Burns | 4.875 | Burns | 5.375 |
| Coldwell | 4.875 | Gardner | 5.375 |
| Gardner | 4.875 | Volcker | 5.375 |
| Jackson | 4.875 | Balles | 5.500 |
| Volcker | 4.875 | Jackson | 5.500 |
| Winn | 4.875 | Kimbrel | 5.500 |
| Balles | 5.000 | Partee | 5.500 |
| Kimbrel | 5.000 | Wallich | 5.500 |
| Wallich | 5.000 | Winn | 5.500 |
| | | | |
| *Individual alternates' desired funds rates* | | | |
| Baughman | 4.725 A | Baughman | 5.375 |
| MacLaury | 4.750 | Mayo | 5.375 |
| Mayo | 4.875 | Guffey | 5.500 |
| Guffey | 5.000 | MacLaury | 5.500 |
| | | Roos | 5.500 |
| | | | |
| | | | |
| *Summary statistics* | | | |
| Target funds rate | 4.875 | Target funds rate | 5.375 |
| Staff proposal | 4.750 | Staff proposal | 5.250 |
| Premeeting funds rate | 4.757 | Premeeting funds rate | 5.191 |
| Number (voters) | 11 | Number (voters) | 11 |
| Mean (voters) | 4.885 | Mean (voters) | 5.420 |
| Median (voters) | 4.875 | Median (voters) | 5.500 |
| Number (alternates) | 4 | Number (alternates) | 5 |
| Mean (alternates) | 4.837 | Mean (alternates) | 5.450 |
| Median (alternates) | 4.813 | Median (alternates) | 5.500 |
| Number (all) | 15 | Number (all) | 16 |
| Mean (all) | 4.872 | Mean (all) | 5.430 |
| Median (all) | 4.875 | Median (all) | 5.500 |

| June 22, 1976 (99, 63, 43) | | July 19, 1976 (99, 63, 43) | |
| --- | --- | --- | --- |
| *Individual voters' desired funds rates* | | | |
| Winn | 5.483 A | Lilly | 5.244 A |
| Balles | 5.500 | Balles | 5.250 |
| Baughman | 5.500 | Black | 5.250 |
| Black | 5.500 | Burns | 5.250 |
| Burns | 5.500 | Coldwell | 5.250 |
| Coldwell | 5.500 | Gardner | 5.250 |
| Gardner | 5.500 | Jackson | 5.250 |
| Jackson | 5.500 | Partee | 5.250 |
| Partee | 5.500 | Wallich | 5.250 |
| Volcker | 5.500 | Winn | 5.250 |
| Wallich | 5.500 | Kimbrel | 5.297 A |
| Lilly | 5.514 A | Volcker | 5.375 |
| *Individual alternates' desired funds rates* | | | |
| Eastburn | 5.500 | MacLaury | 5.250 |
| Fossum | 5.500 | Mayo | 5.250 |
| MacLaury | 5.500 | Guffey | 5.375 |
| Mayo | 5.500 | | |
| Morris | 5.500 | | |
| Roos | 5.723 LT | | |
| Guffey | 5.807 LT | | |
| *Summary statistics* | | | |
| Target funds rate | 5.500 | Target funds rate | 5.250 |
| Staff proposal | 5.500 | Staff proposal | 5.250 |
| Premeeting funds rate | 5.499 | Premeeting funds rate | 5.260 |
| Number (voters) | 12 | Number (voters) | 12 |
| Mean (voters) | 5.500 | Mean (voters) | 5.264 |
| Median (voters) | 5.500 | Median (voters) | 5.250 |
| Number (alternates) | 7 | Number (alternates) | 3 |
| Mean (alternates) | 5.576 | Mean (alternates) | 5.292 |
| Median (alternates) | 5.500 | Median (alternates) | 5.250 |
| Number (all) | 19 | Number (all) | 15 |
| Mean (all) | 5.528 | Mean (all) | 5.269 |
| Median (all) | 5.500 | Median (all) | 5.250 |

| August 17, 1976 (99, 63, 43) | | September 21, 1976 (99, 63, 43) | |
|---|---|---|---|
| *Individual voters' desired funds rates* | | | |
| Volcker | 5.125 | Coldwell | 5.000 |
| Partee | 5.138 LE | Winn | 5.173 A |
| Winn | 5.194 A | Balles | 5.250 |
| Coldwell | 5.223 A | Black | 5.250 |
| Black | 5.250 | Burns | 5.250 |
| Burns | 5.250 | Gardner | 5.250 |
| Gardner | 5.250 | Jackson | 5.250 |
| Guffey | 5.250 | Kimbrel | 5.250 |
| Jackson | 5.250 | Volcker | 5.250 |
| Kimbrel | 5.250 | Wallich | 5.250 |
| Wallich | 5.250 | Lilly | 5.251 A |
| Lilly | 5.260 A | | |
| *Individual alternates' desired funds rates* | | | |
| Eastburn | 5.125 | Baughman | 5.201 A |
| Baughman | 5.250 | Eastburn | 5.250 |
| MacLaury | 5.250 | MacLaury | 5.250 |
| Mayo | 5.250 | Mayo | 5.250 |
| Morris | 5.250 | Morris | 5.250 |
| Williams | 5.250 | | |
| | | | |
| *Summary statistics* | | | |
| Target funds rate | 5.250 | Target funds rate | 5.250 |
| Staff proposal | 5.250 | Staff proposal | 5.250 |
| Premeeting funds rate | 5.253 | Premeeting funds rate | 5.194 |
| Number (voters) | 12 | Number (voters) | 11 |
| Mean (voters) | 5.224 | Mean (voters) | 5.220 |
| Median (voters) | 5.250 | Median (voters) | 5.250 |
| Number (alternates) | 6 | Number (alternates) | 5 |
| Mean (alternates) | 5.229 | Mean (alternates) | 5.240 |
| Median (alternates) | 5.250 | Median (alternates) | 5.250 |
| Number (all) | 18 | Number (all) | 16 |
| Mean (all) | 5.226 | Mean (all) | 5.226 |
| Median (all) | 5.250 | Median (all) | 5.250 |

| October 19, 1976 (99, 63, 43) | | November 16, 1976 (99, 63, 43) | |
|---|---|---|---|
| *Individual voters' desired funds rates* | | | |
| Balles | 4.750 | Coldwell | 4.750 |
| Jackson | 4.750 | Jackson | 4.750 |
| Lilly | 4.750 | Lilly | 4.750 |
| Partee | 4.750 | Partee | 4.750 |
| Wallich | 4.750 | Wallich | 4.750 |
| Winn | 4.750 | Winn | 4.750 |
| Burns | 4.875 | Black | 4.875 |
| Coldwell | 4.875 | Burns | 4.875 |
| Gardner | 4.875 | Gardner | 4.875 |
| Kimbrel | 4.875 | Guffey | 4.875 |
| Black | 5.000 | Kimbrel | 4.875 |
| Volcker | 5.000 | Volcker | 4.875 |
| *Individual alternates' desired funds rates* | | | |
| Baughman | 4.750 | Eastburn | 4.662 LE |
| Eastburn | 4.750 | Baughman | 4.750 |
| Morris | 4.750 | Morris | 4.750 |
| Guffey | 4.875 | MacLaury | 4.875 |
| MacLaury | 4.875 | Mayo | 4.875 |
| Roos | 4.875 | Williams | 5.000 |
| Mayo | 5.000 | Roos | 5.005 A |
| *Summary statistics* | | | |
| Target funds rate | 4.875 | Target funds rate | 4.750 |
| Staff proposal | 5.000 | Staff proposal | 5.000 |
| Premeeting funds rate | 4.977 | Premeeting funds rate | 5.044 |
| Number (voters) | 12 | Number (voters) | 12 |
| Mean (voters) | 4.833 | Mean (voters) | 4.813 |
| Median (voters) | 4.813 | Median (voters) | 4.813 |
| Number (alternates) | 7 | Number (alternates) | 7 |
| Mean (alternates) | 4.839 | Mean (alternates) | 4.845 |
| Median (alternates) | 4.875 | Median (alternates) | 4.875 |
| Number (all) | 19 | Number (all) | 19 |
| Mean (all) | 4.836 | Mean (all) | 4.825 |
| Median (all) | 4.875 | Median (all) | 4.875 |

| December 20, 1976 (99, 63, 43) | | January 17, 1977 (99, 63, 43) | |
|---|---|---|---|
| *Individual voters' desired funds rates* | | | |
| Balles | 4.500 | Black | 4.622 A |
| Coldwell | 4.500 | Jackson | 4.625 |
| Lilly | 4.500 | Winn | 4.625 |
| Partee | 4.500 | Kimbrel | 4.656 A |
| Winn | 4.500 | Balles | 4.750 |
| Black | 4.625 | Burns | 4.750 |
| Burns | 4.625 | Coldwell | 4.750 |
| Gardner | 4.625 | Gardner | 4.750 |
| Jackson | 4.625 | Lilly | 4.750 |
| Kimbrel | 4.625 | Partee | 4.750 |
| Volcker | 4.625 | Volcker | 4.750 |
| Wallich | 4.625 | Wallich | 4.750 |
| *Individual alternates' desired funds rates* | | | |
| Morris | 4.375 | Guffey | 4.625 |
| Baughman | 4.500 | Morris | 4.625 |
| Eastburn | 4.500 | Baughman | 4.750 |
| Mayo | 4.500 | Eastburn | 4.750 |
| Guffey | 4.625 | Mayo | 4.750 |
| MacLaury | 4.625 | | |
| Roos | 4.625 | | |
| *Summary statistics* | | | |
| Target funds rate | 4.625 | Target funds rate | 4.688 |
| Staff proposal | 4.625 | Staff proposal | 4.625 |
| Premeeting funds rate | 4.640 | Premeeting funds rate | 4.547 |
| Number (voters) | 12 | Number (voters) | 12 |
| Mean (voters) | 4.573 | Mean (voters) | 4.711 |
| Median (voters) | 4.625 | Median (voters) | 4.750 |
| Number (alternates) | 7 | Number (alternates) | 5 |
| Mean (alternates) | 4.536 | Mean (alternates) | 4.700 |
| Median (alternates) | 4.500 | Median (alternates) | 4.750 |
| Number (all) | 19 | Number (all) | 17 |
| Mean (all) | 4.559 | Mean (all) | 4.708 |
| Median (all) | 4.625 | Median (all) | 4.750 |

| February 15, 1977 (99, 63, 43) | | March 15, 1977 (99, 63, 43) | |
| --- | --- | --- | --- |
| *Individual voters' desired funds rates* | | | |
| Burns | 4.625 | Burns | 4.688 |
| Coldwell | 4.625 | Coldwell | 4.688 |
| Gardner | 4.625 | Gardner | 4.688 |
| Jackson | 4.625 | Lilly | 4.688 |
| Kimbrel | 4.625 | Mayo | 4.688 |
| Winn | 4.625 | Morris | 4.688 |
| Lilly | 4.688 | Partee | 4.688 |
| Volcker | 4.688 | Volcker | 4.719 |
| Partee | 4.750 | Guffey | 4.750 |
| Wallich | 4.750 | Wallich | 4.750 |
| Black | 4.861 LT | Roos | 4.778 LT |
| Balles | 4.875 | Jackson | 4.875 |
| *Individual alternates' desired funds rates* | | | |
| Baughman | 4.625 | Winn | 4.605 A |
| Eastburn | 4.625 | Baughman | 4.688 |
| Mayo | 4.625 | Black | 4.688 |
| Morris | 4.625 | Balles | 4.750 |
| Roos | 4.625 | Eastburn | 4.750 |
| Guffey | 4.750 | Kimbrel | 4.813 |
| Van Nice | 4.750 | Van Nice | 4.840 LT |
| *Summary statistics* | | | |
| Target funds rate | 4.683 | Target funds rate | 4.683 |
| Staff proposal | 4.625 | Staff proposal | 4.625 |
| Premeeting funds rate | 4.707 | Premeeting funds rate | 4.603 |
| Number (voters) | 12 | Number (voters) | 12 |
| Mean (voters) | 4.697 | Mean (voters) | 4.724 |
| Median (voters) | 4.656 | Median (voters) | 4.688 |
| Number (alternates) | 7 | Number (alternates) | 7 |
| Mean (alternates) | 4.661 | Mean (alternates) | 4.733 |
| Median (alternates) | 4.625 | Median (alternates) | 4.750 |
| Number (all) | 19 | Number (all) | 19 |
| Mean (all) | 4.683 | Mean (all) | 4.727 |
| Median (all) | 4.625 | Median (all) | 4.688 |

| April 19, 1977 (99, 63, 43) | | May 17, 1977 (99, 63, 43) | |
|---|---|---|---|
| *Individual voters' desired funds rates* | | | |
| Burns | 4.750 | Gardner | 5.263 A |
| Coldwell | 4.750 | Coldwell | 5.313 |
| Morris | 4.750 | Jackson | 5.313 |
| Partee | 4.750 | Lilly | 5.313 |
| Roos | 4.750 | Partee | 5.313 |
| Volcker | 4.750 | Burns | 5.375 |
| Lilly | 4.763 A | Guffey | 5.375 |
| Guffey | 4.813 | Mayo | 5.375 |
| Mayo | 4.813 | Volcker | 5.438 |
| Gardner | 4.869 LT | Morris | 5.500 |
| Jackson | 4.875 | Roos | 5.625 |
| Wallich | 5.000 | Wallich | 5.625 |
| *Individual alternates' desired funds rates* | | | |
| Baughman | 4.750 | Winn | 5.313 |
| Black | 4.750 | Baughman | 5.375 |
| Eastburn | 4.750 | Black | 5.375 |
| Willes | 4.750 | Eastburn | 5.375 |
| Kimbrel | 4.875 | Balles | 5.587 LT |
| | | Kimbrel | 5.625 |
| | | Willes | 5.625 |
| *Summary statistics* | | | |
| Target funds rate | 4.750 | Target funds rate | 5.375 |
| Staff proposal | 4.750 | Staff proposal | 5.250 |
| Premeeting funds rate | 4.701 | Premeeting funds rate | 5.323 |
| Number (voters) | 12 | Number (voters) | 12 |
| Mean (voters) | 4.803 | Mean (voters) | 5.402 |
| Median (voters) | 4.757 | Median (voters) | 5.375 |
| Number (alternates) | 5 | Number (alternates) | 7 |
| Mean (alternates) | 4.775 | Mean (alternates) | 5.468 |
| Median (alternates) | 4.750 | Median (alternates) | 5.375 |
| Number (all) | 17 | Number (all) | 19 |
| Mean (all) | 4.795 | Mean (all) | 5.426 |
| Median (all) | 4.750 | Median (all) | 5.375 |

| June 21, 1977 (99, 63, 43) | | July 19, 1977 (99, 63, 43) | |
| --- | --- | --- | --- |
| *Individual voters' desired funds rates* | | | |
| Burns | 5.375 | Burns | 5.375 |
| Coldwell | 5.375 | Gardner | 5.375 |
| Gardner | 5.375 | Guffey | 5.375 |
| Guffey | 5.375 | Lilly | 5.375 |
| Jackson | 5.375 | Mayo | 5.375 |
| Lilly | 5.375 | Morris | 5.375 |
| Mayo | 5.375 | Volcker | 5.375 |
| Morris | 5.375 | Wallich | 5.375 |
| Partee | 5.375 | Coldwell | 5.500 |
| Volcker | 5.375 | Jackson | 5.500 |
| Wallich | 5.375 | Partee | 5.500 |
| Roos | 5.875 | Roos | 5.625 |
| *Individual alternates' desired funds rates* | | | |
| Balles | 5.375 | Balles | 5.375 |
| Black | 5.375 | Winn | 5.375 |
| Eastburn | 5.375 | Baughman | 5.500 |
| Fossum | 5.375 | Black | 5.625 |
| Winn | 5.375 | Eastburn | 5.625 |
| Baughman | 5.650 LT | Kimbrel | 5.625 |
| Willes | 5.875 | | |
| *Summary statistics* | | | |
| Target funds rate | 5.375 | Target funds rate | 5.375 |
| Staff proposal | 5.375 | Staff proposal | 5.500 |
| Premeeting funds rate | 5.389 | Premeeting funds rate | 5.317 |
| Number (voters) | 12 | Number (voters) | 12 |
| Mean (voters) | 5.417 | Mean (voters) | 5.427 |
| Median (voters) | 5.375 | Median (voters) | 5.375 |
| Number (alternates) | 7 | Number (alternates) | 6 |
| Mean (alternates) | 5.486 | Mean (alternates) | 5.521 |
| Median (alternates) | 5.375 | Median (alternates) | 5.563 |
| Number (all) | 19 | Number (all) | 18 |
| Mean (all) | 5.442 | Mean (all) | 5.458 |
| Median (all) | 5.375 | Median (all) | 5.375 |

| August 16, 1977 (99, 63, 43) | | September 20, 1977 (99, 63, 43) | |
|---|---|---|---|
| *Individual voters' desired funds rates* | | | |
| Burns | 6.000 | Burns | 6.125 |
| Coldwell | 6.000 | Gardner | 6.125 |
| Gardner | 6.000 | Lilly | 6.125 |
| Guffey | 6.000 | Partee | 6.125 |
| Jackson | 6.000 | Wallich | 6.125 |
| Lilly | 6.000 | Coldwell | 6.250 |
| Mayo | 6.000 | Guffey | 6.250 |
| Morris | 6.000 | Jackson | 6.250 |
| Partee | 6.000 | Volcker | 6.250 |
| Volcker | 6.000 | Mayo | 6.375 |
| Wallich | 6.000 | Morris | 6.375 |
| Roos | 6.250 | Roos | 6.500 |
| *Individual alternates' desired funds rates* | | | |
| Baughman | 6.000 | Black | 6.125 |
| Eastburn | 6.000 | Baughman | 6.250 |
| Kimbrel | 6.000 | Eastburn | 6.250 |
| Rankin | 6.000 | Winn | 6.250 |
| Winn | 6.000 | Willes | 6.252 LT |
| Balles | 6.250 | Balles | 6.375 |
| Van Nice | 6.250 | Kimbrel | 6.375 |
| *Summary statistics* | | | |
| Target funds rate | 6.000 | Target funds rate | 6.250 |
| Staff proposal | 6.000 | Staff proposal | 6.125 |
| Premeeting funds rate | 5.837 | Premeeting funds rate | 6.080 |
| Number (voters) | 12 | Number (voters) | 12 |
| Mean (voters) | 6.021 | Mean (voters) | 6.240 |
| Median (voters) | 6.000 | Median (voters) | 6.250 |
| Number (alternates) | 7 | Number (alternates) | 7 |
| Mean (alternates) | 6.071 | Mean (alternates) | 6.268 |
| Median (alternates) | 6.000 | Median (alternates) | 6.250 |
| Number (all) | 19 | Number (all) | 19 |
| Mean (all) | 6.039 | Mean (all) | 6.250 |
| Median (all) | 6.000 | Median (all) | 6.250 |

| October 17, 1977 (99, 63, 43) | | November 15, 1977 (99, 63, 43) | |
|---|---|---|---|
| *Individual voters' desired funds rates* | | | |
| Burns | 6.500 | Burns | 6.500 |
| Coldwell | 6.500 | Coldwell | 6.500 |
| Gardner | 6.500 | Gardner | 6.500 |
| Lilly | 6.500 | Guffey | 6.500 |
| Mayo | 6.500 | Jackson | 6.500 |
| Volcker | 6.500 | Lilly | 6.500 |
| Guffey | 6.625 | Mayo | 6.500 |
| Jackson | 6.625 | Morris | 6.500 |
| Partee | 6.625 | Partee | 6.500 |
| Wallich | 6.625 | Roos | 6.500 |
| Morris | 6.750 | Volcker | 6.500 |
| Roos | 6.750 | Wallich | 6.500 |
| *Individual alternates' desired funds rates* | | | |
| Black | 6.625 | Balles | 6.500 |
| Smoot | 6.625 | Black | 6.500 |
| Winn | 6.625 | Eastburn | 6.500 |
| Balles | 6.750 | Kimbrel | 6.500 |
| Baughman | 6.750 | Willes | 6.500 |
| Kimbrel | 6.750 | Winn | 6.528 A |
| Willes | 6.750 | Baughman | 6.767 LT |
| *Summary statistics* | | | |
| Target funds rate | 6.500 | Target funds rate | 6.500 |
| Staff proposal | 6.500 | Staff proposal | 6.500 |
| Premeeting funds rate | 6.463 | Premeeting funds rate | 6.530 |
| Number (voters) | 12 | Number (voters) | 12 |
| Mean (voters) | 6.583 | Mean (voters) | 6.500 |
| Median (voters) | 6.563 | Median (voters) | 6.500 |
| Number (alternates) | 7 | Number (alternates) | 7 |
| Mean (alternates) | 6.696 | Mean (alternates) | 6.542 |
| Median (alternates) | 6.750 | Median (alternates) | 6.500 |
| Number (all) | 19 | Number (all) | 19 |
| Mean (all) | 6.625 | Mean (all) | 6.516 |
| Median (all) | 6.625 | Median (all) | 6.500 |

| December 19, 1977 (99, 63, 43) | | January 17, 1978 (99) | |
|---|---|---|---|
| *Individual voters' desired funds rates* | | | |
| Jackson | 6.486 A | Burns | 6.733 A |
| Burns | 6.500 | Coldwell | 6.750 |
| Coldwell | 6.500 | Guffey | 6.750 |
| Gardner | 6.500 | Lilly | 6.750 |
| Guffey | 6.500 | Mayo | 6.750 |
| Lilly | 6.500 | Morris | 6.750 |
| Mayo | 6.500 | Partee | 6.750 |
| Morris | 6.500 | Volcker | 6.750 |
| Partee | 6.500 | Wallich | 6.750 |
| Volcker | 6.500 | Gardner | 6.938 |
| Wallich | 6.500 | Roos | 7.000 |
| Roos | 6.666 LT | | |
| *Individual alternates' desired funds rates* | | | |
| Eastburn | 6.498 A | Balles | 6.750 |
| Balles | 6.500 | Baughman | 6.750 |
| Baughman | 6.500 | Black | 6.750 |
| Black | 6.500 | Eastburn | 6.750 |
| Kimbrel | 6.500 | Winn | 6.750 |
| Winn | 6.500 | Kimbrel | 7.000 |
| | | Willes | 7.000 |
| *Summary statistics* | | | |
| Target funds rate | 6.500 | Target funds rate | 6.750 |
| Staff proposal | 6.500 | Staff proposal | 6.750 |
| Premeeting funds rate | 6.516 | Premeeting funds rate | 6.767 |
| Number (voters) | 12 | Number (voters) | 11 |
| Mean (voters) | 6.513 | Mean (voters) | 6.788 |
| Median (voters) | 6.500 | Median (voters) | 6.750 |
| Number (alternates) | 6 | Number (alternates) | 7 |
| Mean (alternates) | 6.500 | Mean (alternates) | 6.821 |
| Median (alternates) | 6.500 | Median (alternates) | 6.750 |
| Number (all) | 18 | Number (all) | 18 |
| Mean (all) | 6.508 | Mean (all) | 6.801 |
| Median (all) | 6.500 | Median (all) | 6.750 |

---

February 28, 1978 (99, 63, 43)

---

*Individual voters' desired funds rates*

| Burns | 6.750 |
|---|---|
| Coldwell | 6.750 |
| Jackson | 6.750 |
| Mayo | 6.750 |
| Morris | 6.750 |
| Partee | 6.750 |
| Roos | 6.750 |
| Volcker | 6.750 |
| Wallich | 6.750 |
| Guffey | 6.875 |


*Individual alternates' desired funds rates*

| Balles | 6.750 |
|---|---|
| Baughman | 6.750 |
| Eastburn | 6.750 |
| Kimbrel | 6.750 |
| Willes | 6.750 |
| Winn | 6.750 |
| Black | 6.760 A |

*Summary statistics*

| Target funds rate | 6.750 |
|---|---|
| Staff proposal | 6.750 |
| Premeeting funds rate | 6.793 |
| Number (voters) | 10 |
| Mean (voters) | 6.763 |
| Median (voters) | 6.750 |
| Number (alternates) | 7 |
| Mean (alternates) | 6.751 |
| Median (alternates) | 6.750 |
| Number (all) | 17 |
| Mean (all) | 6.758 |
| Median (all) | 6.750 |

---

*Notes:* The numbers 99, 63, and 43 indicate meetings included in samples of these sizes, as described in the text; LE, A, LT: Desired funds rate was imputed because the member leaned for ease, assented, or leaned for tightness, respectively, relative to the staff proposal.

# Appendix 5
# Greenspan Era Preference
# Profiles by Meeting

| August 18, 1987 | | September 22, 1987 | |
|---|---|---|---|
| *Individual voters' desired funds rates* | | | |
| Angell | 6.625 BS | Heller | 7.063 |
| Boehne | 6.625 BT | Seger | 7.063 BS |
| Boykin | 6.625 BT | Angell | 7.313 BS |
| Heller | 6.625 | Boehne | 7.313 BS |
| Johnson | 6.625 BT | Boykin | 7.313 BS |
| Kelley | 6.625 BT | Corrigan | 7.313 BS |
| Seger | 6.625 BS | Greenspan | 7.313 BS |
| Corrigan | 6.875 BT | Johnson | 7.313 BS |
| Greenspan | 6.875 | Keehn | 7.313 BT |
| Keehn | 6.875 BT | Kelley | 7.313 BS |
| Stern | 6.875 | Stern | 7.313 BT |
| | | | |
| *Individual alternates' desired funds rates* | | | |
| Black | 6.625 BT | Guffey | 7.063 |
| Guffey | 6.625 | Forrestal | 7.188 BT |
| Melzer | 6.625 BT | Melzer | 7.188 BS |
| Forrestal | 6.875 BT | Black | 7.313 BT |
| Hendricks | 6.875 | Eisenmenger | 7.313 |
| Morris | 6.875 BT | Hendricks | 7.313 BT |
| Parry | 7.125 | Parry | 7.813 |
| *Summary statistics* | | | |
| Target funds rate | 6.625 | Target funds rate | 7.313 |
| Committee bias | BT | Committee bias | BS |
| Status quo | 6.625 | Status quo | 7.313 |
| Number (voters) | 11 | Number (voters) | 11 |
| Mean (voters) | 6.716 | Mean (voters) | 7.267 |
| Median (voters) | 6.625 | Median (voters) | 7.313 |
| Number (alternates) | 7 | Number (alternates) | 7 |
| Mean (alternates) | 6.804 | Mean (alternates) | 7.313 |
| Median (alternates) | 6.875 | Median (alternates) | 7.313 |
| Number (all) | 18 | Number (all) | 18 |
| Mean (all) | 6.750 | Mean (all) | 7.285 |
| Median (all) | 6.625 | Median (all) | 7.313 |

| November 3, 1987 | | December 16, 1987 | |
|---|---|---|---|
| *Individual voters' desired funds rates* | | | |
| Seger | 6.625 BE | Seger | 6.625 |
| Boehne | 6.750 BS | Heller | 6.750 BE |
| Boykin | 6.750 BS | Kelley | 6.750 BE |
| Heller | 6.750 BE | Angell | 6.813 BS |
| Johnson | 6.750 BE | Boehne | 6.813 BS |
| Angell | 6.813 | Boykin | 6.813 BS |
| Corrigan | 6.813 | Corrigan | 6.813 BS |
| Greenspan | 6.813 | Greenspan | 6.813 |
| Keehn | 6.813 BE | Johnson | 6.813 BE |
| Kelley | 6.813 BE | Keehn | 6.813 BS |
| Stern | 6.813 BE | Stern | 6.813 BS |
| | | | |
| *Individual alternates' desired funds rates* | | | |
| Forrestal | 6.750 BE | Black | 6.750 BE |
| Black | 6.813 BE | Guynn | 6.813 BE |
| Guffey | 6.813 BE | Morris | 6.813 BS |
| Hoskins | 6.813 | Parry | 6.813 BS |
| Melzer | 6.813 BS | Guffey | 6.875 BS |
| Morris | 6.813 A | Hoskins | 7.000 BS |
| Parry | 6.875 BS | Melzer | 7.000 BS |
| *Summary statistics* | | | |
| Target funds rate | 6.813 | Target funds rate | 6.813 |
| Committee bias | BE | Committee bias | BE |
| Status quo | 6.813 | Status quo | 6.813 |
| Number (voters) | 11 | Number (voters) | 11 |
| Mean (voters) | 6.773 | Mean (voters) | 6.784 |
| Median (voters) | 6.813 | Median (voters) | 6.813 |
| Number (alternates) | 7 | Number (alternates) | 7 |
| Mean (alternates) | 6.813 | Mean (alternates) | 6.866 |
| Median (alternates) | 6.813 | Median (alternates) | 6.813 |
| Number (all) | 18 | Number (all) | 18 |
| Mean (all) | 6.788 | Mean (all) | 6.816 |
| Median (all) | 6.813 | Median (all) | 6.813 |

| February 10, 1988 | | May 17, 1988 | |
|---|---|---|---|
| *Individual voters' desired funds rates* | | | |
| Heller | 6.438 | Angell | 7.000 BT |
| Seger | 6.438 | Forrestal | 7.000 BT |
| Kelley | 6.469 BE | Greenspan | 7.000 BT |
| Corrigan | 6.500 | Heller | 7.000 BT |
| Johnson | 6.500 | Johnson | 7.000 BT |
| Stern | 6.500 | Kelley | 7.000 BT |
| Greenspan | 6.624 A | Seger | 7.000 BT |
| Angell | 6.625 | Black | 7.250 BT |
| Boehne | 6.625 BS | Corrigan | 7.250 BT |
| Boykin | 6.625 | Hoskins | 7.500 |
| Keehn | 6.625 | Parry | 7.500 |
| | | | |
| *Individual alternates' desired funds rates* | | | |
| Forrestal | 6.500 BE | Keehn | 7.000 BT |
| Black | 6.509 LE | Boehne | 7.250 BT |
| Guffey | 6.625 | Boykin | 7.250 BT |
| Hoskins | 6.625 | Guffey | 7.250 BT |
| Melzer | 6.625 | Morris | 7.250 BT |
| Morris | 6.625 | Stern | 7.250 BT |
| Parry | 6.625 | Melzer | 7.500 |
| *Summary statistics* | | | |
| Target funds rate | 6.500 | Target funds rate | 7.000 |
| Committee bias | BS | Committee bias | BT |
| Status quo | 6.625 | Status quo | 7.000 |
| Number (voters) | 11 | Number (voters) | 11 |
| Mean (voters) | 6.543 | Mean (voters) | 7.136 |
| Median (voters) | 6.500 | Median (voters) | 7.000 |
| Number (alternates) | 7 | Number (alternates) | 7 |
| Mean (alternates) | 6.591 | Mean (alternates) | 7.250 |
| Median (alternates) | 6.625 | Median (alternates) | 7.250 |
| Number (all) | 18 | Number (all) | 18 |
| Mean (all) | 6.561 | Mean (all) | 7.181 |
| Median (all) | 6.625 | Median (all) | 7.250 |

| June 30, 1988 | | August 12, 1988 | |
|---|---|---|---|
| *Individual voters' desired funds rates* | | | |
| Angell | 7.375 BT | Angell | 8.125 BS |
| Heller | 7.375 BT | Black | 8.125 BT |
| Johnson | 7.375 BT | Corrigan | 8.125 BT |
| Kelley | 7.375 BT | Forrestal | 8.125 BT |
| Seger | 7.375 BT | Greenspan | 8.125 BT |
| Corrigan | 7.500 BT | Heller | 8.125 BS |
| Greenspan | 7.500 BT | Johnson | 8.125 BT |
| Forrestal | 7.625 BT | LaWare | 8.125 |
| Black | 7.750 | Parry | 8.125 BT |
| Hoskins | 8.000 | Seger | 8.125 BS |
| Parry | 8.000 | Hoskins | 8.625 |
| | | | |
| *Individual alternates' desired funds rates* | | | |
| Boehne | 7.375 BT | Boehne | 8.125 BT |
| Boykin | 7.500 BT | Boykin | 8.125 BT |
| Guffey | 7.500 | Guffey | 8.125 BT |
| Keehn | 7.500 BT | Keehn | 8.125 BT |
| Melzer | 7.500 BT | Melzer | 8.125 BT |
| Morris | 7.500 BT | Stern | 8.125 BT |
| Stern | 7.500 BT | Morris | 8.625 |
| *Summary statistics* | | | |
| Target funds rate | 7.500 | Target funds rate | 8.125 |
| Committee bias | BT | Committee bias | BT |
| Status quo | 7.500 | Status quo | 8.125 |
| Number (voters) | 11 | Number (voters) | 11 |
| Mean (voters) | 7.568 | Mean (voters) | 8.170 |
| Median (voters) | 7.500 | Median (voters) | 8.125 |
| Number (alternates) | 7 | Number (alternates) | 7 |
| Mean (alternates) | 7.482 | Mean (alternates) | 8.196 |
| Median (alternates) | 7.500 | Median (alternates) | 8.125 |
| Number (all) | 18 | Number (all) | 18 |
| Mean (all) | 7.535 | Mean (all) | 8.181 |
| Median (all) | 7.500 | Median (all) | 8.125 |

| September 20, 1988 | | November 1, 1988 | |
|---|---|---|---|
| *Individual voters' desired funds rates* | | | |
| Angell | 8.125 BT | Angell | 8.125 BS |
| Black | 8.125 BT | Black | 8.125 BT |
| Corrigan | 8.125 BT | Corrigan | 8.125 BT |
| Forrestal | 8.125 BT | Forrestal | 8.125 BT |
| Greenspan | 8.125 BT | Greenspan | 8.125 BT |
| Heller | 8.125 BT | Heller | 8.125 BT |
| Johnson | 8.125 BT | Johnson | 8.125 |
| Kelley | 8.125 BT | Kelley | 8.125 BT |
| LaWare | 8.125 BT | LaWare | 8.125 BT |
| Parry | 8.125 BT | Parry | 8.125 BT |
| Seger | 8.125 BT | Seger | 8.125 BS |
| Hoskins | 8.296 BT A | Hoskins | 8.316 A |
| *Individual alternates' desired funds rates* | | | |
| Boehne | 8.125 BT | Boehne | 8.125 BT |
| Boykin | 8.125 BT | Boykin | 8.125 BT |
| Guffey | 8.125 BT | Guffey | 8.125 BS |
| Melzer | 8.125 BT | Melzer | 8.125 BT |
| Morris | 8.125 BT | Morris | 8.125 BT |
| Stern | 8.125 BT | Stern | 8.125 BT |
| Keehn | 8.270 BT LT | Keehn | 8.188 BS |
| *Summary statistics* | | | |
| Target funds rate | 8.125 | Target funds rate | 8.125 |
| Committee bias | BT | Committee bias | BT |
| Status quo | 8.125 | Status quo | 8.125 |
| Number (voters) | 12 | Number (voters) | 12 |
| Mean (voters) | 8.139 | Mean (voters) | 8.141 |
| Median (voters) | 8.125 | Median (voters) | 8.125 |
| Number (alternates) | 7 | Number (alternates) | 7 |
| Mean (alternates) | 8.146 | Mean (alternates) | 8.134 |
| Median (alternates) | 8.125 | Median (alternates) | 8.125 |
| Number (all) | 19 | Number (all) | 19 |
| Mean (all) | 8.142 | Mean (all) | 8.138 |
| Median (all) | 8.125 | Median (all) | 8.125 |

| December 13, 1988 | | February 7, 1989 | |
|---|---|---|---|
| *Individual voters' desired funds rates* | | | |
| Seger | 8.438 | Angell | 9.125 BT |
| Heller | 8.750 | Greenspan | 9.125 BT |
| Angell | 8.938 | Heller | 9.125 BT |
| Black | 8.938 | Johnson | 9.125 BT |
| Forrestal | 8.938 | Kelley | 9.125 BT |
| Greenspan | 8.938 BT | LaWare | 9.125 BT |
| Johnson | 8.938 BT | Seger | 9.125 BT |
| Kelley | 8.938 BT | Corrigan | 9.285 LT |
| LaWare | 8.938 BT | Forrestal | 9.345 LT |
| Hoskins | 9.000 | Black | 9.625 |
| Corrigan | 9.000 LT[a] | Hoskins | 9.625 |
| Parry | 9.076 BT LT[a] | Parry | 9.625 |
| *Individual alternates' desired funds rates* | | | |
| Melzer | 8.563 | Syron | 9.285 LT |
| Guffey | 8.688 | Boykin | 9.288 LT |
| Keehn | 8.750 | Guffey | 9.313 |
| Stern | 8.813 | Keehn | 9.375 |
| Boehne | 8.938 BT | Stern | 9.375 |
| Boykin | 8.938 | Boehne | 9.625 |
| Eisenmenger | 8.938 | Melzer | 9.625 |
| *Summary statistics* | | | |
| Target funds rate | 8.938 | Target funds rate | 9.125 |
| Committee bias | BT | Committee bias | BT |
| Status quo | 8.438 | Status quo | 9.125 |
| Number (voters) | 12 | Number (voters) | 12 |
| Mean (voters) | 8.902 | Mean (voters) | 9.282 |
| Median (voters) | 8.938 | Median (voters) | 9.125 |
| Number (alternates) | 7 | Number (alternates) | 7 |
| Mean (alternates) | 8.804 | Mean (alternates) | 9.412 |
| Median (alternates) | 8.813 | Median (alternates) | 9.375 |
| Number (all) | 19 | Number (all) | 19 |
| Mean (all) | 8.866 | Mean (all) | 9.330 |
| Median (all) | 8.938 | Median (all) | 9.288 |

| March 24, 1989 | | May 12, 1989 | |
|---|---|---|---|
| *Individual voters' desired funds rates* | | | |
| Angell | 9.750 BS | Melzer | 9.563 |
| Greenspan | 9.750 BT | Seger | 9.563 |
| Guffey | 9.750 BT | Heller | 9.750 BS |
| Heller | 9.750 BT | Johnson | 9.750 BS |
| Johnson | 9.750 BT | Angell | 9.813 BS |
| Keehn | 9.750 BT | Corrigan | 9.813 BS |
| Kelley | 9.750 BS | Greenspan | 9.813 BS |
| LaWare | 9.750 BT | Guffey | 9.813 BT |
| Melzer | 9.750 BS | Keehn | 9.813 BS |
| Seger | 9.750 BS | Kelley | 9.813 BS |
| Corrigan | 9.909 LT | LaWare | 9.813 BS |
| Syron | 9.918 LT | Syron | 9.813 BT |
| *Individual alternates' desired funds rates* | | | |
| Black | 9.750 BT | Black | 9.813 BS |
| Boykin | 9.750 BT | Boehne | 9.813 BS |
| Stern | 9.750 BT | Boykin | 9.813 BT |
| Stone | 9.985 LT | Forrestal | 9.813 BT |
| Forrestal | 10.000 | Hoskins | 9.813 BT |
| Parry | 10.097 BT LT | Parry | 9.813 BT |
| Hoskins | 10.190 LT | Stern | 9.813 BS |
| *Summary statistics* | | | |
| Target funds rate | 9.750 | Target funds rate | 9.813 |
| Committee bias | BT | Committee bias | BS |
| Status quo | 9.750 | Status quo | 9.813 |
| Number (voters) | 12 | Number (voters) | 12 |
| Mean (voters) | 9.777 | Mean (voters) | 9.760 |
| Median (voters) | 9.750 | Median (voters) | 9.813 |
| Number (alternates) | 7 | Number (alternates) | 7 |
| Mean (alternates) | 9.932 | Mean (alternates) | 9.813 |
| Median (alternates) | 9.985 | Median (alternates) | 9.813 |
| Number (all) | 19 | Number (all) | 19 |
| Mean (all) | 9.834 | Mean (all) | 9.780 |
| Median (all) | 9.750 | Median (all) | 9.813 |

| July 6, 1989 | | August 22, 1989 | |
|---|---|---|---|
| *Individual voters' desired funds rates* | | | |
| Seger | 9.063 | Angell | 9.063 BE |
| Angell | 9.313 BS | Corrigan | 9.063 BS |
| Corrigan | 9.313 BS | Greenspan | 9.063 BS |
| Greenspan | 9.313 BS | Guffey | 9.063 BS |
| Guffey | 9.313 BS | Johnson | 9.063 BE |
| Johnson | 9.313 BE | Keehn | 9.063 BE |
| Keehn | 9.313 BS | Kelley | 9.063 BE |
| Kelley | 9.313 BS | LaWare | 9.063 BE |
| LaWare | 9.313 BS | Melzer | 9.063 BS |
| Melzer | 9.313 BS | Seger | 9.063 BE |
| Syron | 9.313 BS | Syron | 9.063 BS |
| | | | |
| *Individual alternates' desired funds rates* | | | |
| Black | 9.313 BS | Boehne | 9.063 BS |
| Boehne | 9.313 BE | Boykin | 9.063 BS |
| Boykin | 9.313 BS | Forrestal | 9.063 BS |
| Forrestal | 9.313 BS | Hoskins | 9.063 BS |
| Parry | 9.313 BS | Monhollon | 9.063 BS |
| Stern | 9.313 BS | Parry | 9.063 BS |
| Hoskins | 9.462 A | Stern | 9.063 BS |
| *Summary statistics* | | | |
| Target funds rate | 9.313 | Target funds rate | 9.063 |
| Committee bias | BS | Committee bias | BE |
| Status quo | 9.563 | Status quo | 9.063 |
| Number (voters) | 11 | Number (voters) | 11 |
| Mean (voters) | 9.290 | Mean (voters) | 9.063 |
| Median (voters) | 9.313 | Median (voters) | 9.063 |
| Number (alternates) | 7 | Number (alternates) | 7 |
| Mean (alternates) | 9.334 | Mean (alternates) | 9.063 |
| Median (alternates) | 9.313 | Median (alternates) | 9.063 |
| Number (all) | 18 | Number (all) | 18 |
| Mean (all) | 9.307 | Mean (all) | 9.063 |
| Median (all) | 9.313 | Median (all) | 9.063 |

| October 3, 1989 | | November 14, 1989 | |
|---|---|---|---|
| *Individual voters' desired funds rates* | | | |
| Seger | 8.500 | Seger | 8.000 |
| Angell | 9.000 BE | Angell | 8.500 BS |
| Corrigan | 9.000 BS | Corrigan | 8.500 BE |
| Greenspan | 9.000 BE | Greenspan | 8.500 BE |
| Guffey | 9.000 BS | Guffey | 8.500 BS |
| Johnson | 9.000 BE | Johnson | 8.500 BE |
| Keehn | 9.000 BE | Keehn | 8.500 BE |
| Kelley | 9.000 BE | Kelley | 8.500 BE |
| LaWare | 9.000 BS | LaWare | 8.500 BE |
| Melzer | 9.000 BS | Melzer | 8.500 BS |
| Syron | 9.000 BS | Syron | 8.500 BE |
| | | | |
| *Individual alternates' desired funds rates* | | | |
| Black | 9.000 BE | Black | 8.500 BE |
| Boehne | 9.000 BE | Boehne | 8.500 BE |
| Boykin | 9.000 BS | Boykin | 8.500 BS |
| Forrestal | 9.000 BS | Forrestal | 8.500 BE |
| Hoskins | 9.000 BT | Hoskins | 8.500 BS |
| Parry | 9.000 BS | Parry | 8.500 BS |
| Stern | 9.000 BS | Stern | 8.500 BE |
| *Summary statistics* | | | |
| Target funds rate | 9.000 | Target funds rate | 8.500 |
| Committee bias | BE | Committee bias | BE |
| Status quo | 9.000 | Status quo | 8.500 |
| Number (voters) | 11 | Number (voters) | 11 |
| Mean (voters) | 8.955 | Mean (voters) | 8.455 |
| Median (voters) | 9.000 | Median (voters) | 8.500 |
| Number (alternates) | 7 | Number (alternates) | 7 |
| Mean (alternates) | 9.000 | Mean (alternates) | 8.500 |
| Median (alternates) | 9.000 | Median (alternates) | 8.500 |
| Number (all) | 18 | Number (all) | 18 |
| Mean (all) | 8.972 | Mean (all) | 8.472 |
| Median (all) | 9.000 | Median (all) | 8.500 |

| December 18, 1989 | | February 2, 1990 | |
|---|---|---|---|
| *Individual voters' desired funds rates* | | | |
| Seger | 8.000 | Seger | 7.750 |
| Corrigan | 8.250 BS | Angell | 8.250 BS |
| Greenspan | 8.250 BS | Boehne | 8.250 BS |
| Johnson | 8.250 BS | Corrigan | 8.250 BS |
| Keehn | 8.250 BS | Greenspan | 8.250 |
| Kelley | 8.250 BS | Johnson | 8.250 BS |
| Syron | 8.250 BS | Kelley | 8.250 BS |
| Angell | 8.500 | LaWare | 8.250 BS |
| Guffey | 8.500 BE | Stern | 8.250 BS |
| LaWare | 8.500 BE | Boykin | 8.363 LT |
| Melzer | 8.500 BE | Hoskins | 8.750 |
| | | | |
| *Individual alternates' desired funds rates* | | | |
| Boykin | 8.250 BS | Black | 8.250 |
| Forrestal | 8.250 BS | Forrestal | 8.250 BS |
| Black | 8.500 | Guffey | 8.250 BS |
| Boehne | 8.500 BE | Keehn | 8.250 BS |
| Parry | 8.500 BS | Melzer | 8.250 BS |
| Stern | 8.500 BE | Parry | 8.250 BS |
| Hoskins | 9.000 | Syron | 8.250 BS |
| *Summary statistics* | | | |
| Target funds rate | 8.250 | Target funds rate | 8.250 |
| Committee bias | BS | Committee bias | BS |
| Status quo | 8.500 | Status quo | 8.250 |
| Number (voters) | 11 | Number (voters) | 11 |
| Mean (voters) | 8.318 | Mean (voters) | 8.260 |
| Median (voters) | 8.250 | Median (voters) | 8.250 |
| Number (alternates) | 7 | Number (alternates) | 7 |
| Mean (alternates) | 8.500 | Mean (alternates) | 8.250 |
| Median (alternates) | 8.500 | Median (alternates) | 8.250 |
| Number (all) | 18 | Number (all) | 18 |
| Mean (all) | 8.389 | Mean (all) | 8.256 |
| Median (all) | 8.375 | Median (all) | 8.250 |

| March 27, 1990 | | May 15, 1990 | |
|---|---|---|---|
| *Individual voters' desired funds rates* | | | |
| Angell | 8.250 BS | Angell | 8.250 BT |
| Boehne | 8.250 BS | Boehne | 8.250 BS |
| Corrigan | 8.250 BS | Boykin | 8.250 BT |
| Greenspan | 8.250 BS | Corrigan | 8.250 |
| Johnson | 8.250 BT | Greenspan | 8.250 BS |
| Kelley | 8.250 BS | Johnson | 8.250 BT |
| LaWare | 8.250 BS | Kelley | 8.250 BS |
| Seger | 8.250 BS | LaWare | 8.250 BS |
| Stern | 8.250 BS | Seger | 8.250 BS |
| Boykin | 8.400 LT | Stern | 8.250 BS |
| Hoskins | 8.500 | Hoskins | 8.750 |
| | | | |
| *Individual alternates' desired funds rates* | | | |
| Forrestal | 8.250 BS | Black | 8.250 BT |
| Guffey | 8.250 BT | Forrestal | 8.250 BT |
| Keehn | 8.250 BS | Guffey | 8.250 BT |
| Melzer | 8.250 BT | Keehn | 8.250 BS |
| Syron | 8.250 BT | Melzer | 8.250 |
| Black | 8.445 LT | Parry | 8.250 BS |
| Parry | 8.555 LT | Syron | 8.250 BT |
| *Summary statistics* | | | |
| Target funds rate | 8.250 | Target funds rate | 8.250 |
| Committee bias | BS | Committee bias | BS |
| Status quo | 8.250 | Status quo | 8.250 |
| Number (voters) | 11 | Number (voters) | 11 |
| Mean (voters) | 8.286 | Mean (voters) | 8.295 |
| Median (voters) | 8.250 | Median (voters) | 8.250 |
| Number (alternates) | 7 | Number (alternates) | 7 |
| Mean (alternates) | 8.321 | Mean (alternates) | 8.250 |
| Median (alternates) | 8.250 | Median (alternates) | 8.250 |
| Number (all) | 18 | Number (all) | 18 |
| Mean (all) | 8.300 | Mean (all) | 8.278 |
| Median (all) | 8.250 | Median (all) | 8.250 |

| July 3, 1990 | | August 21, 1990 | |
|---|---|---|---|
| *Individual voters' desired funds rates* | | | |
| Seger | 7.923 LE | Seger | 7.500 |
| Angell | 8.250 BS | Angell | 8.000 BT |
| Boehne | 8.250 BE | Boehne | 8.000 BE |
| Boykin | 8.250 BS | Boykin | 8.000 BE |
| Corrigan | 8.250 BE | Corrigan | 8.000 BE |
| Greenspan | 8.250 BE | Greenspan | 8.000 BE |
| Hoskins | 8.250 BS | Hoskins | 8.000 BS |
| Kelley | 8.250 BE | Kelley | 8.000 BE |
| LaWare | 8.250 BE | LaWare | 8.000 BE |
| Mullins | 8.250 BE | Mullins | 8.000 BE |
| Stern | 8.250 BE | Stern | 8.000 |
| | | | |
| *Individual alternates' desired funds rates* | | | |
| Black | 8.250 BS | Forrestal | 7.792 LE |
| Forrestal | 8.250 BE | Guffey | 8.000 BS |
| Guffey | 8.250 BS | Keehn | 8.000 BE |
| Keehn | 8.250 BE | Melzer | 8.000 BS |
| Melzer | 8.250 BS | Monhollon | 8.000 BS |
| Parry | 8.250 BS | Parry | 8.000 BS |
| Syron | 8.250 BS | Syron | 8.000 BE |
| *Summary statistics* | | | |
| Target funds rate | 8.250 | Target funds rate | 8.000 |
| Committee bias | BE | Committee bias | BE |
| Status quo | 8.250 | Status quo | 8.000 |
| Number (voters) | 11 | Number (voters) | 11 |
| Mean (voters) | 8.220 | Mean (voters) | 7.955 |
| Median (voters) | 8.250 | Median (voters) | 8.000 |
| Number (alternates) | 7 | Number (alternates) | 7 |
| Mean (alternates) | 8.250 | Mean (alternates) | 7.970 |
| Median (alternates) | 8.250 | Median (alternates) | 8.000 |
| Number (all) | 18 | Number (all) | 18 |
| Mean (all) | 8.232 | Mean (all) | 7.961 |
| Median (all) | 8.250 | Median (all) | 8.000 |

| October 2, 1990 | | November 13, 1990 | |
|---|---|---|---|
| *Individual voters' desired funds rates* | | | |
| Seger | 7.500 | Seger | 7.250 |
| Boehne | 7.750 BE | Angell | 7.500 BE |
| Corrigan | 7.750 BE | Boehne | 7.500 BE |
| Greenspan | 7.750 BE | Boykin | 7.500 BE |
| LaWare | 7.750 BE | Corrigan | 7.500 BE |
| Mullins | 7.750 BE | Greenspan | 7.500 BE |
| Stern | 7.922 LT[b] | Kelley | 7.500 BE |
| Angell | 8.000 | LaWare | 7.500 BE |
| Boykin | 8.000 BE | Mullins | 7.500 BE |
| Hoskins | 8.000 | Stern | 7.500 BE |
| Kelley | 8.000 | Hoskins | 7.907 LT[c] |
| | | | |
| *Individual alternates' desired funds rates* | | | |
| Forrestal | 7.750 BE | Forrestal | 7.500 BE |
| Keehn | 7.750 BE | Guffey | 7.500 BS |
| Syron | 7.750 BE | Keehn | 7.500 BE |
| Black | 7.788 LE | Parry | 7.500 BE |
| Guffey | 8.000 BE | Syron | 7.500 BE |
| Melzer | 8.000 BE | Melzer | 7.750 |
| Parry | 8.000 BS | | |
| *Summary statistics* | | | |
| Target funds rate | 7.750 | Target funds rate | 7.500 |
| Committee bias | BE | Committee bias | BE |
| Status quo | 8.000 | Status quo | 7.750 |
| Number (voters) | 11 | Number (voters) | 11 |
| Mean (voters) | 7.834 | Mean (voters) | 7.514 |
| Median (voters) | 7.750 | Median (voters) | 7.500 |
| Number (alternates) | 7 | Number (alternates) | 6 |
| Mean (alternates) | 7.863 | Mean (alternates) | 7.542 |
| Median (alternates) | 7.788 | Median (alternates) | 7.500 |
| Number (all) | 18 | Number (all) | 17 |
| Mean (all) | 7.845 | Mean (all) | 7.524 |
| Median (all) | 7.769 | Median (all) | 7.500 |

| December 18, 1990 | | February 6, 1991 | |
|---|---|---|---|
| *Individual voters' desired funds rates* | | | |
| Seger | 6.755 LE | Angell | 6.250 BE |
| Angell | 7.000 | Black | 6.250 BE |
| Boehne | 7.000 BE | Corrigan | 6.250 BE |
| Boykin | 7.000 BE | Forrestal | 6.250 BE |
| Corrigan | 7.000 BE | Greenspan | 6.250 BE |
| Greenspan | 7.000 BE | Keehn | 6.250 BE |
| Kelley | 7.000 BE | Kelley | 6.250 BE |
| LaWare | 7.000 BE | LaWare | 6.250 BE |
| Mullins | 7.000 BE | Mullins | 6.250 BE |
| Stern | 7.000 BE | Parry | 6.250 BS |
| Hoskins | 7.250 | Seger | 6.250 BE |
| | | | |
| *Individual alternates' desired funds rates* | | | |
| Forrestal | 6.750 | Boehne | 6.250 BE |
| Black | 7.000 BE | Guffey | 6.250 BS |
| Guffey | 7.000 BE | Hoskins | 6.250 BE |
| Keehn | 7.000 BE | McTeer | 6.250 BE |
| Melzer | 7.000 | Melzer | 6.250 BE |
| Syron | 7.000 BE | Stern | 6.250 BS |
| Parry | 7.248 A | Syron | 6.250 BE |
| *Summary statistics* | | | |
| Target funds rate | 7.000 | Target funds rate | 6.250 |
| Committee bias | BE | Committee bias | BE |
| Status quo | 7.250 | Status quo | 6.250 |
| Number (voters) | 11 | Number (voters) | 11 |
| Mean (voters) | 7.000 | Mean (voters) | 6.250 |
| Median (voters) | 7.000 | Median (voters) | 6.250 |
| Number (alternates) | 7 | Number (alternates) | 7 |
| Mean (alternates) | 7.000 | Mean (alternates) | 6.250 |
| Median (alternates) | 7.000 | Median (alternates) | 6.250 |
| Number (all) | 18 | Number (all) | 18 |
| Mean (all) | 7.000 | Mean (all) | 6.250 |
| Median (all) | 7.000 | Median (all) | 6.250 |

| March 26, 1991 | | May 14, 1991 | |
|---|---|---|---|
| *Individual voters' desired funds rates* | | | |
| Angell | 6.000 BT | Angell | 5.750 BS |
| Black | 6.000 BS | Black | 5.750 BS |
| Corrigan | 6.000 BS | Corrigan | 5.750 BS |
| Forrestal | 6.000 BE | Forrestal | 5.750 BE |
| Greenspan | 6.000 BS | Greenspan | 5.750 BS |
| Keehn | 6.000 BE | Keehn | 5.750 BE |
| Kelley | 6.000 BE | Kelley | 5.750 BS |
| LaWare | 6.000 BS | LaWare | 5.750 BS |
| Mullins | 6.000 BS | Mullins | 5.750 BS |
| Parry | 6.000 BS | Parry | 5.750 BS |
| | | | |
| *Individual alternates' desired funds rates* | | | |
| Boehne | 6.000 BS | Boehne | 5.750 BS |
| Guffey | 6.000 BS | Guffey | 5.750 BS |
| Hoskins | 6.000 BS | Hoskins | 5.750 BS |
| McTeer | 6.000 BS | McTeer | 5.750 BS |
| Melzer | 6.000 BS | Melzer | 5.750 BS |
| Stern | 6.000 BS | Stern | 5.750 BS |
| Syron | 6.000 BS | Syron | 5.750 BS |
| *Summary statistics* | | | |
| Target funds rate | 6.000 | Target funds rate | 5.750 |
| Committee bias | BS | Committee bias | BS |
| Status quo | 6.000 | Status quo | 5.750 |
| Number (voters) | 10 | Number (voters) | 10 |
| Mean (voters) | 6.000 | Mean (voters) | 5.750 |
| Median (voters) | 6.000 | Median (voters) | 5.750 |
| Number (alternates) | 7 | Number (alternates) | 7 |
| Mean (alternates) | 6.000 | Mean (alternates) | 5.750 |
| Median (alternates) | 6.000 | Median (alternates) | 5.750 |
| Number (all) | 17 | Number (all) | 17 |
| Mean (all) | 6.000 | Mean (all) | 5.750 |
| Median (all) | 6.000 | Median (all) | 5.750 |

| July 3, 1991 | | August 16, 1991 | |
|---|---|---|---|
| *Individual voters' desired funds rates* | | | |
| Angell | 5.750 BS | Keehn | 5.332 LE |
| Black | 5.750 BS | Angell | 5.500 BS |
| Corrigan | 5.750 BS | Black | 5.500 BE |
| Forrestal | 5.750 BS | Corrigan | 5.500 BE |
| Greenspan | 5.750 BS | Forrestal | 5.500 BE |
| Keehn | 5.750 BS | Greenspan | 5.500 BE |
| Kelley | 5.750 BS | Kelley | 5.500 BE |
| LaWare | 5.750 BS | LaWare | 5.500 BS |
| Mullins | 5.750 BS | Mullins | 5.500 BE |
| Parry | 5.750 BT | Parry | 5.500 BS |
| | | | |
| *Individual alternates' desired funds rates* | | | |
| Boehne | 5.750 BS | McTeer | 5.000 |
| Guffey | 5.750 BS | Hoskins | 5.127 LE |
| Hoskins | 5.750 BS | Boehne | 5.500 BE |
| McTeer | 5.750 BS | Guffey | 5.500 BS |
| Melzer | 5.750 BS | Melzer | 5.500 BS |
| Stern | 5.750 BS | Stern | 5.500 BE |
| Syron | 5.750 BS | Syron | 5.500 BE |
| *Summary statistics* | | | |
| Target funds rate | 5.750 | Target funds rate | 5.500 |
| Committee bias | BS | Committee bias | BE |
| Status quo | 5.750 | Status quo | 5.500 |
| Number (voters) | 10 | Number (voters) | 10 |
| Mean (voters) | 5.750 | Mean (voters) | 5.483 |
| Median (voters) | 5.750 | Median (voters) | 5.500 |
| Number (alternates) | 7 | Number (alternates) | 7 |
| Mean (alternates) | 5.750 | Mean (alternates) | 5.375 |
| Median (alternates) | 5.750 | Median (alternates) | 5.500 |
| Number (all) | 17 | Number (all) | 17 |
| Mean (all) | 5.750 | Mean (all) | 5.439 |
| Median (all) | 5.750 | Median (all) | 5.500 |

| October 1, 1991 | | November 5, 1991 | |
|---|---|---|---|
| *Individual voters' desired funds rates* | | | |
| Angell | 5.250 BS | Corrigan | 4.750 |
| Black | 5.250 BE | Forrestal | 4.750 BE |
| Corrigan | 5.250 BE | Greenspan | 4.750 |
| Forrestal | 5.250 BE | Keehn | 4.750 BE |
| Greenspan | 5.250 BE | LaWare | 4.750 BS |
| Keehn | 5.250 BE | Mullins | 4.750 BE |
| Kelley | 5.250 BE | Parry | 4.750 BE |
| LaWare | 5.250 BS | Angell | 5.000 BE |
| Mullins | 5.250 BE | Black | 5.000 BE |
| Parry | 5.250 BS | Kelley | 5.000 BE |
| | | | |
| *Individual alternates' desired funds rates* | | | |
| Hendricks | 5.018 LE | Boehne | 4.750 BE |
| Boehne | 5.250 BE | Hendricks | 4.750 BS |
| Hoenig | 5.250 BS | McTeer | 4.750 BS |
| McTeer | 5.250 BE | Stern | 4.750 |
| Melzer | 5.250 BS | Syron | 4.750 BE |
| Stern | 5.250 BE | Hoenig | 5.000 BE |
| Syron | 5.250 BE | Melzer | 5.000 |
| *Summary statistics* | | | |
| Target funds rate | 5.250 | Target funds rate | 4.750 |
| Committee bias | BE | Committee bias | BE |
| Status quo | 5.250 | Status quo | 5.000 |
| Number (voters) | 10 | Number (voters) | 10 |
| Mean (voters) | 5.250 | Mean (voters) | 4.825 |
| Median (voters) | 5.250 | Median (voters) | 4.750 |
| Number (alternates) | 7 | Number (alternates) | 7 |
| Mean (alternates) | 5.217 | Mean (alternates) | 4.821 |
| Median (alternates) | 5.250 | Median (alternates) | 4.750 |
| Number (all) | 17 | Number (all) | 17 |
| Mean (all) | 5.236 | Mean (all) | 4.824 |
| Median (all) | 5.250 | Median (all) | 4.750 |

| December 17, 1991 | | February 5, 1992 | |
|---|---|---|---|
| *Individual voters' desired funds rates* | | | |
| Phillips | 3.893 LE | Syron | 3.850 LE |
| Keehn | 4.000 | Angell | 4.000 BE |
| Angell | 4.500 BE | Corrigan | 4.000 BE |
| Black | 4.500 BE | Greenspan | 4.000 BE |
| Corrigan | 4.500 BE | Hendricks | 4.000 BT |
| Forrestal | 4.500 BE | Hoenig | 4.000 BE |
| Greenspan | 4.500 BE | Kelley | 4.000 BE |
| Kelley | 4.500 BE | LaWare | 4.000 BS |
| LaWare | 4.500 BS | Lindsey | 4.000 BE |
| Lindsey | 4.500 BE | Melzer | 4.000 BS |
| Mullins | 4.500 BE | Mullins | 4.000 BE |
| Parry | 4.500 BE | Phillips | 4.000 BE |
| *Individual alternates' desired funds rates* | | | |
| Boehne | 4.000 | Black | 4.000 BE |
| McTeer | 4.000 | Boehne | 4.000 BE |
| Syron | 4.000 | Forrestal | 4.000 BE |
| Hendricks | 4.500 BS | Keehn | 4.000 BE |
| Hoenig | 4.500 BE | McTeer | 4.000 BE |
| Melzer | 4.500 BS | Parry | 4.000 BE |
| Stern | 4.500 BE | Stern | 4.000 BE |
| *Summary statistics* | | | |
| Target funds rate | 4.500 | Target funds rate | 4.000 |
| Committee bias | BE | Committee bias | BE |
| Status quo | 4.500 | Status quo | 4.000 |
| Number (voters) | 12 | Number (voters) | 12 |
| Mean (voters) | 4.408 | Mean (voters) | 3.988 |
| Median (voters) | 4.500 | Median (voters) | 4.000 |
| Number (alternates) | 7 | Number (alternates) | 7 |
| Mean (alternates) | 4.286 | Mean (alternates) | 4.000 |
| Median (alternates) | 4.500 | Median (alternates) | 4.000 |
| Number (all) | 19 | Number (all) | 19 |
| Mean (all) | 4.363 | Mean (all) | 3.992 |
| Median (all) | 4.500 | Median (all) | 4.000 |

| March 31, 1992 | | May 19, 1992 | |
|---|---|---|---|
| *Individual voters' desired funds rates* | | | |
| Angell | 4.000 BS | Angell | 3.750 BS |
| Corrigan | 4.000 BE | Corrigan | 3.750 BS |
| Greenspan | 4.000 BE | Greenspan | 3.750 BS |
| Hoenig | 4.000 BE | Hoenig | 3.750 BE |
| Jordan | 4.000 BS | Jordan | 3.750 BS |
| Kelley | 4.000 BS | Kelley | 3.750 BS |
| LaWare | 4.000 BE | LaWare | 3.750 BS |
| Lindsey | 4.000 BE | Lindsey | 3.750 BE |
| Melzer | 4.000 BS | Melzer | 3.750 BT |
| Mullins | 4.000 BE | Mullins | 3.750 BE |
| Phillips | 4.000 BE | Phillips | 3.750 BE |
| Syron | 4.000 BE | Syron | 3.750 BS |
| *Individual alternates' desired funds rates* | | | |
| Black | 4.000 BE | Black | 3.750 BS |
| Boehne | 4.000 BE | Boehne | 3.750 BS |
| Forrestal | 4.000 BE | Forrestal | 3.750 BS |
| Keehn | 4.000 BE | Keehn | 3.750 BE |
| McTeer | 4.000 BS | McTeer | 3.750 BS |
| Parry | 4.000 BS | Parry | 3.750 BS |
| Stern | 4.000 BS | Stern | 3.750 BS |
| *Summary statistics* | | | |
| Target funds rate | 4.000 | Target funds rate | 3.750 |
| Committee bias | BE | Committee bias | BS |
| Status quo | 4.000 | Status quo | 3.750 |
| Number (voters) | 12 | Number (voters) | 12 |
| Mean (voters) | 4.000 | Mean (voters) | 3.750 |
| Median (voters) | 4.000 | Median (voters) | 3.750 |
| Number (alternates) | 7 | Number (alternates) | 7 |
| Mean (alternates) | 4.000 | Mean (alternates) | 3.750 |
| Median (alternates) | 4.000 | Median (alternates) | 3.750 |
| Number (all) | 19 | Number (all) | 19 |
| Mean (all) | 4.000 | Mean (all) | 3.750 |
| Median (all) | 4.000 | Median (all) | 3.750 |

| June 30, 1992 | | August 18, 1992 | |
|---|---|---|---|
| *Individual voters' desired funds rates* | | | |
| Jordan | 3.473 LE | Hoenig | 2.750 |
| Phillips | 3.500 LE | Phillips | 2.750 |
| Hoenig | 3.530 LE | Lindsey | 3.000 BE |
| Syron | 3.636 LE | Angell | 3.250 BE |
| Angell | 3.750 BS | Corrigan | 3.250 BE |
| Corrigan | 3.750 BE | Greenspan | 3.250 BE |
| Greenspan | 3.750 BE | Jordan | 3.250 BS |
| Kelley | 3.750 BS | Kelley | 3.250 BE |
| LaWare | 3.750 BS | LaWare | 3.250 BS |
| Lindsey | 3.750 BE | Melzer | 3.250 BS |
| Melzer | 3.750 BS | Mullins | 3.250 BE |
| Mullins | 3.750 BE | Syron | 3.250 BE |
| *Individual alternates' desired funds rates* | | | |
| Keehn | 3.250 | Forrestal | 2.750 |
| Black | 3.750 BE | Keehn | 2.750 |
| Boehne | 3.750 BE | Black | 3.250 BE |
| Forrestal | 3.750 BE | Boehne | 3.250 BE |
| McTeer | 3.750 BS | McTeer | 3.250 BE |
| Parry | 3.750 BE | Parry | 3.250 BE |
| Stern | 3.750 BS | Stern | 3.250 BE |
| *Summary statistics* | | | |
| Target funds rate | 3.750 | Target funds rate | 3.250 |
| Committee bias | BE | Committee bias | BE |
| Status quo | 3.750 | Status quo | 3.250 |
| Number (voters) | 12 | Number (voters) | 12 |
| Mean (voters) | 3.678 | Mean (voters) | 3.146 |
| Median (voters) | 3.750 | Median (voters) | 3.250 |
| Number (alternates) | 7 | Number (alternates) | 7 |
| Mean (alternates) | 3.679 | Mean (alternates) | 3.107 |
| Median (alternates) | 3.750 | Median (alternates) | 3.250 |
| Number (all) | 19 | Number (all) | 19 |
| Mean (all) | 3.678 | Mean (all) | 3.132 |
| Median (all) | 3.750 | Median (all) | 3.250 |

| October 6, 1992 | | November 17, 1992 | |
| --- | --- | --- | --- |
| *Individual voters' desired funds rates* | | | |
| Phillips | 2.500 | Jordan | 2.743 LE |
| Hoenig | 2.709 LE | Phillips | 2.759 LE |
| Lindsey | 2.739 LE | Lindsey | 2.786 LE |
| Syron | 2.810 LE | Syron | 2.843 LE |
| Jordan | 2.990 A | Angell | 3.000 BS |
| Angell | 3.000 BS | Corrigan | 3.000 BS |
| Corrigan | 3.000 BE | Greenspan | 3.000 BE |
| Greenspan | 3.000 BE | Hoenig | 3.000 BS |
| Kelley | 3.000 BE | Kelley | 3.000 BS |
| LaWare | 3.000 BS | LaWare | 3.000 BS |
| Melzer | 3.000 BS | Melzer | 3.000 BS |
| Mullins | 3.000 BE | Mullins | 3.000 BE |
| *Individual alternates' desired funds rates* | | | |
| Keehn | 2.733 LE | Parry | 2.781 LE |
| Forrestal | 2.738 LE | Black | 3.000 BS |
| Black | 2.750 | Boehne | 3.000 BS |
| Parry | 2.750 BE | Forrestal | 3.000 BE |
| Boehne | 2.800 LE | Keehn | 3.000 BE |
| McTeer | 3.000 BS | McTeer | 3.000 BS |
| Stern | 3.000 BE | Stern | 3.000 BS |
| *Summary statistics* | | | |
| Target funds rate | 3.000 | Target funds rate | 3.000 |
| Committee bias | BE | Committee bias | BE |
| Status quo | 3.000 | Status quo | 3.000 |
| Number (voters) | 12 | Number (voters) | 12 |
| Mean (voters) | 2.896 | Mean (voters) | 2.928 |
| Median (voters) | 3.000 | Median (voters) | 3.000 |
| Number (alternates) | 7 | Number (alternates) | 7 |
| Mean (alternates) | 2.825 | Mean (alternates) | 2.969 |
| Median (alternates) | 2.750 | Median (alternates) | 3.000 |
| Number (all) | 19 | Number (all) | 19 |
| Mean (all) | 2.869 | Mean (all) | 2.943 |
| Median (all) | 2.990 | Median (all) | 3.000 |

| December 22, 1992 | | February 3, 1993 | |
|---|---|---|---|
| *Individual voters' desired funds rates* | | | |
| Angell | 3.000 BS | Angell | 3.000 BT |
| Corrigan | 3.000 BS | Boehne | 3.000 BS |
| Greenspan | 3.000 BS | Corrigan | 3.000 BS |
| Hoenig | 3.000 BS | Greenspan | 3.000 BS |
| Jordan | 3.000 BS | Keehn | 3.000 BS |
| Kelley | 3.000 BS | Kelley | 3.000 BS |
| LaWare | 3.000 BS | LaWare | 3.000 BS |
| Lindsey | 3.000 BS | Lindsey | 3.000 BS |
| Melzer | 3.000 BT | McTeer | 3.000 BS |
| Mullins | 3.000 BS | Mullins | 3.000 BS |
| Phillips | 3.000 BS | Phillips | 3.000 BS |
| Syron | 3.000 BS | Stern | 3.000 BS |
| *Individual alternates' desired funds rates* | | | |
| Boehne | 3.000 BS | Jordan | 2.758 LE |
| Broaddus | 3.000 BS | Broaddus | 3.000 BS |
| Forrestal | 3.000 BS | Forrestal | 3.000 BS |
| Keehn | 3.000 BS | Hoenig | 3.000 BS |
| McTeer | 3.000 BS | Melzer | 3.000 BT |
| Parry | 3.000 BS | Parry | 3.000 BS |
| Stern | 3.000 BS | Syron | 3.000 BS |
| *Summary statistics* | | | |
| Target funds rate | 3.000 | Target funds rate | 3.000 |
| Committee bias | BS | Committee bias | BS |
| Status quo | 3.000 | Status quo | 3.000 |
| Number (voters) | 12 | Number (voters) | 12 |
| Mean (voters) | 3.000 | Mean (voters) | 3.000 |
| Median (voters) | 3.000 | Median (voters) | 3.000 |
| Number (alternates) | 7 | Number (alternates) | 7 |
| Mean (alternates) | 3.000 | Mean (alternates) | 2.965 |
| Median (alternates) | 3.000 | Median (alternates) | 3.000 |
| Number (all) | 19 | Number (all) | 19 |
| Mean (all) | 3.000 | Mean (all) | 2.987 |
| Median (all) | 3.000 | Median (all) | 3.000 |

| March 23, 1993 | | May 18, 1993 | |
|---|---|---|---|
| *Individual voters' desired funds rates* | | | |
| Boehne | 3.000 BS | Boehne | 3.000 BS |
| Corrigan | 3.000 BS | Corrigan | 3.000 BT |
| Greenspan | 3.000 BS | Greenspan | 3.000 BT |
| Keehn | 3.000 BS | Keehn | 3.000 BS |
| Kelley | 3.000 BS | Kelley | 3.000 BT |
| LaWare | 3.000 BS | LaWare | 3.000 BT |
| McTeer | 3.000 BS | McTeer | 3.000 BT |
| Mullins | 3.000 BS | Phillips | 3.000 BS |
| Phillips | 3.000 BS | Mullins | 3.087 LT |
| Stern | 3.000 BS | Stern | 3.176 LT |
| Lindsey | 3.304 LT | Lindsey | 3.208 LT |
| Angell | 3.500 | Angell | 3.500 |
| *Individual alternates' desired funds rates* | | | |
| Broaddus | 3.000 BS | Forrestal | 3.000 BS |
| Forrestal | 3.000 BS | Hoenig | 3.000 BS |
| Hoenig | 3.000 BS | Parry | 3.000 BT |
| Melzer | 3.000 BS | Syron | 3.000 BT |
| Parry | 3.000 BS | Melzer | 3.217 LT |
| Syron | 3.000 BS | Broaddus | 3.250 |
| Jordan | 3.003 A | Jordan | 3.282 LT |
| *Summary statistics* | | | |
| Target funds rate | 3.000 | Target funds rate | 3.000 |
| Committee bias | BS | Committee bias | BT |
| Status quo | 3.000 | Status quo | 3.000 |
| Number (voters) | 12 | Number (voters) | 12 |
| Mean (voters) | 3.067 | Mean (voters) | 3.081 |
| Median (voters) | 3.000 | Median (voters) | 3.000 |
| Number (alternates) | 7 | Number (alternates) | 7 |
| Mean (alternates) | 3.000 | Mean (alternates) | 3.107 |
| Median (alternates) | 3.000 | Median (alternates) | 3.000 |
| Number (all) | 19 | Number (all) | 19 |
| Mean (all) | 3.042 | Mean (all) | 3.081 |
| Median (all) | 3.000 | Median (all) | 3.000 |

| July 7, 1993 | | August 17, 1993 | |
|---|---|---|---|
| *Individual voters' desired funds rates* | | | |
| Boehne | 3.000 BT | Angell | 3.000 |
| Greenspan | 3.000 BT | Boehne | 3.000 BS |
| Keehn | 3.000 BS | Greenspan | 3.000 BS |
| Kelley | 3.000 BT | Keehn | 3.000 BS |
| LaWare | 3.000 BT | Kelley | 3.000 BS |
| Lindsey | 3.000 BT | LaWare | 3.000 BS |
| McTeer | 3.000 BT | Lindsey | 3.000 BS |
| Mullins | 3.000 | McDonough | 3.000 BS |
| Oltman | 3.000 BT | McTeer | 3.000 BS |
| Phillips | 3.000 BT | Mullins | 3.000 BS |
| Stern | 3.000 BT | Phillips | 3.000 BS |
| Angell | 3.190 LT | Stern | 3.000 BS |
| *Individual alternates' desired funds rates* | | | |
| Broaddus | 3.000 BT | Syron | 2.998 A |
| Forrestal | 3.000 BS | Broaddus | 3.000 BT |
| Hoenig | 3.000 BS | Forrestal | 3.000 BS |
| Melzer | 3.000 BT | Hoenig | 3.000 BS |
| Parry | 3.000 BT | Melzer | 3.000 BS |
| Syron | 3.000 BT | Parry | 3.000 BS |
| Jordan | 3.292 LT | Jordan | 3.012 A |
| *Summary statistics* | | | |
| Target funds rate | 3.000 | Target funds rate | 3.000 |
| Committee bias | BT | Committee bias | BS |
| Status quo | 3.000 | Status quo | 3.000 |
| Number (voters) | 12 | Number (voters) | 12 |
| Mean (voters) | 3.016 | Mean (voters) | 3.000 |
| Median (voters) | 3.000 | Median (voters) | 3.000 |
| Number (alternates) | 7 | Number (alternates) | 7 |
| Mean (alternates) | 3.042 | Mean (alternates) | 3.001 |
| Median (alternates) | 3.000 | Median (alternates) | 3.000 |
| Number (all) | 19 | Number (all) | 19 |
| Mean (all) | 3.016 | Mean (all) | 3.000 |
| Median (all) | 3.000 | Median (all) | 3.000 |

| September 23, 1993 | | November 11, 1993 | |
|---|---|---|---|
| *Individual voters' desired funds rates* | | | |
| Angell | 3.000 BS | Boehne | 3.000 BS |
| Boehne | 3.000 BS | Greenspan | 3.000 BS |
| Greenspan | 3.000 BS | Keehn | 3.000 BS |
| Keehn | 3.000 BS | Kelley | 3.000 BS |
| Kelley | 3.000 BS | LaWare | 3.000 BS |
| LaWare | 3.000 BS | Lindsey | 3.000 BS |
| Lindsey | 3.000 BS | McTeer | 3.000 BS |
| McDonough | 3.000 BS | Mullins | 3.000 BS |
| McTeer | 3.000 BS | Phillips | 3.000 BS |
| Mullins | 3.000 BS | Stern | 3.000 BS |
| Phillips | 3.000 BS | McDonough | 3.002 A |
| Stern | 3.000 BS | Angell | 3.264 LT |
| *Individual alternates' desired funds rates* | | | |
| Broaddus | 3.000 BS | Broaddus | 3.000 BS |
| Forrestal | 3.000 BS | Forrestal | 3.000 BS |
| Hoenig | 3.000 BS | Hoenig | 3.000 BS |
| Melzer | 3.000 BS | Jordan | 3.000 BS |
| Parry | 3.000 BS | Melzer | 3.000 BT |
| Syron | 3.000 BS | Parry | 3.000 BS |
| | | Syron | 3.000 BS |
| *Summary statistics* | | | |
| Target funds rate | 3.000 | Target funds rate | 3.000 |
| Committee bias | BS | Committee bias | BS |
| Status quo | 3.000 | Status quo | 3.000 |
| Number (voters) | 12 | Number (voters) | 12 |
| Mean (voters) | 3.000 | Mean (voters) | 3.022 |
| Median (voters) | 3.000 | Median (voters) | 3.000 |
| Number (alternates) | 6 | Number (alternates) | 7 |
| Mean (alternates) | 3.000 | Mean (alternates) | 3.000 |
| Median (alternates) | 3.000 | Median (alternates) | 3.000 |
| Number (all) | 18 | Number (all) | 19 |
| Mean (all) | 3.000 | Mean (all) | 3.022 |
| Median (all) | 3.000 | Median (all) | 3.000 |

| December 21, 1993 | | February 2, 1994 | |
|---|---|---|---|
| *Individual voters' desired funds rates* | | | |
| Boehne | 3.000 BS | Forrestal | 3.250 BS |
| Greenspan | 3.000 BS | Greenspan | 3.250 BS |
| Keehn | 3.000 BS | Kelley | 3.250 |
| Kelley | 3.000 BS | McDonough | 3.250 |
| LaWare | 3.000 BS | Broaddus | 3.500 |
| McDonough | 3.000 BS | Jordan | 3.500 BS |
| Mullins | 3.000 BS | LaWare | 3.500 |
| Stern | 3.000 BS | Lindsey | 3.500 |
| Lindsey | 3.250 | Parry | 3.500 |
| McTeer | 3.378 LT | Phillips | 3.500 |
| Angell | 3.500 | | |
| Phillips | 3.526 LT | | |
| *Individual alternates' desired funds rates* | | | |
| Forrestal | 3.000 BS | Boehne | 3.250 BS |
| Jordan | 3.000 BS | Keehn | 3.250 BS |
| Parry | 3.000 BT | Syron | 3.250 |
| Syron | 3.000 BS | Hoenig | 3.500 |
| Broaddus | 3.250 | McTeer | 3.500 |
| Melzer | 3.338 LT | Melzer | 3.500 |
| Hoenig | 3.411 LT | Stern | 3.500 |
| *Summary statistics* | | | |
| Target funds rate | 3.000 | Target funds rate | 3.250 |
| Committee bias | BS | Committee bias | BS |
| Status quo | 3.000 | Status quo | 3.000 |
| Number (voters) | 12 | Number (voters) | 10 |
| Mean (voters) | 3.138 | Mean (voters) | 3.400 |
| Median (voters) | 3.000 | Median (voters) | 3.500 |
| Number (alternates) | 7 | Number (alternates) | 7 |
| Mean (alternates) | 3.143 | Mean (alternates) | 3.393 |
| Median (alternates) | 3.000 | Median (alternates) | 3.500 |
| Number (all) | 19 | Number (all) | 17 |
| Mean (all) | 3.138 | Mean (all) | 3.400 |
| Median (all) | 3.000 | Median (all) | 3.500 |

| March 22, 1994 | | May 17, 1994 | |
|---|---|---|---|
| *Individual voters' desired funds rates* | | | |
| Forrestal | 3.500 BS | Jordan | 4.062 LT |
| Greenspan | 3.500 BT | Broaddus | 4.250 BT |
| Kelley | 3.500 BS | Forrestal | 4.250 BS |
| Lindsey | 3.500 BS | Greenspan | 4.250 BS |
| McDonough | 3.500 BS | Kelley | 4.250 BS |
| Phillips | 3.500 BS | LaWare | 4.250 BS |
| Jordan | 3.736 LT[d] | Lindsey | 4.250 BS |
| Broaddus | 3.750 | McDonough | 4.250 BS |
| LaWare | 3.750 BS | Parry | 4.250 BS |
| Parry | 3.750 | Phillips | 4.250 BS |
| | | | |
| *Individual alternates' desired funds rates* | | | |
| Hoenig | 3.500 BS | Boehne | 4.250 BS |
| Keehn | 3.500 BS | Hoenig | 4.250 BS |
| McTeer | 3.500 BS | Keehn | 4.250 BS |
| Minehan | 3.500 BS | McTeer | 4.250 BS |
| Stern | 3.500 BS | Melzer | 4.250 |
| Boehne | 3.750 | Minehan | 4.250 BS |
| Melzer | 3.750 | Stern | 4.250 BS |
| *Summary statistics* | | | |
| Target funds rate | 3.500 | Target funds rate | 4.250 |
| Committee bias | BS | Committee bias | BS |
| Status quo | 3.250 | Status quo | 3.750 |
| Number (voters) | 10 | Number (voters) | 10 |
| Mean (voters) | 3.599 | Mean (voters) | 4.231 |
| Median (voters) | 3.500 | Median (voters) | 4.250 |
| Number (alternates) | 7 | Number (alternates) | 7 |
| Mean (alternates) | 3.571 | Mean (alternates) | 4.250 |
| Median (alternates) | 3.500 | Median (alternates) | 4.250 |
| Number (all) | 17 | Number (all) | 17 |
| Mean (all) | 3.599 | Mean (all) | 4.231 |
| Median (all) | 3.500 | Median (all) | 4.250 |

| July 6, 1994 | | August 16, 1994 | |
|---|---|---|---|
| *Individual voters' desired funds rates* | | | |
| Blinder | 4.250 BT | Blinder | 4.750 BS |
| Forrestal | 4.250 BS | Broaddus | 4.750 BS |
| Greenspan | 4.250 BT | Forrestal | 4.750 BS |
| Jordan | 4.250 BS | Greenspan | 4.750 BS |
| Kelley | 4.250 BT | Jordan | 4.750 BS |
| LaWare | 4.250 BT | Kelley | 4.750 BS |
| Lindsey | 4.250 BS | LaWare | 4.750 BS |
| McDonough | 4.250 BT | Lindsey | 4.750 BS |
| Parry | 4.250 BT | McDonough | 4.750 BS |
| Phillips | 4.250 BS | Parry | 4.750 BS |
| Broaddus | 4.750 | Phillips | 4.750 BS |
| | | Yellen | 4.750 BS |
| *Individual alternates' desired funds rates* | | | |
| Boehne | 4.250 | Boehne | 4.750 BS |
| Hoenig | 4.250 BT | Conrad | 4.750 BS |
| Keehn | 4.250 BS | Hoenig | 4.750 BS |
| McTeer | 4.250 BT | McTeer | 4.750 BS |
| Minehan | 4.250 BS | Melzer | 4.750 BS |
| Stern | 4.250 BS | Minehan | 4.750 BS |
| Melzer | 4.750 | Stern | 4.750 BS |
| *Summary statistics* | | | |
| Target funds rate | 4.250 | Target funds rate | 4.750 |
| Committee bias | BT | Committee bias | BS |
| Status quo | 4.250 | Status quo | 4.250 |
| Number (voters) | 11 | Number (voters) | 12 |
| Mean (voters) | 4.295 | Mean (voters) | 4.750 |
| Median (voters) | 4.250 | Median (voters) | 4.750 |
| Number (alternates) | 7 | Number (alternates) | 7 |
| Mean (alternates) | 4.321 | Mean (alternates) | 4.750 |
| Median (alternates) | 4.250 | Median (alternates) | 4.750 |
| Number (all) | 18 | Number (all) | 19 |
| Mean (all) | 4.295 | Mean (all) | 4.750 |
| Median (all) | 4.250 | Median (all) | 4.750 |

| September 27, 1994 | | November 15, 1994 | |
|---|---|---|---|
| *Individual voters' desired funds rates* | | | |
| Blinder | 4.750 BT | Blinder | 5.250 |
| Forrestal | 4.750 BT | Yellen | 5.250 |
| Greenspan | 4.750 BT | Broaddus | 5.500 |
| Jordan | 4.750 BS | Forrestal | 5.500 |
| Kelley | 4.750 BT | Greenspan | 5.500 BS |
| LaWare | 4.750 BT | Jordan | 5.500 BS |
| Lindsey | 4.750 BT | Kelley | 5.500 BS |
| McDonough | 4.750 BT | LaWare | 5.500 BS |
| Parry | 4.750 BT | Lindsey | 5.500 BS |
| Phillips | 4.750 BT | McDonough | 5.500 BS |
| Yellen | 4.750 BT | Parry | 5.500 BT |
| Broaddus | 5.250 | Phillips | 5.500 BS |
| *Individual alternates' desired funds rates* | | | |
| Boehne | 4.750 BT | Boehne | 5.250 |
| Hoenig | 4.750 BT | Hoenig | 5.500 BS |
| McTeer | 4.750 BS | McTeer | 5.500 |
| Minehan | 4.750 BT | Melzer | 5.500 BS |
| Moskow | 4.750 BT | Minehan | 5.500 BS |
| Melzer | 5.250 | Moskow | 5.500 BS |
| Stern | 5.250 | Stern | 5.500 |
| *Summary statistics* | | | |
| Target funds rate | 4.750 | Target funds rate | 5.500 |
| Committee bias | BT | Committee bias | BS |
| Status quo | 4.750 | Status quo | 4.750 |
| Number (voters) | 12 | Number (voters) | 12 |
| Mean (voters) | 4.792 | Mean (voters) | 5.458 |
| Median (voters) | 4.750 | Median (voters) | 5.500 |
| Number (alternates) | 7 | Number (alternates) | 7 |
| Mean (alternates) | 4.893 | Mean (alternates) | 5.464 |
| Median (alternates) | 4.750 | Median (alternates) | 5.500 |
| Number (all) | 19 | Number (all) | 19 |
| Mean (all) | 4.792 | Mean (all) | 5.458 |
| Median (all) | 4.750 | Median (all) | 5.500 |

| December 20, 1994 | | February 1, 1995 | |
|---|---|---|---|
| *Individual voters' desired funds rates* | | | |
| Blinder | 5.500 BS | Blinder | 5.500 BT |
| Forrestal | 5.500 BS | Yellen | 5.500 BT |
| Greenspan | 5.500 BT | Greenspan | 6.000 BS |
| Kelley | 5.500 BT | Hoenig | 6.000 BS |
| Lindsey | 5.500 BS | Kelley | 6.000 BS |
| McDonough | 5.500 BT | LaWare | 6.000 BS |
| Phillips | 5.500 BT | Lindsey | 6.000 BS |
| Yellen | 5.500 BS | McDonough | 6.000 BS |
| Jordan | 5.519 A | Melzer | 6.000 BS |
| Broaddus | 5.750 | Minehan | 6.000 BS |
| LaWare | 6.000 BS | Moskow | 6.000 BS |
| Parry | 6.000 | Phillips | 6.000 BS |
| *Individual alternates' desired funds rates* | | | |
| McTeer | 5.500 BT | Boehne | 6.000 |
| Melzer | 5.500 BT | Broaddus | 6.000 BS |
| Moskow | 5.500 BT | Forrestal | 6.000 BS |
| Stern | 5.500 BS | Jordan | 6.000 BS |
| Hoenig | 5.865 LT | McTeer | 6.000 BS |
| Minehan | 6.000 | Parry | 6.000 BT |
| | | Stern | 6.000 BS |
| *Summary statistics* | | | |
| Target funds rate | 5.500 | Target funds rate | 6.000 |
| Committee bias | BT | Committee bias | BS |
| Status quo | 5.500 | Status quo | 5.500 |
| Number (voters) | 12 | Number (voters) | 12 |
| Mean (voters) | 5.606 | Mean (voters) | 5.917 |
| Median (voters) | 5.500 | Median (voters) | 6.000 |
| Number (alternates) | 6 | Number (alternates) | 7 |
| Mean (alternates) | 5.644 | Mean (alternates) | 6.000 |
| Median (alternates) | 5.500 | Median (alternates) | 6.000 |
| Number (all) | 18 | Number (all) | 19 |
| Mean (all) | 5.606 | Mean (all) | 5.917 |
| Median (all) | 5.500 | Median (all) | 6.000 |

| March 28, 1995 | | May 23, 1995 | |
|---|---|---|---|
| *Individual voters' desired funds rates* | | | |
| Blinder | 6.000 | Blinder | 6.000 BS |
| Greenspan | 6.000 BT | Greenspan | 6.000 BS |
| Hoenig | 6.000 BT | Hoenig | 6.000 BS |
| Kelley | 6.000 BT | Kelley | 6.000 BS |
| Lindsey | 6.000 BS | Lindsey | 6.000 BS |
| McDonough | 6.000 BT | McDonough | 6.000 BS |
| Melzer | 6.000 BT | Melzer | 6.000 BS |
| Moskow | 6.000 BT | Minehan | 6.000 BS |
| Phillips | 6.000 BT | Moskow | 6.000 BS |
| Yellen | 6.000 BS | Phillips | 6.000 BS |
| Minehan | 6.187 LT | Yellen | 6.000 BS |
| | | | |
| *Individual alternates' desired funds rates* | | | |
| Boehne | 6.000 BT | Boehne | 6.000 BS |
| Broaddus | 6.000 BT | Broaddus | 6.000 BS |
| Forrestal | 6.000 BS | Forrestal | 6.000 BS |
| Jordan | 6.000 BT | Jordan | 6.000 BS |
| McTeer | 6.000 BT | McTeer | 6.000 BS |
| Stern | 6.000 BS | Parry | 6.000 BS |
| Parry | 6.252 LT | Stern | 6.000 BS |
| *Summary statistics* | | | |
| Target funds rate | 6.000 | Target funds rate | 6.000 |
| Committee bias | BT | Committee bias | BS |
| Status quo | 6.000 | Status quo | 6.000 |
| Number (voters) | 11 | Number (voters) | 11 |
| Mean (voters) | 6.017 | Mean (voters) | 6.000 |
| Median (voters) | 6.000 | Median (voters) | 6.000 |
| Number (alternates) | 7 | Number (alternates) | 7 |
| Mean (alternates) | 6.036 | Mean (alternates) | 6.000 |
| Median (alternates) | 6.000 | Median (alternates) | 6.000 |
| Number (all) | 18 | Number (all) | 18 |
| Mean (all) | 6.017 | Mean (all) | 6.000 |
| Median (all) | 6.000 | Median (all) | 6.000 |

| July 6, 1995 | | August 22, 1995 | |
|---|---|---|---|
| *Individual voters' desired funds rates* | | | |
| Blinder | 5.500 BS | Blinder | 5.750 BS |
| Yellen | 5.500 | Greenspan | 5.750 BS |
| Greenspan | 5.750 BE | Hoenig | 5.750 BS |
| Kelley | 5.750 BS | Kelley | 5.750 BS |
| Lindsey | 5.750 BE | Lindsey | 5.750 BS |
| McDonough | 5.750 BE | McDonough | 5.750 BS |
| Moskow | 5.750 BE | Melzer | 5.750 BS |
| Phillips | 5.750 BS | Minehan | 5.750 BS |
| Hoenig | 6.000 BE | Moskow | 5.750 BS |
| Melzer | 6.000 | Phillips | 5.750 BS |
| Minehan | 6.000 BE | Yellen | 5.750 BS |
| | | | |
| *Individual alternates' desired funds rates* | | | |
| McTeer | 5.500 | Boehne | 5.750 BS |
| Parry | 5.500 BS | Broaddus | 5.750 BS |
| Forrestal | 5.636 LE[e] | Forrestal | 5.750 BS |
| Boehne | 5.750 BE | Jordan | 5.750 BS |
| Broaddus | 5.750 | Parry | 5.750 BS |
| Stern | 5.750 BS | Stern | 5.750 BS |
| Jordan | 5.987 A | | |
| *Summary statistics* | | | |
| Target funds rate | 5.750 | Target funds rate | 5.750 |
| Committee bias | BE | Committee bias | BS |
| Status quo | 6.000 | Status quo | 5.750 |
| Number (voters) | 11 | Number (voters) | 11 |
| Mean (voters) | 5.773 | Mean (voters) | 5.750 |
| Median (voters) | 5.750 | Median (voters) | 5.750 |
| Number (alternates) | 7 | Number (alternates) | 6 |
| Mean (alternates) | 5.696 | Mean (alternates) | 5.750 |
| Median (alternates) | 5.750 | Median (alternates) | 5.750 |
| Number (all) | 18 | Number (all) | 17 |
| Mean (all) | 5.773 | Mean (all) | 5.750 |
| Median (all) | 5.750 | Median (all) | 5.750 |

| September 26, 1995 | | November 15, 1995 | |
|---|---|---|---|
| *Individual voters' desired funds rates* | | | |
| Yellen | 5.562 LE | Blinder | 5.508 LE |
| Blinder | 5.750 BS | Lindsey | 5.554 LE |
| Greenspan | 5.750 BS | Greenspan | 5.750 |
| Hoenig | 5.750 BS | Hoenig | 5.750 BS |
| Kelley | 5.750 BS | Kelley | 5.750 BS |
| Lindsey | 5.750 BS | McDonough | 5.750 BE |
| McDonough | 5.750 BS | Melzer | 5.750 BS |
| Melzer | 5.750 BS | Minehan | 5.750 BS |
| Minehan | 5.750 BS | Moskow | 5.750 BS |
| Moskow | 5.750 BS | Phillips | 5.750 BS |
| Phillips | 5.750 BS | Yellen | 5.750 BE |
| | | | |
| *Individual alternates' desired funds rates* | | | |
| Forrestal | 5.500 | Forrestal | 5.611 LE |
| Boehne | 5.750 BS | Boehne | 5.750 BS |
| Broaddus | 5.750 BS | Broaddus | 5.750 BS |
| Jordan | 5.750 BS | Jordan | 5.750 |
| McTeer | 5.750 BS | McTeer | 5.750 BS |
| Parry | 5.750 BS | Parry | 5.750 BS |
| Stern | 5.750 BS | Stern | 5.750 BS |
| *Summary statistics* | | | |
| Target funds rate | 5.750 | Target funds rate | 5.750 |
| Committee bias | BS | Committee bias | BS |
| Status quo | 5.750 | Status quo | 5.750 |
| Number (voters) | 11 | Number (voters) | 11 |
| Mean (voters) | 5.733 | Mean (voters) | 5.710 |
| Median (voters) | 5.750 | Median (voters) | 5.750 |
| Number (alternates) | 7 | Number (alternates) | 7 |
| Mean (alternates) | 5.714 | Mean (alternates) | 5.730 |
| Median (alternates) | 5.750 | Median (alternates) | 5.750 |
| Number (all) | 18 | Number (all) | 18 |
| Mean (all) | 5.733 | Mean (all) | 5.710 |
| Median (all) | 5.750 | Median (all) | 5.750 |

| December 19, 1995 | | January 31, 1996 | |
|---|---|---|---|
| *Individual voters' desired funds rates* | | | |
| Blinder | 5.500 BS | Jordan | 5.215 LE |
| Greenspan | 5.500 BS | Boehne | 5.250 |
| Kelley | 5.500 BS | Greenspan | 5.250 BS |
| Lindsey | 5.500 BS | Kelley | 5.250 BS |
| McDonough | 5.500 BS | Lindsey | 5.250 BS |
| Yellen | 5.500 BS | McDonough | 5.250 BS |
| Phillips | 5.542 LE | McTeer | 5.250 BS |
| Hoenig | 5.750 | Phillips | 5.250 BS |
| Melzer | 5.750 | Stern | 5.250 |
| Minehan | 5.750 | Yellen | 5.250 BS |
| Moskow | 5.750 | | |
| | | | |
| *Individual alternates' desired funds rates* | | | |
| Boehne | 5.500 BS | Guynn | 5.250 |
| Guynn | 5.500 BS | Broaddus | 5.500 |
| Jordan | 5.500 | Hoenig | 5.500 |
| McTeer | 5.500 BS | Melzer | 5.500 |
| Parry | 5.500 BS | Minehan | 5.500 |
| Broaddus | 5.750 | Moskow | 5.500 |
| Stern | 5.750 | Parry | 5.500 |
| *Summary statistics* | | | |
| Target funds rate | 5.500 | Target funds rate | 5.250 |
| Committee bias | BS | Committee bias | BS |
| Status quo | 5.750 | Status quo | 5.500 |
| Number (voters) | 11 | Number (voters) | 10 |
| Mean (voters) | 5.595 | Mean (voters) | 5.247 |
| Median (voters) | 5.500 | Median (voters) | 5.250 |
| Number (alternates) | 7 | Number (alternates) | 7 |
| Mean (alternates) | 5.571 | Mean (alternates) | 5.464 |
| Median (alternates) | 5.500 | Median (alternates) | 5.500 |
| Number (all) | 18 | Number (all) | 17 |
| Mean (all) | 5.595 | Mean (all) | 5.247 |
| Median (all) | 5.500 | Median (all) | 5.250 |

| March 26, 1996 | | May 21, 1996 | |
|---|---|---|---|
| *Individual voters' desired funds rates* | | | |
| Boehne | 5.250 BS | Boehne | 5.250 BS |
| Greenspan | 5.250 BS | Greenspan | 5.250 BS |
| Jordan | 5.250 | Jordan | 5.250 BS |
| Kelley | 5.250 BS | Kelley | 5.250 BS |
| Lindsey | 5.250 BS | Lindsey | 5.250 BT |
| McDonough | 5.250 BS | McDonough | 5.250 BS |
| McTeer | 5.250 BS | McTeer | 5.250 BS |
| Phillips | 5.250 BS | Phillips | 5.250 BS |
| Stern | 5.250 BS | Stern | 5.250 BS |
| Yellen | 5.250 BS | Yellen | 5.250 BS |
| | | | |
| | | | |
| *Individual alternates' desired funds rates* | | | |
| Broaddus | 5.250 | Guynn | 5.250 BS |
| Guynn | 5.250 BS | Moskow | 5.250 BT |
| Hoenig | 5.250 BS | Broaddus | 5.500 |
| Melzer | 5.250 BS | Melzer | 5.500 |
| Minehan | 5.250 BS | Minehan | 5.500 |
| Moskow | 5.250 BS | Parry | 5.500 |
| Parry | 5.250 | Hoenig | 5.581 LT |
| *Summary statistics* | | | |
| Target funds rate | 5.250 | Target funds rate | 5.250 |
| Committee bias | BS | Committee bias | BS |
| Status quo | 5.250 | Status quo | 5.250 |
| Number (voters) | 10 | Number (voters) | 10 |
| Mean (voters) | 5.250 | Mean (voters) | 5.250 |
| Median (voters) | 5.250 | Median (voters) | 5.250 |
| Number (alternates) | 7 | Number (alternates) | 7 |
| Mean (alternates) | 5.250 | Mean (alternates) | 5.440 |
| Median (alternates) | 5.250 | Median (alternates) | 5.500 |
| Number (all) | 17 | Number (all) | 17 |
| Mean (all) | 5.250 | Mean (all) | 5.250 |
| Median (all) | 5.250 | Median (all) | 5.250 |

| July 3, 1996 | | August 20, 1996 | |
|---|---|---|---|
| *Individual voters' desired funds rates* | | | |
| Boehne | 5.250 BT | Boehne | 5.250 BT |
| Greenspan | 5.250 BT | Greenspan | 5.250 BT |
| Jordan | 5.250 BS | Jordan | 5.250 BT |
| Kelley | 5.250 BT | Kelley | 5.250 BT |
| Lindsey | 5.250 BT | Lindsey | 5.250 BT |
| McDonough | 5.250 BT | McDonough | 5.250 BT |
| Meyer | 5.250 BT | McTeer | 5.250 BT |
| Phillips | 5.250 BT | Meyer | 5.250 BT |
| Rivlin | 5.250 BT | Phillips | 5.250 BT |
| Yellen | 5.250 BT | Rivlin | 5.250 BT |
| McTeer | 5.446 LT | Yellen | 5.250 BT |
| Stern | 5.500 | Stern | 5.463 LT |
| *Individual alternates' desired funds rates* | | | |
| Guynn | 5.250 BT | Guynn | 5.250 BT |
| Minehan | 5.250 BT | Moskow | 5.250 BT |
| Moskow | 5.250 BT | Minehan | 5.500 |
| Hoenig | 5.511 LT[f] | Hoenig | 5.665 LT |
| Parry | 5.657 LT[f] | Parry | 5.668 LT[f] |
| Broaddus | 5.750 | Broaddus | 5.750 |
| Melzer | 5.750 | Melzer | 5.750 |
| *Summary statistics* | | | |
| Target funds rate | 5.250 | Target funds rate | 5.250 |
| Committee bias | BT | Committee bias | BT |
| Status quo | 5.250 | Status quo | 5.250 |
| Number (voters) | 12 | Number (voters) | 12 |
| Mean (voters) | 5.287 | Mean (voters) | 5.268 |
| Median (voters) | 5.250 | Median (voters) | 5.250 |
| Number (alternates) | 7 | Number (alternates) | 7 |
| Mean (alternates) | 5.488 | Mean (alternates) | 5.548 |
| Median (alternates) | 5.511 | Median (alternates) | 5.665 |
| Number (all) | 19 | Number (all) | 19 |
| Mean (all) | 5.287 | Mean (all) | 5.268 |
| Median (all) | 5.250 | Median (all) | 5.250 |

| September 24, 1996 | | November 13, 1996 | |
|---|---|---|---|
| *Individual voters' desired funds rates* | | | |
| Boehne | 5.250 BT | Boehne | 5.250 BT |
| Greenspan | 5.250 BT | Greenspan | 5.250 BT |
| Jordan | 5.250 BT | Jordan | 5.250 BT |
| Kelley | 5.250 BT | Kelley | 5.250 BT |
| McDonough | 5.250 BT | Lindsey | 5.250 BT |
| McTeer | 5.250 BT | McDonough | 5.250 BT |
| Phillips | 5.250 BT | McTeer | 5.250 BT |
| Rivlin | 5.250 BT | Meyer | 5.250 BT |
| Lindsey | 5.251 A | Phillips | 5.250 BT |
| Yellen | 5.416 LT | Rivlin | 5.250 BT |
| Stern | 5.500 | Stern | 5.250 BT |
| Meyer | 5.516 LT | Yellen | 5.250 BT |
| *Individual alternates' desired funds rates* | | | |
| Moskow | 5.250 BT | Guynn | 5.250 BT |
| Guynn | 5.305 LT | Moskow | 5.250 BT |
| Parry | 5.500 | Parry | 5.250 BT |
| Hoenig | 5.521 LT | Minehan | 5.455 LT |
| Melzer | 5.572 LT | Broaddus | 5.500 |
| Minehan | 5.625 | Melzer | 5.500 |
| Broaddus | 5.750 | Hoenig | 5.530 LT |
| *Summary statistics* | | | |
| Target funds rate | 5.250 | Target funds rate | 5.250 |
| Committee bias | BT | Committee bias | BT |
| Status quo | 5.250 | Status quo | 5.250 |
| Number (voters) | 12 | Number (voters) | 12 |
| Mean (voters) | 5.307 | Mean (voters) | 5.250 |
| Median (voters) | 5.250 | Median (voters) | 5.250 |
| Number (alternates) | 7 | Number (alternates) | 7 |
| Mean (alternates) | 5.503 | Mean (alternates) | 5.391 |
| Median (alternates) | 5.521 | Median (alternates) | 5.455 |
| Number (all) | 19 | Number (all) | 19 |
| Mean (all) | 5.307 | Mean (all) | 5.250 |
| Median (all) | 5.251 | Median (all) | 5.250 |

## December 17, 1996

*Individual voters' desired funds rates*

| | |
|---|---|
| Boehne | 5.250 BT |
| Greenspan | 5.250 BT |
| Jordan | 5.250 |
| Kelley | 5.250 BT |
| Lindsey | 5.250 BT |
| McDonough | 5.250 BT |
| McTeer | 5.250 BT |
| Meyer | 5.250 BT |
| Phillips | 5.250 BT |
| Rivlin | 5.250 BT |
| Stern | 5.250 BT |
| Yellen | 5.250 BT |

*Individual alternates' desired funds rates*

| | |
|---|---|
| Guynn | 5.250 BT |
| Hoenig | 5.250 BT |
| Minehan | 5.250 BT |
| Moskow | 5.250 BT |
| Parry | 5.250 BT |
| Melzer | 5.591 LT |
| Broaddus | 5.627 LT |

*Summary statistics*

| | |
|---|---|
| Target funds rate | 5.250 |
| Committee bias | BT |
| Status quo | 5.250 |
| Number (voters) | 12 |
| Mean (voters) | 5.250 |
| Median (voters) | 5.250 |
| Number (alternates) | 7 |
| Mean (alternates) | 5.353 |
| Median (alternates) | 5.250 |
| Number (all) | 19 |
| Mean (all) | 5.250 |
| Median (all) | 5.250 |

*Notes:* BE, BS, BT: Bias toward ease, symmetric bias, or bias toward tightness, respectively; LE, A, LT: Desired funds rate was imputed and the member leaned for ease, assented, or leaned for tightness, respectively, relative to the status quo, unless otherwise noted.

[a] Lean is relative to funds rate of 8.9375.  [b] Lean is relative to funds rate of 7.75.
[c] Lean is relative to funds rate of 7.50.  [d] Lean is relative to funds rate of 3.50.
[e] Lean is relative to funds rate of 5.75.  [f] Lean is relative to funds rate of 5.50.

# References

Abrams, Richard, Richard Froyen, and Roger Waud. 1980. Monetary Policy Reaction Functions, Consistent Expectations, and the Burns Era. *Journal of Money, Credit, and Banking* 12:30–42.

Alesina, Alberto. 1987. Macroeconomic Policy in a Two-Party System as a Repeated Game. *Quarterly Journal of Economics* 102:651–678.

Alesina, Alberto, and Jeffrey Sachs. 1988. Political Parties and the Business Cycle in the United States, 1948–1984. *Journal of Money, Credit, and Banking* 20:63–82.

Alesina, Alberto, and Lawrence H. Summers. 1993. Central Bank Independence and Macroeconomic Performance: Some Comparative Evidence. *Journal of Money, Credit, and Banking* 25:151–162.

Alt, James E., and John T. Woolley. 1982. Reaction Functions, Optimization, and Politics: Modelling the Political Economy of Macroeconomic Policy. *American Journal of Political Science* 26:709–740.

Andersen, Leonall C., and Jerry L. Jordan. 1968. Monetary and Fiscal Actions: A Test of Their Relative Importance in Economic Stabilization. *Review* (Federal Reserve Bank of St. Louis) 50 (November): 11–24.

Barro, Robert J., and David B. Gordon. 1983. A Positive Theory of Monetary Policy in a Natural Rate Model. *Journal of Political Economy* 91:589–610.

Barth, James, Robin Sickles, and Philip Wiest. 1982. Assessing the Impact of Varying Economic Conditions on Federal Reserve Behavior. *Journal of Macroeconomics* 4:47–70.

Beck, Nathaniel. 1982. Presidential Influence on the Federal Reserve in the 1970s. *American Journal of Political Science* 26:415–445.

Beck, Nathaniel. 1984. Domestic Political Sources of American Monetary Policy: 1955–1982. *Journal of Politics* 46:786–817.

Beck, Nathaniel. 1987. Elections and the Fed: Is There a Political Monetary Cycle? *American Journal of Political Science* 31:194–216.

Beck, Nathaniel. 1990. Congress and the Fed: Why the Dog Does Not Bark in the Night. In *The Political Economy of American Monetary Policy*, ed. Thomas Mayer, 131–150. New York: Cambridge University Press.

Belden, Susan. 1989. Policy Preferences of FOMC Members as Revealed by Dissenting Votes. *Journal of Money, Credit, and Banking* 21:432–441.

Bergstrom, Theodore C., and Robert P. Goodman. 1973. Private Demand for Public Goods. *American Economic Review* 63:280–296.

Bernanke, Ben. 2003a. Constrained Discretion and Monetary Policy. Speech given to the Money Marketeers of New York University, New York, February 3. http://www.federalreserve.gov/boarddocs/speeches/2003/20030203/default.htm.

Bernanke, Ben. 2003b. Speech at the twenty-eighth annual policy conference of the Federal Reserve Bank of St. Louis, Inflation Targeting: Prospects and Problems, October 17. http://www.federalreserve.gov/boarddocs/speeches/2003/20031017/default.htm.

Bernanke, Ben, and Alan Blinder. 1992. The Federal Funds Rate and the Channels of Monetary Transmission. *American Economic Review* 82:901–921.

Blinder, Alan. 1997. What Central Bankers Could Learn from Academics—and Vice Versa. *Journal of Economic Perspectives* 11, no. 2:3–19.

Blinder, Alan. 1998. *Central Banking in Theory and Practice.* Cambridge: MIT Press.

Board of Governors of the Federal Reserve System. 1994. *The Federal Reserve System: Purposes and Functions.* 8th ed. Washington, DC: Board of Governors of the Federal Reserve System.

Board of Governors of the Federal Reserve System. 2002. *Eighty-Ninth Annual Report: 2002.* Washington, DC: Board of Governors of the Federal Reserve System.

Borcherding, Thomas E., and Robert T. Deacon. 1972. The Demand for the Services of Non-Federal Governments. *American Economic Review* 62:891–901.

Canterbery, E. Ray. 1967. A New Look at Federal Open Market Voting. *Western Economic Journal* 6:25–38.

Chang, Kelly H. 2003. *Appointing Central Bankers: The Politics of Monetary Policy in the United States and the European Monetary Union.* New York: Cambridge University Press.

Chappell, Henry W. Jr., Thomas M. Havrilesky, and Rob Roy McGregor. 1993. Partisan Monetary Policies: Presidential Influence Through the Power of Appointment. *Quarterly Journal of Economics* 108:185–218.

Chappell, Henry W. Jr., Thomas M. Havrilesky, and Rob Roy McGregor. 1995. Policymakers, Institutions, and Central Bank Decisions. *Journal of Economics and Business* 47:113–136.

Chappell, Henry W. Jr., Thomas M. Havrilesky, and Rob Roy McGregor. 1997. Monetary Policy Preferences of Individual FOMC Members: A Content Analysis of the *Memoranda of Discussion. Review of Economics and Statistics* 79:454–460.

Chappell, Henry W. Jr., and William Keech. 1986. Party Differences in Macroeconomic Policies and Outcomes. *American Economic Association Papers and Proceedings* 76:71–74.

Chappell, Henry W. Jr., and William Keech. 1988. The Unemployment Consequences of Partisan Monetary Policies. *Southern Economic Journal* 55:107–122.

Chappell, Henry W. Jr., and Rob Roy McGregor. 2000. A Long History of FOMC Voting Behavior. *Southern Economic Journal* 66:906–922.

Chappell, Henry W. Jr., and Rob Roy McGregor. 2004. Did Time Inconsistency Contribute to the Great Inflation? Evidence from the FOMC Transcripts. *Economics and Politics,* forthcoming.

Chappell, Henry W. Jr., Rob Roy McGregor, and Todd Vermilyea. 2004. Majority Rule, Consensus Building, and the Power of the Chairman: Arthur Burns and the FOMC. *Journal of Money, Credit, and Banking* 36:407–422.

Chopin, Marc C., Steven Cole, and Michael A. Ellis. 1996a. Congressional Influence on U.S. Monetary Policy: A Reconsideration of the Evidence. *Journal of Monetary Economics* 38:561–570.

Chopin, Marc C., Steven Cole, and Michael A. Ellis. 1996b. Congressional Policy Preferences and U.S. Monetary Policy. *Journal of Monetary Economics* 38:581–585.

Christian, James W. 1968. A Further Analysis of the Objectives of American Monetary Policy. *Journal of Finance* 23:465–477.

Cox, D. R. 1961. Tests of Separate Families of Hypotheses. In *Proceedings of the Fourth Berkeley Symposium on Mathematical Statistics and Probability*. Berkeley: University of California Press.

Cukierman, Alex. 1992. *Central Bank Strategy, Credibility, and Independence*. Cambridge: MIT Press.

Cukierman, Alex. 2000. The Inflation Bias Result Revisited. Working paper.

Cukierman, Alex, Steven Webb, and Bilin Neyapti. 1992. Measuring the Independence of Central Banks and Its Effect on Policy Outcomes. *World Bank Economic Review* 6:353–398.

Davidson, R., and J. G. MacKinnon. 1981. Several Tests for Model Specification in the Presence of Alternative Hypotheses. *Econometrica* 49:781–793.

DeLong, J. Bradford. 1997. America's Peacetime Inflation: The 1970s. In *Reducing Inflation: Motivation and Strategy*, ed. Christina D. Romer and David H. Romer, 247–280. Chicago: University of Chicago Press.

Dewald, William G., and Harry G. Johnson. 1963. An Objective Analysis of the Objectives of American Monetary Policy, 1952–61. In *Banking and Monetary Studies*, ed. Deane Carson, 171–189. Homewood, IL: Richard D. Irwin, Inc.

Drazen, Allan. 2000. *Political Economy in Macroeconomics*. Princeton, NJ: Princeton University Press.

Fair, Ray C. 1984. *Specification, Estimation, and Analysis of Macroeconomic Models*. Cambridge: Harvard University Press.

Federal Reserve Bank of Minneapolis. 1992. Interview with Mark H. Willes. http://www.minneapolisfed.org/info/mpls/history/willes.cfm?js=0.

Federal Reserve Bank of Minneapolis. 1995. Interview with Janet Yellen, *The Region* (June). http://www.minneapolisfed.org/pubs/region/95-06/int956.cfm.

Friedlaender, Ann F. 1973. Macro Policy Goals in the Postwar Period: A Study in Revealed Preference. *Quarterly Journal of Economics* 87:25–43.

Friedman, Milton. 1960. *A Program for Monetary Stability*. New York: Fordham University Press.

Friedman, Milton. 1968. The Role of Monetary Policy. *American Economic Review* 58:1–17.

Gilbert, R. Alton. 1985. Operating Procedures for Conducting Monetary Policy. *Review* (Federal Reserve Bank of St. Louis) 67 (February): 13–21.

Gildea, John. 1990. Explaining FOMC Members' Votes. In *The Political Economy of American Monetary Policy*, ed. Thomas Mayer, 211–227. New York: Cambridge University Press.

Goodfriend, Marvin. 1986. Monetary Mystique: Secrecy and Central Banking. *Journal of Monetary Economics* 17:63–92.

Goodfriend, Marvin. 1991. Interest Rates and the Conduct of Monetary Policy. In *Carnegie-Rochester Conference Series on Public Policy*, ed. Allan H. Meltzer and Charles I. Plosser, 34:7–30. Amsterdam: North-Holland.

Gordon, Robert J. 1981. *Macroeconomics*. 2nd ed. Boston: Little, Brown, and Company.

Gordon, Robert J. 1997. The Time-Varying NAIRU and its Implications for Economic Policy. *Journal of Economic Perspectives* 11, no. 1:11–32.

Greider, William. 1987. *Secrets of the Temple: How the Federal Reserve Runs the Country*. New York: Simon and Schuster.

Grier, Kevin. 1987. Presidential Elections and Federal Reserve Policy: An Empirical Test. *Southern Economic Journal* 54:475–486.

Grier, Kevin. 1989. On the Existence of a Political Monetary Cycle. *American Journal of Political Science* 33:376–389.

Grier, Kevin. 1991. Congressional Influence on U.S. Monetary Policy: An Empirical Test. *Journal of Monetary Economics* 28:201–220.

Grier, Kevin. 1996. Congressional Oversight Committee Influence on U.S. Monetary Policy Revisited. *Journal of Monetary Economics* 38:571–579.

Grier, Kevin, and Howard E. Neiman. 1987. Deficits, Politics, and Money Growth. *Economic Inquiry* 25:201–214.

Hakes, David R. 1990. The Objectives and Priorities of Monetary Policy under Different Federal Reserve Chairmen. *Journal of Money, Credit, and Banking* 22:327–337.

Hamilton, James D. 1994. *Time Series Analysis*. Princeton, NJ: Princeton University Press.

Havrilesky, Thomas M. 1967. A Test of Monetary Policy Action. *Journal of Political Economy* 75:299–304.

Havrilesky, Thomas M. 1987. A Partisanship Theory of Monetary and Fiscal Policy Regimes. *Journal of Money, Credit, and Banking* 19:308–325.

Havrilesky, Thomas M. 1988. Monetary Policy Signaling from the Administration to the Federal Reserve. *Journal of Money, Credit, and Banking* 20:83–101.

Havrilesky, Thomas M. 1995. *The Pressures on American Monetary Policy*. 2nd ed. Norwell, MA: Kluwer Academic Publishers.

Havrilesky, Thomas M., and John Gildea. 1991a. The Policy Preferences of FOMC Members As Revealed by Dissenting Votes. *Journal of Money, Credit, and Banking* 23:130–138.

Havrilesky, Thomas M., and John Gildea. 1991b. Screening FOMC Members for their Biases and Dependability. *Economics and Politics* 3:139–150.

Havrilesky, Thomas M., and John Gildea. 1992. Reliable and Unreliable Partisan Appointees to the Board of Governors. *Public Choice* 73:397–417.

Havrilesky, Thomas M., and James Granato. 1993. Determinants of Inflationary Performance: Corporatist Structure vs. Central Bank Autonomy. *Public Choice* 76:249–261.

Havrilesky, Thomas M., Robert Sapp, and Robert Schweitzer. 1975. Tests of the Federal Reserve's Reaction to the State of the Economy: 1964–1974. *Social Science Quarterly* 55:835–852.

Havrilesky, Thomas M., and Robert Schweitzer. 1990. A Theory of FOMC Dissent Voting with Evidence from the Time Series. In *The Political Economy of American Monetary Policy*, ed. Thomas Mayer, 197–210. New York: Cambridge University Press.

Haynes, Stephen E., and Joe A. Stone. 1989. An Integrated Test for Electoral Cycles in the U.S. Economy. *Review of Economics and Statistics* 71:426–434.

Hetzel, Robert L. 1998. Arthur Burns and Inflation. *Economic Quarterly* (Federal Reserve Bank of Richmond) 84 (Winter): 21–44.

Hibbs, Douglas A. Jr. 1977. Political Parties and Macroeconomic Policy. *American Political Science Review* 71:1467–1487.

Hibbs, Douglas A. Jr. 1986. Political Parties and Macroeconomic Policies and Outcomes in the United States. *American Economic Association Papers and Proceedings* 76:66–70.

Hibbs, Douglas A. Jr. 1987. *The American Political Economy*. Cambridge: Harvard University Press.

Ireland, Peter N. 1999. Does the Time-Consistency Problem Explain the Behavior of Inflation in the United States? *Journal of Monetary Economics* 44:279–291.

Jordan, Jerry L. 2001. Darryl Francis: Maverick in the Formulation of Monetary Policy. *Review* (Federal Reserve Bank of St. Louis) 83 (July/August): 17–22.

Judd, John P., and Glenn D. Rudebusch. 1998. Taylor's Rule and the Fed: 1970–1997. *Economic Review* (Federal Reserve Bank of San Francisco), no. 3:4–16.

Kahaner, Larry. 2000. *The Quotations of Chairman Greenspan*. Holbrook, MA: Adams Media Corporation.

Kane, Edward. 1980. Politics and Fed Policymaking: The More Things Change the More They Remain the Same. *Journal of Monetary Economics* 6:199–212.

Karamouzis, Nicholas, and Raymond Lombra. 1989. Federal Reserve Policymaking: An Overview and Analysis of the Policy Process. In *Carnegie-Rochester Conference Series on Public Policy*, ed. Karl Brunner and Allan H. Meltzer, 30:7–62. Amsterdam: North-Holland.

Keech, William R. 1995. *Economic Politics: The Costs of Democracy*. New York: Cambridge University Press.

Keech, William R., and Irwin L. Morris. 1997. Appointments, Presidential Power, and the Federal Reserve. *Journal of Macroeconomics* 19:253–267.

Kettl, Donald F. 1986. *Leadership at the Fed*. New Haven, CT: Yale University Press.

Khoury, Salwa S. 1990. The Federal Reserve Reaction Function: A Specification Search. In *The Political Economy of American Monetary Policy*, ed. Thomas Mayer, 27–49. New York: Cambridge University Press.

Knott, J. H. 1986. The Fed Chairman as a Political Executive. *Administration and Society* 18:197–231.

Krause, George A. 1994. Federal Reserve Policy Decision Making: Political and Bureaucratic Influences. *American Journal of Political Science* 38:124–144.

Krause, George A. 1996. Agent Heterogeneity and Consensual Decision Making on the Federal Open Market Committee. *Public Choice* 88:83–101.

Kydland, Finn E., and Edward C. Prescott. 1977. Rules Rather than Discretion: The Inconsistency of Optimal Plans. *Journal of Political Economy* 85:473–491.

Laney, Leroy O. 1990. The FOMC Dissent Voting Record: Reserve Bank Presidents versus the Governors. Unpublished paper, First Hawaiian Bank.

Lapp, John S., and Douglas K. Pearce. 2000. Does a Bias in FOMC Policy Directives Help Predict Intermeeting Policy Changes? *Journal of Money, Credit, and Banking* 32:435–441.

Lucas, Robert E. 1980. Rules, Discretion, and the Role of the Economic Advisor. In *Rational Expectations and Economic Policy*, ed. Stanley Fischer, 199–210. Chicago: University of Chicago Press.

MacKinnon, J. G. 1983. Model Specification Tests against Nonnested Alternatives. *Econometric Reviews* 2:85–110.

Maisel, Sherman J. 1973. *Managing the Dollar*. New York: W. W. Norton and Company.

Mayer, Thomas. 1999. *Monetary Policy and the Great Inflation in the United States: The Federal Reserve and the Failure of Macroeconomic Policy, 1965–79*. Cheltenham, UK: Edward Elgar.

McGregor, Rob Roy. 1996. FOMC Voting Behavior and Electoral Cycles: Partisan Ideology and Partisan Loyalty. *Economics and Politics* 8:17–32.

McKelvey, Richard, and William Zavoina. 1975. A Statistical Model for the Analysis of Ordinal Level Dependent Variables. *Journal of Mathematical Sociology* 4:103–120.

Meade, Ellen E., and D. Nathan Sheets. 2002. Regional Influences on U.S. Monetary Policy: Some Implications for Europe. Unpublished paper, Center for Economic Performance, London School of Economics and Political Science.

Meltzer, Allan H. 2003. *A History of the Federal Reserve, Volume 1: 1913–1951*. Chicago: University of Chicago Press.

Mishkin, Frederic S. 2003. *The Economics of Money, Banking, and Financial Markets*. 6th ed. update. Boston: Addison-Wesley.

Morris, Irwin. 2000. *Congress, the President, and the Federal Reserve: The Politics of American Monetary Policymaking*. Ann Arbor: University of Michigan Press.

Nixon, Richard. 1962. *Six Crises*. Garden City, NY: Doubleday.

Nordhaus, William D. 1975. The Political Business Cycle. *Review of Economic Studies* 42:169–190.

Orphanides, Athanasios. 2001. Monetary Policy Rules Based on Real-Time Data. *American Economic Review* 91:964–985.

Orphanides, Athanasios. 2002. Monetary Policy Rules and the Great Inflation. Working paper, Board of Governors of the Federal Reserve System.

Peek, Joe, and James A. Wilcox. 1987. Monetary Policy Regimes and the Reduced Form for Interest Rates. *Journal of Money, Credit, and Banking* 19:273–291.

Persson, Torsten, and Guido Tabellini. 2000. *Political Economics: Explaining Economic Policy*. Cambridge: MIT Press.

Phelps, Edmund S. 1968. Money-Wage Dynamics and Labor Market Equilibrium. *Journal of Political Economy* 76:678–711.

Poole, William, and Robert H. Rasche. 2003. The Impact of Changes in FOMC Disclosure Practices on the Transparency of Monetary Policy: Are Markets and the FOMC Better "Synched"? *Review* (Federal Reserve Bank of St. Louis) 85 (January/February): 1–9.

Posen, Adam S. 2002. Six Practical Views of Central Bank Transparency. Working paper, Institute for International Economics.

Puckett, Richard. 1984. Federal Open Market Committee Structure and Decisions. *Journal of Monetary Economics* 14:97–104.

Reuber, G. L. 1964. The Objectives of Canadian Monetary Policy, 1949–1961: Empirical "Trade-offs" and the Reaction Function of the Authorities. *Journal of Political Economy* 72:109–132.

Rogoff, Kenneth. 1985. The Optimal Degree of Commitment to an Intermediate Monetary Target. *Quarterly Journal of Economics* 100:1169–1189.

Rogoff, Kenneth, and Anne Sibert. 1988. Elections and Macroeconomic Policy Cycles. *Review of Economic Studies* 55:1–16.

Romer, Christina D., and David H. Romer. 2002. A Rehabilitation of Monetary Policy in the 1950s. *American Economic Association Papers and Proceedings* 92:121–127.

Romer, Christina D., and David H. Romer. 2004. Choosing the Federal Reserve Chair: Lessons from History. *Journal of Economic Perspectives* 18:129–162.

Romer, Thomas, and Howard Rosenthal. 1979. The Elusive Median Voter. *Journal of Public Economics* 12:143–170.

Shughart, William F. II, and Robert D. Tollison. 1983. Preliminary Evidence on the Use of Inputs by the Federal Reserve System. *American Economic Review* 73:291–304.

Sims, Christopher A., James H. Stock, and Mark W. Watson. 1990. Inference in Linear Time Series Models with Some Unit Roots. *Econometrica* 58:113–144.

Taylor, John B. 1993. Discretion versus Policy Rules in Practice. *Carnegie-Rochester Conference Series on Public Policy* 39 (December): 195–214.

Thornton, Daniel L., and David C. Wheelock. 2000. A History of the Asymmetric Policy Directive. *Review* (Federal Reserve Bank of St. Louis) 82 (September/October): 1–16.

Tobin, James. 1958. Estimation of Relationships for Limited Dependent Variables. *Econometrica* 26:24–36.

Toma, Mark. 1982. Inflationary Bias of the Federal Reserve System: A Bureaucratic Perspective. *Journal of Monetary Economics* 10:163–190.

Tootell, Geoffrey M. B. 1991a. Regional Economic Conditions and the FOMC Votes of District Presidents. *New England Economic Review* (March/April): 3–16.

Tootell, Geoffrey M. B. 1991b. Are District Presidents More Conservative than Board Governors? *New England Economic Review* (September/October): 3–12.

Tootell, Geoffrey M. B. 1996. Appointment Procedures and FOMC Voting Behavior. *Southern Economic Journal* 63:191–204.

Tootell, Geoffrey M. B. 1999. Whose Monetary Policy Is It Anyway? *Journal of Monetary Economics* 43:217–235.

Waller, Christopher J. 1989. Monetary Policy Games and Central Bank Politics. *Journal of Money, Credit, and Banking* 21:422–431.

Waller, Christopher J. 1992a. A Bargaining Model of Partisan Appointments to the Central Bank. *Journal of Monetary Economics* 29:411–428.

Waller, Christopher J. 1992b. The Choice of a Conservative Central Banker in a Multisector Economy. *American Economic Review* 82:1006–1012.

Weintraub, Robert E. 1978. Congressional Supervision of Monetary Policy. *Journal of Monetary Economics* 4:341–362.

Wells, Wyatt C. 1994. *Economist in an Uncertain World: Arthur F. Burns and the Federal Reserve, 1970–78*. New York: Columbia University Press.

West, Kenneth D. 1988. Asymptotic Normality, When Regressors Have a Unit Root. *Econometrica* 56:1397–1417.

Willes, Mark. 1978. Eliminating Policy Surprises: An Inexpensive Way to Beat Inflation. In *1978 Annual Report*, Federal Reserve Bank of Minneapolis. http://www.minneapolisfed.org/pubs/ar/ar1978.cfm.

Woodward, Bob. 2000. *Maestro: Greenspan's Fed and the American Boom*. New York: Simon and Schuster.

Woolley, John. 1984. *Monetary Politics*. New York: Cambridge University Press.

Yohe, William P. 1966. A Study of Federal Open Market Committee Voting. *Southern Economic Journal* 12:396–405.

# Index